Places and Politics
in an Age of Globalization

Places and Politics in an Age of Globalization

EDITED BY
ROXANN PRAZNIAK
AND
ARIF DIRLIK

ROWMAN & LITTLEFIELD PUBLISHERS, INC.
Lanham • Boulder • New York • Oxford

ROWMAN & LITTLEFIELD PUBLISHERS, INC.

Published in the United States of America
by Rowman & Littlefield Publishers, Inc.
4720 Boston Way, Lanham, Maryland 20706
http://www.rowmanlittlefield.com

12 Hid's Copse Road
Cumnor Hill, Oxford OX2 9JJ, England

Chapter 3 was previously published in *TAJA: Australian Journal of Anthropology* 10:1
(1999). Reprinted by permission. Chapter 12 was previously published in *Social Justice*
vol. 25, no. 4 (1999) as "Transcommunality: From the Politics of Conversion to the
Ethics of Respect..." Reprinted by permission.

British Library Cataloguing in Publication Information Available

Library of Congress Cataloging-in-Publication Data

Places and politics in an age of globalization / edited by Roxann Prazniak and Arif
Dirlik.
    p. cm.
    Includes bibliographical references and index.
    ISBN 0-7425-0038-1 (alk. paper) — ISBN 0-7425-0039-X (pbk. : alk. paper)
    1. Group identity. 2. Globalization. I. Prazniak, Roxann. II. Dirlik, Arif.

    HM753 .P53 2000
    305.8—dc21
                                                                            00-0445?

Printed in the United States of America

♾™ The paper used in this publication meets the minimum requirements of American
National Standard for Information Sciences—Permanence of Paper for Printed Library
Materials, ANSI/NISO Z39.48–1992.

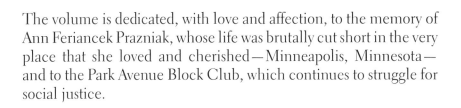

The volume is dedicated, with love and affection, to the memory of Ann Feriancek Prazniak, whose life was brutally cut short in the very place that she loved and cherished—Minneapolis, Minnesota—and to the Park Avenue Block Club, which continues to struggle for social justice.

Contents

Prelude: Beware of the M Word

Russell C. Leong

Beware of the M word
    Motherfucker
    Multiculturalism

Everyone's wearing it
on their lips
and on their cheeks
it's the latest cosmetic

Revlon offers seventy-five
shades of foundation
from palest ivory
to deepest ebony
& yellow, red, & olive in between.

Beware of the M word
watch out for Benetton
the clothing company
with colorful clothing
They say:
"We own multiculturalism"
    but
    who owns it?
    who created it?
    who sold it?

On with the M word
In yesterday's *New York Times*
Chanel put it this way:

"We tried to plug in some holes
  in the lighter and darker areas."
Now remember
  we're just talking about foundation
  women's makeup, the base coating
  and the colors of hip clothing.

We're talking right on
about the consumer
color line
  color without politics
  color without contradictions
  color without clashes
  color without classes
is blind
is no color at all
it's just powder
  in four to eight hours
  the sweat & smog
  will wipe it off your face

Color is the latest trick
  faster than a hustler or a whore
  on Hollywood Boulevard
  you don't even get any ass
  for your money

Beware of the M word
  Conglomerates
  clothing companies
  colleges
who use it

Motherfucker
Multiculturalism
nothing is sacred
no land, no ocean
That word
can sell anything from
  poverty to poetry
  pain to politicians

It's a new form
a nuevo color line

multiculturalism
so why not
multiracism
multisexism
multifeminism
multinationalism
multiples
that multiply geometrically
like the bombs that befell
Nagasaki Hiroshima
Okinawa Seoul
Saigon Bach Mai
Haiphong
Basra Baghdad

places we once called home.

And closer to home
in the City of Fallen
Angels
multiple fires
light our eyes
Watts
Compton
South Central
Hollywood
Pico Union
Koreatown.

Beware of the M word
multiple serial killings
of black and Asian boys
split and skewered
by the multiple
stabs of a crazy pale man

The Word
everyone is wearing it
smeared on their lips
pressed on their cheeks
at the tip of their tongues

Beware
your mamma tells you

of the bogie man
with the sweet seductive
M Word
    Mmmm
    it melts in your mouth
    not in your hands

The M Word
    takes more than it ever gives
    kills more than it ever loves
    takes to motion
    without emotion
reduces us to notions
of pure color
blind to our
    politics
    contradictions
    classes
    clashes
    & cultures

We cannot be reduced
to a single definition
    to one word
    one vision
    one spirit
for
We were multiple and cultural
compounded
in Asia, Africa, Americas
before the M word wuz ever born

We are the mothers and the fathers
who tell our children
wipe your mouth of the M word
wash your hands of it
before you come to the table
and give thanks
for all the dead before you
and all the living to come.

Acknowledgments

This volume is a product of a conference held at Duke University April 13–15, 1995—"Asia-Pacific Identities: Culture and Identity Formation in the Age of Global Capital." Some of the participants in the conference are not represented in the volume, and other names have been added to it since the original conference. We would like to thank Stanley Abe, Karin Aguilar-San Juan, Glenn Alcalay, Gerald Alfred, Anne Allison, Frank Chin, Leo Ching, Hae Joang Cho, Tim Costello, Mariana Guerrero (Annette Jaimes), Harry Harootunian, Yuji Ichioka, Maivan Lam, Ralph Litzinger, Maurice Meisner, Donald Nonini, Charles Piot, Marianna Torgovnick, Peter Wood, and Cui Zhiyuan for their contributions to the original conference. Russell Leong, who was one of the original participants, contributed the poem "Beware of the M Word," which captures the general sense of the discussion at the conference and was devoted to questioning some of the fashionable and, we feel, politically retrograde ideas of our times. We would also like to thank the contributors to the volume who joined the project later for their willingness to share their research and ideas with us.

The conference was sponsored by a number of offices at Duke University. We would like to thank the Asian/Pacific Studies Institute, Asian Students Association, Center for International Studies, the Departments of Cultural Anthropology, English, and History, the Duke University Student Union Major Speakers Committee, the Mary Lou Williams Center, the Office of the Vice-Provost for Academic and International Affairs, and the Josiah Charles Trent Memorial Foundation, Inc., for their generosity. The staff of the Asian Pacific Studies Institute helped with organizational matters with their usual competence, making life much easier for the organizers. We are grateful.

"Beware of the M Word" was first published in *High Performance Magazine*, Summer 1992 issue, which was a special issue focusing on writers of color and the Los Angeles Rebellion edited by Wanda Coleman.

Finally, Susan McEachern, editor and friend, has been supportive of the publication project with her usual grace and enthusiasm.

The editing of the volume was completed during Arif Dirlik's tenure as fellow of the Netherlands Institute for Advanced Studies in the Humanities and the Social Sciences. We thank the institute for its congenial intellectual atmosphere, which facilitated the task of editing.

Part I

Introduction: Theoretical Issues

1

Introduction: Cultural Identity and the Politics of Place

Arif Dirlik and Roxann Prazniak

The chapters in this volume address issues of contemporary cultural identity in relation to the politics of place. We are not concerned with questions of "identity politics" or "the politics of location." Rather, the chapters inquire into the challenges presented to collective identities by social and cultural developments under the regime of Global Capitalism and how, conversely, such identities may be rethought in place-based ways to serve as ingredients of a counterhegemonic, democratic politics. Cultural nationalism, ethnicity, and indigenism are the three modes of contemporary cultural identity formation that appear in the following chapters. The chapters for the most part draw on manifestations of these identity formations in the politics of places in and around the Pacific. They also seek to bring together theoretical and activist concerns.

Collective identities have come under suspicion in recent years among putative radicals infatuated by postmodern/postcolonial critiques of subjectivity, so that even to speak of collective identities is to risk charges of "essentialism." It should be evident from the discussions that follow that the contributors to this volume share in the concern over the oppressive implications of collective identity formation where they do in fact presuppose dehistoricized and desocialized essences in the definition of collective identities—as in the case of "cultural nationalisms" of various kinds, which would seem to be the most culpable in this regard. Nevertheless, we also feel that it is necessary to move beyond a politically nihilistic preoccupation with "essentialism" to rephrase the problem of identity in politically more productive ways. "Identity politics" or the "politics of location," however useful they may have been in bringing to the surface aspects of oppression disguised or ignored in earlier radical politics, have by now exhausted their critical power and serve little purpose beyond an involutional elitist narcissism. Divorced from problems of collective identity, identity politics ends up with a methodological individualism that is barely distinguishable from libertarian approaches to the question of identity. In their repudiation of larger structures of power and inequality, moreover, advocates of identity politics draw on paradigms of the market to render identity formation into a process of negotiation, which in the name of returning subjectivity to the oppressed suppresses the many inequalities that shape social encounters—much the same as the conservative ideology of the market is intended to disguise the inequalities of capitalism. Defeated by the many failures of the radical promises of the past and complicit in contemporary structures of power, radicals of the postmodern/postcolonial variety not only are oblivious to contemporary popular struggles but in many ways undermine them by denying their claims to collective identity and representation. While it may not be fair in all cases to suggest that identity politics represents the hijacking of radicalism by conservatives and liberals, it is nevertheless the case that contemporary radicalism has become as indistinguishable from liberalism as the latter has been blurred by its flirtation with conservatism.

In arguing for renewed attention to collective identities, the following chapters emphasize a need to distinguish between hegemonic and antihegemonic cultural practices as well as between those of the powerful and the powerless. The charge of "essentialism," used indiscriminately against all claims to cultural identity, often overlooks that in many contemporary cases, claims to identity, while expressed in the language of the past, nevertheless have their point of departure in the present and represent projects to be realized in the future; the past, in such cases, serves as a source of utopian longings that point to the future. This is the case most prominently with indigenism, which, as far as many indigenous peoples are concerned, rejects Euro-American notions of past, present, and future, but nevertheless articulates its aspirations with a historical consciousness in which the traces of modernity are clearly visible. It is also clear in the case of radical versions of indigenism that there is a recognition in the project of the need to account for inequalities and oppressions inherited from the past or produced in the present.

Even where such recognition is not explicitly forthcoming, it is still necessary to distinguish between the claims to identity of the powerful and the powerless, because the powerless may face such threats, including on occasion the threat of extinction, that it is intellectually, politically, and morally irresponsible to encompass within one notion of "essentialism" (emanating from centers of power, we may note) every reification of collective identity from the civilizations of Samuel Huntington to the cultural nationalisms of states and diasporic elites to the claims to identity of the Lumbee of North Carolina or the Tasmanians.[1] Since such claims to identity are an irreducible reality of the contemporary world, regardless of what postmodern or postcolonial theory may assert, we need to recognize and account for them. Since such claims are made within structures of unequal power, we need to distinguish among them according to their circumstances and aspirations. The alternative is not just an evasion of politics and complicity in contemporary power; it is also a disavowal of the world.

Claim of identity are made within structures of inequality.

In addressing these questions, finally, the following chapters share a common concern to challenge a contemporary culturalism that has not only endowed culture with priority over questions of political economy but has rendered it into an autonomous realm in consideration of questions of identity. The avoidance of questions of political economy has serious implications in addressing questions of relations between societies; not least among which are questions of colonialism and neocolonialism that were crucial historically to the redefinition of cultural identities. It also has implications for relations within societies, especially class relations, which have receded from the field of vision as questions of political economy have been replaced (once again) by questions of culture. Almost by definition, different classes in society have different visions of that society, its historical meaning and trajectory. As the definition of cultural identity is reified into nationalist or ethnic identity, what results is a hegemonic suppression or appropriation of differences in cultural identity that also ends up identifying culture with ethnicity, nation, race, or religious grouping. The ironic consequence of culturalism is that in its very separation of culture from questions of political hegemony, it ultimately denies to culture its autonomy through these identifications.

Cultural nationalism, ethnicity, and indigenism are the three modes of cultural identity formation that are important to grasping the problems addressed in the following chapters. We describe them here as "modes," rather than as types or some other equivalent, because the social and cultural realities that are encompassed within the terms *cultural nationalism, ethnicity,* and *indigenism* are not antithetical or even clearly distinguishable in terms of some objective reality. These realities overlap, and the term we deploy to depict the same social entity may be contingent upon circumstances. The terms refer not to fixed entities but to historically shifting positions. And if distinguishing them makes sense, it is only in terms of concrete structural locations. The terms themselves are fluid in meaning; they may refer to different entities, they may refer to different modes in which the same entity formulates its own self-image or the way in which it presents itself to the outside. What we insist on, however, is that these various modes of representation are not politically innocent and that the naming itself carries different implications both in terms of the relationships between groups and in terms of their own internal constitution. To offer a concrete illustration: the Hmong may be described as an indigenous group in Laos, an ethnic group when they are relocated in the United States, and as cultural nationalists when they claim a diasporic Hmong identity. We may be speaking of the same group of people, but under different circumstances. The choices, however, are not arbitrary, but refer to the changing historical and social/structural locations of the Hmong. The choices also refer to changing self-images of the Hmong, which are not to be separated from the images that others may hold of them.

A few words are in order here on cultural nationalism, ethnicity, and indigenism as abstractions that may also help explain the way we understand and deploy them in this volume. The term *cultural nationalism* is used to depict a mode of cultural identity formation that is more or less "off-ground"; in other words, a cultural abstraction that does not have a necessary location. Cultural nationalism is understood, therefore, in its contrast with a political nationalism and, in a significant sense, in its avoidance of politics, which is not to say that it does not have serious political consequences. This is the sense in which cultural nationalism appears in discussions of East Asian societies. In his *Cultural Nationalism in Colonial Korea*, Michael Robinson discusses the ways culture emerged as a focus of concern in Korea under Japanese colonial rule where, unable to express themselves politically, Korean intellectuals devoted themselves to the investigation of culture in the definition of Koreanness.[2]

But such an enforced condition of depoliticization is not crucial to cultural nationalism. For nearly two decades in the 1970s and 1980s, Japanese intellectuals were preoccupied with the question of "Japaneseness" (*Nihonjinron*), which also has been described as "cultural nationalism." In this case, the effort to establish a Japanese essence (not for the first time, historically speaking) was a product of internally generated needs to establish an identity that seemed to be evaporating quickly as Japan became a major player in Global Capitalism and Japanese society began to show all the complications and strains of capitalist production and consumption. "Japaneseness," according to Yoshino Kosaku, was promoted equally by the state and corporations.[3] To the outside world, it was a declaration that Japan was different even as it became less different; ironically feeding Orientalist images of Japan through "self-Orientalization." Internally speaking, "Japaneseness" was a reminder of an essentialized national identity to a citizenry who were becoming increasingly more conscious of themselves not just as Japanese but also as workers, women, consumers, polluters, and so forth; in other words, as the source of a national discipline that was in the process of evaporation. Harumi Befu puts it pithily when he observes that "intellectuals write *Nihonjinron* as prescriptions for behavior. Government turns it into a hegemonic ideology. And the corporate establishment disseminates it."[4] It is also interesting that, throughout, "Japaneseness" was defined in terms of an agrarian society that was destroyed by Japan's very success at capitalism.

The most recent East Asian manifestation of cultural nationalism is in China, where it appears with even greater complexity in the bringing together of concerns over loss of national identity with success at capitalism and concerns over the meaninglessness of national identity with a diasporic dispersal of Chinese populations around the world. In this case, also, cultural nationalism, expressed this time in the concept of a "cultural China," is articulated against non-China and, simultaneously, against Chinese disappearing into the many places of the Chinese diaspora.[5] It also has strong disciplinary hints, as Chinese populations, discovering the joys of capitalist consumption, show signs of losing their "Chineseness." Chinese cultural nationalism is similar to the Japanese in that it is at once the product of a new sense of empowerment that comes with success in the capitalist world economy and of a response to the threat of dissolution into a capitalism without cultural boundaries. What makes it different, and interesting, is that its promoters are Chinese Overseas who seek "to capture the center from the periphery"; adding a diasporic dimension to the idea of cultural nationalism. The diasporic dimension is especially important to the notion of cultural nationalism (in contradistinction to the political), because in this case culture becomes the means to unifying populations scattered into four states (soon to become three) and many other locations. The task of culture under the circumstances is not so much avoiding as transcending politics. On the other hand, the disassociation of "culture" in cultural China from any territory defined by Chinese states and its affirmation of a reified Chineseness against the dispersal of Chinese into many local cultures is also revealing of a fundamental premise that may be common to all cultural nationalism but appears with particular egregiousness in this case: the identification of culture with a racial category (which itself is unsustainable except at the level of some imagined physical identity: anyone who looks Chinese is Chinese, which recapitulates the worst assumptions of Euro-American racism) renders the idea of culture itself meaningless. To use a distinction offered by Partha Chatterjee, the problematic of cultural nationalism may be how to deal with national culture in its relationship to the state and capitalism, but its thematic rests upon categories of Orientalism that are not just cultural but also strongly racial.[6]

Ethnicity is much more problematic, for the very simple reason that if, on the one hand, it partakes of the deterritorialized notion of culture characteristic of cultural nationalism (and the more diasporic it becomes, the more it does so), it refers, on the other hand, to localized forms of cultural identity that are, in common usage anyway, cultures of the dispossessed and the marginal. Ethnicity gives credence to cultural nationalist arguments, but it also undermines the idea of both national and transnational cultures. Ethnic Chineseness, for example, may offer support to a Chinese cultural nationalism. It may also make the idea irrelevant, especially if ethnicity is stripped of its racial connotations, or abstract definitions in terms of some criterion or other, and viewed instead in terms of concrete localized cultural formations. From the perspective of such local or place-based ethnicity, nation-building itself may appear as a colonial project that seeks to erase all cultural differences associated with places. (We are not referring here just to other "nationalities" but to differences within supposedly the same ethnicity, such as a Han ethnicity.)[7] On the other hand, today, when ethnicity is defined in transnational contexts, ethnicity has emerged as a major challenge to the organization of the world in terms of nation–states. Ethnicity, therefore, always involves challenges to cultural identity formation. The question is, where does it serve productive political purposes, and where does it become the cause for genocidal conflict?

We are not interested here in recapitulating the tired debate between primordialism and constructivism. We take the constructivism (which is to say, the historicity) of ethnicity for granted. But does that make ethnicity any less real? The answer, we think, is that in the case of ethnicity, more than with either cultural nationalism or indigenism, the answer must be situational, contingent upon the interaction of internal and external circumstances. The treatment of ethnicity calls for a good dose of common sense, however unrealizable that may seem from a strictly "scientific" perspective.[8] We all know that although a definition of ethnicity on the basis of history, language, religion, locational origin, and the like may not be sustainable (because it is not that difficult in each case to find exceptions), under certain situations all of those characteristics used in the definition of ethnicity in their different ways do create affinities that become the basis for "ethnic action." In these senses, ethnicity presents problems similar to that of creating a nation, but without a state to enforce it, or to forcefully create homogeneity out of difference. Hence ethnicity is much more subject to the vagaries of circumstances than nations with states, which can freeze time and space in their self-definitions. Not only that, but ethnicities are usually at the mercy of others, since stateless peoples usually find themselves at a disadvantage when compared with people with states; it is usually the former, as a matter of fact, who find themselves described as ethnics of one kind or another. Or they are minorities, regarded as ethnic outsiders, even where they capture state power, as with the non-Han rulers of China.[9] What is most important from the perspective of the problems addressed later in this text is that ethnics are forever caught in a choice between "placing" or "deterritorializing" themselves, becoming part of the places in which they are located, or asserting their identification with some supra-place identity, the cultural nationalisms discussed previously. In this particular sense, it may be suggested that the use of the concept of ethnicity in identity formation is bound at one extreme by indigenism and at the other by cultural nationalism and, where the nation may be equated to civilization, by the notion of civilization itself.

Some comment is necessary, finally, on the values associated with ethnicity. From certain perspectives, in particular the perspective of the nation–state, ethnic identification is undesirable. And it is also the case, especially today, that we encounter ethnicity more often than not in its less-desirable or even murderous manifestations in the form of ethnic conflict. It is important to remember, however, that ethnicity may appear also as a utopian project, associated with the presumed values of an ethnic group, in which case ethnicity may also appear in its more positive guises, so long as it does not result in a nihilistic insularity or a chauvinistic denial of the values claimed by other ethnic groups. In such cases, ethnicity, rather than resulting in conflict, may serve as a basis for community building. This is a case argued in the chapter by Margaret Zamudio, which suggests that ethnicity may serve as a basis for coalitions in place-based people's movements.

Indigenism is seemingly the most concrete and, therefore, the least problematic of these modes of identity formation. After all, to be indigenous is to be rooted in place, and attachment to the land in a very concrete sense is a prescriptive component of indigenism as concept. Such rootedness in place implies that, even more so than in the case of ethnicity, indigenism is inconsistent with the notion of the modern nation–state. As John Brown Childs argues, indigenism implies not the absence of trans- or extra-local organization, but federated forms of governance from the bottom up. Statelessness has meant in the case of indigenous peoples that they have been vulnerable to the power of the aggressive modern nation–state, and indigenous people everywhere have been colonized over the last few centuries and continue to exist in subordinate positions, in denial of their claims to sovereignty. It is for the same reason that indigenous forms of organization continue to provide a radical challenge to modern political organization—in particular the nation–state—and offer possibilities that need to be considered seriously in any speculation over place-based democratic alternatives to the abstractions of both national and transnational political identities. Such consideration does not negate the possibility of translocal or transnational activity and organization, but simply draws attention to the necessity for any democratic society of organization from the bottom up that does not erase but is founded upon place-based differences.[10]

Nevertheless, the dislocations of indigenous peoples over the last few centuries renders indigenism, too, into an abstract formulation. Not only are there many indigenous peoples who have voluntarily or involuntarily relocated to urban areas, but indigenous people too are participants in contemporary diasporic motions. Indigenous origins, in other words, do not necessarily coincide with indigenism as a cultural and political orientation. Indigenousness at one location may translate into ethnic status at another, as we have observed, and indigenism itself, articulated as a general ideology, may partake of the abstractness of cultural nationalism. Thus the Samoan/Fijian writer Epeli Hau'ofa proclaims:

> Oceania is vast, Oceania is expanding. Oceania is hospitable and generous, Oceania is humanity rising from the depths of brine and regions of fire deeper still, Oceania is us. We are the sea, we are the ocean, we must wake up to this ancient truth and together use it to overturn all hegemonic views that aim ultimately to confine us again, physically and psychologically, in the tiny spaces which we have resisted accepting as our sole appointed place, and from which we have recently liberated ourselves. We must not allow anyone to belittle us again, and take away our freedom.[11]

To Hau'ofa, the diasporas of South Pacific peoples are signs of Oceania once again asserting its vastness. He does not tell us how a Samoan relocated to Los Angeles retains his/her Samoanness, but there is an assumption here nevertheless of the expansion of indigenism into a cultural nationalism of sorts.

Indigenism, too, makes certain claims to reified cultural characteristics, "bodies of knowledge and corresponding codes of values—evolved over many thousands of years by native peoples the world over."[12] Nevertheless, it is the place-rootedness of indigenism (without which it must become merely another form of ethnicity) that in the end differentiates it from the other two modes of identity formation. Diversity on the basis of concrete location is built into the very definition of indigenism. And while indigenist ideology may stipulate certain "bodies of

"Place based

knowledge and . . . codes of values," based upon a particular relationship to nature, as characteristics of all indigenous peoples, what is implied is not a homogeneity of knowledge and values. Consequently, indigenous "nationalism" represents political alliances of various kinds, rather than the imposition of the same cultural and political values on all those who claim indigenousness.[13] It also follows that indigenism as movement cannot be exclusive in its politics on the basis of cultural difference without betraying its own premises; not of those adherents at any rate, who share in the premise of local self-determination. In this, indigenism may have something in common with ethnicity against cultural nationalism (as in ethnically based politics). Indigenism and ethnicity in turn differ in terms of relationship to place; even where it appears in placeless manifestations, indigenism nevertheless retains the ideal of place—with all its implications in terms of relation to nature and social relations—as a mark of identity.

Cultural nationalism and place-based consciousness provide the two poles in identity formation, the interplay of which informs the discussions in the chapters that follow. The chapters are organized around contemporary problems of ethnicity and indigenism. But ethnicity and indigenism serve in most of the discussions as sites of contestation between cultural reification and place-based practices within the context of Global Capitalism, diasporas, and state-sponsored identities. While the term *cultural nationalism* does not appear very often in the discussions, it is implicit in those manifestations of ethnicity and indigenism, especially of ethnicity, where cultural identity is reified into an abstraction, serves to disguise divisions internal to the group, and plays a hegemonic part in the definition of group identity. Places appear much more explicitly and mostly in the deconstruction of such reification. It is not that place-consciousness is immune to reification; the idea of community, for example, may serve hegemonic purposes at the local level as powerful as, or more powerful than, any cultural nationalism. The politics of place, moreover, may issue in any number of positions on the political spectrum, including right-wing politics. Nevertheless, it is an assumption shared by most of the contributors to this volume that places provide the most important locations in our day for lasting solutions to conflicts based on cultural identities.

Places are important for a number of reasons. With the attenuation of nation–states' roles in mediating between capital and place, places have acquired a special prominence at a moment when Global Capitalism, and globalization, seem to have acquired hegemonic status in locations of power. Not the least important manifestation of this new development is the proliferation of place-based movements. These movements, nourished by a number of concerns that range from the ecological to the social and political to most basic problems of livelihood, also need to confront questions of cultural identity because it is in places that groups claiming different identities confront one another. These confrontations are not to be resolved by political fiat from above, but require a recognition of a common destiny at the local level. Reification of cultural identity is a powerful obstacle to such a recognition. Conversely, recognizing a common destiny is perhaps the most plau-

sible argument against such reification, and a compelling reason for "placing" identities. What is at issue is not multiculturalism, which is another mode of reification through symbols of identity divorced from history, but the recognition of a common history to be produced in response to problems of everyday life.

Some of the implications of place-based consciousness and its affinities with an indigenist outlook are discussed in the chapters that follow. It will suffice to note here that given what is by now a tradition of reliance on the state, or a faith in the resolution of local problems at the national or even the international level, any advocacy of place-based practices meets with immediate suspicion if not hostility. It is important, in the first place, to draw a distinction between place-based and place-bound. To argue for the priority of the place-based is not to close out options for action at the level of national or global spaces, but merely to reassert the priority of place-based practices for any democratic resolution of the problems of livelihood and social coexistence. Conversely, those who are suspicious of the "anarchistic" implications of place-based activity often overlook the ways in which states themselves serve as sources of oppression and disorder. They also overlook the ways in which states contribute to disorder indirectly: as objects of plunder, which leads different ethnicities, real or imagined, into competition for the conquest of states, therefore contributing further to the ethnicization of politics.

The two chapters that directly follow this introduction deal with theoretical issues raised by place-based consciousness and its opposite, the abstraction of identity and culture on sites that, in their very representations of the past, negate any meaningful notion of history.

The chapters in the following sections examine these theoretical issues as they appear in concrete contexts. The common concern of the chapters in Part II is the relationship of identity and the mode in which it is expressed to differential relationships of class, gender, and colonial power; the reification of identity that may be oppressive in one context may serve purposes of political struggle and resistance in another. These chapters illustrate the limitations of theoretical discussions of identity, which may point to the problems that might be anticipated in practice, but are no substitute themselves for investigation of concrete situations that shape the mode, and the meaning, of cultural politics. This is indeed a fundamental difficulty presented by place-based politics, which, even in its theorization, needs to recognize the differences that are not to be subsumed in theoretical generalizations. The difficulty may be the difficulty of all genuinely democratic politics. As far as area coverage is concerned, what is being discussed in this section could be expanded indefinitely, as places are practically inexhaustible, if not infinite. This, of course, is not feasible, and may not even be necessary. The sampling offered here hopefully illustrates the contradictory meanings associated with cultural nationalism, ethnicity, and indigenism in different contexts.

The chapters in Part III turn to questions of indigenism in relationship to problems of development and ecology. These discussions seek to show that while indigenism, too, is subject to reification (as argued also in the chapter by Elizabeth

Rata in Part II), it nevertheless retains a connection to places. In its very ground-edness, indigenism offers ways to unthink the assumptions of a developmentalist ideology that currently finds expression in slogans of globalism and professes an illusory global integration even as it nourishes off the fragmentation of the globe into cultural entities in accordance with the productive and consumptive needs of a globalized capitalism.

The concluding chapter, by Wendy Harcourt, reflects off the issues raised in the previous sections with a particular focus on problems of women. Harcourt's discussion, enriched by her experiences of activism, brings out two important points of concern in this collection: how places provide locations of activity for those who, however disenfranchised in formal politics, are the bearers of life at the everyday level, and how the very processes of globalization through such media as the Internet, while not an unmixed blessing, have served to bring places to the forefront of global activity.

NOTES

1. The reference here is to Samuel Huntington's "The Clash of Civilizations?" *Foreign Affairs* 72(3)(1993): 22–49. Huntington's reification of culture at the level of "civilization" is in many ways symptomatic of the times and is a foremost example of the hegemonic uses of cultural identity (which also distracts from questions of political economy, state power, class, gender, and race issues, etc.).

2. Michael E. Robinson, *Cultural Nationalism in Colonial Korea, 1920–1925* (Seattle: University of Washington Press, 1988). This may be reading more into Robinson's argument than he intends, for he never states clearly why he uses the term *cultural nationalism*, except that the ideological movement he takes up dealt with issues of culture and was encouraged by the "cultural policy" of the colonial regime. We would like to suggest here that whether or not under colonial circumstances, a "culturalist" approach to change presupposes, often explicitly, a disavowal of problems that rest in the realism of political economy, the state, and society; in other words, a change in attitudes within an existing structural status quo. This may be the case even where the goals are radical, as in the case, for example, of the Cultural Revolution in China.

3. Kosaku Yoshino, *Cultural Nationalism in Contemporary Japan: A Sociological Enquiry* (London: Routledge, 1992).

4. Harumi Befu, "Nationalism and *Nihonjinron*," in *Cultural Nationalism in East Asia*, ed. Harumi Befu (Berkeley, Calif.: Institute of East Asian Studies, 1993), 107–35, here 118.

5. For "Cultural China," see Tu Wei-ming, "Cultural China: The Periphery as Center," *Daedalus* (Spring 1991): 1–32. For critical commentaries, see Arif Dirlik, "Confucius in the Borderlands: Global Capitalism and the Reinvention of Confucianism," *Boundary 2*, 22(3) (November 1995): 229–73 and "Critical Reflections on 'Chinese Capitalism' as Paradigm," *Identities*, 3(3) (1997): 303–30. For an argument in favor of grounding Chinese ethnicity, see Ling-chi Wang, "Roots and Changing Identity of Chinese in the United States," *Daedalus* (Spring 1991): 181–206.

6. Partha Chatterjee, *Nationalist Thought and the Colonial World: A Derivative Discourse?* (Minneapolis: University of Minnesota Press, 1993), chap. 2. For an illuminating

study of deterritorialized "transnations," see L. Basch, N. Glick Schiller, and C. Szanton Blanc, *Nations Unbound: Transnational Projects, Postcolonial Predicaments, and Deterritorialized nation–states* (New York: Gordon and Breach, 1994).

7. For an interesting study that stresses intra-Han ethnicity in China, see Emily Honig, *Creating Chinese Ethnicity: Subei People in Shanghai, 1850–1980* (New Haven, Conn.: Yale University Press, 1992). For nation-building as a colonial project, see Eugen Weber, *Peasants into Frenchmen: The Modernization of Rural France, 1870–1914* (Stanford, Calif.: Stanford University Press, 1976), especially 485–96.

8. For an example of such "common sense" use of ethnicity, see Stuart Hall, "Cultural Identity and Diaspora," in *Contemporary Postcolonial Theory: A Reader*, ed. Padmini Mongia (London: Arnold Press, 1996): 110–21, where Hall acknowledges the constructedness of ethnicity, without denying its reality, and its "situational" political utility.

9. Pamela K. Crossley, "Thinking about Ethnicity in Early Modern China," *Late Imperial China* 11(1) (June 1990): 1–34. See also, Mark Elliott, "Bannerman and Townsman: Ethnic Tension in Nineteenth-Century Jiangnan," *Late Imperial China* 11(1) (June 1990): 36–74.

10. For the radical implications of indigenism for the modern system of international relations, see Franke Wilmer, *The Indigenous Voice in World Politics* (Newbury Park, Calif.: Sage Publications, 1993). These implications are responsible, we think, for the ways in which indigenous movements have become prominent in contemporary radical politics (as in the case, most dramatically, of the Zapatista Uprising in Chiapas) and have caught the imagination of those involved in the so-called new social movements, which share with indigenism an emphasis on groundedness in places.

11. Epeli Hau'ofa, "Our Sea of Islands," in *A New Oceania: Rediscovering Our Sea of Islands*, ed. Eric Waddell, Vijay Naidu, and Epeli Hau'ofa (Suva, Fiji: School of Social and Economic Development, University of the South Pacific, 1993), 2–16, here 5.

12. Ward Churchill, "I Am Indigenist: Notes on the Ideology of the Fourth World," in *The Struggle for the Land: Indigenous Resistance to Genocide, Ecocide and Expropriation in Contemporary North America*, Ward Churchill (Monroe, Maine: Common Courage Press, 1993), 403–51, here 403.

13. Churchill, "I Am Indigenist."

2

Place-Based Imagination: Globalism and the Politics of Place

Arif Dirlik

The past decade has witnessed the irruption of place consciousness into social and political analysis. Place consciousness, one recent philosophical inquiry suggests, is integral to human existence, for it is nearly impossible to "imagine what it would be like if there were no places in the world."[1] On the other hand, places are not given, but produced by human activity, which implies that how we imagine and conceive places is a historical problem. In its most recent manifestation, place consciousness is closely linked to, and appears as the radical other of, that other conspicuous phenomenon of the last decade, globalism.

In this chapter I inquire into the relationship between globalism and place consciousness and the implications of this relationship for contemporary configurations of the ways in which we seek to grasp the world. The discussion has three goals. The first goal is to bring some terminological clarity to discussions of place, which I for one find somewhat confusing in their juxtapositions of the global and the local, or the spatial and the place-based, while using such terms as *local, spatial*, and *place-based* interchangeably. Second, I seek on the basis of such clarification to rephrase the problem of the global and the local, specifically, to address a certain asymmetry in the formulation of the relationship between the two. This will require also a consideration that it may be more productive intellectually and politically to view these terms as signifiers for processes, rather than as locations conceived in narrow geographical terms—as globalization and localization, in other words, rather than as the global and the local—which raises questions about a tendency in much of the existing literature to counterpose spatiality to temporality. Finally, I will make a case for a specifically place-based consciousness, by considering the implications of places for conceptions of development, for categories of social analysis such as class, gender, and ethnicity, and for the ways in which we deal with questions of culture in cultural criticism. I will suggest on the

15

basis of these three sets of questions that it may be best to conceive of places and place-based consciousness not as a legacy of history or geography, the givens of time and space that provide the context for intellectual and political activity, but as a project that is devoted to the creation and construction of new contexts for thinking about politics and the production of knowledge.

I argue that changes in attitude on questions of development, social categories, and culture, under conditions of a global capitalism, are largely responsible for contemporary manifestations of place consciousness. The latter, in turn, opens up new avenues for the ways in which we think about these questions. At a time of intellectual uncertainty and political despair, moreover, place consciousness offers a critical perspective from which to reevaluate long-standing assumptions in social and political analysis and to formulate alternatives both to the hegemony of an abstract modernity and the political defeatism if not nihilism of a ludic post-modernity.

GLOBAL/LOCAL: SPATIAL/PLACE-BASED

As the terminology of place is by no means self-evident, I would like to begin with a few words on my understanding of this term, in the process distinguishing *place* from kindred terms such as *space* and *locality*, with which it is often used inter-changeably. Under contemporary circumstances, this terminology invites, un-avoidably, the concept of the global, which provides the context for most discussions of place. I will, therefore, take the juxtaposition of the global and the local as my point of departure.

I will begin with the rather mundane observation that for all their supposed concrete referentiality, *the global* and *the local* are terms that derive their meanings from one another, rather than from reference to any specifically describable spatiality.[2] The term *global* used as a signifier for certain processes (economic, political, social, and cultural) obviously does not refer to the globe as a representation of the whole world conceived geometrically. Not only are large parts of the world left out of those processes, but even in those parts of the world that are included in the processes, the processes appear as pathways in networks of one kind or another that leave untouched or even reduce to marginality significant surfaces of what is implied by a term such as *global*. The global, therefore, is something more than national or regional, but it is by no means descriptive of any whole; at its most abstractly discursive, it may refer to anything other than the local. Projected onto realms beyond that of the physically geographic, such as realms of culture and psychology, it is also not universal.[3] To burden it with further complications, it is moreover in constant motion.

The global, nevertheless, would seem in our day to call into question spaces defined by the political boundaries of the nation, which has called into question the meaning of its spatial other, the local. The local in an earlier usage derived its meaning from its contradiction to the national, or the universal. Increasingly, however, the local derives its meaning from its juxtaposition to the global. The very uncertainty about the meaning of the global condemns it to ambiguity. Unless the boundaries of the local may be drawn by fiat, as in national administrative structures, which are blurred by globalization, however, the local is as difficult to locate as the global, which endows it with meaning. Hence it is not surprising, unlike in an earlier day when the local derived its meaning from the national, to find that nations and entire extranational regions may qualify as referents for the local.[4]

It is not surprising, given the conflation of the language of *space* and *place* with that of the *global* and the *local*, that those terms too should be imbued through and through with the ambiguities of the latter juxtaposition. In much of the discussion about places, local, spatial, and place-based are used interchangeably. The conflation is not just intellectual; it is also, and even more deeply, political. The very conceptualization of globalism is revealed upon closer examination to be a kind of spaceless *and* timeless operation,[5] which rather than render it vacuous as a concept, ironically bolsters its pretensions to a new kind of universalism, rendering it into a point of departure for all other spatializations. It is not very surprising that anything less than the global should be mobilized in juxtaposition to it as its other, confounding the possibility of profound differences among the spatial, the local, and the place-based. Thus it becomes possible to speak of the spatial, the local, and the place-based in the same breath, forgetting that while the local derives its meaning from the global, spatial itself derives its meaning from a parallel with globality and stands in the same oppositional relationship to the place-based as the global does to the local. This privileging of the global is even more evident in the literature in that alternative perspective that seeks to differentiate the spatial and the place-based in the association of space with capital, history, and activity, while the place-based is the realm of labor, stasis, and immobility.

In his monumental work on space, which has inspired theoretically a great deal of the discussion on space and place, Henri Lefebvre recognized a need for a differentiation of space from place in the distinction he drew between the "representation of space" and "representational space." As he puts it, "Representational space is alive: it speaks, it has an effective kernel or centre: Ego, bed, bedroom, dwelling, house; or: square, church, graveyard. It embraces the loci of passion, of action and of lived situations, and thus immediately implies time. Consequently, it may be qualified in various ways: it may be directional, situational or relational, because it is essentially qualitative, fluid and dynamic."[6] Lefebvre's distinction between the two kinds of space, both within the context of the production of capitalist relations, parallels two further distinctions between appropriated and dominated spaces and space as product and work; the one set relating space to power, the other to psychology and esthetics.[7] While Lefebvre uses the word *place* only occasionally, representational and appropriated spaces and space as work clearly

correspond in the discussion to places in their groundedness in nature and their intimate relationship to the immediacy of everyday life.[8]

Space is product, the geographical equivalent of the commodity; place, on the other hand, is product *and* work, with the uniqueness of the work of art or the craft of the artisan. Space and place stand in opposition to one another, as the opposition of different kinds of labor (and different stages in the production of space). What appears on first sight as the opposition of the production of space under capitalist and precapitalist formations is revealed on closer examination as opposition between different kinds of labor as well; one that distinguishes capitalist from precapitalist modes of production, but involves also an evaluation of labor with divisive implications for the laborers themselves. It is also interesting that "time," in this case, is the "time" of place as against what Walter Benjamin described as the "empty, homogeneous time" of modernity. Time and space coincide in place, against the timelessness of space.

The juxtaposition of space and place in this original discussion, which took capitalism as its premise, is intended to promote the radical cause of social transformation: "any revolutionary 'project' today, whether utopian or realistic, must, if it is to avoid hopeless banality, make the reappropriation of the body, in association with the reappropriation of space, into a non-negotiable part of its agenda."[9] But Lefebvre introduces almost a note of hopelessness to this project in observing that this struggle is delimited already by the conquest of space by "the power of the negative," so that the struggle may take place only within the conditions set by the history of its production, for "there is in any case no way of turning back."[10] On the other hand, his conflation of the political, the psychological, and the esthetic suggests the possibility that places may provide the occasions for esthetic experiments or unfulfillable longings, which, rather than return to the political, may end up further excluding the political from everyday life by substituting for it public play and private nostalgia. The challenge of the conflation is how to recapture places for politics (and use-value) against their consumption into postmodernist privatization, where one place is scarcely distinguishable from another in an unending chain of exchange-values.

Lefebvre's work put space on the agenda of radical politics and cultural criticism by arguing that natural or social spaces were not locations for historical activity but, on the contrary, were themselves products of human activity that must be understood not just geographically but historically. His juxtaposition of space and place, on the other hand, underlined the complexity of radical agenda in its hints that a radical agenda is not to be conceived merely in terms of social categories (of class, gender, ethnicity, whatever), because place (unlike space) is a social product but not just a social product; place is the location, I would like to suggest here, where the social and the natural meet, where the production of nature by the social is not clearly distinguishable from the production of the social by the natural. This ambiguity may be responsible for much of the discussion over space and place over the last decade. The globalization of capital has placed the production of space on the agenda of radical politics with unprecedented intensity. As this process has become unavoidably visible in the almost daily making and unmaking of places at a frenetic pace, the question of place has acquired a parallel urgency. The questions raised by the juxtaposition of space and place, under the circumstances, are not merely questions of theory, but of practical politics, of daily survival. Unlike in the ideology of capital, where globalization appears as a means to maximize exchange values and places are merely means to that end, in radical politics the new awareness of place is an urgent issue because places in the past played only a marginal part, or, more accurately, were marginalized in a hegemonic consensus over the location of significant political activity at supraplace levels, which in its derogation of places differed little from the consignment of places to ultimate oblivion by the motions of capital. Interestingly, while space or spatiality has acquired a new respectability with the reconfiguration of global economies, place continues to be consigned to the margins, as a subcategory of the spatial, rather than as a challenge to the latter. The problem is as visible in the defense of place-based politics as in its repudiation.

David Harvey, most influential in his introduction of space into thinking on political economy, politics, and culture, was to resolve the space/place ambiguity by assigning space into the realm of capital and place into the realm of the laborer, including women and ethnicities; but unambiguously translating into the language of class (and capitalist development) problems that involved different kinds of labor as well (therefore erasing contradictions within labor, regardless of the hegemonic circumstances that may have created such contradictions):

> the capacity of most social movements to command place better than space puts a strong emphasis upon the potential between place and social identity. This is manifest in political action. The defensiveness of municipal socialism, the insistence on working-class community, the localization of the fight against capital, become central features of working-class struggle within an overall patterning of uneven geographical development. The consequent dilemmas of socialist or working-class movements in the face of a universalizing capitalism are shared by other oppositional groups—racial minorities, colonized peoples, women etc.—who are relatively empowered to organize in place but dis-empowered when it comes to organizing over space. In clinging, often of necessity, to a place-bound identity, however, such oppositional movements become a part of the very fragmentation which a mobile capitalism and flexible accumulation can feed upon.[11]

Harvey's opposition of space to place is not unique; it is stated with even less ambiguity in a recent discussion of European economies, where the authors state that "it may be helpful, terminologically and theoretically, to understand *space* as the domain of capital—a domain across which capital is constantly searching in pursuit of greater profits—and *place* as the meaningful situations established by labor."[12]

The equation of space with capital and place with labor (among other subaltern groups) in these usages makes for a level of precision in the relationship of geographical to social categories, but only at the cost of three reductionisms (at least three that are immediately obvious to me): a reductionist conception of the mode of production that erases the complex relationships between labor and capital, and within labor itself; the economistic exclusion from consideration the rich interplay between politics, psychology, and esthetics in Lefebvre's juxtaposition of these categories—including the place of nature in places that has disappeared in these characterizations of place; and a social reductionism, in the implication that class relations between capital and labor are sufficient to explicate the relationship between space and place.

This delineation of space from place has come under criticism from socialist-feminists. In a recent article, Laura Chernaik writes that:

> Harvey's distinction between place and space interacts with the way that he considers class differently from race and gender, as an analytical category as well as identity form; race and gender are only treated as forms of identity, not as analytical categories in their own right. It is only universalization which is treated as spatialization; universalization is considered as the prerogative only of capitalism and, in potential, of labour. . . . However, 'place-bound' identities are spatial practices and thus, according to Harvey and Lefebvre's theory, part of the production of space. Harvey's expression, 'place-bound', is quite misleading; local practices can produce spatializations. Local practices are not bound to place but are potentially possible to articulate across space, globally. The form that this global articulation takes, though, is more often a network than a system; a coalition of specific, different groups rather than a universalization of any one political identity.[13]

In her defense of place, Chernaik returns us to a more complicated understanding of the relationship between place and space in two ways. First is her multiplying of the social categories that need to be taken into consideration in analyzing the dynamic relationship between place and space. Second, she reunifies place and space through these same social categories, which is contingent on the important distinction that she draws between system and network. I will return to this later.

The socialized conception of space, which must be the inevitable concomitant of the spatialization of the social, has been theorized most extensively by Doreen Massey, who similarly reintroduces a place/space ambiguity against their separation into exclusive spheres. Massey's influential analysis of places grows directly out of struggles over the politics of place between global capital and local communities in England. Her definition of places is especially important not only because she seeks to "socialize" places thoroughly in order to relieve them of any association with nostalgic yearnings for a past that was never there but also because she defends places against globalization by rephrasing the relationship between temporality and spatiality, namely, by denying their separability analytically. As she puts it in a recent work,

> If . . . the spatial is thought of in the context of space-time and as formed out of social interrelations at all scales, then one view of a place is as a particular appreciation of

those relations, a particular moment in those networks of social relations and understandings. But the particular mix of social relations which are thus part of what defines the uniqueness of any place is by no means all included within that place itself. Importantly, it includes relations which stretch beyond—the global as part of what constitutes the local, the outside as part of the inside. Such a view of place challenges any possibility of claims to internal histories or to timeless identities. The identities of places are always unfixed, contested and multiple. And the particularity of any place is, in these terms, constructed not by placing boundaries around it and defining its identity through counterposition to the other which lies beyond, but precisely (in part) through the specificity of the mix of links and interconnections *to* that 'beyond'. Places viewed in this way are open and porous.[14]

Massey's conceptualization of space is directed at those who would view place "as bounded, as in various ways a site of authenticity, as singular, fixed and unproblematic in its identity . . . a conceptualization of place which rests in part on the view of space as stasis."[15] In other words those views of place, we might add, that were products of modernity, that produced places as locations for parochialism and changelessness in ways that the inhabitants of places never intended and in the end resulted in an inexorable urge to erase places by incorporating them into the spaces of modernity (defined by capitalism, or its statist counterpart in socialism, as well as nationalism). Not surprisingly, under the regime of modernity, the defense of place was to come to be linked to conservative opposition to modernity—or, what amounts to the same thing politically, to a nostalgic yearning for a past lost irrevocably. From the perspective of a modernist radicalism, moreover, the concern for place appears as an impediment to the struggle against capitalism, which, in its very "realism," accepts the destruction of places as a condition of its success.

Massey's conceptualization is one manifestation of an effort to break this link between place consciousness and conservative politics and to redirect radical attention to the importance of place, aided by a specifically feminist radicalism. It represents, if only on these grounds, a postmodern venture, which is also suggested by its rejection of fixity, boundedness, and essentialized interiority to the concept of place.[16]

This postmodernism is in the end a virtue and a liability. Massey's well-considered defense of place consciousness against modernist criticism, the context for her argument, also places limitations on her defense of place consciousness. That place-consciousness does not of necessity require spatial boundedness or the exclusion of the extra-local, temporal stasis, or social homogeneity are important reminders that these putative characteristics of place consciousness were more a fabrication of modernist prejudice than a description of the realities of premodern (and modern) local societies.[17] On the other hand, this critique of the marginalization of places in a modernist radicalism does not quite abolish the problematic of place; places may not be "place-bound," but the abolition of the distinction between place-based and spatial reintroduces an ambiguity at another level by denying the distinctiveness of the place-based: the effort to salvage place ends up by declaring that there is nothing special about place after all.[18] Massey's conceptualization needs to be amended by a further critique of postmodern abstraction of places, which, in the process of affirming difference and a "politics of location," is overly zealous, I think, in disassociating place from fixed location. This is where ecological conceptions of place, which are almost totally absent from these discussions (and marginalized by them in the preoccupation with the "social construction of space"), have some crucial insights to contribute by once again bringing nature (even if it is only a "myth of nature," in Lefebvre's terms) into the conceptualization of place.

In contrast to concepts of space and local, the ecological conception insists, an important aspect of the concept of place is its groundedness in topography.[19] Most theoretical discussions of place of which I am aware (including Massey's) take place within the context of urban geography and sociology, with the consequence that this aspect of place consciousness disappears into the background of discussions driven by easily observed phenomena of ceaseless urban dislocations and relocations. Ecologically conceived discussions of places, by contrast, are of necessity attentive to questions of the fixity of places and the limitations set on the production of place by its immediate environment.[20]

The topographical grounding of place immediately points to a second question, the question of boundaries. If place is not enclosed within exclusive boundaries, can the concept of space therefore dispense with the problem of boundaries? Massey's reconceptualization of space and place in terms of social relations ("the spatial is social relations 'stretched out'")[21] is quite fruitful and enables a questioning of the modernist prejudices against place. Without some delimitation of how far social relations may be "stretched out," however, place may be meaningless, especially in these days of diasporas where even kinship relations, for example, may be stretched out over the globe, making place indistinguishable from the global. This may be the reason that, for all her effort at specifying place, Massey's discussion continues to use place-based, spatial, and local interchangeably, where place is on occasion equated with the territory of the nation.[22] Here, too, attention to the groundedness of places in ecology and topography is important. This is not to return to some kind of geographic determinism or bounded notion of place, but to suggest that any intellectually and politically critical notion of place must recognize some notion of boundary; porosity of boundaries is not the same as the abolition of boundaries.

Groundedness, which is not the same thing as immutable fixity, and some measure of definition by flexible and porous boundaries, I suggest, are crucial to any conceptualization of place and place-based consciousness. Place as metaphor suggests groundedness from below, and a flexible and porous boundary around it, without closing out the extralocal, all the way to the global. What is important about the metaphor is that it calls for a definition of what is to be included in the place from within the place—some control over the conduct and organization of everyday life, in other words—rather than from above, from those placeless abstractions such as capital, the nation–state, and their discursive expressions in the realm of theory. It is these features, I think, that justify attention to the place-based against kindred notions of local and spatial. The latter may serve in certain usages as equivalents to place-based, but they also may be, and are, mobilized as projects or qualifications of those placeless abstractions, which both in intention and effect negate places conceived in terms of control over everyday life. No less than "the struggle of memory against forgetting" in the temporal realm, in the words of Milan Kundera, the struggle for place in the concrete is a struggle against power and the hegemony of abstractions.

The political implications of place consciousness may carry greater significance than ever in our day. Neil Smith concludes his study of space with the observation that, "capitalism has always been a fundamentally geographical project. It may not be too soon to suggest, and I hope not too late, that the revolt against capitalism should itself be 'planning something geographical.'"[23] If capitalism has always been geographical as a project, the manipulation and production of spaces have become more visible than ever as a global capitalism has abstracted itself from lived places into transnational spaces, but strives chameleon-like to assume localized colorings that enable unprecedented penetration of the local by the global, remaking places in accordance with its own marketing and production needs while flaunting a new-found concern for place and community, which serves only to confound further the relationship between places and global marketing strategies and to disguise the power relations between corporation and community.

Ironically, the very effort to manipulate places in the marketing of commodities and images is responsible also for the renewed awareness of places. My insistence on a grounded conception of place derives from a particular appreciation of this situation. The distinguished French historian of China Jean Chesneaux in a recent work uses the paradigm of Hong Kong to describe the contemporary global economy as "an off-ground economy." In light of recent developments in Hong Kong, I am not sure of what Chesneaux has to say about Hong Kong, but I think he is on the mark where it concerns the new phase of capitalism, which has taken the essential placelessness of capitalism to unprecedented proportions.[24] His metaphor suggests that regrounding the economy may be an important first step in the radical geographical project to which Smith draws attention. Far more than an object of nostalgia for a past lost irrevocably, place in this perspective appears as a project that, rather than resign to modernist prejudices against it, insists on the importance of the past as a source of critical perspectives on the present, while reworking the past with present concerns.

Place conceived as project provides a context in which we may reformulate the ways in which we think of spaces presently. What the project may be is best enunciated through a consideration of the implications of place or place-based consciousness for the categories through which the modernist project expresses itself: development, categories of social analysis, and culture. But first a reformulation of the problem that recognizes the intractability of the problem of the local and

Local
Place-based

global
spatial

the global or the place-based and the spatial and presents us with choices that may not be disentangled sociologically or at the level of abstract theory, which is a problem with existing discussions of place/space in which the defense and the repudiation of place both carry considerable theoretical plausibility and for that same reason seem in their opposition to be confined within a theoretical world of their own out of which there is no exit that is to be revealed by theory.

HYBRIDITY AND CONTRADICTION: THE UNITY OF THE GLOBAL AND THE LOCAL

There is an asymmetry in almost all discussions of the problem of the global and the local, in which I must include a previous discussion of mine.[25] The asymmetry is in the relegation of the local to subordinate status against the global, which is also associated with the universal, which almost inevitably issues in the objectification of the local that must then be explained or defended. If Casey is right in his observation that it would be impossible to imagine a world without places, the local as place-based should not even need a defense. And yet, such is the hegemony of the modernist marginalization of places that this task emerges as the primary task in disentangling the relationship of the local to the global. Places then need to be explained/defended not on their own terms, but in terms of the operations of the global, which introduces an asymmetry to the analysis before it has even begun in the very formulation of the problem. What if the global were local, or place-based, just as the local or place-based were global?

This is the question raised in a central way by Bruno Latour in his book *We Have Never Been Modern*. Latour addresses the question of the global and the local as part of a broader project of deconstructing modernity (*Western* modernity), which was made possible by dividing humans from nonhumans (culture/nature), that enabled another divide, the West and the Rest (Us and Them). These two divides that underlie "the modern constitution," as he puts it, necessitated procedures of "purification" and "translation" (separating the various realms in thought, followed by mediating their relationships), which ironically was to result in the proliferation of hybrids, negating the whole project of modernity. As he puts it, "those [non- or premoderns] who think the most about hybrids circumscribe them as much as possible, whereas those [modern Westerners] who choose to ignore them by insulating them from any dangerous consequences develop them to the utmost."[26] The global and the local provide just such a case of hybridity, which, in their separation, enable an illusion of the universal against the parochial, in the process disguising its own affinities with the pre- and the nonmodern:

> Just as the adjectives "natural" and "social" designate representations of collectives that are neither natural nor social in themselves, so the words "local" and "global" offer points of view on networks that are by nature neither local nor global, but are more

or less long and more or less connected. What I have called the modern exoticism consists in taking these two pairs of oppositions as what defines our world and what would set us apart from all others.[27]

We may recall here Chernaik's distinction between system and network, which enabled a bridging of the divide between the global and the local. For Latour, the metaphor of the network assumes a far more crucial epistemological part in questioning not only the division between the global and the local but the very idea of a distinct modernity, for "the moderns have simply invented longer networks by enlisting a certain type of nonhumans."[28] He observes, moreover, that "as concepts, 'local' and 'global' work well for surfaces and geometry, but very badly for networks and topology."[29] His own conception of the relationship between the global and the local is expressed through the deceptively simple "railroad model." "Is a railroad local or global? Neither. It is local at all points, since you always find sleepers and railroad workers, and you have stations and automatic ticket machines scattered along the way. Yet it is global, since it takes you from Madrid to Berlin or from Brest to Vladivostok. However, it is not universal enough to take you just anywhere."[30]

If the railroad is neither local nor global, it is arguably though not necessarily both local and global. In conflating the two, Latour's goal is to bring down to size claims to globality and attendant epistemological claims to universality. Thus, he queries, "could IBM be made up of a series of local interactions?" He continues: "The capitalism of Karl Marx or Fernand Braudel is not the total capitalism of the Marxists. . . . It is a skein of somewhat longer networks that rather inadequately embrace a world on the basis of points that become centres of profit and calculation. In following it step by step, one never crosses the mysterious *lines* that should divide the local from the global."[31] The conclusion is to deny to IBM (or to science, the Red Army, the Ministry of Education in France, or whatever) the omniscience and omnipotence that follows from the illusion of controlling spaces:

> The moderns confused products with processes. They believed that the production of bureaucratic rationalization presupposed rational bureaucrats; that the production of universal science depended on universalist sciences; that the production of efficient technologies led to the effectiveness of engineers; that the production of abstraction was itself abstract; that the production of formalism was itself formal. We might just as well say that a refinery produces oil in a refined manner, or that a dairy produces butter in a butterly way.[32]

That Latour uses the metaphor of the railroad to illustrate his argument, instead of, say, the footpath or the airplane, may alert us immediately to some of the problems in his conceptualization of networks and his suppression of historicity in deconstructing modernity. But it may be fruitful for the moment to pursue the line of thought he offers where the global and the local are concerned.

The ultimate indistinguishability of the global and the local may be more pertinent presently, as a distinctive characteristic of the regime of global capitalism. *Glocal* expresses cogently what Latour has in mind by the hybridity of the global and the local. What it forces us to think about is a double process at work in shaping the world: the localization of the global and the globalization of the local, neither, as Latour warns us, to be confounded by the product.

However "off-ground" global capitalism may be, as Jean Chesneaux suggests, most of the transactions of transnational corporations are indeed conducted in places, subject to place-based contingencies and considerations. Transnational corporations have sought to "deterritorialize" their operations, but it still seems to matter in terms of national identification where their centers and branches are located. While transnationalism is a new ideal of capital, there are still U.S. corporations, Japanese corporations, British corporations, and so on. Even in that most "off-ground" of economic activities, financial transactions, a Great Britain with a powerful banking system can exert global influence out of all proportion to its place in production or its status in political power.

The global/local overlap is important in other ways. The effort of transnational corporations to "domesticate" themselves in localities of their operations may be a product of simple business calculations, but it nevertheless creates problems of its own. IBM, in its transnationalization, had to face the problem of "multiculturalism" of its workforce, which could not be contained within received managerial practices. The problem of the global and the local may be most intractable in the realm of communications, where it has led to the prolonged, and possibly irresolvable, debate over homogenization of cultures versus their local appropriations; irresolvable because the very transnational economic motivations of communications corporations necessitate the production of programs directed at places, making it impossible to distinguish places as autonomous markets from places as produced markets. In the process, however, the corporations as agents of globalization internalize the contradictions that are implicit in the incorporation of different cultural situations within their own productive procedures.

Similar observations could be extended to other realms of globalization, from the rapidly spreading idea of civil society to the operations of NGOs. Most importantly, the very movements that struggle against capital and its globalizing forces are themselves globalized in significant ways. Contrary to those depictions of space/place in terms of categories of capital versus class, gender, and ethnicity, it is quite obvious that these latter are themselves globalized in various measures, internalizing in the categories themselves the contradictions between their locally concrete manifestations. What is important is that the very process of globalization results in a situation where place-based differences, which must be addressed to make globalization possible and feasible, are incorporated into the very process of globalization, abolishing the boundary between the external and internal, bringing differences into the interior of the process of globalization, and presenting the global with all the contradictions of the local. Globalization as process, in other words, is not to be confounded with globality as product, let alone universalization of economic, political, social, and, especially, cultural forms.

The reverse process, the globalization of the local, is equally visible. Amitai Etzioni's "communitarian movement" seeks to promote community reorganization from its headquarters in Washington, D.C., while Robert Bellah and company's *Habits of the Heart* becomes a best-seller for the place-based values it advocates, with little relationship to real places except those that are white and affluent. Hillary Clinton promotes village-based family values, apparently oblivious to the destruction of real villages by transnational corporations, of which the Clinton administration is an enthusiastic advocate globally. Boulder, Colorado, is probably a greater consumer of local religious and medical practices from around the world than anywhere else, while it is also assiduous about keeping out the locals who hail from those places. Ecological escapees into the wilderness provide well-heeled New Age yuppies with pilgrimage sites wherein to reconnect with places, so as to render more tolerable their participation in global pillage.

The local in these instances is rendered into a commodity available for global circulation. But it would be mistaken to think that it is First World consumption alone that is responsible for the globalization of the local. Local products and cultural practices from handmade baskets to yogic exercises are now available for global circulation. The corporate government of Mexico awards the National Export Prize to indigenous coffee producers in Chiapas, in spiteful challenge to the Zapatistas, which is reported without comment in a North American magazine with the unlikely title of *Grassroots Development*. The Zapatistas of Chiapas themselves, in order to render place-based existence plausible and possible, go on television and the Internet to advertise their cause, earning them the plaudit of the "first postmodern revolution." Indigenous peoples, seeking to affirm their ties to the land, not only find the definition of indigenism complicated by urbanized indigenes, but seek to represent themselves in state capitals and way out in Geneva at UN headquarters. A leader of an Apache tribe legitimizes his defense of Apache lands serving as radioactive waste dumps on the grounds that indigenous people have a special relationship to land and will be better able to dispose of such waste. The people themselves, however they may appropriate the cultural messages that come from the outside, nevertheless end up around television sets that globalize them even without the necessity of motion. Even kinship, that most local and primordial of affinities, may be globalized as members of the same family find themselves scattered around the globe, not out of contingency but as part of strategic family planning to maximize resources.

The global, in other words, appears as the local, while the local in terms of networks appears as the global. Under such circumstances, the effort to sort out the global from the local, and to find social constituencies for each, may indeed end up with the modernist prejudice against which Latour's argument serves as a warning. It also exposes the futility of searching for theoretical answers to the problems of the global and the local, to the either/or logic that would seem to dominate so

Critique of hybridity

much of the debate between the global and the local, or space and place, that I discussed previously. The question here is whether or not hybridity, as Latour proposes, provides a resolution of these problems. Hybridity itself as a concept, no less in Latour's than in postcolonial conceptualizations, is a static resolution of the problem of difference in naturalized boundaries that does not recognize the contradictions produced by hybridity, the ways in which hybridity produces its own structural contexts, and how those contexts, themselves products of human activity, come to delimit the resolution of the problems it presents.

Why hybridity may be deceptively appealing but nevertheless insufficient or even misleading may be illustrated with reference to any hybrid fruit or flower or whatever. The hybrid does not abolish the original stocks of which it is a product, but presents us with new problems. It is the third space, in Homi Bhabha's metaphor, that does not eliminate the other two spaces but enriches and complicates choice. At this level, the presence of the hybrid in addition to the original stocks presents new marketing problems; but such problems only add to the dynamism of the market and legitimize its claims to offer ever more prolific choices; a liberal market pluralism in the guise of a fruit or flower, so to speak.

But what if the hybrid were to lead to the extinction of the originals out of which it was produced, which is a daily condition of products of nature and society that promises to assume even greater daily relevance in these days of genetic and social engineering? Given what the hybrid is, a dialectical reconceptualization of it may offer only an occasion for the lighthearted playfulness that is so dear to postmodernists and postcolonialists. But there is a world of difference between the description of a fruit or flower as a hybrid and its representation in terms of the multiple contradictions implied by the relationships between the hybrid and the original stocks. Phrased in the terminology of dialectics, it is a unity of opposites that is expressed in the hybrid, with all the dynamism implicit in such an unstable unity. Hybridity suggests merely a proliferation of alternatives, but in real life may also lead to the extinction of alternatives. Contradiction, in its recognition of such eventualities, calls for its anticipation, and purposeful intervention in its resolution (this is what Latour may have in mind in his observation that the precapitalist premoderns sought to control hybrids). The question is no longer one of marketing, it is more fundamentally one of production. It is also a good bit more serious because it necessarily invites considerations of power.

At this more serious level, I can think of no better way of illustrating the problem of power in hybridity than by reconsidering what Latour has to say about corporations as networks. The idea of corporations as networks of localized and contingent operations may be useful in the deconstruction of corporate claims to a universal rationality. But that itself says little about corporate power. Corporate leaders are quite prepared themselves to concede that globalization brings with it "new contradictions" between the global and the local, but they do not conclude that they should cease to maximize power; on the contrary, the recognition of the contradiction leads to the search for new management techniques to restore lost

power, or to maximize it.[33] The global may be a hybrid, as may the local. But the differences that account for hybridity in each case are different, to which Latour is indifferent in spite of his observation that postmodernism may be culpable for eradicating difference between differences. And this is most evident at the level of place. The corporation, seeking domestication, strives for an abolition of the boundary between corporation and community, which almost inevitably ends up in the conversion of community into corporate town, or worse.[34] Contrary to the logic of theory, which calls for the erasure of boundaries, the inequality of power calls in practice for the delineation of those same boundaries, for without them, spaces must invade places, and an "off-ground" economy must put an end to the groundedness of everyday life, because those very managers of the corporation, who in daily life are part of everyday place existence, are also part of a network that is informed by a geography of power to which places are mere inconveniences. Latour is wrong not because of his stress on networks against surfaces, but because he employs a reductionist notion of networks.

The ultimate virtue of this line of analysis, which confronts us simultaneously with the locality of the global and the globality of the local, is to confirm that the debate over the global and the local, or the spatial and the place-based, does not lend itself to theoretical resolutions. Dressing the problem in academic garb merely disguises the real nature of the problem and becomes a way of avoiding it. David Harvey is quite right in saying that the stress on place, in voiding supraplace organization, renders everyone vulnerable to a mobile capital that does not recognize limits to its motions. Chernaik and Massey are quite right in saying that place and space are not to be distinguished with such precision, because space socialized permits a less restrictive notion of place that, for all its ambiguity, is richer in the imagination of political possibilities. Finally, Latour is right in providing a theoretical justification for either position, by bridging through networks the division of space from place—by globalizing place and placing globality—which in the end recognizes the epistemological ambiguity but has little to say about questions of power.[35] His deconstruction of modernity, in the name of a more accurate representation of power against modernist prejudice, may even be an enabling of the legitimation of contemporary configurations of power, one that confirms the configurations of power created by modernity even as he questions the validity of its epistemological justification.

In spite of all these problems, Latour's phrasing of the problem of the local and the global yields an important conclusion: the question of the local cannot be eliminated or marginalized without an equal elimination or marginalization of the global, which restores to the problematic of the local/global a symmetry that is missing from most discussions; if the local is not to be conceived without reference to the global, it is possible to suggest that the global cannot exist without the local, which is the location for its producers and consumers of commodities, not to speak of the transnational institutions themselves. The question then is not the confrontation of the global and the local, but of different configurations of "glocality."

Instead of assigning some phenomena to the realm of the global and others to the realm of the local, it may be necessary to recognize that in other than the most exceptional cases these phenomena are all both local and global, but that they are not all local and global in the same way. Such recognition may also help clarify what is distinctive about place-based thinking or imagination. The task that follows immediately is to inquire into the meaningfulness of any social analysis that does not take place seriously as not just a location for, but as a determinant of the ways in which we think, social categories.

PLACE IN SOCIAL AND CULTURAL ANALYSIS

Massey's reminder that what makes a place unique is a "particular mix of social relations" is well taken but one-sided. If places are produced, as Lefebvre tells us, and are not merely preordained locations where things happen, the production of place includes as part of its very constitution the production of that "particular mix of social relations," which implies that social relations, and the categories in terms of which we conceive them, make sense most if we conceive them in terms of place-based manifestations, if not only in place-bound ways. That particular mix, in turn, produces the particular set of structures that gives concrete meaning to social relations represented in categories of class, gender, race, and so on—and to place itself.[36] This has become more and more inescapable as (a) the production of places under global capitalism (as either creation or destruction) become a condition of life and (b) dissatisfaction with this situation has led to the questioning of the hegemonic implications of concepts divorced from places.

Most conspicuous in this regard are questions that have been raised concerning what Arturo Escobar calls "development discourse." Development discourse, assuming universality for its own particular definitions of poverty and wealth, stagnation and progress, and ultimately what constitutes a good life, has led to an invasion of the world by Euro-American capitalism (now joined by others), which ultimately has had destructive consequences for societies and natures.[37] In a similar vein, Stacy Pigg argues that essential to the development discourse is an erasure of differences, in her case, the erasure of differences between living villages in Nepal to create a "generic village" that is more easily comprehended by developmentalist bureaucrats (foreign or Nepalese), and that lends itself more easily to development schemes directed from afar.[38] The erasure of difference, however, is not just the responsibility of far-away development bureaucrats, because it is "localized" through the complicity of the state and native leaders who have internalized the culture of developmentalism, which is a problem that is not peculiar to Nepal but describes the complicity in erasing differences of all modernizing nation–states. Indeed, it is difficult to say in historical hindsight which—a voracious capitalism ever invading places or a nation–state inventing homogeneities—has been the bigger problem in the creation of such generic categories. This might ultimately be a moot question, because the complicity of state and capital (or, in the case of existing socialisms, of state and managerial bureaucrats) extends over the history of modernity.[39] Closer attention to difference, which implies closer attention to place, leads Escobar to conclude that while developmentalism has already destroyed much (in Latin America), it has not destroyed everything, and the hybrid forms that place-based native traditions have forced on a universalist developmentalism may yet provide alternative ways of thinking about life and change against a development discourse that recognizes no exterior.[40] Place in any case is essential to the critique of developmentalism and imagining alternatives to it.[41]

The questioning of developmentalist universalism, which is one aspect, albeit a fundamental one, of the questioning of universalist social categories, inevitably raises questions about the universality of categories of social analysis, which are all products of the same modernity that produced developmentalism and are implicated in it one way or another. In this case, however, there is greater complexity to both the sources of such questioning and to its consequences, which has played a major part in the debates over the global and the local, the spatial and the place-based. Are classes conceivable without reference to places? Are genders, races, and ethnicities? Is the obliviousness to places in the use of such categories responsible for the rendering of critical categories into instruments of hegemony? The sources of such questions are complex, because the questions do not arise unmediated from the conditions of capitalism or the state, but are mediated by differences that emerge simultaneously with the enunciation of the categories themselves: for instance, questions of gender and race in class, questions of race and class in gender, questions of gender and class in race. Place appears as one more such critical question.

The consequences are also complex. Places that define themselves in terms of communities, or some kind of *place-bound* (I use this term intentionally) identity, also end up disguising and suppressing inequalities and oppressions that are internal to place. The ease with which "communities" blame internal dissensions on outside agitators has the obviousness of a cliché. Social categories such as class, gender, and race are divisive against the self-image of the community. Could the inequalities that they articulate be faced, let alone resolved, without a sense of the categories as universals?[42] On the other hand, viewed from a supracommunity perspective, these categories are also integrative, providing bonds between places, which may be the only defense against supraplace forces (of capital and the state) playing communities against one another to maximize their own powers, as David Harvey warns.

It may be because such categories have assumed hegemonic implications in their complicity with supraplace power that place has begun to intrude insistently into their constitution. But the structural conditions of global capitalism and the gradual abandonment by nation–states of the responsibilities they had assumed briefly for remedying spatial inequalities in national territories have done much to underline the placedness of categories of social analysis. Such abandonment has brought places face-to-face with capital without the intermediation of the state, set places against one another in the competition for attracting capital, and, in the process, revealed the fracturing of categories of social analysis along place differences. Hence the arguments heard frequently these days: that classes and class relations are best understood in their place-based manifestations, that gender has a place aspect to it that is not addressed in its qualifications by class and race, that ethnicity, which has been globalized in contemporary diasporic motions, needs to be understood also in terms of places, which is where different ethnicities confront one another, and race, which has always been a meaningless category, carries different meanings in different locations. The questioning of hegemony that place makes possible is not an alternative to, but an additional moment—albeit a most fundamental one—in the questioning of the hegemony of homogenizing abstractions, this time directed at the very antihegemonic categories themselves.[43]

Finally, the question of culture and of the organization and transmission of knowledge that is an integral part of any conceptualization of culture as a dynamic force. If we are to engage the question of culture in any antihegemonic, critical sense, can we dispense with places? I realize that the notion of culture has been used for long to imprison places, to render place-bound cultural identities into markers of backwardness, which then has provided the excuse for opening them up to "civilization"—global and national. But having gone through the latter process already, is it time once again to reaffirm culture as a place-based (not place-bound) phenomenon? Culture being a prime weapon in the struggles over hegemony, the question has a particular urgency in this, the age of global capitalism.

In the attack on place-based culture, the modernizing nation–state has been complicit with the developmentalist ideology of capital and its socialist counterpart, both assuming a developmentalist universality against places in spite of their own mutual oppositions. Place-based culture has been important in the whole issue of developmentalism because of the part assigned to culture as an element in promoting or obstructing progress; hence the evaluation of cultures in hierarchies in terms of their conduciveness to development. While this is by now recognized widely in critiques of modernizationist modes of apprehending culture, has such evaluation been abandoned? I think not, because conversations about culture are conducted still, now in the context of a transnationalized elite, in ways that marginalize places. Postcolonial criticism, which has made much of its own attentiveness to difference and the politics of location, continues to slip in by the backdoor reified notions of culture that presuppose national homogeneities. The plays, negotiations, localized encounters—porous boundaries that mark that depoliticized approach to cultural criticism—usually take as their subjects the European and the Indian, the European and the Chinese, the European and the African, or the White Australian and the Aborigine, but rarely the Bengali and the Gujarati, the Shanghaiese and the Beijinger, the cosmopolitan urban intellectual and the villager, or Chinese and African. In its preoccupation with "Europe" and its others, this approach is thoroughly Eurocentric. In its preoccupation with "negotiating" differences at that reified level, it is thoroughly elitist and informed by a market paradigm of individual subjectivity. The multiculturalism of postcolonial criticism does indeed consist of negotiating for power that assumes already the existence of a global power structure that is to be apportioned according to more complex notions of gender, ethnicity, and color.

These cultural assumptions also shape the kind of knowledge that is deemed valuable, which further bolsters the cultural assumptions that produce it. There has been a striking tendency in recent years in the United States to privilege the knowledge of the displaced, the "traveling theorist," against place-based knowledge.[44] As Edward Said has written,

> liberation as an intellectual mission, born in the resistance and opposition to the confinements and ravages of imperialism, has now shifted from the settled, established and domesticated dynamics of culture to its unhoused, decentered, and exilic energies, whose incarnation today is the migrant, and whose consciousness is that of the intellectual and artist in exile, the political figure between domains, between forms, between homes, and between languages.[45]

This is quite in keeping with long-standing traditions in modern learning to privilege off-ground, abstract, knowledge against "referential" knowledge, the point of departure for which is not some abstract notion of identity difference, but the immediate environment of life. The privileging of such knowledge has obvious reasons; its recipients are expected to operate in environments that have little to do with places: as corporate executives, government officials, or development economists, or maybe even as literary theorists writing about ethnicities without any connection to the ethnicities in their backyards, let alone in the lands that they have left behind.

The encounter between global and place-based assumes its greatest complexity and urgency for those who work in the production of knowledge, where it makes a difference whether the encounter leads to preoccupations with personal identity ("home"), with the struggle against localized oppressions, or with the concern for the problems presented by homogeneity and heterogeneity in global relations. In the midst of a "globalism" craze, it may be important to consider what it is that a place-based imagination has to offer and what may be the conceptualization of places that contributes the most to this end.

The urgency of this question may be illustrated through the recent conflict between globalism and area studies. Area studies in the United States, themselves products of hegemonic constructions of the world in the post–World War II period (but with longer roots in Orientalist conceptualizations of the globe), do not lend themselves to any easy defense against the current calls for globalization. It is important nevertheless to underline where these calls are coming from. Unlike in an earlier day, when the critique of area studies issued mostly from left positions against First World hegemonies, what empowers them presently is the call for globalization in the organization of learning by capital and its various institutional and ideological apparatuses. Ironically, also, while the construction of area studies was informed by the hegemonic needs of capital and First World states, area studies specialists did not just analyze the world in the service of power; many of them turned in the course of analysis to the defense of Third World societies against their subordination to First World domination and hegemony. To erase area studies in the name of globalization is to erase also the possibilities of their divisive consequences within First World institutions. Interestingly, the earlier opposition of area specialists to hegemony was empowered to a large extent by political movements outside of academia: from socialist to labor movements, from peasant insurgencies to struggles for national liberation. The decline in radical political movements seems to have cut academics off from this source of empowerment, which also accounts for the frequently heard expressions of despondency these days concerning the victory of reaction globally.

If any kind of resistance to this new form of hegemony is to be possible, it seems to me that the assertion of places against globalization is a crucial starting point. It is necessary, to begin with, to "place" globalism so as to counteract its mystification of its own location. The agenda of globalism, which seeks further to erase difference even while eulogizing the latter, gives away its continuities with earlier discourses of development. If globalism is more efficient as a developmentalist ideology, it is because it seeks to conceal, with some success, that this agenda is set still within the old locations of power, but now with the complicity of Third World states, corporations, intellectuals, and experts, who are allowed increasingly to participate in the discourse and processes of development; partly as an unavoidable consequence of their incorporation into a global capitalism, and partly because their participation is deemed to be necessary to the efficient operation of transnationalism. The condition of their participation, nevertheless, is their internalization of the knowledge and norms of the system. This is most readily evident in the training of such Third World experts in First World institutions such as economics departments, business schools, and even law schools of First World universities, which themselves are now in the process of branching out over the globe for more efficient integration of a globalized knowledge. It follows that the stress on place also entails the reconceptualization of those societies not only against First World domination but also against the domination of places by nation–states *and* against transnationalized classes, genders, ethnicities (e.g., "diasporic identities"), and so on.[46]

The second aspect is that, under such conditions, places have come to face the operations of global power more directly, as nation–states become more complicit in globalism and gradually abandon the task they had assumed earlier of mediating the global and the local. In contrast to, say, earlier ideologies of national liberation that rested in the nation–state the responsibility for the defense of places,

places now must fend for themselves. This is not to say that the nation–state has become irrelevant, or that it should be conceded to the forces of globalism. But it is more urgent than ever to "place" the nation–state itself, demystify its claims, and organize against it, if only as a means to resuscitating the connection between place and nation—this time from below. It is also necessary, to this end, to reconsider relations between places, between places and transplace or supraplace organizational forms and, finally, across national boundaries, to imagine alternative possibilities in the reorganization of spaces. Such alternatives may be novel, products of contemporary circumstances, or they may draw upon and rework through contemporary needs earlier organizational forms that have been marginalized and condemned to oblivion by modernist regimes of power. At any rate, they call for political and intellectual agenda that break not only with the "cognitive maps" of area studies, and of other spatial configurations associated with area studies, but also presuppose a countermapping to that of a contemporary hegemonic globalism.

A DEFENSE OF PLACE

Implicit in my analysis is a suggestion that there may be no places anymore, since globality is a condition of places. We speak of places out of negativity. Places come to attention at the moment of their extinction: destruction through deindustrialization, or through the deprivation of identities in the rendering of villages into "generic" villages in development discourse. The "positive" angle in the production of places, *creating* places, does not offer much comfort either. A recent study of place, quite serious in its intentions, states that:

> This book presents a fresh approach—called *strategic place marketing*—for the revitalization of towns, cities, regions and nations. Strategic marketing calls for designing a community to satisfy the needs of its key constituencies. Place marketing succeeds when stakeholders such as citizens, workers and business firms derive satisfaction from their community, and when visitors, new businesses, and investors find their expectations met.[47]

What is a place, one is tempted to ask, that is made and remade on a daily basis in order to attract tourists and investors? And what is a mentality that does not even consider the question? The questions bring into relief the two underlying premises of my discussion: it is difficult to imagine life without places; so that it is necessary to keep the idea of place alive even when it has been rendered into exchange value without any meaning of its own. It is even more necessary, however, to question and transcend such notions that make places into playthings of a globalizing capital and to reaffirm places in terms of the values implied by the concept of place, not out of a utopian or nostalgic urge to restore to places some irrecoverable (or even unimaginable) pristine purity, but in order to differentiate clearly places as projects. This requires, if only as a point of departure, the reassertion of the autonomy of place against the invasion of states and capital; in other words, a recollection that the only way to reappropriate place is to reassert use against exchange value.

The previous discussion indicates, I hope, that the defense or advocacy of place-based imagination here is not a product of a utopian project, but a response to a very real systemic crisis. The global pressures over the past decade to abandon the myth of the national market have deprived places of the protection they enjoyed under the regime of welfare states, bringing them face-to-face with the operations of a transnational capitalism and its cultures. The blurring of national boundaries with the "downsizing" of the nation–state has been exacerbated by motions of peoples globally, by the demands for sovereignty of stateless ethnicities, by indigenous peoples who have placed on the agenda of global politics a need to reconsider the international system as it was established by the Treaty of Westphalia in 1648 and globalized in the course of the nineteenth and twentieth centuries.[48] To speak of places and new forms of politics informed by places, therefore, is to answer a need for new ways to reorganize political space, which of necessity may be contingent in form, but nevertheless address problems of a systemic nature. Places, by their very logic, also raise anew the question of the relationship between society and nature. While we may by now know nature only as "second nature," a social product, as Neil Smith argues, it is also necessary, I would like to suggest, to imagine the naturalness of the natural so as to produce social and political forms that enable a harmonious coexistence between nature and society, rather than blur the boundaries between nature and society by rendering nature into a purely social construct, or by a "cyborgian" metaphorization of the human/nonhuman relationship, which, however well-intentioned, nevertheless leaves the door open for the further invasion of nature by technology.[49]

The advocacy of place presently covers a broad spectrum of social and political movements. They range from indigenous, ecological, and social movements (informed widely by women's concerns) around the world that articulate basic concerns for survival in their reaffirmation of spirit, nature, and place against developmentalism, to urban movements that seek to protect neighborhoods, to recollectivization efforts in China within the context of relations to global markets, to elitist communitarian movements and militia movements of displaced farmers in the United States that also draw on earlier religious values.[50] Politically, they cover the whole range from place-based anarchism to right-wing elitism. It is those movements, including indigenism, that have reasserted the priority of abolishing the alienation of humans from nature (Latour's "first divide"), with a corresponding reevaluation of relationships between humans (doing away with "us" and "them," Latour's second divide), that in my view offer the most radical and possibly the only meaningful criticism of modernist developmentalism—so long as they avoid reification of nature and society, of essentialized communitarianism, and of constructed tradition, and instead view their undertaking as projects without naturalizing them.

What is at issue here is not some kind of primordial purism, but a simple question of which we are all aware: the question of imagining life without development, which at this stage in history may be as difficult as imagining life without places. And this is the most fundamental contradiction that may be at issue. Politics of place is very much visible in our day. So is talk of community. So even are efforts in formerly socialist states such as China toward some measure of recollectivization against the privatizing forces that emanate from a global economy. While these phenomena all issue from a recognition of the devastating effects of globalization, and together put the issue of place back on a global agenda, they all entail also some compromise with "reality," which translates in practice into an inability or reluctance to imagine an outside to global capitalism. Thus elite communities seek to ensconce themselves in walled places, places market themselves, and recollectivization takes as its premise a more effective integration with the global economy. Under the circumstances, David Harvey's observation that emphasis on place only makes place more vulnerable to manipulation goes unchallenged, and the debate over space and place merely produces its own recycling without addressing the most basic question of all: Could there be any meaning to the discussion of place without a simultaneous and uncompromising repudiation of the very idea of development? The question immediately invites a second one that is equally basic: If places isolated from one another must be condemned to manipulation from the outside, is there any point to discussing place without also bringing in new forms of supraplace relationships as an alternative to existing institutional mechanisms, whether of capital or the nation–state? The transformation of place, in other words, may be inconceivable without a simultaneous transformation of space, because place and space, while analytically distinct, are nevertheless linked in intimate ways. Here, too, there have been efforts recently to discover such alternatives in indigenous forms of organization.[51] But at the bottom of all is a necessity to recognize the fundamental contradictions as a point of departure for reconceptualizing life against the hegemony of the modernist erasure of its most important dimensions.

I would like here to return to the statement I made about phenomena being inextricably global and local, but that they are not global and local in the same way. While Latour and Escobar use the concept of hybridity with close attention to its structural contexts and consequences, there is nevertheless a constant possibility imbedded in the concept itself of slippage into a dehistoricized and decontextualized localization of encounters between place and space similar to that in much of postcolonial criticism. Escobar struggles with this problem explicitly but, I think, without a clear resolution, because he is unwilling to confront the question that the possibility of alternative developments he perceives in hybridization may be prefigured already by the development discourse of which he is critical. He is conscious of differences between different kinds of hybridities, and even the possibility that the static, naturalized, concept of hybridity may suppress the contradictions presented by difference, but he nevertheless stops short of engaging these differences, and hybridity itself, in terms of their internal contradictions, which themselves are inextricable from the contradiction between the inside and the outside, as is implicit in the globalization of the local, and the localization of the global. The contradiction is both structural and historical. If development discourse already has hybridized places, is it possible to sustain hybridity, let alone return to a predevelopment past? Are we then condemned to endless encounter and play between the local and the global, without place, without a past or a future, where the "politics of location" itself is "off-grounded" or relocated at the level of individual identities, negating the possibility of meaningful politics because all it can promise is the production of politically meaningless differences or hybridities? Why do we not speak about contradictions any longer? Against hybridity, contradiction presents us with the problem of recognizing difference, but also demanding their resolution, since contradictions may not be sustained indefinitely without reconfiguring difference.

In a fundamental sense, the resolutions offered by these various critiques of modernity are all nonresolutions that take refuge in hybridity without considering its contradictory implications. Earlier ways of positing the global (capital) against the local (labor) may be insufficient to represent a contemporary situation when the glocal meets the glocal, but the latter terms also conceal significant historical differences and the changing configurations in the structuring of power. To say that IBM differs from the British East India Company only in the reach of its networks is to ignore the power of IBM over surfaces as well; to say that we have always been hybrids is to ignore that there is a difference between exchange and appropriation. I think there is something very wrong with arguments that natives appropriate for their own meanings the cultural meanings propagated by transnational communication companies, which, in the name of restoring subjectivity to natives (which may be empirically valid), proceed nevertheless to declare that power is inevitably localized and that it affects all sides equally. It does ignore in analysis an asymmetry of power, which appears in its full nakedness only after a symmetry is established in analysis. The global is localized, and the local is globalized. That is the symmetry. But the globalization of the local does not compensate in terms of politics, economy, and culture for the localization of the global. That is the asymmetry, that requires for its appreciation a sense of context and structure, even if the context is a product of the content, as the content is a product of the context. It requires also a sense of history, that what appears today as something of an exchange, in which both sides participate, may turn out to be less than an exchange because it is *unequal* exchange, because one side will see its life transformed by television while the other side will through the same television invade the world and create a new structural context for its operations.[52]

Hybridity, then, itself begs the question of resolution. Under conditions of "unequal exchange," the resolution itself is likely to be more in favor of space over place, of abstract power over concrete everyday existence, where the former may even produce the "differences" of the latter in a process of maximizing its power while mystifying its location.[53] For all its empirical validity and its promise in re-thinking modernity, hybridity without contradiction may end up legitimating the inequalities that must of necessity be part of its constitution under conditions of "unequal exchange." It also defuses claims to "pure" identities that may be essential to struggles against existing structures of power and the imagination of alternatives to it.

If hybridity is problematic as an effective response to developmentalism under conditions of unequal power, what are the alternatives? In terms of radical imaginings, it seems to me that there are only two: the total repudiation of development in the name of the autonomy of places and the projection of places into spaces to create new structures of power, which may provide protection to places, because, rather than repudiate places in the name of abstractions, they incorporate places into their very constitution. The one alternative finds expression most dramatically in the arguments of the deep ecologists; the other has yet to get the hearing it deserves, because of the tendency to set place against space, as in the debates to which I previously referred. In other words, against the either/or approach to questions of place and space, it is necessary to reintegrate the two in new reorganizations of space—from below. There is no guarantee that this may be accomplished, but one wonders what the alternatives to it might be. Radicals are as bound by the legacies of the past as anyone else and need to rethink the relationship to place and space of the constituencies for whom they claim to speak. This is as good a "place" to start as any other. Whether they take as their point of departure places or spaces, the working class or capital, or the complex gendered, ethnic, or racial constituents of places and spaces, it seems to me that a strategy that reintegrates place and space (and these many constituencies) is indispensable against the abstractions of modernity. One thing seems to me to be unavoidable: just as it is impossible if not pointless to reaffirm places without questioning development (life as it is, in other words) at its very fundamentals, it is equally meaningless to pretend that places may reappropriate nature and society unless they also project themselves into the spaces that are presently the domains of capital and modernity. Escaping from society is not the best way of changing it. On the other hand, radical disassociation from society as it is may be inevitable as a first step before any meaningful reconstruction of society even appears on the horizon as a possibility. In either case, radical movements of the present may have much to learn from indigenous paradigms of the relationship between nature and society as well as from indigenous forms of social and political organization.[54] The radicalism I speak of, needless to say, is not to be confounded with New Age consumptions of indigenism as it presupposes fundamental social and political reorganization. Fundamental to such reorganization is a recognition of the primacy of place, and of its autonomy, and, *on that irreducible basis*, to produce translocal or, better still, transplace alliances and cooperative formations. "Critical regionalism," in cultural forms or social formations, may in this perspective take as its point of departure not globalism, but places.[55]

Against the grain of much of contemporary thinking on "binary oppositions," I would like to suggest here that, for all the risks they entail in encouraging social conflict, such oppositions have an important part to play in considerations of alternatives to the present. This fact was widely recognized in revolutionary ideologies but has become unfashionable in postrevolutionary thinking on culture and society.[56] Failure to address questions raised by conflicts driven by essentialist notions of identity in fact undermines claims to validity of a postmodernist or postcolonialist epistemology that refuses to recognize that for all its insistence on collage, fluidity, and hybridity, the real world on a daily basis reveals the continued importance of essentialized identities in politics. I am not referring here just to the multitudinous conflicts around identities of class, gender, ethnicity, race, religion, and so on, but more to the point in the present context, to confrontations between the forces of globalism and the forces of place. To mobilize hybridity as alibi against such conflicts does not just deconstruct power, as a postrevolutionary shadow left would like to think it is doing; it also deconstructs claims to identity in legitimation of rethinking modernity and the designing of alternative projects. Postmodernity is an efficient way, under the circumstances, to defuse the claims to alternative possibilities of newcomers to modernity. Binary oppositions, albeit inspired by different configurations of power than those that promoted modernist developmentalism, may indeed be the condition for producing new forms of hybridity that are driven by and promote new social and cultural visions. The juxtaposition of purity/hybridity is itself a binary opposition that precludes thinking of binarism and hybridity in radically new ways that defers indefinitely the possibility of realizing more egalitarian constitutions of hybridity and excludes by fiat the reconstitution of the world according to a different set of rules. The problem may not be that "we have never been modern," but that all of a sudden we are not the only ones who are modern. And that calls for choices against the teleologies of a Euro-American modernity; which, by now, are hardly just Euro-American in compass.[57]

This is where the insistence on groundedness, fixity, and the "myth of nature" assume strategic significance if counterresolutions to the contradictions of hybridity are to be even conceivable; for they point to the reconquest of space by place as an irreducible goal. This is also where indigenism and other movements inspired by it assume an unprecedented significance, both in their reaffirmation of groundedness in land and in the possibilities that they may offer in the restructuring of space.[58] Having recognized, however, that it may no longer be possible to go back to place, or to a past that was constructed in places, the past itself no less than space may serve only as a source for future projects that do not repudiate the present but seek social construction or the construction of nature in place-based ways with the past always before—not behind—it.

Given all the uncertainties that a place-based notion of change invokes, nay, demands, the question of place is not one to be resolved at the level of theory, not only because difference is nearly impossible to theorize but also because to theorize is to abolish difference and to appropriate it to an academic discourse that has its own priorities, which do not coincide with the priorities of everyday life. Politics of place is practical politics, where the categories of abstract social analysis may serve as impediments to the resolution of questions of everyday life if used inflexibly, but may have much to offer if used with regard to specific context in cognizance of the world at large. This is in keeping with a recognition of places as projects that reaffirm the necessity of reconstructing life from below in its very connectedness with nature.[59]

The imagination of place itself calls for a humility in the conceptualization of knowledge if only we recall Paolo Freire's reminder that truth is inconceivable except in terms of its contribution to humanity. And humanity itself, in such conceptualization, is not an abstracted humanity but living human beings, whose needs have to be addressed before we may even engage in speculations about humanity, in other words, humanity as a "concrete universal," rather than an abstract notion of humanity that brackets living people, their relationships to nature, to nonhumans, and to one another.

The project as I describe it here is itself open to the charge of abstraction and worse—utopian dreaming. That may well be the case, but the dismissal of radical opposition to the present as utopian engages in a closure of alternatives to the present that disguises its own location in power. The question raised by it is very difficult and also very simple: Whom do we speak for when we speak? And what choices do we make? If utopianism is fraught with the dangers of the unforeseen, the closure on utopianism represents little more than resignation to power as it is, in which we are all complicit, perhaps more so when we deny that when we speak we always speak for something or someone and that we make choices in doing so.

The most compelling reason for speaking about places is that there are already many living people out there who are engaged in defending places and their lives against the encroachment of states and capital. Even where such encroachment seems total, as in the United States, for instance, struggle of this kind is very much a way of life. The institutions in which we work, given their attachments and links to power, speak for the global and engage in constant derogation of places, which, from the perspective of power, must be consigned to oblivion of one kind or another—or, better still, to exchange values, susceptible to calculation by economists who are wedded to the capitalist mode of production with which their learning is intertwined. For all its complexities, which are no more complex than those of globality, place-based imagination enables a critique of power that is thoroughly radical in its questioning of the very fundamentals of life and knowledge that inform contemporary existence.[60] The question for those who speak from academic sites, such as ourselves, is not a choice between reality versus utopianism, or practicality versus nostalgic recovery of what is not to be recovered, oppositions that silence rather than empower, but a much simpler choice: Whose voices are to be the more audible in the ways in which we play the world, the voices of globalism that erase both people and places or the voices of the weak who are straining to be heard? Who the "weak" may be, and how we hear them, are themselves complicated questions that may call for complex and contradictory answers—many of them possibly unacceptable to the people thus depicted. It is important nevertheless to keep the questions in the foreground of conversation—if only to preserve or, more ambitiously, to create those discursive spaces that enable the thinking of alternatives to "the power of the negative."

Arguments for hybridity offer one possible answer to such questions. They seem to me to be insufficient under the circumstances, because even where they question the positivistic assumptions of developmentalism, they still shy away from breaking with its consequences, sounding like a throwback to the past is another great fear of modernism, especially among radicals. Globalism is uncompromising in its desire, and to answer such uncompromising desire with a negotiation of hybridity only nourishes its appetite for conquest. As Latour reminds us, moreover, modernity both produces hybridity and confronts it as its negation. Hybridity is a halfway resolution that contains, through a biological metaphor, contradictions that call for resolutions, the primary contradictions being, to return to Latour's "Great Divides" in the definition of modernity, that between nature and humanity and that between human and human. Where but in places, where nature meets society and human beings confront one another in the concreteness of everyday existence, is such a resolution to be expected?

The answer to this question, if there is an answer, calls for unthinking the ways in which we have become accustomed to thinking the world and our places in it. A modernity driven by capitalism has rendered places into inconveniences in the path of progress to be dispensed with, either by erasure or, better still, by rendering them into commodities, which may mark the difference between modernity and postmodernity. But this very notion of progress, in the words of David Noble, is "progress without people." Places offer a way to recenter people in full recognition of the nondivisibility of humans and nonhumans. The way back to such a recognition, which must of necessity also be a way forward, may start with questioning if capital, and the globalism off which it nourishes, are inconveniences on the way to places.

NOTES

*Shorter versions of this chapter have been published in *Review* 22(2) (Spring 1999): 151–82; K. Olds, P. Dicken, P. F. Kelly, Lily Kong, and H. W. C. Yeung, eds., *Globalization and the Asia Pacific* (London: Routledge, 1999); and a special issue of *Development* 41(1) (1998), devoted to the issue.

1. Edward S. Casey, *Getting Back into Place: Toward a Renewed Understanding of the Place-World* (Bloomington, Ind.: University of Indiana Press, 1993), ix.

2. Similarly with space and place: "The ideas 'space' and 'place' require each other for definition." Yi-fu Tuan, *Space and Place: The Perspective of Experience* (Minneapolis: University of Minnesota Press, 1977), 6.

3. My distinctions here between the global and the universal and surface and network owe much to the discussion of the problem of modernity in Bruno Latour, *We Have Never Been Modern*, tr. Catherine Porter (Cambridge, Mass.: Harvard University Press, 1993).

4. See, for example, Masao Miyoshi, "A Borderless World? From Colonialism to Transnationalism and the Decline of the nation–state," *Critical Inquiry* 19 (Summer 1993): 726–51.

5. Anthony Smith notes that globalism has a notion of the past, but one that does not call upon history. See Anthony D. Smith, "Towards a Global Culture?" in *Global Culture: Nationalism, Globalization and Modernity*, ed. Mike Featherstone (London: Sage, 1990), 171–91, here 177. Somewhat more problematically, considering its contributions to the concern with space, it may be suggested that globalism does not have a spatiality either, but contributes only to the further abstraction of notions of space. For an enthusiastic advocacy of such abstraction, see Roland Robertson, "Mapping the Global Condition: Globalization as the Central Concept," in *Global Culture*, 15–30.

6. Henri Lefebvre, *The Production of Space*, tr. Donald Nicholson-Smith (Oxford: Basil Blackwell, 1991), 42.

7. Lefebvre, *Production of Space*, 164–8, for appropriated and dominated spaces, and 68–99, for space as product and work. A further distinction, between "natural space" and "social space" (30–1), receives less attention in the discussion, in spite of the suggestion that the natural space is the "common point of departure," because of the unknowability of nature "before the intervention of humans with their ravaging tools" (32).

8. In a different sense, everyday life is also crucial to the distinction between space and place that Michel deCertau draws in his *The Practice of Everyday Life* (Berkeley: University of California Press, 1984). See especially, chapter 9, where deCertau describes space as "practiced place," in contrast to which place appears as the realm of motionless objects (117–18). Lefebvre's own ambivalence toward real places is quite audible in "Notes Written One Sunday in the French Countryside," in *Critique of Everyday Life*, vol. I, tr. John Moore (London: Verso, 1991), 201–27. This interesting piece begins with an almost lyrical description of places and ends up with a condemnation of their domination by religion, to which Lefebvre suggests Marxism is the answer.

9. Lefevbre, *The Production of Space*, 166–7.

10. Lefevbre, *The Production of Space*, 109. By the "negative," Lefebvre has in mind the coercive dominations of space by the state, bureaucracies, military, etc.

11. David Harvey, *The Postmodern Condition* (London: Basil Blackwell, 1989), 302–3.

12. Huw Beynon and Ray Hudson, "Place and Space in Contemporary Europe: Some Lessons and Reflections," *Antipode* 25(3) (1993): 177–90, 182.

13. Laura Chernaik, "Spatial Displacements: Transnationalism and the New Social Movements," *Gender, Place and Culture* 3(3) (1996): 251–75, here 257.

14. Doreen Massey, *Space, Place, and Gender* (Minneapolis: University of Minnesota Press, 1994), 5.

15. Massey, *Space, Place, and Gender*, 5.

16. I use postmodernism here advisedly and in a limited sense, without its associations with poststructuralism. Otherwise such a description might come as a surprise to Massey, who is very much concerned with material circumstances and structural conditions.

17. For a similar argument, see A. Dirlik, "The Global in the Local," in *Global/Local: Cultural Production and the Transnational Imaginary*, ed. Rob Wilson and Wimal Dissayanake (Durham, N.C.: Duke University Press, 1996), 21–45.

18. Massey is not very ambiguous on this question. In the recent revised edition of her influential *Spatial Divisions of Labor: Social Structures and the Geography of Production* (New York: Routledge, 1995, first published in 1984), she complains that that work was "misread" by those who perceived her defense of place in terms of a "geological metaphor"—places, in other words, rendered particular by the sedimentations of their pasts. Against this "misreading," she reaffirms the priority of social relations in the definitions of place and space, in other words, structural relations over the histories of places. See pages 321–2.

19. For a critical discussion of efforts to reconcile Marxism to "green" thought, see Noel Castree, "The Nature of Produced Knowledge: Materiality and Knowledge Construction in Marxism," *Antipode* 27(1) (1995): 12–48.

20. Such discussions are voluminous and represent a spectrum from the bizarre to the eminently sensible. For a sampling of reasoned defenses of ecologically conceived places, see Andrew Dobson, ed., *The Green Reader: Essays toward a Sustainable Society* (San Francisco: Mercury House, 1991).

21. Massey, *Space, Place, and Gender*, 2.

22. E.g., Massey, *Space, Place, and Gender*, 8, where national liberation movements are described as "the classic case of place-based struggles," which also ignores the part nationalism has played in erasing places.

23. Neil Smith, *Uneven Development: Nature, Capital and the Production of Space* (Cambridge, Mass.: Basil Blackwell, 1990), 178.

24. Jean Chesneaux, *Brave Modern World: The Prospects for Survival*, tr. Diana Johnstone, Karen Bowie, and Francisca Garvie (London: Thames and Hudson, 1992). The people of Hong Kong, in spite of the "off-groundedness" of the Hong Kong economy, have in recent years shown a remarkable awareness of place consciousness, which goes against both the old colonial regime and the nationalist rhetoric of the Beijing regime. The class aspect of this awareness is not to be ignored, as the nationalist rhetoric of the Communist Party of China in this case seeks to disguise an alliance, unprecedented in its explicitness, between the state and transnational capital (Chinese and non-Chinese) against an emergent civil society that unites around the idea of Hong Kong as place of daily life. Giovanni Arrighi, in *The Long Twentieth Century: Money, Power and the Origins of Our Time* (New York: Verso, 1994), reminds us that the "deterritorialization" of capital (in contrast to its perennial ally, the territorial state) is not new, but is endemic to capitalism. I would like to insist nevertheless that contemporary technologies have created a new situation in abetting capital to achieve its dreams.

25. Dirlik, "The Global in the Local."

26. Latour, *We Have Never Been Modern*, 41.

27. Latour, *We Have Never Been Modern*, 122.

28. Latour, *We Have Never Been Modern*, 117.

29. Latour, *We Have Never Been Modern*, 119.

30. Latour, *We Have Never Been Modern*, 117.

31. Latour, *We Have Never Been Modern*, 121.

32. Latour, *We Have Never Been Modern*, 115–16.

33. For an elaboration of this point and its implications, see A. Dirlik, "The Postmodernization of Production and Its Organization," in Arif Dirlik, *The Postcolonial Aura: Third World Criticism in the Age of Global Capitalism* (Boulder, Colo.: Westview Press, in print).

34. For an in-depth study, see Bryan D. Palmer, *Goodyear Invades the Backcountry: The Corporate Takeover of a Rural Town* (New York: Monthly Review Press, 1994). A corporation such as Wal-Mart, which invades places waving the American flag to cover its transnationalism, is especially noteworthy in its efforts to create company towns. This invasion of space has its counterpart in the invasion of time in new notions of work. Much of the literature on globalization is taken by the possibilities created by new technologies for new forms of work, which supposedly recreate artisanal or entrepreneurial forms of work that may be relocated in the home, or even on the beach, with the aid of a laptop computer. Conceived dialectically against these ideological glorifications of new kinds of work, it is apparent also that such "decentralization" of work is possible because the new technologies enable an invasion of all temporalities, at home, on the beach, and in its abolition of any significant distinction between work and leisure. Unlike the artisan, the worker on the beach has little control over his/her time, being only a press of the button away from the overseers. For more on this, see "The New World of Work," *Business Week* (17 October 1994): 76–104.

35. These multiple affirmations present a theoretical dilemma that needs to be spelled out further to avoid confusion. My reference to the dressing of these problems in academic garb is intended to question the many ways in which problems of everyday life are distanced from their life situations by their appropriation into the problematics and languages of academic disciplines, as in the case of the "development discourse" yet to be discussed. While the abstraction implicit in such appropriation also raises questions of theory and practice, the problem of theory I have in mind in these multiple affirmations is in some ways much more acute and intractable. I may express it best by citing what Jameson has to say about the theoretical dilemmas presented by the "new social movements," which are especially pertinent here because these movements have played a significant role in raising the question of place: "[A]re the 'new social movements' consequences and aftereffects of late capitalism? Are they new units generated by the system itself in its interminable inner self-differentiation and self-reproduction? Or are they very precisely new 'agents of history' who spring into being in resistance to the system as forms of opposition to it, forcing it against the direction of its own internal logic into new reforms and internal modifications? But this is precisely a false opposition, about which it would be just as satisfactory to say that both positions are right; the crucial issue is the theoretical dilemma, replicated in both, of some explanatory choice between the alternatives of agency and system. In reality, however, there is no such choice, and both explanations or models—absolutely inconsistent with each other—are also incommensurable with each other and must be rigorously separated at the same time that they are deployed simultaneously." Fredric Jameson, *Postmodernism; Or, the Cultural Logic of Late Capitalism* (Durham, N.C.: Duke University Press, 1994), 326. The dilemma in radical theory is also a dilemma of practice. If I understand Jameson correctly, the "new social movements" are significant as agency as they respond to "real" problems presented by the system, but they are also products of systemic "self-differentiation" and are likely to contribute further to such differentiation, taking the movements ever farther away from the confrontation of the system. Much the same could be said of the dilemmas presented by places. See also, fn. 57.

36. For illuminating discussions of the implications of place-basedness for social categories, see Dick Walker and The Bay Area Study Group, "The Playground of U.S. Capitalism? The Political Economy of the San Francisco Bay Area in the 1980s," in *Fire in the Hearth: The Radical Politics of Place in America*, ed. Mike Davis, Steven Hiatt, Marie

Kennedy, Susan Ruddick, and Michael Sprinker (New York: Verso, 1990), 3–82. See also, Beatrix Campbell, "New Times Towns," in *New Times: The Changing Face of Politics in the 1990s*, ed. Stuart Hall and Martin Jacques (London: Verso, 1990), 279–99.

37. Arturo Escobar, *Encountering Development: The Making and Unmaking of the Third World* (Princeton, N.J.: Princeton University Press, 1995).

38. Stacy Leigh Pigg, "Inventing Social Categories through Place: Social Representations and Development in Nepal," *Comparative Study of Society and History* 34(3) (July 1992): 491–513.

39. For a study of the confrontation between the modernizing state and rural resistance in the initial phase of modernization in China, see Roxann Prazniak, *Of Camel Kings and Other Things: Rural Rebels against Modernity in Late Imperial China* (Boulder, Colo.: Rowman and Littlefield, 1999).

40. Escobar, *Encountering Development*, 217–22.

41. That this is not just a left, or radical, concern is cogently expressed in Thomas Friedman, "Balancing NAFTA and Neighborhood," *Rocky Mountain News* (from *The New York Times*) (Saturday, 13 April 1996): 44A. The initial success of the Pat Buchanan campaign for presidency in 1996 did much, I think, to draw the attention to places among establishment commentators. Friedman's title is inspired by Michael J. Sandel, *Democracy's Discontent: America in Search of a Public Philosophy* (Cambridge, Mass.: The Belknap Press of Harvard University, 1996). See especially the last chapter.

42. For a recent critique of the reification of "community," see Iris Marion Young, "The Ideal of Community and the Politics of Difference," *Social Theory and Practice* 12(1) (Spring 1986): 1–26. Like most critics of community, Young takes individualism and the affirmation of difference as her point of departure. This ignores, first, that the preoccupation with individualism and difference may be quite limited (mostly to the affluent, especially in First World societies) and largely irrelevant in a global perspective. It also rules out the possibility of negotiating difference once it enters community awareness. Even at their most despotic, moreover, the tyranny of community where people have to live together may be "benign" as compared with the tyranny of states. For an argument that anticipates such criticisms and many other of the criticisms directed at place and community, see Leopold Kohr, *The Breakdown of Nations* (New York: Rhinehart, 1957). For a passionate denunciation of the ways in which modernity and capitalism have exacerbated the oppression of women—not just by exacerbating premodern forms of oppression but also by breaking down customary limits on oppression—see Maria Mies, *Patriarchy and Accumulation on a World Scale* (London: ZED Books, 1986).

43. For an example of the question of place in class, see the debate between Ron Martin, Peter Sunley, and Jane Wills, "Unions and the Politics of Deindustrialization: Some Comments on How Geography Complicates Class Analysis," and Andrew Herrod, "Further Reflections on Organized Labor and Deindustrialization in the United States," *Antipode* 26(1) (1994): 59–95; for the question of place in gender, see Geraldine Pratt and Susan Hanson, "Geography and the Construction of Difference," *Gender, Place and Culture*, 1(1) (1994): 5–29; for the question of ethnicity, see Arif Dirlik, "Transnational Capital and Local Community in the Making of Asian America," *Amerasia* 22(3) (1996): 1–24; and for race, see Paul Gilroy, *The Black Atlantic: Modernity and Double Consciousness* (Cambridge, Mass.: Harvard University Press, 1993). For a revealing discussion of the relationship between changes wrought by the motions of capital and the need for place-based social analysis, see also the work cited in fn. 37.

44. *Traveling theory*, a term that I believe was coined by Edward Said, was elaborated further in the volume edited by James Clifford and Vivek Dareshwar, *Traveling Theories/Traveling Theorists, Inscriptions*, No.5 (1989).

45. Edward Said, *Culture <u>and</u> Imperialism* (New York: Vintage Books, 1994) 332. I choose Edward Said's eloquent assertion of this kind of knowledge *because* of his distinction as an intellectual who has been sharply and sensitively cognizant of his own intellectual itinerary. It may be because of his preoccupation with imperialism and colonialism, rather than with capitalism, that the statement comes easily. It is possible, of course, to be displaced without changing physical location, which is the more general problem. And what kind of knowledge is at issue here is not clear. What of the knowledge that is crucial to the sustenance of life, albeit of a different kind than the one that Said has in mind, that is erased by "traveling theory"?

46. For a longer discussion, see "No Longer Far Away: The Reconfiguration of Global Relations and Its Challenges to Asian Studies," Working Papers of the Center for Asian Studies—Amsterdam (forthcoming).

47. Philip Kotler, Donald H. Haider, and Irving Rein, *Marketing Places: Attracting Investment, Industry, and Tourism to Cities, States and Nations* (New York: Free Press, 1993), 18.

48. For the latter, see Franke Wilmer, *The Indigenous Voice in World Politics* (Newbury Park, Calif.: Sage, 1993). The national market, if only as a myth, has been crucial to our ideas of nationalism, a point ignored in Benedict Anderson's influential *Imagined Communities*, which downplayed both the state and the national market in the constitution of nations, somewhat reductively rendering nationalism into a cultural phenomenon.

49. This is the implication as I read it of the otherwise quite important work of Donna Haraway on the ways we have sought to know nature. See especially, "A Cyborg Manifesto: Science, Technology, and Socialist Feminism in the Late Twentieth Century," in *Simians, Cyborgs, and Women: The Reinvention of Nature* (New York: Routledge, 1991), 149–81. For a critique, see David Simpson, *The Academic Postmodern and the Rule of Literature: A Report on Half-Knowledge* (Chicago: University of Chicago Press, 1995), 166–8.

50. For a sampling of this literature, very much limited in geographical coverage, see Jeremy Seabrook, *Victims of Development: Resistance and Alternatives* (London: Verso, 1993); Franke Wilmer, *The Indigeneous Voice in World Politics* (Newbury Park, Calif.: Sage, 1993); Vandana Shiva, *Staying Alive: Women, Ecology and Development* (London: Zed Books, 1989); Gail Omvedt, *Reinventing Revolution: New Social Movements and the Socialist Tradition in India* (Armonk, N.J.: M. E. Sharpe, 1993); Cui Zhiyuan, "China's Rural Industrialization: Flexible Specialization, Moebius-Strip Ownership and Proudhonian Socialism," in *Identity Production under Global Capitalism: Theories and Practices*, ed. Arif Dirlik and Roxann Prazniak (fortcoming); Minor Sinclair, ed., *The New Politics of Survival: Grassroots Movements in Central America* (New York: Monthly Review Press, 1995); Frank Bardacke, Leslie Lopez, and the Watsonville, California, Human Rights Committee, eds. and trans., *Shadows of Tender Fury: The Letters and Communiqués of Subcomandante Marcos and the Zapatista Army of National Liberation* (New York: Monthly Review Press, 1995); John Gyford, *The Politics of Local Socialism* (London: George Allen & Unwin, 1985); Daniel Kemmis, *Community and the Politics of Place* (Norman: University of Oklahoma Press, 1990); Robert N. Bellah, Richard Madsen, William M. Sullivan, Ann Swidler, and Steven M. Tipton, *Habits of the Heart: Individualism and Commitment in American Life* (Berkeley: University of California Press, 1996), 2nd. edition; Amitai Etzioni, *The Spirit of Community: The Reinvention of American Society* (New York: Simon and Schuster, 1993).

51. See, for instance, John Brown Childs's paradigm of "transcommunalism" in his contribution to this volume. For another indigenism-inspired discussion, see Silvia C. Rivera, "Liberal Democracy and *Ayllu* Democracy in Bolivia: The Case of Northern Potosi," *Journal of Development Studies* 26(4) (July 1990): 97–121. For the increasingly significant challenge to the international system of indigenism, see Franke Wilmer, *The Indigenous Voice in World Politics.*

52. This may be an appropriate place to note a tendency in recent scholarship to inflate the idea of resistance to include everything that the "weak" do, which in the end makes the very idea of resistance irrelevant politically. James Scott's *Weapons of the Weak: Everyday Forms of Peasant Resistance* (New Haven, Conn.: Yale University Press, 1985) has been used as an occasion in some historical writing to render everything from cross-dressing to gambling into some kind of resistance. While there is an important reminder here that resistance may take a variety of forms against earlier tendencies to equate resistance with radical or revolutionary political activity, it is also necessary to bear in mind that "resistance without anticipated transformation" (as Choi Chungmoo has put it) may be inflated to the point where the whole idea is meaningless. Michael Adas, himself an advocate of greater attention to "nonconfrontational" kinds of resistance, cautions nevertheless against a new kind of romanticism that overstates "the extent to which these responses can ameliorate the plight of the exploited and permit them to punish their oppressors." Michael Adas, "South Asian Resistance in Comparative Perspective," in *Contesting Power: Resistance and Everyday Social Relations in South Asia,* ed. Douglas Haynes and Gyan Prakash (Berkeley: University of California Press, 1991), 290–305, here 300. It is also necessary to note that while attention to nonconfrontational resistance is partly a consequence of greater cognizance of "subalterns" other than the working class and peasant subjects of revolutionary resistance, in good postrevolutionary fashion "subalternity" as concept erases differences between different kinds of "subalternity" and the forms of resistance associated with different groups that have vastly different political implications. There also seems to be a hint in Adas's remarks of some kind of competition between different realms of "area studies," as he seeks (along with the contributors to the volume mentioned) to foreground the nonconfrontational styles of resistance in South Asia against the preoccupation in East and Southeast Asian studies with violent, confrontational (in other words, revolutionary) styles. The association has much to tell us about the origins and visibility of postcoloniality, which, I have argued elsewhere, may be described more accurately as postrevolutionary. See Arif Dirlik, "Postcolonial or Postrevolutionary: The Problem of History in Postcolonial Criticism," in Arif Dirlik, *The Postcolonial Aura: Third World Criticism in the Age of Global Capitalism* (Boulder, Colo.: Westview Press, 1997), 163–85. One might suggest, in the present context, that nonconfrontational resistance, which may in fact be quite functional to systemic health, is about the most logical kind of resistance permitted under conditions of "hybridity."

53. To move away from capital to view this problem in the context of modernity generally, it may be interesting to note here the case of the Chinese Revolution, which was to dramatize the contradiction between place and supraplaced organization and theory as a very condition of a guerilla strategy of revolution. Mao Zedong's writings are replete with references to the contradiction between place and state, place and party, and place and development, all of which have remained as abiding concerns of the history of Chinese communism, and persists even among Mao's successors who have otherwise repudiated the in-

tensity with which he confronted place and various supraplace spaces. In spite of this awareness, the developmentalism of the Communist Party of China and its commitment to the nation–state, not to speak of its own interests as an organization, led repeatedly to the sacrifice of places to larger considerations of power. Nevertheless, the Maoist revolutionary legacy retains a paradigmatic power in spite of its discrediting because of directions it would take after 1949. It may not be surprising that those in China and abroad who are most anxious to erase this legacy are also those who are committed to globalism of one kind or another. For an alternative reading, see Wim F. Wertheim, *Third World Whence and Wither? Protective State versus Aggressive Market* (Amsterdam: Uitgeverij Spinhuis, 1997), chap. 3. In both a positive and a negative sense, the role of places in the Chinese Revolution may provide the best argument for the priority of place in the consideration of meaningful change.

54. For example, against the notion of "sustainable development," which represents the adjustment of developmentalism to ecological and social necessity, the Yaqui scholar Mariana Jaimes Guerrero suggests "sustainable self-sufficiency," which inverts the relationship between self-sufficiency and development and offers a resolution of the contradictions of developmental hybridity radically different from that in "sustainable development." This inversion also calls forth inevitably new relationships between places and new organizational forms to express those relationships. See "The 'Patriarchal Nationalism' of Transnational Colonialism: As Imperialist Strands of Genocide/Ethnocide/Ecocide," paper presented at the conference "Asia-Pacific Identities: Culture and Identity Formation in the Age of Global Capital," Duke University, April 13–15, 1995. Given the context of the discussion here, it is important to note that I do not intend by this contrast any suggestion that a scholar such as Escobar is given to advocating "sustainable development." For his own trenchant criticism of this idea and defense of "sufficiency," see Escobar, *Encountering Development*, 192–211.

55. For "critical regionalism," see Kenneth Frampton, "Towards a Critical Regionalism: Six Points for an Architecture of Resistance," in *The Anti-Aesthetic: Essays on Postmodern Culture*, ed. Hal Foster (Port Townsend, Wash.: Bay Press, 1983), 16–30. Existing supraregional organizations, such as labor unions, have also become increasingly conscious of places. For an example of such "social unionism," see CAW (Canadian Autoworkers) Union, "Discussion Papers," 4th. Constitutional Convention, Quebec City, 23–26 August 1994, 15. I am indebted to John French for providing me with this source. The dialectic between place-based movements and supralocal—to national and even transnational levels—is also examined in Tomoji Nishikawa, "Diversifying the State: American Grassroots Groups and Japanese Companies," Ph.D. Dissertation, Department of Sociology, University of California–Berkeley, 1995.

56. Place-based consciousness, even if reified, is an antidote to many of the supraplace essentializations of identity around ethnicity, race, religion, etc., precisely because it insists on the location of culture in grounded places. On the other hand, the move away from the centrality of the nation–state in place-based consciousness is viewed quite frequently as an invitation to ethnic and other kinds of conflict at the local level, which ignores the status of states as objects of plunder, which, rather than contain ethnic conflicts, encourages them.

57. Partha Chatterjee has offered an argument that (probably wisely) stays away from specific resolutions, but otherwise parallels this reasoning. Chatterjee's argument is for-

mulated in a critical reading of Arjun Appadurai's case for a transnationalism "beyond the nation." In the process, he questions both the idea of "postnational formations" and received ideas of civil society, which are intimately tied in with modernizing projects. His own case draws attention to efforts within nations to formulate alternative strategies of democratic politics. I would add here that such alternative efforts become even more meaningful if we look "beyond the nation," which will confront places and globalism more directly without the mediation of the nation–state. See "Beyond the Nation? Or Within?" *Economic and Political Weekly* (4–11 January 1997): 30–4.

58. It is important to note here a problem that is too complex to incorporate in the text in the present context. Indigenous arguments for political restructuring provoke far greater resistance, and even incredulity, in contrast to indigenous beliefs that would seem to have enormous psychological and cultural appeal, at least in First World societies. This, I think, is related to the psychological dimensions of place to which Lefebvre pointed. It may be useful to add to Latour's two "great Divides" of modernity, another—the division of the self that follows from these divides, what Marx described as humans' alienation from their "species-being." Marx had work and production in mind when he made that statement, but place may be a significant aspect of such alienation, as is evident in those psychologized versions of place-consciousness that express themselves in the quest for "home"; in which place stands in juxtaposition to deterritorialized existence. We may add to Marx's alienation from humans' species-being an equally important alienation from nature, which, as Latour argues, issues in alienation from other human beings ("them") and, as I suggest here, in a self divided. While the "us" and "them" distinction is not particularly modern, the divided self may be, precisely because it is consequent on Latour's two Great Divides. It is also interesting that modernity distinguishes "state of nature" from "human nature," associating the latter with naturalness, while consigning the former to prehistory, as an unnatural condition. It may not come as much of a surprise that societies Euro-Americans came upon in their expansion that they deemed to be living in a "state of nature" were societies that were marked by a high level of collective existence, while "human nature" becomes the location for naturalized acquisitiveness and competition. The psychological and cultural attraction to indigenism articulates a deep unhappiness with the latter. The solution, however, may ultimately lie in the recovery of the material and political associations of the "state of nature," which is far more radical in its challenges, including its challenges to those who consume indigenism culturally.

59. To avoid confusion here, the question is not one of the irrelevance of theory but of the contradiction between theory and practice (in the sense of a "unity of opposites"). Theoretical analysis of space, as in the case of Lefebvre, Smith, etc., calls for a "spatial response" to the spatializations of capital, but does not offer a direct answer to the kind of response that may be appropriate. This may be viewed as a further extension of the theoretical dilemma referred to in fn. 35. Two considerations further complicate the dilemma. At the level of theory, a nonreductionist analysis requires, in addition to the analysis of capitalism, an analysis of the spaces of nations, patriarchy, racism, ecologies, etc. The complexity is further overdetermined by the mediation of places, with their "particular mixes" of ecological and social relations, that rules out any uniformity in the resolutions of the spatial problem and calls for particular readings of particular places with the aid of theory, but without rendering theory into a substitute for practice. Practice is complicated

further by the reminder that the categories of analysis themselves are metaphors for highly differentiated human realities.

60. Note, for instance, Vine Deloria Jr.'s critique of science and history in *Red Earth, White Lies: Native Americans and the Myth of Scientific Fact* (New York: Scribner, 1995), which, unlike Latour's critique of science, seeks not just to deconstruct modernity, but to set a clear alternative against it.

3

Indigenous Struggles and the Discreet Charm of the Bourgeoisie

Jonathan Friedman

INTRODUCTION

Since the mid-1970s there has been a massive increase in the activities of indigenous minorities in the world. Their struggles have become global news, and they have entered numerous global organizations so that they have become an international presence. This, I shall argue, does not mean that they have been globalized and that they are just like everyone else in today's globalizing world. They have been part of many a national scene for many decades. They have been marginalized in their own territories, boxed and packaged and sometimes oppressed even unto death. But this has changed in many parts of the world, because the indigenous is now part of a larger inversion of Western cosmology in which the traditional Other, a modern category, is no longer the starting point of a long and positive evolution of civilization, but a voice of wisdom, a way of life in tune with nature, a culture in harmony, a gemeinschaft, that we have all but lost. Evolution has become devolution, the fall of civilized man. But there is a social reality to this change as well, since the voices of the Other are the voices of real people struggling for control over their conditions of existence, conditions that have been denied to them at the very least. This struggle is not about culture as such, but about social identity of a particular kind, indigenous identity, which is constituted around cultural and experiential continuities that are only poorly mirrored in Western categories, not least, in anthropological categories. Fourth World struggles have been partially, and in some cases very, successful, but they do not operate in a simple structure where the only larger context is the nation–state or some other kind of state. They are also part of a dynamic global system, one that is multiplex and contains a number of related processes. There has been a more general inflation of cultural politics and ethnic conflict in the world, but there are also substantial increases in class stratification, economic polarization, and major shifts in capital accumulation. All of these changes constitute a field of analysis that must, I believe, be our central focus of understanding.

We need always to struggle to gain and maintain a perspective on reality, especially in periods, like this one, when it seems to be escaping at such great speed. This is a period of rapid change. It is heralded as the age of information, the age of globalization. Anthropologists have been much taken by the current transformations but have not done much in the way of research on them. This is unfortunate because the changes or experienced changes have certainly impacted on the discipline. What is going on? Is culture dead? Is consumption where it's all at? Are we entering a new urban civilization in which hybridity is the rule and the indigenous interesting primarily because it can be incorporated into a larger global celebratory machine, like world-music incorporates its various themes. It is necessary to step back, take it easy, look at the contours of the world we inhabit, and investigate seriously the mechanisms that seem to be steering our history. What may appear as chaos, or as "disjuncture" is truly an appearance, the starting point and not the end point of our attempt to grasp the nature of social reality.

ON GLOBALIZATION

The first appearance that strikes many of us today is captured by the slogan "globalization," which is bandied about in business economics (where it really developed), to cultural studies, and even anthropology. Some work on globalization is analytically and theoretically significant, but much more of it consists of simple opinions and reflections on the immediate. Cultural globalization thinking is based on a rather myopic view rooted in intellectual experience of the media, the Internet, and travel. It correctly understands that the world has become smaller (but this is always relative: Fernand Braudel made speed of transport a key to his notion of world "systems," a theme also well developed among geographers, not least David Harvey, whose concept of "time-space compression" does enough to account for much of what globalization consciousness is all about). Roland Robertson, who was one of the first out in these discussions, places globalization at the turn of the twentieth century, although he has now pushed this back to the ancient world. He is primarily interested in consciousness of a larger world and the way in which people increasingly identify with a larger global unity as well as the way the local expresses the global. The establishment of the League of Nations and many of our new global cults are examples of globalization, but so is the Meiji Restoration's importing of European concepts of governance. Cultural form moves and is adopted into increasingly larger places. Now, of course this has been going on for quite a long time. Even the conceptual apparatus of globalism is present in the universalism of the Enlightenment or the Ecumenism of the late Mediaeval Church, to say nothing of Alexander the Great. So, the historical demarcation of globalization does not hold water, since there is no historical disjuncture involved, or, on the contrary, there may be innumerable such breaks. Robertson, at least, explores the ideological structures of globalization, although without any concrete research material to support his interpretations. In anthropology, globalization discourse is even more limited in historical and intellectual scope. It usually refers to a very recent period, the 1970s perhaps, and is closer to CNN in its intellectual breadth, the latter having been first with much of the jargon. Here it is used, very much following cultural studies arguments, to dislocate and deconstruct common notions of culture. The latter is no longer anchored in territory. Nor is anything else, according to Arjun Appadurai. Instead we are all in movement, not just our migratory selves, but our meanings, our money, and our products. And all of these various "scapes" seem to have gotten lives of their own, leading to a chaotic disjuncture. More pedestrian approaches, such as that of Ulf Hannerz, make no clear statements, except that the world has suddenly become culturally hybridized because of the various movements of cultural things, including here, subjects. This is indeed a global vision of matter out of place. Mary Douglas should have seen it coming. (Mary Douglas introduced the expression "matter out of place" to define formally the notion of dirt in her well-known *Purity and Danger.*) But it is also an enjoyable chaos of variable mixtures that has become an identity among certain intellectuals and nonintellectuals that are part of the reason that a larger perspective is needed. Globalizing intellectuals are significant actors in the world today, and they do not seem like indigenous movements. John Kelly (1995), after citing Appadurai to the effect that "we need to think ourselves beyond the nation" (1993: 411), goes on to make his case against the indigenes:

> Across the globe a romance is building for the defense of indigenes, first peoples, natives trammeled by civilization, producing a sentimental politics as closely mixed with motifs of nature and ecology as with historical narratives. . . . In Hawaii, the high water mark of this romance is a new indigenous nationalist movement, still mainly sound and fury, but gaining momentum in the 1990's. . . . This essay is not about these kinds of blood politics. My primary focus here is not the sentimental island breezes of a Pacific romance, however much or little they shake up the local politics of blood, also crucial to rights for diaspora people, and to conditions of political possibility for global tansnationalism. (Kelly, 1995: 476)

This is an issue of class or elite position to which I shall return. As an introduction to the issue it should merely be noted that globalizing cosmopolitan identity appears to be very much intertwined with the discourse of globalization, and that is not a scientific way to go about understanding the global.

Let us take a step backward here and ask a few questions. Has the world become globalized so recently? Is everything really different today? Are there not territorial practices or (God help me) "cultures" anymore? In much of the discourse the answer is normative. There are plenty of nationalists and ethnics and indigenous radicals around, but they have got it all wrong! They haven't caught up with progress! And progress is globalization, the formation of a global village, and the village is really a world city. Oh what fun! But for whom?

There is another side to this and another approach to the global as well. That approach is not, I would argue, so caught up in the categories that it posits, but maintains an old-fashioned distance from them. First, globalization is not new at all, according to those who have actually researched the question. While there is much debate over the issue, there is also an emergent argument that the world is no more globalized today than it was at the turn of the twentieth century. Harvey who has done much to analyze the material bases of globalization puts the information revolution in a continuum that includes a whole series of other technological time-space compressions. Paul Hirst and Grahame Thompson (1996) go much farther in trying to despectacularize the phenomenon.

> Submarine telegraphy cables from the 1860's onwards connected inter-continental markets. They made possible day-to-day trading and price-making across thousands of miles, a far greater innovation than the advent of electronic trading today. Chicago and London, Melbourne and Manchester were linked in close to real time. Bond markets also became closely interconnected and large-scale international lending—both portfolio and direct investment—grew rapidly during this period. (Hirst, 1996: 3)

Foreign direct investment, which was a minor phenomenon relevant to portfolio investment, reached 9 percent of world output in 1913, a proportion that was not surpassed until the early 1990s (Bairoch and Kozul-Wright, 1996: 10). Openness to foreign trade was not markedly different in 1993 than in 1913. In the 1890s the British were very taken with all the New World products that were inundating their markets (Briggs and Snowman, 1996)—cars, films, radio, X rays, and lightbulbs.

> As in the late 20th Century trade was booming, driven upwards by falling transport costs and by a flood of overseas investment. There was also migration on a vast scale from the Old World to the New.
>   Indeed, in some respects the world economy was more integrated in the late 19th Century than it is today. The most important force in the convergence of the 19th Century economies . . . was mass migration mainly to America. In the 1890's, which in fact was not the busiest decade, emigration rates from Ireland, Italy, Spain and Scandinavia were all above 40 per thousand. The flow of people out of Europe, 300,000 people a year in mid-century, reached 1 million a year after 1900. On top of that, many people moved within Europe. True, there are large migrations today, but not on this scale. (*Economist*, December 20–January 2, 1997-98: 73)

This was a period of instability, to be sure, of enormous capital flows, like today. It was also a period of declining British hegemony and increasing British cultural expansion. Britain had no enemies as such, except those that it was helping to create by its own export of capital. Giovanni Arrighi argues on the basis of historical research that massive financial expansions have accompanied all the major hegemonic declines in the history of the European world system.

> To borrow an expression from Fernand Braudel (1984: 246)—the inspirer of the idea of systemic cycles of accumulation—these periods of intensifying competition, financial expansion and structural instability are nothing but the 'autumn' of a major capitalist development. It is the time when the leader of the preceding expansion of world trade reaps the fruits of its leadership by virtue of its commanding position over world-scale processes of capital accumulation. But it is also the time when that same leader is gradually displaced at the commanding heights of world capitalism by an emerging new leadership. (Arrighi, 1997: 2)

This kind of argument has been central for the kind of historical global systemic analysis that we have engaged in since the mid-1970s. If our argument dovetails with Arrighi here, it is because of a certain equifinality of research results and not a mere theoretical similarity. In this model East Asia should be the next center of the world system, but many are arguing today that what historically appears as a periodical globalization may be becoming a permanent state of affairs (Sassen, 1997; Friedman, 1998a, 1998b). As a result of speedup, the cycles of accumulation may have so decreased in periodicity as to make geographical shifts a mere short-lived tendency rather than a process that can be realized. This should not detract from acknowledging the degree to which East Asia has grown to a dominant economic position. It might even be argued that the current crisis is a result of precisely this region's rapid growth in a period of shrinking real world markets.

The purpose of starting with all of this is to set the stage for a perspective. Globalization has occurred previously. It does not necessarily indicate that we are entering a new era in evolutionary terms, and it is certainly structurally comprehensible in terms of what is known about the world system. Globalization is a structural phenomenon in the terms set out here. In economic terms, it refers primarily to the decentralization of capital accumulation. The unification of the world in technological terms is a process that is financed by decentralizing capital investment, not by some autonomous cultural or even technological process. And while it certainly generates a global perspective for those who travel along the upper edges of the system, there are other processes that are equally global in terms of their systematicity, but exceedingly local/national/ethnic/indigenous in terms of their constitution. This is the crux of the problem: the current situation is one that is producing both globalized and localized identities. Now, in sociological terms both of these phenomena are local. Globalization is in fact a process of local transformation, the packing in of global events, products, and frameworks into the local. It is not about delocalizing the local but about changing its content, not least in identity terms. A cosmopolitan is not primarily one who constantly travels the world, but one who identifies with it in opposition to his own locality. That is why so many working-class border crossers in the world

are so blatantly innocent of such an identity. They are less interested in celebrating their border crossing than in avoiding precisely the borders that are so
deadly dangerous in their lives. The true cosmopolitans are, as always, members
of a privileged elite, and they are not so in objectively cultural terms, if such
terms make any sense, but in terms of their practices of identity.

FRAGMENTATION AND INDIGENEITY

In global perspective, there is not that much disagreement today concerning the
fact that the world is pervaded by a plethora of indigenous, immigrant, sexual,
and other cultural political strategies aimed at a kind of cultural liberation from
the perceived homogenizing force of the state. In a certain perverted sense this
is as true of the new elites as of the regional minorities, but in very different
ways. The rise of indigenous movements is part of this larger systemic process,
which is not to say that it is a mere product in a mechanical deterministic sense.
There are two very different but related aspects to this process. The social
process consists of the disintegration of homogenizing processes that were the
mainstays of the nation–state. This has led to increasing conflicts about particular rights and of the rights of "particular" people, a real conflict between individual versus collective rights and of the national versus ethnic. Cultural politics in general is a politics of difference, a transformation of difference into
claims on the public sphere, for recognition, for funds, for land. But the differences are themselves differentiated in important and interesting ways, not least
in relation to extant structures of identification. Both regional and indigenous
identities in nation–states make claims based on aboriginality. These are claims
on territory as such, and they are based on a reversal of a situation that is defined as conquest. Roots here are localized in a particular landscape. There are
important ambivalences here. All nationals can also be regionals, and many nationals can identify as indigenes. All of this is a question of the practice of a particular kind of identity, an identity of rootedness, of genealogy as it relates to territory. It is in the very structure of the nation–state that such identities are prior
identities. No nation can logically precede the populations that it unified in its
very constitution. This, of course, is a logical and not an empirical structure.
There is no guarantee that the nation–state did not itself generate regional identities. In fact in much of the "Invention of Tradition," tradition consists of arguing precisely in such terms. Just as colonial governments created regional and
state-to-be identities in Africa, so did nation–states create regional minorities at
home. What is overlooked in this intellectualist tradition is the way in which
identities are actually constituted. The latter consist of linking a matrix of local
identifications and experiences to a higher order category, which then comes to
function as a unifying symbol. The logic of territorial identity is segmentary. It
moves in terms of increasing encompassment, and it depends on a practice of

creating fields of security. It expresses a certain life-orientation, an intentionality, that cannot be waved away by intellectual flourishes.

The differential aspect of indigeneity is not a mere social struggle for recognition of difference. It is about the way difference must be construed and incarnated in real lives. There are extreme examples of this process that are expressive of the deep structures of the nation–state. It has led the Afrikaners of South Africa to apply for membership in the World Council of Indigenous Peoples. One of the most spectacular is the formation referred to as the Washitaw nation. The Washitaw, according to Göran Dahl (1997), are a self-identified tribe, inhabiting the Louisiana, Mississippi, Oklahoma area. They are black and are affiliated with the extreme right "Republic of Texas." They claim to be descended from West Africans who moved to America when the continents were still joined, that is, before the Indians: "We are the aborigines—the dark-skinned, bushy-haired original inhabitants of 'so-called' north and south America (Muu, Afrumuurican)" (Bey, 1996: 4).

They have an empress who claims not only land but also an aristocratic descent for her tribe. Dahl shows that there are early references to Indians from the early nineteenth century that indeed describe the Choctaw as somehow different than their neighbors, but it is not clear that they were black. On the other hand, there are black Indian tribes in Suriname who are descendants of runaway slaves, and it is not unlikely that blacks may have been adopted into the Indian tribes of the area. What is more important is the fact that there is a local identity that may well be one that resulted from historical relations between blacks and Indians, but that it has been transformed into tribal identity in which the African is paramount and more indigenous (previous to) than the Indian. The structure of the identity is what is important here, and its association with the Republic of Texas is significant. For such groups, the major enemy is the state, representative of the cosmopolitan and antipopular oppressor of real people, imperial and positively against the kind of aboriginal difference represented by the Washitaw and similar organizations. Their political aim is control over territory and governmental autonomy. They make their own license plates (as do certain Hawaiian groups) and refuse the entire tax system of the United States.

The structure that is constructed here is one whose logic is organized by the very structure of nationhood, a relation between cultural identity and territory as opposed to the territorial state, which is perceived as usurper and conqueror. This kind of a structure emerges in conditions in which the state is clearly not representative of the people involved. Such conditions are variable, not only in space, but in time as well. The logic linking peoplehood and indigeneity to the constitution of the nation–state is the same logic as well as a structure of opposition. Bruce Kapferer, in his discussion of Sinhalese and Australian forms of nationalism suggests that Australia, as a variant of the modern nation–state, is based on an absolute distinction between nation and state. The people identify as separate and subordinate to the state, which is perceived as a foreign body. Australia is exemplary because it is a country that was not just a colony, but a penal colony, peopled by the powerless and clearly not associated in an organic way with statehood, any more than prisoners can be said to own the prison that they inhabit. Australia is pervaded by an ambivalence that is quite complex. The core of the country, the nation, is alienated from the state that it has tried to capture. Its relation to both territory and empire places it in a fragile position. If its primary identity is established in relation to its main country of origin as a penal colony, it is also, by definition, an immigrant country. Alienated not only from the state, but even from Nature associated with the savage and uncontrollable outback that can only be conquered but not adapted to or understood (Lattas, 1997). Caught between and opposed to the state, the Aborigines, and new immigrants, this is a potentially volatile structure of identification that produces both primitivist and antiprimitivist ideologies. It may help account for a state-organized multiculturalism whose policy expressed in *Creative Australia* is aimed at recreating a new national identity based on a notion of combined differences that are not weighted in any clear way, thus alienating both a significant core of Australians and the Aborigines as well. It might also help account for the particular racism directed against Aborigines, which places immigrants and Aborigines in the same category of threat-to-the-nation (Blainey, 1995). The other extreme is represented by "homogeneous" countries like Germany and the Scandinavian countries, where peoplehood, nature, and the state are fused, and in which the modern state can be said to have been captured by the people, at least until quite recently. Now, of course this is a historical process as well. In Sweden, the patriarchal structure was not imbued with a strong notion of representativity until the working-class movements transformed their patriarchal organization into an antistate of sorts. (It should be noted, however, that the patriarchal state was strongly oriented to the "people" and to the formation of a national unity of an organic type based very much on the responsibility of the national elites toward the people.) Where the early patriarchal structure was one in which the ruling class attempted to own the people, its capture inverted this relation. This is of course more complicated, since the state itself is essentially a representative governmental body and not a class. The real conflict relates to the control of the state as a political instrument. The social democratic state, the "people's home" became a power in itself, just as Pierre Clastres's antichief did. The latter is the transparent instrument of peoplehood and also an instrument of violent control and leveling. The Swedish state reorganized much of social and economic life in striving to create the "good society" in the name of the people. This representativity was maintained until recently at the same time as state functions were defined actively as extensions of the will of the people. As Clastres and others have pointed out, such a structure accords an enormous potential for the transformation of the state into an autonomous and self-directed organism. The practice of homogeneity in Sweden was successful largely because it resonated with local identities. The ruling class was in important respects, excepting here the nobility, an outgrowth of the "people." Indigeneity is only fragmenting when it is a separate identity within the state (as with the Saami). The indigenous as a general form of intentionality is about rooting. In certain conditions it produces alternative identities against the state, in other conditions it can produce extreme nationalism within the state. This accounts for the strange fact that the ideology of the New European Right is so similar to that of some indigenous movements. As a strategy it is more general than indigenous movements as such. Self-directedness is what makes such movements distinct. There is no logical way that national states and indigenous movements can coexist without a change in the larger structure of the state itself, or by making compromises that simply accentuate the ambivalence of the situation. The articulation of indigeneity and the world system produces a whole set of new contradictions that are becoming salient in the current situation.

This simplified continuum is a continuum of positions in the global system as well as a continuum of logical variation. It is not a static or general typology but refers to an organization of identification that can itself change over time. The globalized identities of today are those that have stressed the superiority of hybridity and then of multiculturalism, which, from their point of view, is an encompassment of difference that depends on "being above it all." But such positions are only possible with reference to the nation–state itself. They are those who define themselves as going beyond the nation–state and who declare that the latter is a dying or dead institution and even blame it for the major ills of the world, usually summed up in the word *essentialism*. But this is merely one position in a spectrum of possibilities too large to explore here. At the other end of the spectrum is indigeneity itself. The relation between national elites and the nationalist position is highly ambivalent insofar as it is ideologically egalitarian at the same time that it is hierarchical in practice.

I suggested that the major operator in this continuum is the dynamics of class formation in the global system. Globalizers are those who identify with the top of the system, whereas localizers tend to identify with the bottom. There is more to this, however, than mere identity politics.

GLOBAL PROCESS AND THE UNIFICATION OF FRAGMENTS UNDER CAPITALISM: THE NEW CLASSES

In a recent and very important thesis, Elizabeth Mary Rata has described what she refers to as the emergence of tribal capitalism. Her hypothesis is that a new class has emerged, a postindustrial class, whose wealth and power are based in the new sectors of economic development, the media, the Internet, and other software sectors and the professions surrounding these sectors. This class is the bearer of a new ideologythat must at first oppose itself to old capitalist elites. This class occupies an ambivalent position, a combination of particular elite status and a universalistic ideology of equality used in the struggle against the old hegemonic class. This leads to the emergence out of a guilt complex typical for this class position of a bicultural ideology for New Zealand—the idea that we are all both white and Maori, we are special. This is very interesting insofar as it captures the notion of hybridity that is common in other elite ideologies, for example, Australia, Canada, and now increasingly among a certain similar cultural elite in the United States (not least academics). This is the global orientation that I described previously in relation to the establishment of globalization as an ideology. Rata traces the way in which this class ideology articulated with the strengthening of Maori identity via the establishment of a separate cultural project, language schools, a national cultural revival, and then land rights and access to capital on established tribal lands. This is a movement from cultural identity to tribal property. The Waitangi Amendment Act established the tribes as corporate, political, and economic entities and the later Maori Fisheries Commission became the means of transfer of property rights and funds for the establishment of fishing enterprises. The effects of juridification were increasing potential conflicts within the tribes as people struggled to define their genealogical rights to means of production. The issue of exclusion versus inclusion with respect to such rights is an expression of the tendency toward class division among the Maori. This is a theme that appears throughout the rest of the chapter and is interesting to compare to peoples such as the Saami, in which access to reindeer and herding territories is a basis of privilege that severely divides the population, even though the colonial history is somewhat different. The combination of tribal organization and capital accumulation and transfers is important in understanding the way a local movement can become reorganized into the global system. The class structure that seems to be emergent is one in which those who control capital within the tribes introduce wage labor among lower ranked kin, tending to turn them into a subordinate class, if these relations are reproduced. The second class division emerges between those with and without access to tribal property—more than half of the Maori who still inhabit urban ghettos. Rata makes use of Marxism and especially Regulation Theory to develop her thesis that there is a new form of accumulation emerging here, the "tribal capitalist mode."

There is a third process that Rata touches on as well—the formation of a Maori middle class based on the control over specialized knowledge in the matrix linking the new national cultural class referred to previously, the cultural apparatuses of the state, and the reconstruction of Maori society. These are intellectuals who played and continue to play key roles in the Maori movement, but who also function as consultants to both tribes and government, as mediators and teachers. It is, of course, to be expected that intelligentsia should emerge within such movements and that they should become increasingly established as the movements become institutionalized. They are, after all, the focal points for political unity and often political action as well, pivots in the competition for funding and rights. It would be a sign of incomprehension, not untypical of anthropologists, to critique such developments on the grounds that they deviate from the anthropologist's conception of traditional culture. Even the class aspect of this development is quite logical in terms of the process of integration itself. On the other hand, such divisions are bound to be sources of potential conflict within the emerging larger political community.

But there is more to this development that has everything to do with the state of global capitalism today. This is related to the extreme decentralization of capital accumulation and the spectacular shift from real investment to fictitious accumulation. Saskia Sassen estimates that there are at least 75 trillion dollars in financial circulation. Since the 1980s financial assets have grown 2.5 times faster than the gross domestic product of the richest nations, and they are growing, and continuing to grow logarithmically, in this period of real overproduction, as evidenced by the Asian crisis. Much of this money is transferred in the form of pork barrel projects to firms dealing with all kinds of nonproductive activity, not least among which are the so-called consultancies and NGOs that have developed explosively in the past decade. There are of course many NGOs that are engaged in productive activities or in genuinely effective activities related to the survival of indigenous peoples, but there is no hindrance to the massive development of carpetbaggers and treasure hunters. One example of this is the recent history of an organization calling itself Uhaele, which came to the Office of Hawaiian Affairs (OHA) with an offer to help them organize the approaching Hawaiian sovereignty for a sizeable fee. A contract was almost consummated but the situation came to light suddenly, and the whole affair was called off amidst a throttle of scandalous accusations concerning who had signed the agreement with the firm. The same organization had had some earlier dealings in Vanuatu, where, after signing a lease for an offshore island, it proceeded to advertise the island as a tax haven for people of superior intelligence and sell shares in the island, which was soon to be declared the independent country of Aurora. Lawrence Nevels, a lawyer specializing in these kinds of operations, and his family were to be the royalty of this constitutional monarchy.

> It is intended to create an independent country called AURORA, with minimal government, maximum personal freedom and a laissez-faire economy. . . . It is intended that the population of Aurora will be very cosmopolitan; admission as first citizens will be based upon needed skills, professions and talents and belief in the political and economic principles upon which the country is founded. Men and women of numerous races, of varied religions, will be invited to apply. (Nevels, n.d.: 1)

Needless to say, the independence never materialized. Vanuatu stopped it with military threats. Nevels disappeared, and his investors lost their money. Nevels is a lawyer, and when Uhaele surfaced, its home base was Reno, Nevada, . . . of course. The group entered into elaborate negotiations with OHA, which was scheduled to receive several hundred million dollars as reparations from the federal government as well as other funds from the state government. The negotiations specified ultimately that Uhaele would by and large control the administration of OHA's economy in exchange for 20 percent of the net proceeds. Now, since Uhaele had no capital, no employees, no equipment, to say the least, this arrangement was clearly a gold mine for them—their talent for a piece of the action. "Uhaele was a letterhead and a telephone" (*Ke Kia'i*, 1991: 8).

The world is full of firms like this, on the hunt after the masses of financial wealth that is circulating into "good causes," whether at the national or international level. In all of this there is always a tendency toward class formation, however little this may be manifested. It has certainly led to the formation of global elite representatives of various groups who are immediately implicated in a field of tension, between their very rooted places of origin and the inordinate power of global funds to incorporate them into the global cocktail circuit. The United Nations and a host of other megaorganizations have been gathering places for the formation of global identities, places, as well, for the destruction of local accountability. The vitality of certain indigenous movements is measurable by the degree to which indigenous peoples manage to capture or replace their representatives in such situations. But this is truly a field of contradictory forces. The process of fragmentation via indigenization is subject to processes of social *verticalization* that is related to the institutions and funds that circulate in this period of globalization of capital.

VERTICALIZATION, FRAGMENTATION, AND THE SOCIAL TRANSFORMATION OF THE GLOBAL SYSTEM

Verticalization, or class polarization, is a vector of the global system, and it affects all of the forms of fragmentation that represent the other major vector in the system. Ethnification and class formation are the paired processes that characterize this simultaneous development. The transformation of the nation–state into a modern form of the absolutist state is an expression of the same process. The increase in clientelism in European states, and between the states and regions and the Union, is part of the disintegration of the homogeneous nation–state. The notion of a Europe based on regions rather than states is part of this and would transfer power to Brussels while undermining the relation between states and their subregions. Thus, the notion pushed by some of the cultural globalists, that we have somehow moved beyond the obsolete nation–state and are entering a new world of the postnational, is a misconstrual of a more complex situation. While it is true that global capital exercises increasing power over national conditions of reproduction, this does not spell the end of the nation–state as such, but its transformation, from a homogeneous entity in which common goals link the "people" and their state, to a separation of the state from the nation. The state itself, according to ongoing research, is becoming increasingly oriented to international capital flows, to the regulation of such flows as they relate to conditions of maintenance of territorial economic units. The recent Asian crisis has made this resoundingly evident. George Soros apparently lost more than 100 million dollars in Asia, and he has, more generally, clamored for increasing international controls over financial flows.

> Although I have made a fortune in the financial markets, I now fear that untrammeled intensification of laissez-faire capitalism and the spread of market values to all areas of life is endangering our open and democratic society. The main enemy of the open society, I believe, is no longer the communist but the capitalist threat. . . . Too much competition and too little cooperation can cause intolerable inequities and instability. . . . The doctrine of laissez-faire capitalism holds that the common good is best served by the uninhibited pursuit of self-interest. Unless it is tempered by the recognition of a common interest that ought to take precedence over particular interests, our present system . . . is liable to break down. (Soros, 1997: 45, 48)

This expresses a desire, at present being implemented by many states, for a stronger regulation of the conditions of equilibrium in the world market. Work by Sassen indicates that nation–state functions are increasingly shifting from national to international issues. This is what might be called a liftoff of the state. In Europe it is related in its turn to the emerging relation between nation–states and the European Union. European governmental organs are not tied to constituencies as are national organs. They have experienced problems of corruption, problems in uncontrolled use of power, and problems in inordinately high remunerations for their members, but this is also reflected in the many credit card crises at the national level: there is a general accountability crisis in the nation–state that is expressed in declining respect for politicians who are considered increasingly to be a class with their own interests. Politicians, on the other hand, have in various ways, expressed their distaste for ordinary people, whom they often accuse of being rednecked and nationalist.

That this could occur in a country like Sweden is ample evidence of the forces involved. Carl Bildt, European Bosnia negotiator and leader of the Conservative Party, has written that a European government is the ultimate solution for the continent and that its form could well take a form reminiscent of the Hapsburg Empire. Similar statements have come from social democrats and others. Sweden, which is officially multicultural, has, in a government bill, stated categorically that Sweden no longer has a common history since there were so many different immigrant groups present on Swedish soil (where does that put the United States or Canada?). The bill goes on to formulate a new structure for the state that moves clearly in the direction of a plural society based on the association of different cultural groups. There are tendencies in the media elite and in the state to classify any opposition to this planned transformation as racism. The overall impact of the transformation of the global system is one that places the state in a new kind of vortex of global forces, one where it becomes a focal point for an association of different groups rather than the representative of what one comedian has called "that special interest group, the people." This structural tendency is one in which the political class and the other cultural elite class factions identify increasingly with the global, in which, as has been said of the U.S. situation, "They have more in common with their counterparts in Brussels or Hong Kong than with the masses of Americans not yet plugged into the network of global communications" (Lasch, 1995: 35).

Now the state, transformed in this way, becomes the focal point of certain distributions of favors, funds, and positions to an increasingly fragmented nation–state. The clientelism to which I referred previously is very much the product of this transformation. Regional, immigrant, and indigenous minorities all become subject to this changing field of forces. The field tends to create new elites that move within the global sphere, ranked lower than the real big shots, since they are clients to the real sources of power and money. They may have global spheres of their own, like the W.C.I.P. (World Council of Indigenous Peoples), and they sometimes mingle with higher ranked elites, but they are primarily local clients in the global mesh of neofeudal dependencies.

The rise of indigenous movements was part of a general process of transformation in the world system, in which the weakening of the Western nation–state took the form of the rise of cultural politics. This was, as suggested at the start, part of a common decline in hegemony, which was also expressed in a rapid increase in economic globalization. Whether this is a temporary or permanent change cannot be determined here, because the general periodicity of accumulation has increased and because globalization has become more rapid, cheaper, and increasingly institutionalized. It has, in any case, produced major transformations of class relations, the emergence of a new cosmopolitan elite or congeries of elites that have been sucked into the globalization process and who are the producers of globalizing representations of the world, and understandings that challenge the very existence of the nation–state and proclaim a new postnational era at the same time as fragmentation and cultural conflict are more pervasive than ever at lower levels of the system. The articulation of verticalizing and fragmenting process produces the paradox of class division at all levels, including movements that begin in urban ghettos. It is important to take these contradictions into account when trying to understand the trajectory of indigeneity in today's world.

MAKING THE WORLD SAFE FOR CAPITALISM

The processes of vertical and horizontal polarization that I have discussed here dovetail with the work of many other authors who have written about the cultural state of the world. Appadurai, as I have indicated, has noted a certain aspect of this transformation, which he understands as an increasing confrontation between new diasporic and old national structures. His position, however, is more ideological than scientific. He does concede that the future may indeed entail a bloody conflict, but he assumes that the result of the conflict will necessarily be a new world of "cultural freedom." Others have stressed the marvels of cultural mixture and multiculturalism and have transformed former progressive ideology into a struggle for cultural plurality and cultural mixture. The new transnational ideology is certainly a force in the world, but it comes not from the grass roots but from the world's various political and cultural elites. The forces in the processes of polarization involved the conversion of status from local to global for many — for rising middle classes and even indigenous representatives. For the latter, of course, such a shift implies a contradiction in identity, a contradiction between the rootedness of indigeneity and the cosmopolitan life of the higher circulatory elites of the world arena. But even the economic forces involved here can easily lead to a stratification of indigenous groups within more restricted arenas where pork barrels and state funding can be used to cement hierarchical control over the resources won by indigenous movements. This is an important issue for indigenous movements themselves, and many of the participants in such movements are acutely aware of these issues.

Much new research is needed, and this is not merely a statistical question. The understanding of new social connections, new circles of friends, and increasingly relatives is in order. The role of the intellectuals is also crucial in understanding these developments. When Tony Giddens becomes an important advisor for Tony Blair in the name of the return of a socialist agenda, we might take a closer look at the agenda itself—the fact that Bill Clinton, Tony Blair, and Romano Prodi have joined forces, leaving more "traditional" socialists such as Lionel Jospin out in the cold. When George Soros calls for a new global regulation of capitalism, he is not calling for socialism but for a stable program to make the world safe for his investments. The new alliance of the left might well be a new example of the structural adjustment of the elites.

CONCLUSION: ROUTES VERSUS ROOTS

I have tried to suggest that there is a certain systematicity in the world arena that can account for phenomena that have often been left within the discourses that produced them. Some years ago Arif Dirlik suggested that the new postcolonial discourse was engendered within a particular class position, that of the new postcolonial elites themselves, and that it was extraordinarily adequate to the current phase of globalized capitalism. I suggested in another article that the ideologies of hybridity were integral parts of an emergent cosmopolitan perspective that combined an antimodernist culturalism with an experienced globalization of identity, producing an ideology of global cultural encompassment. If former internationalists and cosmopolitans were primarily modernists and not terribly concerned with their cultural identities, the new variety is just as concerned as all others about discovering its roots. For the cosmopolitan the roots become necessarily multiple and entwined in their worldly journeys; roots with routes. James Clifford's recent collection of essays, *Routes*, expresses and explores the interaction of roots and routes, even if he is primarily concerned with the identities of objects. Diasporas, for example, can certainly be understood as the culturalization of migration, but as identities they usually imply some form of placedness or point of origin. This is the rather trivial paradox in the notion that somehow we can move from the national to the transnational in the sense of superseding the former, when it is, of course, impossible to even conceive of the transnational without the national. The only nonrooted cosmopolitans are the older variety of internationalists who identified entirely with social projects, such as socialism, or with some other form of future orientation, but never with any form of culturally framed identity. The unease in the identity of today's cultural cosmopolitans may account for their obvious dislike for the indigenous identities that, numerically at least, are clearly on the rise and in the great majority.

My argument is that all of these emergent identities are existentially authentic, true to themselves. They have an experiential force that accounts for their ability to attract new members. From cosmopolitan hybrids to Chiapas, all are true to themselves, even taking account of the complexities and variations of such identities. And in order to understand these real identities, which are not mere products of invention and manipulation, we must try to understand the social conditions from which they arise. These are conditions that shape experience and, thus, channel cultural production. On the other hand we must also be cognizant of the nature of ideological struggle in the present conjuncture. This is a struggle that is being waged in different ways and from different positions. While indigenous struggles are primarily locally focused, they have been globalized in the channels of international political organizations that have amplified their voice. While this produces a formidable contradiction in opening up a field of social identity for global representatives of the local, the latter has continuously produced forms of resistance to the formation of a new global power structure within the indigenous political sphere. Indigenizing identities and ideologies make no pretensions about reorganizing the world. The cosmopolitan struggle is quite different insofar as it is based in a rising elite faction, a globalized elite that self-identifies as encompassing the cultural variety of the world. This struggle concerns ideological hegemony, an attempt to reenvision the world as a multicultural-based, yet hybridized, unity-in-diversity. Elites are well placed to assert such a vision, but this placement is one that is increasingly questioned by those who do not occupy or wish to occupy such positions. Lest we be taken in by the curious logical fallacy that would encourage us to move "beyond place," to shift our thinking from roots to routes, it might be noted that routes connect places, that they have origins (roots) as well as end points, and that to move beyond place entails the question "And where do we end up then?"

REFERENCES

Appadurai, A. "Patriotism and Its Futures." *Public Culture* 5(3) (1993): 411–29.

Arrighi, G. "Globalization, State Sovereignty, and the 'Endless' Accumulation of Capital." Unpublished ms., 1997.

Bairoch, Paul, and R. Kozul-Wright. "Globalization Myths: Some Historical Reflections on Integration, Industrialization and Growth in the World Economy." UNCTAD discussion paper #113, Geneva, Switzerland, 1996.

Bey, Umaralli Shabazz. "We Are the Washitaw. Columbia via USA." The Washitaw Nation, unpublished ms., 1966.

Blainey, G. "The New Racism." *The Australian* (8 April 1995).

Braudel, Fernand. *The Perspective of the World.* New York: Harper and Row, 1984.

Briggs, A., and D. Snowman. *Fins de Siecle: How Centuries End, 1400–2000.* New Haven, Conn.: Yale University Press, 1996.

Dahl, G. "God Save Our County! Radical Localism in the American Heartland." Unpublished ms., 1997.

"The Century the Earth Stood Still." *Economist.* 346 (1997–98): 71–3.

Friedman, J. "Class Formation, Hybridity and Ethnification in Declining Global Hegemonies." In *Globalisation and the Asia Pacific*, edited by K. Olds, P. Dickin, P. Kelly, L. Kong, and H. Young. London: Routledge, 1998a, 230–55.

———. "The Hybridization of Roots and the Abhorrence of the Bush." In *Spaces of Culture: City, Nation, World*, edited by M. Featherstone and S. Lash. London: Sage, 1998b, 70–89.

Hannerz, U. "The World in Creolization." *Africa* 57 (1987): 546–59.

Harvey, D. *The Postmodern Condition.* Oxford: Blackwell, 1989.

Hirst, P. "Global Market and the Possibilities of Governance." Paper presented at the Conference on Globalization and the New Inequality, University of Utrecht, Utrecht, Holland, November 20–22, 1996.

Hirst, P., and G. Thompson. *Globalization in Question.* Cambridge: Polity, 1996.

Ke Kia'i (the Guardian). "The Odd Couple: Uhaele and OHA." In *Ke Kia'i, "The Guardian."* Vol. 2, 9. Honolulu, 1991.

Kelly, J. "Diaspora and World War, Blood and Nation in Fiji and Hawaii." *Public Culture* 7 (1995): 475–97.

Lasch, C. *The Revolt of the Elites.* New York: Norton, 1995.

Lattas, A. "Aborigines and Contemporary Australian Nationalism: Primordiality and the Cultural Politics of Otherness." In *Race Matters*, edited by G. Cowlishaw and B. Morris, 223–55. Canberra: Aboriginal Studies Press, 1987.

Nevels, L. N. *The Aurora Corporation.* Unpublished manuscript, n.d.

Rata, E. M. "Global Capitalism and the Revival of Ethnic Traditionalism in New Zealand: The Emergence of Tribal-Capitalism." Ph.D. thesis, University of Auckland, 1997.

Robertson, R. "Glocalization." In *Global Modernities*, edited by Mike Featherstone, Scott Lash, and Roland Robertson. London: Sage, 1992.

Sassen, S. "Territory and Territoriality in the Global Economy." Unpublished ms., 1997.

Soros, George. "The Capitalist Threat." *The Atlantic Monthly* 279(2) (1997): 45–58.

Part II

Transnationalism and Ethnic Identities: Labor, Capital, and the Problem of Community

4

Asians on the Rim: Transnational Capital and Local Community in the Making of Contemporary Asian America

Arif Dirlik

An issue of *AsianWeek* in January 1996 contained two items that cogently illustrate the problem I would like to discuss in this chapter. One was an invited editorial by Matt Fong, California state treasurer and "one of the nation's highest elected Asian American officials." Entitled "From Gold Mountain to the Golden Door," Fong's editorial outlined his vision of making California into "the capital of the Pacific Rim." He wrote,

> California's strategic location, coupled with its huge and diverse economic base and available capital, make it an ideal gateway to the Pacific Rim to facilitate trade and capital flows between the Pacific and the rest of the world.
>   California has the opportunity to lead the charge toward dramatically expanded global trade by developing its role as a financial services center to increase the sophistication, speed, volume, reliability, and cost-effectiveness of international commerce. Business, labor, government, and the academic community must aggressively work together to seize this opportunity and chart a new course for California. . . . As the global economy changes, we must provide a vision and take advantage of opportunities that will make California a better, more prosperous place in which to work, live and do business. California's Golden Door to the Future is the Gateway to the Pacific Rim.[1]

The other was a news item about the appointment to a post with the California Department of Education of Henry Der, who had served as the executive director of Chinese for Affirmative Action in San Francisco since 1974. The Superintendent of Education Delaine Eastin, who was able to appoint Der in spite of opposition from the office of Governor Pete Wilson, described Der as "progressive . . . dedicated to the community and to minorities . . . who's not afraid to speak for the community." Der himself stated that while his new job made it inappropriate for him to serve as a spokesperson for the Asian American community, "I'm so much rooted in this community that I'm not going to that new job to forget that I am an Asian American." His concerns, however, transcended his Asian Americanness: "I firmly believe we must do everything possible to close the gap between the haves and the have-nots in American society . . . I feel very, very strongly that education is one strategy."[2]

For *AsianWeek,* Fong and Der are equally illustrations of Asian American success, two of "50 Asian Americans who'll make a difference in the new year."[3] But the success story also conceals deep contradictions that bear directly on our understanding of Asian America, and its meaning in the contemporary world, which is the problem I would like to discuss here. I am not concerned about Fong's and Der's political affiliations or about their trajectories as individuals.[4] My concern, rather, is with their contrasting orientations, which are informed by quite different self-images as Asian Americans: the one looking out to the Pacific and the future, through the "Golden Door" of California; the other looking to communities rooted in California and their historical legacies, centered around but not restricted to Asian Americans. The difference is spatial, but not in an inert geographical sense (east-west), or even in the sense of spaces defined by national boundaries. The spaces in this case derive their meaning from associations that are quite contemporary in their implications, and the contradictions that they present: the global, and globalizing, spaces of transnational capital versus the local spaces of communities. Given the significant part that the ideal of community played in the formation of an Asian American consciousness historically, the spatial contradiction appears also as a temporal contradiction between a contemporary Asian American consciousness and the originary assumptions of Asian America.

The contrast between the two orientations, I would like to suggest, is paradigmatic of fundamental contradictions that are essential to grasping contemporary Asian America as social and ideological formation. The contradiction between the global and the local as structuring moments in contemporary society is not exclusive to Asian America, which is also a reminder that the Asian American experience is but one instance of what is increasingly a common phenomenon not just in the United States but worldwide; the problem of Asian America as I conceptualize it is not a cultural or a regional problem but a problem in global postmodernity.[5] What is specific to Asian America is its relationship to new centers of global economic power in Pacific and, to a lesser extent, South Asia, that have been responsible for bringing the Pacific to the forefront of global consciousness, in the process challenging Eurocentric conceptions of modernity that were themselves empowered by the apparently unchallengeable supremacy of Euro-American capitalism. What this challenge implies remains to be seen, but in an immediate sense, the emergence of Pacific Asian economies as key players in the global economy has had a transformative effect on the Asian American self-image, as well as on the perceptions of Asian Americans in the society at large. While the most visible effect may be the elevation in Asian American status vis-à-vis other minority groups, the transformation has not put an end to earlier problems in the conceptualization of Asian America, which persist in reconfigured forms, has introduced new burdens on being Asian American, and has complicated the very notion of Asian America to the point where it may break apart under the force of its contradictions. Especially important, I will suggest, is the increasing ambiguity in the conceptualization of Asian America of Asian populations as members of grounded communities versus as diasporic Rimpeople.

I will argue that while earlier conceptualizations of Asian America seem irrelevant under current circumstances, and have come under criticism for being outdated, those conceptualizations may be more relevant than ever, if for different reasons than those which inspired them in the first place. We need to rethink earlier conceptualizations because they no longer seem to be capable of containing the changes either within Asian America or in its relationship to its local and global environments. On the other hand, "forgetting" the past is hardly a way to rethink it, which requires that we remember differently. Especially important in my view is the community ideal in Asian American consciousness, which has been all but swept away by the enthusiasm over Asian Americans as Rimpeople.

THE PACIFIC AND ASIAN AMERICAN ETHNICITY
IN HISTORICAL PERSPECTIVE

A spatial contradiction has shaped the history of Asian America from the arrival of significant numbers of Asians on Pacific shores in the mid-nineteenth century. For the larger part of this history this contradiction was expressed in the language of a racist Orientalism. I have argued elsewhere that emigration from Asia from the beginning represented a Pacific component in U.S. national history that was suppressed, literally, by repression and eventual exclusion and, ideologically, by the ideology of a Western moving frontier.[6] Already by the mid-nineteenth century the Pacific appeared as an extension of an expanding Western frontier, which would not allow for any alternatives to the idea of "civilization" that propelled it, let alone a counter frontier emanating from across the Pacific. It was across the Pacific that a "Western civilization" destined to rule the world met once again its ancient nemesis, the "Orient."[7]

Gary Okihiro has argued at length the ways in which the Orientalist legacy shaped American views of those who obstructed this frontier, including Amerindians, but especially of the immigrants from Asia.[8] The very term *Asian* was an invention of this Orientalism. The people who immigrated from across the Pacific did not think of themselves in continental and, until the late nineteenth century, even in national terms, their primary identifications being with their origins in local societies. Asians were rendered into a racial and cultural formation in their construal as "Asians," "Orientals," or "Mongolians" by the hegemonic discourse.[9] This discourse also rendered Asians into permanent foreigners, incapable culturally and even genetically of becoming "real" Americans, which would serve as justification for their exclusion from 1882 through World War II. The exclusion did not extinguish memories of ties to native origins, or even involvement in the politics of nations of origin, but it rendered affirmation of such ties into a further liability. Even where consciousness of origins was weak, as with generations born in the United States, the very "Asianness" of Americans of Asian descent was deemed to preclude their becoming "real" Americans, as in the social scientific "dual personality" thesis, which assumed an Asian coding in the personalities of this group of Americans, regardless of their cultural orientations. The most tragic manifestation of this racist Orientalism was the incarceration in concentration camps of Americans of Japanese descent.

These Orientalist assumptions were to prevail against egregious evidence that Asians themselves did not have a sense of unity as Asians, or even the explicit recognition that different groups of Asians could be used against one another in perpetuating their exploitation and oppression, a tactic employed by white capital against Asian laborers. While they were able occasionally to unify in struggles against their oppression, there is little evidence that Asians of different nationalities had a sense of kinship for one another on account of being "Asian." On the contrary, to the extent that they identified with their national origins in Asia, conflicts within Asia pitted different groups of Asians against one another, resulting in "disidentification," whereby members of one group distanced themselves "from another group so as not to be mistaken and suffer the blame for the presumed misdeeds of that group."[10]

Grounded very much in U.S. soil, Americans of Asian descent were excluded from a U.S. national history for more than a century. It was the radical struggles of the 1960s that eventually rephrased the terms of the discourse on Asian America and also produced the idea of Asian Americanness as concept and vision. Once it had been coined, the term *Asian American* would acquire enormous power in shaping the discourse on the past, the present, and the future of Asian America. Yet its origins seem to have been fortuitous. According to the distinguished Japanese American historian Yuji Ichioka, who was to become one of the pioneers in Asian American studies, he coined the term in a meeting in Berkeley in 1968, out of analogy with other terms of ethnic identification, especially African American, which was at the source of much of the ethnic vocabulary of the time.[11] The term would be crucial in uncovering and reconstructing, to borrow the title of one of Ichioka's works, the "buried past" of Asian America. It would also have far-reaching political and intellectual consequences in mobilizing an "Asian American movement" as well as serious institutional consequences in official definitions of Asian America.

The term *Asian American* nevertheless bore upon it the imprint of its historical legacy. The *Asian* component was derivative of the hegemonic discourse on

Asians rather than the actual experiences and self-images of the Asian peoples covered by it and by implication at least shared a commonality with the Orientalist reification of Asia in erasing the significant differences among these peoples. But this is where the similarity ended. Where the Orientalism of the hegemonic discourse had nourished off a culturalist denial of history to Asia and, by extension, to Asians in the United States, the discourse spawned by the reconceptualization of Asian as Asian American was informed by a radical historicism that repudiated the fundamental assumptions of the hegemonic discourse. If it bore traces of an earlier hegemonic discourse, the new discourse was informed in its "rearticulation" of the problems of Asian America by the radical challenge to existing social relations of the radical thinking of the 1960s.[12]

The historicism of the new discourse was expressed at the most fundamental level in "claiming America"(in Maxine Hong Kingston's words) by rooting Asian Americanness in the ground of U.S. history. In his preface to *Roots: An Asian American Reader*, which was the first collection of its kind, Franklin Odo wrote that "this volume was written and edited with the intent of going to the 'roots' of the issues facing Asians in America. It may, therefore, strike the reader as 'radical'—a term which derives from the Latin *radix*, meaning, appropriately enough, roots." Tortured by questions of identity, he continued, "increasing numbers [of Asian Americans] . . . look to their 'roots.' The central section of this volume deals with the history of Asian Americans, from the emigration period to the present. This was another facet of the title's significance—our 'roots' go deep into the history of the United States and they can do much to explain who we are and how we became this way."[13]

Asian Americans, in other words, rather than being transplantations in the United States of racially and culturally marked Asian peoples without history, were the very products of the history of the United States in the making of which they had been participants from the beginning. What justified the inclusion of these different peoples in one category was also historical experience: "All Asians have much in common: the history of their exploitation. . . . But there are unique qualities to each of the ethnic groups which make united struggles difficult."[14]

If a common historical experience of oppression and exploitation justified speaking of an Asian America, this discourse also presupposed that Asian America was not to be taken for granted, as Odo's statement suggests, but was something that was to be created in the course of struggles against oppression and exploitation; Asian America, in other words, was not simply a product of past legacy, but a vision of the future. As John Liu was to write a decade later, in connection with the problems of Asian American studies:

These attempts at delineating a common culture should admonish Asian American studies instructors to focus on what Asian American meant at its inception: *a political choice.* Asian American studies arose from a *commitment* to build a common identity and a common culture. Most of the people who first worked toward building

Asian American studies consciously tried to create a culture that challenged the cultural hegemony of the dominant society. Because many of the early people were political activists, they knew Asian Americans could only be successful in their struggles if they developed an alternative way of seeing and living along with their political demands. It was no accident that the counter culture movement developed during the student, civil rights, women and ethnic movements. The demand for political change was simultaneously a call to transform the ways in which people did and saw things — that is, a call for a different cultural nexus.[15]

The grounding of Asian America in U.S. history underlined the commonality of the Asian American experience with the experiences of other oppressed groups in American society, while it problematized the relationship of Asian Americans to distant origins in Asia. In the same essay cited previously that affirmed the Americanness of Asians, Odo phrased the latter problem in the form of questions: "What should be a 'proper' stance toward the inculcation or maintenance of a cultural heritage? How closely, if at all, and in what ways should Asian Americans relate to Asia? Responses vary from 'back to Asia' types to a strictly Americanist, localized point of view."[16]

The "localized point of view" by far had the greater weight in the originary conceptualization of Asian America. Paraphrasing a statement by Eugene Genovese that "all good Marxist writing leads to an explication of class," Gary Okihiro wrote that "all ethnic studies history may, from one point of view, be judged good or poor by the extent to which it contributes to our understanding of community."[17] What was at issue, however, was much more than an "understanding" of community in the usual academic sense; the fundamental issue was the political one of strengthening communities. A work such as Yuji Ichioka's *Issei: The World of the First Generation Japanese Immigrants, 1885–1924* carefully delineates in great detail the history of Japanese Americans of the first generation so as to preserve and promote memories of community.[18] The community concerns of the generation of scholars informed by the idea of Asian America, it needs to be emphasized, were not parochial concerns, but saw in the community ideal a concern that was common to all ethnic groups. Community represented for all such groups a basis for resistance to racial and cultural oppression as well as the source of alternative visions of social organization for the future.

Finally, the idea of community was very much tied in with the perception of ethnic communities as objects of an "internal colonialism," that gave them a commonality with colonialized societies worldwide. The Asian American movement, like other ethnic movements of the 1960s, identified externally not with Asia per se, but with other Third World societies that were the objects of colonial oppression. Within the context of the U.S. war in Vietnam, Asian Americans felt a special sense of kinship with the Vietnamese, which distinguished their responses to the war from others who protested against it, but their responses were couched in terms of Third World solidarity in general, as evidenced in the vocabulary of the

Third World employed by political protesters in San Francisco State University and the University of California–Berkeley in 1968, which also produced the idea of Asian America.[19]

In her *Asian American Panethnicity*, Yen Le Espiritu has offered a thoughtful account of the successes and limitations of the Asian American movement. Rearticulating the dominant society's exclusionary idea of "Asian," the movement created a new ideological and institutional context for Asian America:

> Although the pan-Asian concept may have originated in the minds of non-Asians, it is today more than a reflection of this misperception. Asian Americans did not just adopt the concept but also transformed it to conform to their ideological and political needs . . . young Asian American activists rejected the stereotyped term "Oriental" and coined their own term, "Asian American." Although both terms denote the consolidation of group boundaries, Asian American activists insisted on their term because they wanted to define their own image—one that would connote political activism rather than passivity. . . . Not only did Asian Americans consolidate, but they also politicized, using the very pan-Asian concept imposed from the outside as their political instrument.[20]

Initially consisting mostly of Chinese, Japanese, and (to a lesser extent) Filipino Americans, by the mid-1970s the movement made efforts to include other groups such as Koreans, South Asians, and even Pacific Islanders, spawning another term, *Asian Pacific Americans*.[21] Movement activity and publications gave Asian Americans visibility on the political scene and spawned institutions that gave its achievements permanence—Asian American studies programs on university campuses and social and political organizations of various kinds around which to unite Asian Americans and ensure their representation on government programs. Asian American scholarship was to reconstruct the history of Asians in the United States, putting an end to long-standing notions of Asians as temporary residents of the United States, as well as demonstrating Asian participation in and contributions to U.S. history. Asian American literature did much to reveal the complexities of the inner lives of Asians in their efforts to make homes for themselves against oppression and discrimination. And "Asian American" was quickly assimilated into official language in government programs and censuses.

The movement also faced critical problems almost immediately. In spite of conscious efforts to respect diversity, the rearticulation of Asianness in the language of radicalism did not eliminate the contradiction between the homogenizing implications of an Asian American panethnicity and nationally defined ethnic self-perceptions. Filipino Americans were uncomfortable from the beginning with their inclusion under categories of "yellow" or "Asian," their discomfort exacerbated by the Japanese and Chinese American domination of the movement.[22] Within the Chinese and Japanese American groups themselves, there was a disjuncture between the perceptions and aspirations of the young radical intellectuals who defined the movement and the ethnic and political identifications of the peoples for whom they spoke; the disjuncture implicit in the term also brought forward generational and class differences.

Other problems were products of the success of the movement. As with other radical movements at the time, the movement in its unfolding brought out significant gender differences, with women demanding that their multiple-layered oppression not be dissolved into categories of ethnic, racial, or class oppression. The institutionalization of the movement, which required also some assimilation to existing structures of power, quickly distanced activists further from the communities for which they spoke. By the early 1980s, Asian American scholars were already acutely aware of the ways in which academic demands distanced them from the radical, community-oriented scholarship that had given rise to Asian American studies programs in the first place. Espiritu has argued cogently that those involved in community programs faced this problem in even more critical ways: success in dealing with government programs required professionalization, which not only distanced community activists from the communities for which they worked, but also exacerbated class divisions between an emergent professional-managerial group and the communities at large.[23] Rather than being defined by the originary radical vision of the movement, the discourse on Asian America was shaped increasingly by the dialectics of state policy and the professional-managerial commitments of an Asian American elite—which, incidentally, further undermined panethnic unity, as the more established groups of Chinese and Japanese continued to dominate this new elite.

Still, it is important to underline here that these contradictions were informed by a new ideological and structural context that had been established by the Asian American movement, which continues to this day to serve as a frame of reference for understanding Asian America. The movement imbedded the problems of Asian America in U.S. soil. In doing so, it also endowed panethnic identification with normative status so that while ethnic "disidentification" is ever-present as an option (and perhaps also in everyday practice), it no longer seems "natural" but calls for explanation and justification against this new frame of reference. The new ideological and institutional framework, of course, also facilitates panethnic unity when needs and interests require it. Having started as political fiction, in other words, panethnicity has come to be a source of political legitimacy.

These contradictions may not be significantly different from those of other minority groups in the United States whose struggles likewise led to new unities but also to new divisions and conflicts. Asian America, however, was to experience another radical transformation that would lead to a break with the situation created by the struggles of the 1960s, which has called into question the possibility of thinking of the problems of Asian America in the language of those struggles. I am referring here to the already widely recognized demographic transformation of Asian America, itself bound up with radical changes in the relationship of the United States to Asia, as expressed in the new language of the Pacific. What may be less widely recognized is that this new transformation, the future of which is highly unpredictable, may be in the process of constructing new ethnicities that are no longer containable within the national framework that earlier bounded thinking about ethnicity and giving new meaning to older divisions as well.

The idea of Asian America faced a critical challenge from the outside almost as soon as it had come into existence—the challenge of the new immigration from Asia, made possible by the immigration law of 1965 that was to result in a dramatic increase in the number of Asian immigrants. On the surface, the new immigration boosted the power of Asian America by rapidly inflating the numbers of Asians in the United States: from a total of around 1,357,000 in 1970, the number of Asian American Pacific Islanders in the United States would increase to around 3,700,000 in 1980 to approximately 7,274,000 in 1990. Because of certain preferences in the immigration law, the new immigrants also included a high percentage of educated professionals who were less likely to keep silent in the face of discrimination and more likely to add their voices to calls for Asian American empowerment.[24]

Equally important, however, was the fact that the new immigration almost immediately made irrelevant the fundamental assumption that had guided the struggle for Asian America: the rootedness of Asian Americans in U.S. history. In 1970, U.S.-born and -educated Asians made up about two-thirds of the population of Asian America. By 1980, the percentage had been reversed, with the foreign-born constituting 73 percent of the population, up dramatically for all groups except Japanese Americans. The immigration also transformed the relative numerical strength of the various national ethnic groups, moving Chinese and Filipinos way ahead of Japanese Americans as well as adding immense numbers to formerly numerically marginal groups such as Koreans, South and Southeast Asians and Pacific Islanders. "Roots" for this new population was more likely to mean roots somewhere in Asia or the Pacific than in the United States or in U.S. history.

The new immigration to the United States coincided with crucial transformations within the Pacific. The United States was to play a crucial part in the new Pacific formation, and from a U.S.-based perspective, what is most striking is the flow across the Pacific of Asian peoples; indeed, the new immigration, with its economic and cultural implications, appears if not as a reversal of the nineteenth-century frontier, then at least as a revival of the eastern flow of Asian peoples that was aborted by the ideology of a Western-moving frontier. Nevertheless, it is important to remember that now, as then, the flow of Asian peoples to the United States is part of a larger process of motions of peoples that is at once a product and a constituent of a Pacific formation. The major difference between the present and the past is the economic and political emergence of Pacific Asian societies, which has resulted in a restructuring not only of the Pacific but of global economic, political, social, and cultural relations in general and endowed these motions of Asian peoples with a new meaning. The new Asian immigration to the United States partakes of this altered meaning and represents an unprecedented challenge to the very idea of an Asian America.

There is no space here to elaborate on the multiple dimensions of a contemporary Pacific formation, and little need to do so, since my concern is with the consequences of the new Pacific formation for people's motions, rather than for its inner workings per se. Suffice it to say here that past legacy and present circumstances have interacted in complex ways in shaping new patterns of immigration—and in blurring the differences between the present and the past, especially in the United States. For nearly two centuries, during which a Pacific formation coincided with the U.S. national formation, a Eurocentric racism excluded Asians from the United States, which was to become untenable after World War II. By the end of the war, the United States had achieved its goal of making the Pacific (including East Asia) into an American Lake, but policy by then was dictated by considerations of containing the spread of Communism in Asia, which called for a reconsideration of domestic policies that were informed by racism (in the same manner that the fight against Nazi racism had called forth a reconsideration of racism at home). Two tragic wars in Asia would help speed up the process whereby those people who were already part of the American Lake could become Americans as well. The 1965 immigration law made up for past injustices by allowing foreign relatives of American citizens to become American citizens. The same law allowed for the immigration of those who sought to escape under one guise or another circumstances of economic deprivation and political oppression. Filipinos, colonialized by U.S. aspirations to rendering the Pacific into an American Lake, but long denied their Americanness nevertheless, would benefit from these provisions; so would Chinese, released from controls by a Communist regime opening up to capitalism and not knowing how to dispose of a "surplus" population. In these and other cases, immigration has followed an earlier push-pull model of motions of peoples from poor to rich countries in search of economic or political survival. The parallels with the past do not end there; people's motions across the Pacific once again have become an occasion for business, reviving earlier practices of indentured servitude, most notably in the case of Chinese migration to the United States, but with other groups as well.[25]

The burden of the past may weigh heavily on the poor, but the parallels with the past must not be exaggerated, for the new migrations take place in a Pacific restructured by contemporary economic forces. United States domination provided the context for the new Pacific formation, but it is clear in hindsight that the United States could not dictate the outcome of its own policies. The strengthening of the Western Rim economies to contain Communism was to end up creating economic powers that have come to challenge U.S. economic domination of the Pacific. The emergence of these powers has also created a Pacific formation that has brought societies of the rim much closer economically and culturally, has rendered their relations much more systemic, and has introduced a multidimensionality to the flows of capital, commodities, and people. Commodity chains, capital flows, and even transfers of people under the aegis of transnational corporations have bound Pacific economies together. Pacific Asian economies are active players in this economic activity. They are no longer the exporters of merely labor, but also of capital. And they are crucial to the productive activity of U.S. corporations, which have become major exporters of jobs across the Pacific.[26]

Two important consequences of this systemic integration of the Pacific are relevant to the discussion here. First is the generation of diasporic populations or, where such populations already existed, their transformation into transnational ethnicities. The term *diaspora* has become increasingly current over the past decade, in connection mainly with Chinese but also with Asian Indian and Filipino populations. In the case of the first two groups in particular, migration abroad is not a new phenomenon but goes back to the nineteenth century and even earlier. But they have acquired a new significance in light of global economic developments, and the localized identities that they had acquired in their settlements abroad have been overwhelmed in reassertions of cultural nationalism that stress their "essential" unity across global spaces.[27]

The other consequence is the emergence of a highly vocal and visible trans-Pacific professional-managerial class that is the product of the new Pacific formation. As Paul Ong, Edna Bonacich, and Lucie Cheng put it,

> as the Asian countries have emerged from their peripheral status within the world economy, their focus on scientific and technical innovation is luring back many of their professional expatriates from the United States. This phenomenon has three consequences. For the developing Asian countries, the return of highly educated and experienced people helps relieve a significant shortage of professionals in selected fields. For the United States, the departure of these highly trained professionals with experience in the most advanced areas of research presents a potential threat. Finally, for the world system as a whole, the frequent movement back and forth of professionals contributes to the internationalization of the professional-managerial stratum.[28]

We need to remember that, in addition to family members, the 1965 immigration law gave preference to this group, whose immigration was to make a major impact on Asian American communities as well as on perceptions of Asian Americans. Their presence would do much to bolster the idea of Asian Americans as a "model minority." Their "movement back and forth"(which is not equally available to the poorer immigrants) has also contributed to the reshaping of Asian American ethnicity.

As it has come to include these groups that are no longer containable within national boundaries, Asian America is no longer just a location in the United States, but is at the same time a location on a metaphorical rim constituted by diasporas and motions of individuals. To understand Asian Americans it is no longer sufficient to comprehend their roots in U.S. history or, for that matter, in countries of origin, but a multiplicity of historical trajectories that converge in the locations we call Asian America that may diverge once again to disrupt the very idea of Asian Americanness. It is multiple location in the same physical space that has introduced a new fundamental contradiction to the idea of Asian America, overdetermining the inherited contradictions of panethnicity and nationally or more locally defined ethnicities. This multiplicity of location is evident in even a cursory examination of Asian American publications, which, unlike in an earlier day, include within their compass everything from local U.S. news and events to happenings in remote locations in Asia, and even elsewhere so long as they involve "Asians."[29] It also finds a counterpart in discussions of Asian American identity in the new positive value assigned to the idea of hybridity, which in its "dual personality" manifestation provided the occasion for rejecting the Americanness of Asians, and which Asians earlier struggled against in claiming their history as Americans.[30] While few would object to the openness implicit in cultural inclusiveness, or a hybridity that allows for individual or group "multiculturalism," the diffuseness of Asian American identity that they imply simultaneously may end up, against earlier efforts to construct such an identity, encouraging the everpresent possibility of ethnic insularity.

It seems clear that the idea of Asian America today requires a different mapping of the United States, Asia, the Pacific, and the world than that which produced the idea less than three decades ago. The old political and economic units, and spatial directionalities, that informed the older mapping are no longer sufficient to grasp the forces that are in the process of reshaping nationalities, racial affinities, and ethnicities.[31] Ironically, these same changes have revived some of the earlier problems in reconfigured forms. I have already referred to the significant class differences in the experience of the new trans-Pacific motions. Another important problem arises out of the closer relationships to societies of origin in Asia. To the extent that the contemporary Asian American populations identify with their societies of origin in Asia, they are once again vulnerable in their relationships to one another to replicating the divisions and conflicts that beset Asian societies. At the same time, closeness to Asia opens up the possibility of distancing themselves from their immediate environments in the United States, especially in their relations to other minority groups. Finally, a kind of Orientalism in reverse, or a self-Orientalization, has reappeared in discussions of Asian American populations. Gary Okihiro has argued that the idea of "model minority" is a product of just such an Orientalist stereotyping of Asian Americans:

> yellow peril and the model minority are not poles, denoting opposite representations along a single line, but in fact form a circular relationship that moves in either direction. . . . Moving in one direction along the circle, the model minority mitigates the alleged danger of the yellow peril, whereas reversing direction, the model minority, if taken too far, can become the yellow peril.[32]

Perhaps the most blatant example of a revived Orientalism is the dehistoricized culturalism that traces the economic success of Asian societies and, with them, of Asian Americans, to some vaguely defined "Asian" characteristic. In the case of

Pacific Asian societies, this has taken the form of erasing crucial historical and structural differences under the rubric of "Confucian" values. The same kind of culturalism is visible, as I noted previously, in cultural nationalist homogenizations of diasporic populations.[33]

FROM JOHN HUANG TO BEIJING:
THE PITFALLS OF DIASPORA DISCOURSE

The reconceptualization of Asian Americans in terms of diaspora or transnationality responds to a real situation: the reconfiguration of migrant societies and their political and cultural orientations. But diaspora and transnationality as concepts are also discursive; not only do they have normative implications, but they also articulate—in a very Foucauldian sense—relations of power within populations so depicted, as well as in their relationship to societies of origin and arrival. Diaspora discourse has an undeniable appeal in the critical possibilities it offers against assumptions of national cultural homogeneity, which historically has resulted in the denial of full cultural (and political) citizenship to those who resisted assimilation into the dominant conceptualizations of national culture, were refused entry into it, or whose cultural complexity could not be contained easily within a single conception of national culture. This critical appeal, however, also disguises the possibility that diasporic notions of culture, if employed without due regard to the social and political complexities of so-called diasporic populations, may issue in reifications of their own, opening the way to new forms of cultural domination, manipulation and commodification. The problems presented by diaspora discourse may be illustrated through the recent case of John Huang, the Chinese American fund-raiser for the Democratic National Committee. When Huang was charged with corruption on the grounds that he raised funds from foreign sources, the Democratic National Committee proceeded immediately to canvas all contributors with Chinese names to ascertain whether or not they were foreigners, turning a run-of-the-mill case of political corruption into a racial issue. The committee's action reactivated the long-standing assumption that anyone with a Chinese name might in all probability be foreign, reaffirming implicitly that a Chinese name was the marker of racial foreignness. What followed may not have been entirely novel, but seemed quite logical nevertheless in terms of contemporary diasporic "networks" (perhaps, more appropriately in this case, "webs"). John Huang's connections to the Riady family in Indonesia, which surfaced quickly, not only underlined the probable foreignness of Chinese contributors but also suggested further connections between Chinese Americans and other Chinese Overseas that seemed to be confirmed by revelations that several other Chinese American fund-raisers, or contributors, had ties to Chinese in South and Southeast Asia. As these overseas Chinese had business connections in the People's Republic of China, before long a petty corruption case turned into a case of possible conspiracy that extended from Beijing, through Chinese Overseas to Chinese Americans.[34]

This linking of Chinese Americans to diasporic Chinese and the government in Beijing has provoked charges of racism among Asian Americans and their many sympathizers. Racism is there, to be sure. But is this racism simply an extension of the historical racism against Asian Americans, or does it represent something new? If so, is it possible that at least some Asian Americans have been complicit in producing a new kind of racist discourse? The question is fraught with difficulties—chief among them shifting responsibility to the victim—but it must be raised nevertheless.

The linking of John Huang, Chinese Overseas, and the Beijing government, I would like to suggest here, has been facilitated by the new discourse on the Chinese diaspora, which, in reifying Chineseness, has created fertile grounds for nourishing a new racism. The idea of diaspora is responsible in the first place for abolishing the difference between Chinese Americans and Chinese elsewhere (including in China). In response to a legacy of discrimination against Chinese Americans, which made them hesitant even to acknowledge their ties to China and other Chinese, some Chinese Americans and their sympathizers have been all too anxious to reaffirm such ties, in turn suppressing the cultural differences arising from the different historical trajectories of different Chinese populations scattered around the world. The antiassimilationist mood (expressed most fervently in liberal "multiculturalism") itself has contributed in no small measure to such cultural reification. The question, moreover, is not merely that of culture. *Because* of the fact that the very phenomenon of diaspora has produced a multiplicity of Chinese cultures, the affirmation of "Chineseness" may be sustained only by recourse to a common origin, or descent, that persists in spite of widely different historical trajectories, which results in the elevation of ethnicity and race over all the other factors—often divisive—that have gone into the shaping of Chinese populations and their cultures.

In its failure to specify its own location vis-à-vis the hegemonic, self-serving, and often financially lucrative reification of "Chineseness" in the political economy of transnationalism, critical diaspora discourse itself has fallen prey to the manipulation and commodification made possible by cultural reification and contributes to the foregrounding of ethnicity and race in contemporary political and cultural thinking. There has been a tendency in recent scholarship, publications industry, and arts and literature, for instance, to abolish the difference between Asians and Asian Americans. In scholarship, contrary to an earlier refusal of Asian studies specialists to have anything to do with Asian American studies, there have been calls recently to integrate Asian American studies into Asian studies, which partly reflects the increased prominence of trans-Pacific population flows, but also suggests the increasingly lucrative promise of reorienting Asian American studies in that direction. Publishers' catalogs, especially those devoted to "multiculturalism" and ethnic relations, freely blend Asian with Asian American themes, and it is not rare to see these days a catalog in which *Woman Warrior* is placed right next to *The Dream of the Red Chamber*. A film series on "Asian American film" mysteriously includes many more films from Asia than from Asian America.

Moreover, and more fundamentally, within the context of flourishing Pacific economies (at least until very recently), some Asian Americans—most notably Chinese Americans—have been assigned the role of "bridges" to Asia; which role they have assumed readily for its lucrative promises. I referred previously to the homogenization of Chinese populations in the recent Confucian revival, which attributes the economic success of Chinese, without regard to time or place, to the persistence of "Confucian values," which were viewed earlier as obstacles to capitalism but have been rendered now into the source of everything from economic development to the production of "model minorities."[35] Thus, one promoter of Pacific economies writes, "With their cultural, linguistic, and family ties to China, Chinese-American entrepreneurs like [Henry Y.] Hwang are proving to be America's secret weapon in recapturing a predominant economic role in the world's most populous nation."[36] It may not be very far from a portrayal of Chinese Americans as American economic moles in China to William Safire's depiction of John Huang as a Chinese political mole in Washington, D.C. Finally, widely different Chinese populations have in recent years been endowed with supposedly identical cultural characteristics that further erase their differences. Networked through *guanxi*, and driven by Confucianism, Chinese around the world in this representation have been rendered into a "tribe" (in the same Kotkin's description) in relentless search for wealth and power.[37]

The attitudes that lie at the root of these recent tendencies are not the less products of racism for being produced by or sympathetic to Chinese and other Asian populations. Chinese populations are no less divided by class, gender, and ethnic differences than other populations. Not the least among those differences are differences of place and history. If these differences are erased by the shifting of attention from these categories to a general category of diaspora, it is necessary to raise the question of whom such erasure serves. There is no reason to suppose that the government in Beijing (or, for that matter, Taiwan) is any more reluctant than the government in Washington or U.S. transnational corporations to use diasporic Chinese for its own purposes. On the other hand, both from a political and an economic perspective, some diasporic Chinese are obviously of greater use than others and in turn benefit from the erasure of differences among Chinese, which enables them to speak for all Chinese.[38] Reconceptualization of Chinese populations in terms of diasporas, in other words, serves economic and political class interests (it is not accidental that the Chinese American John Huang was connected with the Riady family, which made him useful in a number of ways).

In this context, it is also important to raise the question of the relationship between diaspora and national boundaries, for as the notion of diaspora erases differences among Chinese, it seeks also to question national boundaries. Here, too, there is a question of who stands to benefit the most from the erasure of national boundaries. Whatever its own colonizing tendencies, the nation–state is still capable, properly controlled from below, to offer protection to those within its boundaries. It is not very surprising, therefore, that those Chinese Americans devoted to social issues and community building (such as Henry Der) should be suspicious of the claims of diasporas or the questioning of national boundaries.[39]

What I am suggesting here is not a return to the nation with its colonial, homogenizing, and assimilationist ideology, but the qualification of diasporic with place consciousness. To raise the question of places is to raise the issue of difference on a whole range of fronts, including those of class, gender, and ethnicity. It is also to raise the question of history in identity. Identity is no less an identity for being historical (is there any other kind?). Contrary to a hegemonic cultural reification or a whimpering preoccupation with the location of "home," which seem to have acquired popularity as alternative expressions of diasporic consciousness, what is important is to enable people to feel at home where they live.[40] This does not require that people abandon their legacies, only that they recognize the historicity of their cultural identities and that those identities are subject to change in the course of historical encounters.

Diasporas are dispersals from some remembered homeland, from some concrete place, which after the fact is conceived in terms of the nation (at least over the past century), although concrete places of origin retain their visibility even in their incorporation into the language of the nation or of diaspora. The dispersed also land in concrete places in the host society, which, too, is captured in national terms, even if the very fact of diaspora if nothing else disturbs efforts to define nation and national culture. Ling-ch'i Wang tells us that one Chinese metaphor for the diasporic condition is "growing roots where landed" (*luodi shenggen*).[41] While a prejudice for the nation makes it possible to speak of "national soil" and demands assimilation to some "national culture," rootedness as a metaphor points inevitably to concrete places that belie easy assumptions of the homogeneity of national soil or culture. Kathleen Neil Conzen writes of German immigrants to the United States that,

> as change occurred, it could proceed without the kinds of qualitative shifts implied by the familiar notions of acculturation and assimilation. Culture was more strongly localized—naturalized in the literal botanical sense of the term—than it was ethnicized, and the structures of everyday life, rather than being assimilated to those of some broader element within American society, responded to the transforming pressures of modern life on a parallel trajectory of their own.[42]

The statement points to both the concrete place-basedness and the historicity of diasporic identity. James Clifford uses the metaphor of "routes" to capture the spatiotemporality of cultural identity; I will describe it simply as "historical trajectory through places."[43] Encounters in places traversed involve both forgetting and new acquisitions. The past is not erased, therefore, but rewritten. Similarly, the new acquisitions do not imply disappearance into the new environment, but rather the proliferation of future possibilities.

What attention to place suggests is the historicity of identity. The "assimilation theory" to which Conzen objects presupposed dehistoricized and placeless notions of culture; assimilation implied motion from one to the other. One could not be both Chinese and American, but had to move from being Chinese (whatever that might mean) to being American (whatever that might mean). Hence failure to become "fully American" could produce such notions as "dual personality," which precluded being American—as well as suggesting that such an identity represented the degeneration of the components out of which it was formed.

Such cultural assumptions in the end could only rest on the principle of descent, in other words, race. Ironically, contemporary critiques of assimilation theory, to the extent that they ignore place and history, end up with similar assumptions. A case in point is the currently fashionable idea of hybridity, which "multiculturalism" evaluates differently than monoculturalism permitted earlier, but which nevertheless retains similar culturalist assumptions (some notion of Chineseness conjoined to some notion of Americanness to produce a hybrid product). And since culturalism still runs against the evidence of difference, it may be sustained only by the reification of ethnicity and, ultimately, race. Diasporic identity in its reification does not overcome the racial prejudices of earlier assumptions of national cultural homogeneity, but in many ways follows a similar logic, now at the level not of nations but offground "transnations." The "children of the Yellow Emperor" may be all the more of a racial category for having abandoned its ties to the political category of the nation.[44]

The insistence on places against diasporic reification has consequences that are not only analytical in an abstract sense. It draws attention, in the first place, to another, place-based, kind of politics. One of the dangerous consequences of undue attention to diasporas is to distance the so-called diasporic populations from their immediate environments, to render them into foreigners in the context of everyday life. Given the pervasiveness of conflicts in U.S. society that pitch different diasporic populations against one another, rather than retreat behind reified identities that further promote mutual suspicion and racial division, it is necessary to engage others in political projects to create political alliances where differences may be "bridged," and common social and cultural bonds formed to enable different populations to learn to live with one another.[45] A Chinese living in Los Angeles has more of a stake in identifying with his/her African or Hispanic American neighbors than with some distant cousin in Hong Kong (without implying that the two kinds of relationships need to be understood in zero-sum terms). Following the logic of this argument, I suggest that place-based politics offers the most effective means to achieving such ends. Place-based politics does not presuppose communities that shut out the world, but refocuses attention on building society from the bottom up.

The other consequence is also political, but within the context of academic politics, for there is a pedagogic dimension to realizing such political goals. It is rather unfortunate that recent ideological formations, backed by the power of foundations, have encouraged the capturing of ethnicities in "diasporic" American or cultural studies. In the case of studies of Asian Americans in particular, the most favored choices these days would seem to be to recognize Asian American studies as a field of its own, to break it down into various national components (Chinese, Japanese, Filipino, etc.), or to absorb it into American or Asian studies. Each choice is informed by political premises and goals. Asian American studies as a field is under attack from the inside for its homogenizing implications as well as its domination by some groups over others. Breaking it down, however, does not offer any readily acceptable solution, as it merely replaces continental homogeneity with national homogeneities; why should there be a Chinese American rather than, say, a Fuzhounese American studies? And why stop at Fuzhou? On the other hand, absorbing Asian American studies into either Asian or American studies would seem to achieve little more than bringing it as a field under the hegemony of the study of societies of origin or arrival.

If education has anything to do with politics, and it does have everything to do with it, the wiser course to follow in overcoming ethnic divisions would be to reinforce programs in ethnic studies, which initially had the bridging of ethnic divisions and the pursuit of common projects (based in communities) to that end as fundamental goals. Ethnic studies since its inception has been viewed with suspicion by the political and educational establishments and suffered from internal divisions as well. Whether or not these legacies can be overcome is a big question, embedded as they are in the structures of U.S. society and academic institutions. The irony is that while ethnic studies might help ideologically in overcoming ethnic divisions, it is not likely to receive much support unless interethnic political cooperation has sufficient force to render it credible in the first place. The ideology of globalization, of which diasporic ideology is one constituent, further threatens to undermine its promise (and existence). Here, too, place-based politics may have something to offer in countering the ideologies of the age.

THE LOCAL AND THE GLOBAL IN ASIAN AMERICA

By way of conclusion, I would like to return to what I described in the introduction as a contradiction between the present and the past, the originary vision of community that defined the term *Asian American* when it first emerged in the 1960s and the contemporary understanding of Asian America, to which recalling that vision appears now as "the trope of nostalgic history."[46] The original vision of Asian America may no longer be able to contain the forces reshaping Asian America. But is it, therefore, irrelevant? The question is not an abstract question of ethnicity, it is a deeply political one. So is the answer.

As I noted previously, the forces that have restructured Asian America over the past three decades have boosted the power of Asian America, but also created new strains on an already problematic social formation. The new immigration was to create new problems in Asian American relations with other minority groups (the African/Korean American conflict comes readily to mind)[47], but also between different national ethnic groups within a Pan-Asian ethnicity as well as within individual groups. Karen Leonard has documented conflicts between settled Punjabi groups and new immigrants from South Asia, while Peter Kwong has shown the ways in which Chinatowns have been remapped by conflicts between the older residents from Guangdong and the new immigrants from Fujian.[48] The conflicts include basic economic and class issues but, ironically, are expressed in the language of cultural authenticity: "real Americans" versus "real Asians."

The discourse on Asian America has stayed clear of the language of authenticity, but has undergone noticeable changes in its efforts to accommodate the restructuring of Asian America. As early as the 1980s, Asian American scholars recognized the problems presented to the idea of Asian America by the new immigration and sought to find ways of incorporating the problems and orientations of the new immigrant population into ways of speaking about Asian America. New immigrants, and the need to include them in Asian American studies, was very much on the minds of the scholars (some of whom were themselves new immigrants) contributing to the volume *Reflections on Shattered Windows*, published in 1988. The title is itself indicative of their concerns (and an affirmation of the origins of the movement in windows shattered in San Francisco State). Nevertheless, they were also wary of the consequences for Asian America of the Pacific connection ushered in by the same immigration. The volume was prefaced by a poem by Russell Leong titled "Disarmed/1968–1987: San Francisco State College," which included the lines

Those who understand
America today
hesitate
before crossing
the Pacific bridge
tomorrow.
Forty years ago
the tinge of our skin
wrongly imprisoned us
under the shadow of the rising sun
across the sea.
Yet today
we bargain our lives
for an inflated currency:
Human capital.
Transnational investment.
Economic migrants.
What does this mean—
Where does it end?

The "dominoes" of a defunct theory
reincarnated into building blocks
of the Pacific Century
As Asians, once again
form the bridge
toward a new manifest destiny.
But bridges have been burnt
whole villages napalmed before.[49]

Or, as Michael Omi put it in the same volume, less poetically but with equal passion:

> Asian American studies should contribute to an understanding of, and perhaps help to define, the emergent political, economic, and cultural relations between the U.S. and Asia. With the demise of the "Atlantic era," Pacific Rim studies is "hot." The crucial task for Asian American studies will be to define an approach that avoids the exploitative developmental outlook endemic to international capital. If Asian American studies does not intervene, Pacific Rim studies will be monopolized by the wolves.[50]

The effort to draw a distinction between the new immigration and the Pacific idea that accompanied it was an important one, and one that has continued to inform the debate on Asian America. The effort seems in hindsight to have been quixotic in its urge to preserve the radical vision of communities rooted in an Asian *American* history for, in the interesting observation of Kent Ono, "The argument that Asian Americans try to make immigrants subjects of the state as quickly as possible may, in fact, work in reverse. In the process of normalizing immigrants, 'Asian Americans' may in fact be socialized to become more like those they serve, more migrant."[51] This is indeed what seems to have happened over the past decade, when Asian Americans have appeared increasingly, in the words of Edna Bonacich, as a "middleman minority." The strong affirmation of identity at the origins of the Asian American movement seems also to have retreated before a situation where the postmodern presents "the moment for the ethnic to be conjoined with the universal, as everything is now in a correlate condition of fragmentation and revision," or erases "at that very moment the specificity of ethnicity."[52]

What is interesting is that the questions raised about Asian American ethnicity currently, expressed now in the language of postmodernism and postcoloniality, still take as their frame of reference the ideological and institutional structures created by the Asian American imaginary of the 1960s. This is no doubt partially because of the persistence of organizational structures (including Asian American studies) that were products of the movement. I would like to venture here, however, that the continuing concern is also because of the persistence of structures of racial, class, and gender division, embedded in the capitalist organization of society, that perpetuate in reconfigured forms the problems that gave rise to the

Asian American movement in the first place and necessitate the preservation of that frame of reference.[53]

The reconfiguring of the problems, nevertheless, calls for a reconfiguring of the answers, and this is what necessitates a new understanding, if not a new vision, of Asian America. In her contribution to the special issue of *amerasia journal*, "thinking theory in asian american studies,"[54] from which I have previously quoted generously, Sau-ling Wong offers a thoughtful appraisal of the problems of reconsidering Asian America that bears some comment. Wong's argument is similar to the argument I have offered previously in the necessity of drawing a distinction between what she calls *diasporic* and *domestic* perspectives in the understanding of contemporary Asian America; the one stressing the global dimensions of Asian America, the other focusing on the national context.[55] Arguing the ways in which these perspectives confound easy definitions of Asian American identity and undermine cultural nationalism, Wong nevertheless returns to a reaffirmation of identity as a necessity of meaningful political action. In this case, the meaningful political action implies not just a return to earlier notions of community, but the defense of the very notion of community against the developmentalist ideology of a transnational capitalism that is in the process of engulfing the local by the global (in the specific case of Asian Americans, by an ideology of the Pacific, which has become the most recent location for the legitimization of "developmentalism").[56]

Given the strategic importance that Asian America has been assigned in a Pacific economic formation, it may also have a very significant part to play in the reassertion of local welfare against the globalizing forces of transnational capitalism, which returns this discussion to where it started. As the contrasts between Matt Fong and Henry Der reveal, the question of a Pacific versus a community orientation is no longer simply a question of Asian America as expressed in the vision of the 1960s, or perpetuated in racially or nationally conceived notions of ethnicity. Those questions are themselves embedded in the confrontations between futures mortgaged to the promises of a utopianized transnational capitalism and the very concrete realities of everyday existence at the level of the local, in which there are few differences between old-timers and newcomers, between Asians and others. Where "bridges" are placed under such circumstances is a matter not of ethnic destiny, but of political choice. I will conclude here with a long quotation, that I hope embodies in the concrete the many themes, and the complex history, of an idea that is Asian America:

Kathy Nishimoto Masaoka is standing in front of the twelve-foot-tall "Friendship Knot," a double helix of concrete anchored in the mall next to the New Otani. She is scowling at the bronze plaque that dedicates the sculpture to Morinosuke Kajima, the wartime boss of the Hanaoke slaves, but here described as an "international businessman, whose vision and generosity initiated the revitalization of Little Tokyo."

"This used to be the heart of the community," she explains, pointing toward a courtyard of glitzy tourist shops selling Armani suits and English hunting gear under

the shadow of the New Otani. "Three old hotels provided affordable housing for elderly Issei [first-generation immigrants] as well as young Latino families. There were
scores of traditional, family-run storefronts and cheap restaurants.

"But then, in 1973, Kajima created the East-West Development Corporation to
oversee the redevelopment of this area. The residents wanted replacement senior
housing and the preservation of existing business. The Downtown corporate leaders
and the city's Community Redevelopment Agency (C.R.A.), on the other hand,
pushed Kajima's plan for a luxury hotel and shopping center. They saw Little Tokyo
as a conduit for Japanese corporate investment, not as a vibrant Japanese-American
neighborhood. Kajima eventually selected the New Otani chain, headed by a
wealthy Japanese family, to manage the hotel."[57]

According to Mike Davis, Little Tokyo activists, led by a female Salvadoran immigrant, were in touch with elderly Chinese men who had been victims of Kajima operations during World War II, to establish solidarity against Kajima, welcomed otherwise through the "Golden Doors" of the Pacific. That, too, may be
trans-Pacific panethnicity, but one that is defined by a different kind of politics
that grounds transnationalism in the welfare of local communities.

NOTES

*This is a revised version of an essay that was commissioned by the Asia Society, but
initially published in *Amerasia* 22(3) (1996). I would like to thank the Asia Society, especially Vishakha Desai, vice president in charge of cultural programs, for permission to publish the essay first in *Amerasia*. The views expressed in this chapter are strictly my own and
implicitly or explicitly at odds with those of the Asia Society, which initially sponsored the
"Bridges with Asia" project. I hope the differences are productive in consequence; institutions such as the Asia Society may make important contributions to the resolution of the
problems I discuss in the chapter.

1. Matt Fong, "From Gold Mountain to the Golden Door," *AsianWeek* 17(12) (January 19, 1996): 7.

2. Alethea Yip, "APA [Asian Pacific American] Spokesman," *AsianWeek* 17(12) (January 19, 1996): 9. Governor Wilson's office objected to Der for the latter's views on "affirmative action, 'English-only' legislation, Proposition 187, and Wilson himself," which obviously differed from those of the governor.

3. See *AsianWeek* 17 (19) (January 5, 1996): 13–18, for the list.

4. It is noteworthy here that while many of the changes I discuss, especially the revi-
talized orientation to Asia and the Pacific, are associated with the post-1965 immigrant
population, with its immediate ties to countries of origin. This is not the case with Matt
Fong, who, according to *AsianWeek*, is a fourth-generation Chinese American. The question, in other words, is not one of being more or less American, conceived in generational
or other terms.

5. For further discussion of this problem, see Arif Dirlik, "The Global in the Local,"
and the other essays in the collection *Global/Local: Cultural Production and the Transnational Imaginary*, ed. Rob Wilson and Wimal Dissayanake (Durham, N.C.: Duke Uni-

versity Press, in print). My interpretation here obviously places structural relationships ahead of culturalist arguments that promote an "Asian" exceptionalism, which is popular especially among non-Asian writers on Asian Americans and the contemporary Pacific.

6. Arif Dirlik, "Asia-Pacific in Asian-American Perspective," in *What Is in a Rim? Critical Perspectives on the Pacific Region Idea, Second Edition*, ed. Arif Dirlik (Lanham, Md.: Rowman & Littlefield, 1997), 283–308.

7. For a recent (and still unabashedly triumphalist) discussion, see Arrell Morgan Gibson, *Yankees in Paradise: The Pacific Basin Frontier* (Albuquerque: University of New Mexico Press, 1993), completed with the assistance of John S. Whitehead.

8. Gary Y. Okihiro, *Margins and Mainstreams: Asians in American History and Culture* (Seattle: University of Washington Press, 1994), chap. 1.

9. I owe the term *racial formation* to Michael Omi and Howard Winant, *Racial Formation in the United States: From the 1960s to the 1980s* (New York: Routledge, 1986). In the article cited previously in endnote 6, I explain at some length why, given the legacy of Orientalism, culture is also an important element in considerations of Asian America.

10. Yen Le Espiritu, *Asian American Panethnicity: Bridging Institutions and Identities* (Philadelphia: Temple University Press, 1992), 20. Espiritu derived the idea from David M. Hayano, "Ethnic Identification and Disidentification: Japanese-American Views of Chinese Americans," *Ethnic Groups* 3(2) (1981): 157–71.

11. At a conference at Duke University, "Asia-Pacific Identities: Culture and Identity Formation in the Age of Global Capital," April 13–15, 1995. Other terms of identity available at the time included *yellow* and even *Oriental.*

12. Omi and Winant have usefully defined "rearticulation" as "the process of redefinition of political interests and identities, through a process of recombination of familiar ideas and values in hitherto unrecognized ways." Omi and Winant, *Racial Formation*, 146, fn 8.

13. Franklin Odo, "Preface," *Roots: An Asian American Reader*, ed. Amy Tachiki, Eddie Wong, Franklin Odo, and Buck Wong (Los Angeles: UCLA Asian American Studies Center, 1971), vii, viii.

14. Odo, "Preface," *Roots*, ix.

15. John M. Liu, "The Relationship of Migration Research to Asian American Studies: Unity and Diversity within the Curriculum," in *Reflections on Shattered Windows: Promises and Prospects for Asian American Studies*, ed. Gary Y. Okihiro, Shirley Hune, Arthur A. Hansen, and John M. Liu (Pullman: Washington State University Press, 1988)), 117–25, here 123–4.

16. Odo, "Preface," *Roots*, x–xi.

17. Gary Y. Okihiro, "The Idea of Community and a 'Particular Type of History,'" in *Reflections on Shattered Windows*, 175–83, here 181.

18. Yuji Ichioka, *Issei: The World of the First Generation Japanese Immigrants, 1885–1924* (New York: Free Press, 1988).

19. See Odo, "Preface," *Roots*, x, for the Third World. For differences of Asian American responses to the war in Vietnam, see Espiritu, *Panethnicity*, 44. For the student movement in 1968, see the special issue of *Amerasia* 15(1) (1989).

20. Espiritu, *Panethnicity*, 162.

21. See Emma Gee, ed., *Counterpoint: Perspectives on Asian America* (Los Angeles: UCLA Asian American Studies Center, 1976), pref. I should note here that this inclusiveness has not always been welcomed by those so included. Native Hawaiians, for example,

who identify with indigenous rather than ethnic causes, see Asian Americans in Hawaii as participants in the expropriation of Hawaiian lands and part of the structure of foreign domination. From this perspective, the idea of Asian Pacific American is another instance of the imperialistic erasure of Hawaiian indigenism. For an example, see the essays in Haunani Kay-Trask, *From a Native Daughter: Colonialism and Sovereignty in Hawaii* (Monroe, Maine: Common Courage, 1993). Other Pacific Islanders, too, often identify more closely with indigenism, and their relationship to Asians is shaped by local experiences with Asian populations that are direct rather than intermediated by what happens in the United States (e.g., Asian Indians in Fiji, or Japanese and, more recently, Taiwanese investments in the South Pacific).

22. Espiritu, *Panethnicity*, 104. Already in 1976 an examination of the movement by a Filipino writer challenged its panethnic assumptions. See Lemuel F. Ignacio, *Asian Americans and Pacific Islanders (Is There Such an Ethnic Group?)* (San Jose, Calif.: Pilipino Development Associates, 1976).

23. See, especially, chap. 4.

24. See, for example, Leland T. Saito and John Horton, "The New Chinese Immigration and the Rise of Asian American Politics in Monterey Park California," in *The New Asian Immigration in Los Angeles and Global Restructuring*, ed. Paul Ong, Edna Bonacich, and Lucie Cheng (Philadelphia: Temple University Press, 1994), 233–63, here 243.

25. Peter Kwong, "China's Human Traffickers," *The Nation* (October 17, 1994): 422–5. In other cases, as with Filipinas or women from Southeast Asia, indentured servitude would seem to be more gender specific.

26. In his testimony before an incredulous congressional committee in 1877, Henry George argued against Chinese immigration while at the same time defending "free trade" on the grounds that while the import of the products of cheap labor benefited the United States, the import of the labor itself did not. George nevertheless backed away from a suggestion that employers should "employ where they can the cheapest." More than a century later, the latter has become the common practice in the Pacific economy, which is what I mean here by the export of jobs. While there may not be much difference between the export of capital and the import of labor, as some of the congressmen suggested to George in 1877, labor immigration still meets with immediate opposition while the free mobility of capital usually goes unnoticed. See Philip S. Foner and Daniel Rosenberg, eds., *Racism, Dissent and Asian Americans from 1850 to the Present: A Documentary History* (Westport, Conn.: Greenwood, 1993), 25–9.

27. For further discussion, see Arif Dirlik, "Critical Reflections on 'Chinese Capitalism' as Paradigm," *Identities* (forthcoming). Cultural nationalism is complicated, and contradicted, by simultaneous claims to an "Asian" legacy as an explanation of success that seeks to dislodge a Eurocentric conceptualization of capitalism. For a discussion of the complexities of diasporic identities, see Ling-chi Wang, "Roots and Changing Identity of the Chinese in the United States," *Daedalus* (Spring 1991): 181–206.

28. Paul Ong, Edna Bonacich, and Lucie Cheng, "The Political Economy of Capitalist Restructuring and the New Asian Immigration," in *New Asian Immigration*, 3–35, here 13.

29. This blurring of boundaries between Asia and Asian America may be typical of a phenomenon that pertains to ethnic studies in general. Young Mexican Americans, according to one source, "reject the 'Chicano' label and, even more vociferously, 'Hispanic' and 'Latino.' 'We're Mexicans,' they say." Ana Castillo, "Impressions of a Xicana Dreamer," *The Bloomsbury Review* (November/December 1995), 5, 13, here 5. A 1995 Bantam Dou-

bleday Dell catalog for "ethnic studies" is divided into sections that include "Asian studies" (the "core curriculum," which includes Chinese novels such as the *Dream of the Red Chamber* and *Wild Swans*), "Middle Eastern studies," "Native American Studies," and "Hispanic/Latino/Chicano studies." With the exception of Native American studies, all the sections draw freely on literature from the "areas" from which the ethnicities presumably hail. In the case of Asian Americans, there have been calls in scholarly circles to bring Asian American studies closer to Asian studies. Asian American studies are much in demand these days, mostly in response to student protests. Very often, however, the impression given by these demands is that Asian American studies should be studies of Rimpeople, rather than Asian Americans within the context of ethnic relations within the United States. I have stressed the importance of the Pacific dimension of Asian America, but as an element that disturbs national histories on both sides of the ocean. There is something quite dangerous politically in overemphasizing the Asianness of Asian Americanness, which renders them "foreign," even if that "foreignness" may be more acceptable presently than in the nineteenth century, and may even be marketable under the rubric of "multiculturalism,"(at least of a transnational corporate multiculturalism). It also distances ethnic groups in the United States from one another, by identifying them with their various areas of origin, rather than with the locations that they share, and which provides the point of departure for any kind of common political action. There is a good case to be made here that the blurring of area boundaries plays into the hands of existing hegemonic constructions of globalism and "multiculturalism," rather than challenging them, which also reflects the needs of an Asian American elite in complicity with existing structures of power. Against this construction, the call for the original goals of "ethnic studies" seems radical indeed. For an example by a Korean American student activist who stresses the need for "ethnic studies," rather than "area studies," see Ronald Kim, "The Myth and Reality of Ethnic Studies," *AsianWeek* (February 16, 1996): 7.

30. For an example, see the influential essay by Lisa Lowe, "Heterogeneity, Hybridity, Multiplicity: Marking Asian American Differences," *Diaspora* 1(1) (Spring 1991): 24–44. For an early discussion of "hybridity" that stresses its disabling consequences for young Asian Americans, see William Carlson Smith, *Americans in Process: A Study of Our Citizens of Oriental Ancestry* (New York: Arno and the *New York Times*, 1970), chap. xvii, "Cultural Hybridism." Originally published in 1937.

31. While different groups may experience this remapping differently, it is clear that the phenomenon itself is not exclusive to any one group, but a product of what I referred to as global postmodernity. A seminal work to address the question, this time in relation to the African diaspora, is Paul Gilroy's *The Black Atlantic: Modernity and Double Consciousness* (Cambridge, Mass.: Harvard University Press, 1993).

32. Okihiro, *Margins and Mainstreams*, 142. For an earlier critique that emphasizes the conservative implications of the model minority idea, see Keith Osajima, "Asian Americans as the Model Minority: An Analysis of the Popular Press Image in the 1960s and 1980s," in *Reflections on Shattered Windows*, 165–74.

33. For a more detailed discussion, see Arif Dirlik, "Confucius in the Borderlands: Global Capitalism and the Reinvention of Confucianism," *Boundary* 2 22(3) (Fall 1995): 229–73.

34. There is a great deal of material on the John Huang case, although no studies as yet. For a blatant example of the unscrupulous linking of John Huang with the Riadys and the PRC, see William Safire, "Listening to Hearings," *New York Times* (13 July 1997).

35. It is noteworthy that with the so-called meltdown of Asian economies in late 1997, "Asian Values," among them Confucianism, have once again lost their luster. It turns out once again that Asian values have been responsible for creating a corrupt "crony capitalism" that inevitably led to economic breakdown.

36. Joel Kotkin, "The New Yankee Traders," *INC* (March 1996): 25.

37. For critiques of these tendencies in connection with the John Huang case, see Ling-ch'i Wang, "Foreign Money Is No Friend of Ours," *AsianWeek* (November 8, 1996): 7, and Nick Cullather, "The Latest 'Peril' From Asia," *AsianWeek* (November 15, 1996): 7.

38. For an important discussion, see Peter Kwong, *Forbidden Workers: Illegal Chinese Immigrants and American Labor* (New York: New Press, 1997), especially chap. 5, "Manufacturing Ethnicity."

39. Such suspicion is not limited to Chinese Americans. In a recent conference in Singapore, one paper presentation that foregrounded diasporas and "transnations" was challenged by the well-known Singapore sociologist and activist Chua Beng-huat, who declared without qualification that he was a Singaporean, not a transnational or diasporic.

40. I am referring here to the title of a conference held in early November 1997 at New York University, "Where Is Home?" (previously the title of an exhibition on the Chinese in the United States). The preoccupation has its roots in a particularly narcissistic and manipulative offshoot of cultural studies.

41. Ling-ch'i Wang, "Roots and Changing Identity," 199–200.

42. Kathleen Neils Conzen, "Making Their Own America: Assimilation Theory and the German Peasant Pioneer," German Historical Institute, Washington, D.C., Annual Lecture Series, No. 3 (New York: Berg Publishers, 1990), 9.

43. See the collection of his essays in *Routes: Travel and Translation in the Late Twentieth Century* (Cambridge, Mass.: Harvard University Press, 1997).

44. For a recent trenchant critique of "hybridity," see Jonathan Friedman, "Global Crises, the Struggle for Cultural Identity and Intellectual Porkbarrelling: Cosmopolitans versus Locals, Ethnics and Nationals in an Era of De-hegemonisation," in *Debating Cultural Identity: Multi-Cultural Identities and the Politics of Anti-Racism*, ed. Pnina Werbner and Tariq Madood (London: ZED, 1997), 70–89. My critique here, needless to say, refers not to the intentions of those who employ the concept of hybridity, but rather to the logic of the metaphor.

45. The divisive effects of diasporic discourse as I approach it here are similar to the divisive effects of the idea of a "model minority."

46. Kent A. Ono, "Re/Signing 'Asian American': Rhetorical Problematics of Nation," *amerasia journal* 21(1 & 2) (1995): 67–78, here 77, fn. 20.

47. For a critical (and sensitive) discussion of the African/Korean American conflict, see Nancy Abelmann and John Lie, *Blue Dreams: Korean Americans and the Los Angeles Riots* (Cambridge, Mass.: Harvard University Press, 1995). I am grateful to Mette Thunoe for bringing this work to my attention.

48. Karen I. Leonard, *Making Ethnic Choices: California's Punjabi Mexican Americans* (Philadelphia: Temple University Press, 1992); Peter Kwong, "The Wages of Fear," *The Village Voice* (April 26, 1994): 1–5. See also his more recent *Forbidden Workers*.

49. Okihiro et al., *Reflections on Shattered Windows*, xiv.

50. Michael Omi, "It Just Ain't the Sixties No More: The Contemporary Dilemmas of Asian American Studies," in Okihiro et al., *Reflections on Shattered Windows*, 31–6, here 35.

51. Ono, "Re/Signing," 75.

52. David Palumbo-Liu, "Theory and the Subject of Asian American Studies," *amerasia journal* 21(1 & 2) (1995): 55–65, here 58.

53. For a passionate reaffirmation of the movement's original goals, see Glenn Omatsu, "The 'Four Prisons' and the Movements of Liberation: Asian American Activism from the 1960s to the 1990s," in *The State of Asian America: Activism and Resistance in the 1990s,* ed. Karin Aguilar-San Juan (Boston: South End, 1994), 19–69.

54. This interesting collection contains contributions that range from near rejection of the idea of Asian America to an affirmation of "Asiacentrism." If I may rephrase the subtitle of Sau-ling Wong's essay, what the collection reveals is not that theory is at a crossroads, but that Asian America is. I would like to take note of the essay by Paul Wong, Meera Menvi, and Takeo Hirota Wong, "Asiacentrism and Asian American Studies?" (137–47), which argues for an Asiacentrism comparable to Afrocentrism. While the argument replicates some of the worst excesses of Orientalism in its reductionist argument for a spiritual Asia, it is important in the case it makes for an alternative development (as well as its suspicion of "theory" for its inevitably hegemonic premises), which was a goal of the Asian American movement in its radical phase. Interestingly, the idea of Asia proposed here is also radically different from the idea of Asia promoted by the likes of Lee Kuan Yew of Singapore, to whom the defining feature of the Asian spirit is its unquestioning commitment to capitalism.

55. Sau-ling C. Wong, "Denationalization Reconsidered: Asian American Cultural Criticism as a Theoretical Crossroads," *amerasia journal* 21(1 & 2) (1995): 1–27, here 2.

56. The vocabulary of the local and the global is mine, but I think it is consistent with what Professor Wong is arguing; I hope, at any rate, that my vocabulary does not distort her intentions. Unlike her, and others such as Lisa Lowe, I think also that "cultural nationalism" is more a product of contemporary developments than of the original aspirations of the Asian American movement, which, as I have argued, had a much more historicized notion of both nation and culture than seems to prevail currently. The polemics against cultural nationalism should be part of a present-day struggle against the homogenization of identities, rather than directed at straw targets in the past. Wong uses the example of Frank Chin and the *Big Aiiieeeee!* editors as the foremost examples of cultural nationalism. It is arguable that Frank Chin at any rate has moved from an earlier historicist representation of Asian America to a culturalist position; his essentialist culturalism in his introduction to the *Big Aiiieeeee!* contrasts sharply with the historicist representations in his fiction, but most importantly, with the 1971 essay that he and Jeffrey Chan coauthored, "Racist Love," published in the volume, *Seeing through Shuck,* ed. Richard Kostelanetz (New York: Ballantine Books, 1972), 65–79. The shift may well have something to do with the resurgent Orientalism of the present, not least of all in the works of writers such as Amy Tan, against whom Chin positions himself.

57. Mike Davis, "Kajima's Throne of Blood," *The Nation* (February 12, 1996): 18–20, here 19. The contradiction between community and transnational capital affects all ethnicities and has become an inescapable issue of contemporary politics. For a recent discussion, see Thomas Friedman, "Balancing NAFTA and Neighborhood," *Rocky Mountain News* (from the *New York Times*) (Saturday, 13 April 1996): 44A

5

Chinese Illegals Are American Labor

Peter Kwong

It was only on June 6, 1993, when a rusty tramp steamer named *Golden Venture* carrying 286 would-be Chinese illegals lurched aground off Rockaway Beach in Queens, New York, a few hundred yards from a Coast Guard station, that the problem of Chinese smuggling of illegals gained national attention. But in New York's Chinese community, the residents had been witnessing the rapid influx of illegals from Mainland China ever since the mid-1980s. They were known as the "Eighteen-Thousand Men," meaning the suckers who had paid the Snakeheads (the human smugglers) $18 thousand to come to this country. In the early 1990s, New York–area law enforcement authorities had their hands full dealing with the increasing number of gruesome crimes of murder, torture, and kidnapping perpetrated by the Snakeheads against the Snake-people (the illegals), usually as a result of debt payment disputes.

The largest group of illegals came from the rural areas surrounding the southern Chinese city of Fuzhou, on the northern coast of Fujian Province. New York City has been the destination for most of them. The smuggling network, first established in the 1970s, has since been perfected so as to be able to funnel thousands of illegals on short order.

The image of invading hordes of Asians wading through U.S. coastal waters deepened the U.S. sense of vulnerability caused by the nagging apprehension over the daily onslaught of Mexican aliens coming across the southern border of the United States. After the initial shock over the *Golden Venture* fiasco, the public demanded quick action.

Politicians took full advantage of this national anxiety as a cost-free popular issue. Governor Pete Wilson of California pushed through Proposition 187 in the state of California to limit public services available to illegals. Riding on the momentum of that proposition's successful passage, he thrust himself forward as a presidential candidate for the Republican Party—pointedly announcing his candidacy in front of the Statue of Liberty. Meanwhile, Pat Buchanan promised his supporters that he would erect a great wall along the Mexican border as his effort to "take back America," if he were elected president of the United States.

In 1994, the U.S. Commission on Immigration Reform announced its recommendation proclaiming "the immediate need for more effective prevention and deterrence of unlawful immigration" by urging the beefing up of border controls and the development of a computerized fraud-resistant verification system. In the summer of 1996, just before congressional recess, when all the legislators returned to their home states to prepare for national elections, the Republican-dominated House and Senate had been in conference for the passage of an "immigration reform bill." Aside from the far-reaching and costly efforts to tighten control over U.S. borders, it also contained a provision proposed by Representative Elton Gallegly that aimed to deny undocumented children the right to public education. "Our goals are to do all we can to discourage the unchecked flow of illegal immigrants and to encourage those illegal immigrants already here to go home," said Gallegly.

This contest to see who is tougher on the illegals has turned ugly. The target has now expanded to include legal immigrants as well. Senator Allen Simpson and others have proposed a 25 percent reduction in the number of legal immigrations allowed, eliminating slots for siblings and adult children of U.S. citizens. The Congressional Task Force on Immigration Reform has introduced legislation that would deny rights and services to U.S.-born individuals who are children of illegals. The provision was incorporated into the 1996 Republican National Election Platform. This legislation would in effect repeal the 14th Amendment to the Constitution, which guarantees citizenship rights to persons born in the United States. However, punitive attacks against legal and illegal immigrants do not stop there. The new Welfare Reform Bill, which was signed into law by Bill Clinton, would end federal welfare benefits and social services for legal immigrants during their first five years in the United States. Supplemental Security Income (SSI) and food stamps would end for noncitizens now receiving benefits. About 500 thousand legal immigrants who are not citizens would be cut off from SSI, and at least one million legal immigrants would lose their eligibility for food stamps.

President Clinton has certainly not shied away from using the immigrant issue to advance his political support. A few weeks after the Chinese shipping incident, amid the outcry over illegal immigration, notably in the key electoral states of California and Florida, President Clinton unveiled a major initiative by classifying Chinese human smuggling as a threat to national security to be countered by a coordinated effort under the direction of the National Security Council. He declared: "We must not—we will not—surrender our borders to those who wish to exploit our history of compassion and justice."

By presidential instruction, twelve departments and agencies of the U.S. government are to work under the coordination of the White House Domestic Policy Council and the National Security Council to stem illegal migration and human smuggling. The CIA (Central Intelligence Agency), long the single most important agency fighting against international communism, was given the task of developing plans to "identify the smugglers and disrupt their operations." The FBI (Federal Bureau of Investigation) is now the lead enforcement agency against illegal immigration on land, and the Coast Guard serves the same function at sea.

The most powerful countermeasure against human smuggling is actually embodied in the antiterrorist bill passed by the U.S. Congress. The Anti-Terrorism and Effective Death Penalty Act of 1996 stipulates that the penalties against smugglers be increased from five to ten years. The act identifies smuggling as a RICO (Racketeer Influenced and Corrupt Organizations Act) predicated felony, and it also charges the courts to give law enforcement agencies the authority to use wiretaps when dealing with such crimes. To deter illegals expeditiously, much to the civil libertarians' dismay, the act permits aliens seeking admission to be summarily excluded and deported and their asylum claims administratively determined before a nonjudicial officer while the aliens are detained. Americans seem to suspect that terrorism is usually the work of illegals who have infiltrated their midst. Illegal immigration and terrorism have thus taken the place of communism as our number one national security concern.

Public debates on the immigration issue have been emotional, usually lacking in balance, fairness, or even logic. Serious and rational voices have not been heard—only loud extremist organizations like FAIR (Federation for American Immigration Reform) and people like Peter Brimelow, author of *Alien Nation*, and Chilton Williamson, author of *The Immigration Mystique*, both of whom unabashedly argue that Americans have the right to stop immigrants in order to return to the original American racial balance (by which they mean only the blue-blooded Anglo-Saxons), get attention.

In all the debates the assumption is always that everyone wants to immigrate to this country, even though we have done nothing to encourage that. The immigrants' presence, the argument goes, is solely the result of the generosity of the American people and the leniency of American laws. For instance, American and European countries are now arguing that they have been "too generous" to refugees and illegal aliens, although this generosity has been the legacy of the Cold War years, when political defections from the other side were encouraged. Cubans seeking political asylum and East Germans running across the Berlin Wall were "freedom" fighters worthy of medals and cash rewards. It is this kind of self-righteous attitude that has kept the public from knowing who the *Golden Venture* Chinese illegals were and what they intended to do had they not been arrested. And the public does not care what is happening to them. After more than three years, half of these Chinese illegals are still imprisoned in York, Pennsylvania, and in federal detention centers elsewhere. On the practical ground level, human smuggling from Mainland China has not stopped. While the U.S. Navy and Coast Guard were able to shut off the illegal boat traffic, smuggling from Asia continues to come by land through Central America, Mexico, and the Caribbean basin as well as via multiple combinations of alternative air routes. Some reports estimate that there are thousands of Chinese in temporary residence in Moscow at any time, waiting to travel to the United States. This is partly because Aeroflot, the Russian airline, offers daily flights to Cuba and Nicaragua—both strategic staging points for smuggling illegals into the United States. Hundreds of Chinese illegals are entering the United States each month. By now, the estimated number of Chinese illegals in the United States is around 200 thousand, and the Snakeheads in Fuzhou are still as busy recruiting as ever—the smuggling fee has been escalating steadily: from $18 thousand in the early 1980s, to $35 thousand in 1989, and now as high as $40 thousand per person.

Tough talk on immigration aside, there is neither effective law enforcement nor a national will to stop the illegals. U.S. industries, especially agrobusinesses, have always relied on cheap immigrant labor. Before 1965, migrant "guest workers" could come in legally through the Bracero Program. The 1965 Immigration Act, however, was formulated in the belief that the U.S. economy had matured and no longer needed menial labor. In the new law there was no provision for unskilled individuals to enter the country legally. The only criterion for legal immigration became either family unity (i.e., entering the country as close blood relative of a citizen) or a professional skill. Without the Bracero guest worker program or any other programs, unskilled immigrant workers had to come in through the "back door," illegally.

U.S. businesses today rely on low-wage laborers more than ever to supposedly increase productivity and meet global competition. Businesses, in those labor-intensive, declining manufacturing and low-tech service industries especially opt for cheap, less demanding, and less organized workers, which usually means illegals. Without illegals, U.S. agrobusinesses in the border states and garment industries in New York and Los Angeles would not exist. Without their assistance as kitchen help, busboys, and dishwashers in many of the nation's cities, half of the restaurants would close. Moreover, many Americans hire house-cleaners, private nurses, nannies, and gardeners without bothering to find out their legal status, as long as they can get their services cheaply. Governor Pete Wilson, for all his self-righteous grandstanding on immigration, used an illegal as domestic help some years ago but has conveniently shifted the blame to his wife for the "mistake."

Illegals, segregated and shunned by the native-born workers, are kept apart from the rest of the American society. They are invisible and unprotected. In addition, illegals are often employed by their coethnics. This ethnic dimension further conceals their role as part of the U.S. labor force and part of the U.S. economy, although Chinese illegals working as garment seamstresses produce garments for U.S. manufacturers to sell to U.S. consumers, and those who work in Chinese take-out restaurants serving U.S. urban and suburban clienteles are just as much a part of the U.S. labor force as those working for Denny's or McDonald's.

To be sure, Chinese illegals have introduced a number of disturbing problems. They are not just illegals but have come to this country with an extraordinary amount of debt. If debts are not paid, the "enforcers," usually youth gang members contracted by the Snakeheads, threaten and often physically torture the debtors. Chinese illegals, living in constant fear, are willing to take any job to pay off their debts. Because of the Chinese illegals' vulnerable position of indentured servitude, employers clamor for their services. This demand has pushed the human smuggling business into a $3 billion-a-year industry. Thus Chinese illegals come virtually unimpeded.

Their impact is felt in New York's Chinatown and various other Chinese American communities, where they have been displacing the jobs of earlier legal immigrants. The indebted illegals have penetrated the garment, construction, domestic, and restaurant trades. Chinatown wage earnings, already low by U.S. standards before the influx of the illegals, have declined to as low as two dollars an hour for garment seamstresses. Homework, thought to have disappeared from the United States fifty years ago, is a common phenomenon in Chinatown. It is also common in Chinatown for children under eighteen to work long hours after school in factories. The phenomenon of withholding wages at garment factories has developed to epidemic proportions. In the meantime, the burden of their indebtedness has driven some of the illegals to vicious crime—including drug trafficking, kidnapping, and extortion of their fellow immigrants.

These illegal Chinese pose serious immigration, labor, and law enforcement problems. So far criminal prosecution of the human smugglers has been ineffective, because the smugglers belong to a very sophisticated organized crime network. Its global structure operates smuggling not only to the United States but also to Japan, Germany, Australia, and the Netherlands. The network's safe houses and staging areas spread from Moscow and Budapest, Bangkok and Hong Kong, to Mexico City, Peru, and Bolivia. Unlike most organized crime systems with clear membership—Italian Mafia based on family, Chinese triads based on secret fraternal organizations—the human smuggling network has no set structure, only functional arrangements.

The smuggling network is further protected by the nonintervention attitude of the present Chinese government, which has long considered overseas Chinese a national asset. Emigration lowers China's unemployment and increases foreign-exchange reserves from remittances. In fact the Chinese government officially and unofficially facilitates the smuggling process. And the global Fuzhounese connections provide the smugglers with finance, transportation links, safe houses, and local contacts. These contacts furnish the most up-to-date information on law enforcement movement, enabling the Snakeheads to adopt an array of alternative routes to infiltrate the U.S. borders.

The network, which is masterminded in Asia, does not operate directly in this country. Once illegals cross the U.S. border, they are under the control of "enforcers," who are members of local youth gangs. New York–area gangs, such as the White Tigers and the Fuching, are paid to do the Snakeheads' dirty work, but they are not knowledgeable about the Snakeheads' affairs. Their arrests by U.S. authorities have no effect on the international smuggling operations.

U.S. law enforcement is not up to speed in dealing with the smuggling problem. Different branches of the government each specialize in their own responsibility with no overall coordination. The INS (Immigration and Nationalization Service) is interested in interdiction, whereas the FBI is only interested in illegals if they have committed crimes such as kidnapping, and the Customs Department is only interested in smugglers' money-laundering schemes. Local police may know more about the illegal situation than other law enforcement agencies do but have no authority to intervene unless the illegals have committed robbery or extortion. When the agencies do cooperate in a task-force situation, they spend months working on one single case under the RICO statute. The case is then thrown to the district attorney's office, which is interested in quick convictions, preferably through plea bargaining. U.S. law enforcement as a whole lacks coordination and institutional memory.

In 1986 Congress passed the Employers' Sanction Act to shut down sources of employment for illegals. This act would penalize employers for knowingly employing undocumented workers. The problem is that since the law's passage, the Labor Department has done little to enforce it. Ultimately, in the current national procapital political climate, none of the agencies has the incentive for strict enforcement against the illegals.

The Chinese illegals are hidden away from U.S. workers in ethnic ghettos and segregated workplaces. Controlled by Chinese organized crime, they do not even work alongside legal Chinese workers. Unseen and unheard, they are America's sublevel labor force, totally unprotected. Stricter immigration laws would only drive them further underground, deeper under the control of Chinese crime syndicates.

The indebted Chinese illegals are therefore situated in a complex multistrata configuration. As illegals they belong to a subdivision within the U.S. working class, working for coethnics, they are hidden within ethnic enclaves, and as indebted laborers they belong to a subclass even within the Chinese ethnic community. And most of all they work under a predicament akin to indentured servitude—a condition that has been outlawed in this country since 1886.

The Chinese situation may be unusual considering the exorbitant amount charged by the smugglers, but it is by no means unique or restricted to the Chinese. According to one report smuggling systems among the Indians and Pakistanis charge $28 thousand.[1] There is no doubt that given the U.S. demand for cheap labor and given the ineffective counteraction against smuggling, the Chinese variety of indentured servitude can be repeated elsewhere. Seventy-two illegal Thai seamstresses, who were incarcerated and forced to work around the clock in a barbwire-fenced-off factory compound in Elmonte, California, are a case in point.

The issue here is no longer just about stopping Chinese illegals from coming. In fact, the question is not about the illegals any more. U.S. employers are using the illegals as an excuse to depress wages for *all workers*. The presence of the illegals and the lack of labor enforcement have totally destroyed U.S. labor standards. However, this is exactly what was intended. Free market advocates, like the editors of the *Wall Street Journal*, promote unregulated labor immigration with the implicit understanding that awarding jobs to the undocumented will have disciplinary effects on legal U.S. workers.

In the current debates, conservatives such as those associated with the Manhattan Institute, challenge Americans who demand affirmative action by pointing to the immigrants' willingness to do the work Americans won't. Moreover, the immigrants don't insist on the market wage rate, and they don't ask for government assistance or even expect the protection of a social safety net. Illegal immigrants are being used in U.S. domestic debates on racial and labor policies.

The most insidious attack against the illegals is the promotion of the theory of ethnic enclaves. Sociologists like Min Zhou, in her book *Chinatown: The Socioeconomic Potential of an Urban Enclave*, argues that Chinese ethnic social relations regulate economic behavior to the mutual benefit of all. In Chinatown, she claims, economic behavior is not purely self-interested, and it is not based on strict calculation in dollars. Min Zhou defends sweatshops and low wages by asserting that Chinese do not see themselves as exploited because "the work ethic of immigrant Chinese is built on a value standard from Chinese culture" and not on the one from the U.S. culture.[2] In fact, Chinese business leaders insist that U.S. labor standards are not applicable to the Chinese since most of them have a strong sense of ethnic solidarity and do not mind hard work if it is for other Chinese. What is being advanced here is ethnic exceptionalism—the idea that inside of immigrant communities there is neither class division nor exploitation.

No wonder the Chinese have been promoted as a "model minority," fit for other minorities to emulate. Many even argue that in today's global economy, Americans in general are too soft and expect too much. The U.S. business community would like to transform U.S. work ethics into those of the Japanese, the Koreans, or the Singaporians. This is ironic, because at the beginning of the twentieth century, Americans tried to "assimilate" the "new immigrants" from Eastern and Southern Europe by obliging them to conform to Anglo-Protestant values. It was thought that unless the immigrants acquired these "American values," they would not have the capacity to be upwardly mobile. Now, at the beginning of the twenty-first century, the Americans are being told that unless they acquire the immigrant or Asian work ethics, they will not prosper. It is in this same spirit that some social scientists see nothing wrong with using "neoauthoritarian" regimes like those in China and Singapore as models for economic development.

The working people within the Chinese community, however, have not been docile. Against all odds—including the language problem, the indifference of law enforcement, the dominant political power of the Chinese economic elite, the intimidation of organized crime, and the overwhelming procapital ideology of this country, not to mention the defeatist and compromising attitude of the organized labor—the new immigrants never lose their spirit of resistance. There is at present in Chinatown a small but significant labor movement demanding intervention by

U.S. law and labor enforcement agencies to protect and maintain U.S. standards in the Chinese community. Yet, what they really expect is even more basic: protection against employers holding back wages, blacklisting, physical intimidation, and violations of occupational health and safety rules.

There are those who oppose the public exposure of those intraethnic issues in fear of further stereotyping of the Chinese community. In fact, Asian American leaders have taken a very defensive posture in face of the present anti-immigrant attacks. They have continued to emphasize the positive contributions of Asian legal immigrants to the U.S. economy, particularly by Asian professionals and small business entrepreneurs. Their main concern is to make sure that Congress does not eliminate several categories in the family unity provisions for legal immigration. In the meantime, they have kept silent on Asian labor and illegal immigrant issues.

But this is not an Asian American issue; it is an American issue. Chinese illegals are strategically located in multiple fractures in American society. Their presence exposes the problems with American immigration, criminal, racial, labor, ethnic, and intraethnic conditions in the United States. On an immediate level, I am calling for the prompt and coordinated effort on the part of the federal government to eradicate smuggling of humans and the practice of indentured involuntary labor. However, this alone is not enough. As with the fight against illegal drugs—where interdiction alone would not work if the demand side is not dealt with—so it is with the immigration issue.

How do we stop employers from wanting to use cheap and exploitable labor? The instinctive response is through immigration restriction. That would lead us right back to the sorry records of U.S. immigration history. Legal restriction in the past was always achieved at the cost of ugly and hostile anti-immigrant movements.

Anti-immigrant fever is not new in U.S. history. Every ethnic group confronts hostility upon their arrival, for they are perceived as competitors and replacements for the groups that came earlier. This type of tension often plays out in ethnic hatred and violence. Its more notable examples in the past were the bigotry against the Germans, the Know-Nothing movement against the Irish and Catholics, and in the 1920s, the nativist movement against Jews and Eastern Europeans. A more violent form of bigotry was the reaction against the Chinese in the late 1880s, when U.S. workers and labor unions rallied around the slogan "Chinamen Must Go!" accusing the Chinese of being "strikebreakers" and allies of monopoly capital. In each case the working people picked on the new immigrants as their enemy, rather than uniting with them to fight the employers who had induced the conflict in the first place. The confronting groups remain vengeful and prejudiced against each other for decades to come. In each instance the American people were divided and defeated. Capital, on the other hand, has maintained the upper hand.

Racial and ethnic restriction in the United States began with the Chinese Exclusion Act in 1882. Subsequently, exclusions were placed on every single group of Asian immigrants—the Japanese, the Koreans, the Asian Indians, and finally, the Filipinos. The ultimate restriction against all ethnic and racial immigrants came in the 1924 National Origins Act, which placed limited quotas on the number of immigrants allowed from Eastern and Southern Europe and called for the prohibition of legal entry of virtually all colored immigrants from Asia and the Caribbean. The 1924 act was a blot in the claim of the United States to be a country of equality and opportunity.

A landmark reversal came in 1965, when Congress passed the 1965 Immigration Act right after the passage of the 1964 Civil Rights Act, in the spirit of America's struggle for racial equality. The new immigration law was purged of all ethnic and racial provisions. An English person is just as eligible as a Chinese person to apply to become a legal immigrant, leading to eventual citizenship. It is this act that has transformed the historical pattern of immigrant flow from Europeans to mainly Asians and Latinos.

However, the bubbling anti-immigrant movement of the 1990s threatens to reopen an old wound. The present demand for immigrant restriction would affect mostly Asians and Latinos just as they are beginning to redress their past exclusion. This new nativist movement has already rekindled the racial intolerance of the past.

The source of current problems with immigration is the fact that the 1965 reform, while it has eliminated racial discrimination, never resolved the issue of immigration of unskilled laborers. Over the past thirty years, the compromise has been to use their labor without giving them legal status. In effect, this encourages people to break the law and allows employers to take advantage of them. The social consequence has been the development of a segregated class of people who are poor and politically unprotected.

Ironically, the immigration reform of 1965 suffered from the same shortcomings as the 1964 Civil Rights act—both had eliminated legal discrimination, and both had provided opportunities for the emergence of middle-class minorities. Vernon Jordan and I. M. Pei might be prosperous and socially accepted as members of the U.S. mainstream. But just as the civil rights movement has left a moribund underclass trapped in inner cities, the 1965 Immigration Act has left a degraded caste of illegals.

In view of this history, there has to be a different approach. Instead of restrictions against illegals, the policy that would be more beneficial to numbers of constituencies would be to include them as part of the U.S. working class to be protected. That means universal application of labor laws to all workers—be they native-born Americans or immigrants, legal or illegal.

Therefore, Americans should support the Chinese fight for labor enforcement. The Chinese struggle is the frontline defense against capital's attempt to use immigrants to degrade the conditions of all U.S. workers. If the enforcement of labor standards is successful, then it will take away the incentive of employers to hire and exploit illegals. This will, in turn, dry up the business of smuggling humans. Such a strategy would also avoid people turning racial and ethnic hostilities against each other. The power of the working people would thereby be strengthened. United, U.S. labor can turn the tables and put capital on the defensive by demanding a different direction for U.S. economic development. The common call should be the promotion of U.S. productivity through investment in science and technology, rather than the competition with the Third World on wage cutting, which has already led to a downward spiral with an ominous outcome.

Erecting a proimmigrant position like the one proposed here should lead the United States to a better economic future, and for the first time, the United States would have an enlightened immigration policy that upholds the value of equality and democracy.

NOTES

1. Sam Dillon, "U.S. Cracks Ring That Smuggled Asians via Mexico," *International Herald Tribune* (31 May 1996): 2.

2. Min Zhou, *Chinatown: The Socioeconomic Potential of an Urban Enclave* (Philadelphia: Temple University Press, 1992), 222.

6

Organizing Labor among Difference: The Impact of Race/Ethnicity, Citizenship, and Gender on Working-Class Solidarity

Margaret M. Zamudio

Theoretical understandings of the impact of categories of difference, race/ethnicity, citizenship, and/or gender, on organizing labor have ranged from viewing these categories as disruptive to the universal ends of class solidarity (Bonacich, 1972, 1973; Olzak, 1992) to recognizing the central role these categories play in building working-class solidarity (Delgado, 1992, 1993; Ruiz, 1987; Zamudio, forthcoming; Zavella, 1987). The broad range of effects that race/ethnicity, citizenship, and gender possibly have on working-class solidarity suggests the complex and fluid nature of these political categories. These categories of difference can function either to undermine or to facilitate working-class solidarity.

The struggle to organize the largely immigrant Latina/o and Asian workers at the New Otani Hotel in Los Angeles in the midst of aggressive employer resistance captures the complex and often contradictory roles that race/ethnicity, citizenship, and gender play in shaping working-class solidarity. Successful labor organization in industries where difference is salient requires the development of strategies to diffuse racism, nativism, and sexism. Strategies that tap into the resources of ethnic/racial, immigrant, and gendered communities in order to build coalitions of resistance are of particular importance in an industry with a rigid social division of labor. The New Otani Hotel exemplifies the rigid social division of labor along racial/ethnic, citizenship, and gendered boundaries and thus provides a test case for developing and implementing strategies that foster organized working-class solidarity and resistance.

The ethnic/racial, immigrant, and gender composition of the actors involved represents an almost extreme sample of workplace diversity. The ownership and management of the hotel are exclusively Japanese. Up to 90 percent of the "back-of-the-house" workers are immigrant Latina/o from several Latin American countries, but mostly from Mexico, El Salvador, and Guatemala. Immigrant Japanese workers also make up a significant segment of the workforce, although they are mainly concentrated in the higher paying, yet labor intensive, positions in the hotel's upscale specialty theme restaurants as waitresses and chefs. The inclusion of immigrant Asian workers from the Philippines and Korea in white-collar positions further stratifies the hotel. The salience of race/ethnicity and citizenship in occupational segmentation at the New Otani is further complicated with the rigid gendered positions pervasive in the service industry, where women are concentrated in traditional domestic positions like housekeeper and waitress.

The management of the New Otani has actively followed the oppressive tradition of segmenting jobs along salient categories of difference and then drawing on the antiunion strategy of manipulating these differences in order to promote conflict between workers and consequently maintain control over the labor force. At various points, the union campaign has felt the disorganizing effects that racism, nativism, and sexism have on working-class solidarity. However, in line with what has been dubbed the New Labor Movement, the workers at the New Otani Hotel and Local 11 have resisted falling victim to old strategies. Rather, they have relied on the ethnic/racial, immigrant, and gendered experiences of workers and their communities to build solidarity. In the process of tapping into these experiences as resources for mobilization, the organizers have turned to the Japanese American and immigrant and native Latina/o communities for support. The effort to develop strong community relations and build progressive coalitions has effectively met the challenge of organizing among difference and stands out as a model for grassroots organizing.

This chapter examines a moment of the unresolved union campaign at the New Otani Hotel, where since 1993 the hotel's working-class leadership along with Local 11 of the Hotel Employees, Restaurant Employees Union (HERE) have been organizing workers and struggling for a union contract. While the hotel's vast resources and staunch antiunionism presents a formidable obstacle in this "David and Goliath" matchup, the workers' persistence, commitment, and organizing strategies nevertheless stand out as a model for organizing labor when race/ethnicity, citizenship, and gender categories are salient. Thus, the following analysis suggests the structural conditions and political practices that intervene to shape the role that race/ethnicity, citizenship, and gender play when organizing a diverse workforce.

The New Otani provides a setting for examining theories that point to the difficulties of organizing a workforce divided along racial/ethnic, citizenship, and gender lines, traditionally used to explain the U.S. failure to establish progressive unionism. Much of our understanding about the relationship between difference and class formation stems from the analysis of labor struggles during the period of industrial capitalism. The two main theories that either explicitly or implicitly ex-

plain the lack of progressive unionism and the active exclusion of minorities, immigrants, and women focus either on split labor markets and competition or segmentation and structural stability. Both of these theories examine the relationship
between a diverse workforce and the reproduction of capitalist relations of production. While each theory differs in its assumptions about this relationship, they
both highlight the disorganizing effects of a diverse workforce.

However, the transition from a goods-producing to service-producing economy, demographic shifts in the labor force, and the consolidation of a history of
political struggles for union democracy, pave the way for a reinterpretation of the
impact of difference on working-class solidarity. The willingness and commitment of unions like Local 11 to organize traditionally ignored low-wage minority and immigrant workers reflects the success of prior union struggles for union
democracy and provides a reasonable basis for anticipating that the union's organizing strategies will produce outcomes that influence the tendencies for the
experience of difference to foster solidarity. Local 11's strategies involve building
community-based coalitions and drawing on the vast ethnic and racial resources
within a community. These strategies demonstrate the great potential in organizing a diverse workforce.

This study relies on two related sets of data. The first source of data is from a
yearlong ethnographic study of Local 11's campaign to organize the New Otani
Hotel, an effort that continues today. The study was conducted between February 1995 and January 1996, using participatory research methods, such as attending meetings and rallies, participating in the picket lines, and traveling with organizers and workers as they attempted to build support for the union. During this
period, interviews were conducted with hotel workers, Local 11 organizers working on the New Otani campaign, Local 11's President Maria Elena Durazo, and
Local 11 Staff Director Jennifer Skurnik. In order to maintain confidentiality, the
names of workers who continue to work at the hotel have been changed. In addition, forty in-depth interviews with hotel employers in the Los Angeles area provide a second and complementary source of data for this project. The interviews
are part of a study on the attitudes of employers toward various groups of workers,
including immigrant Latina/os. The following section provides a qualitative description of the struggle at the New Otani and sets up the case for analysis.

THE NEW OTANI: HISTORY AND SOCIAL FEATURES

The luxury New Otani Hotel sits in the middle of Little Tokyo in downtown Los
Angeles. City Hall and Parker Center, the home of the Los Angeles Police Department, are a short walk away and supply the hotel and its restaurants with a regular walk-in clientele. However, on a January afternoon in 1996, three weeks after Local 11 of the Hotel Employees Restaurant Employees International Union
along with a long list of supporters, including several elected officials, called for

an international boycott against the hotel, the action seems to be having an effect. On any given Friday during the lunch and dinner hours picket lines of about fifty workers, union organizers, and community supporters shouting boycott slogans line the main entrances to the New Otani Hotel. The workers are mostly Latino, while the community supporters are split between Asian Americans, Latinos, blacks and whites. As I arrive to join the multiethnic picket line during the height of the lunch hour, one of the hotel's main restaurants appears deserted. I sign in and get my picket from Manual and join Ana, a thirty-five-year-old mother of three who emigrated from El Salvador in 1978 and who was fired from the hotel after working there for seventeen years.

Ana was one of three lead organizers in the hotel fired two years ago on trumped up charges that she allowed another worker to punch out her time card. She is now a union organizer for Local 11 and a symbol for the New Otani struggle. Her picture along with the other two women that were fired make up one of the three, approximately 10-by-5-foot panels in the "wall of shame" erected outside of the hotel. Another panel depicts Chinese slaves imprisoned during World War II by Kajima Corporation, the Japan-based corporate owner of the New Otani. The third panel is a picture of Japanese Americans, who, after a long struggle with the New Otani owners, were displaced from their low-income homes in the 1970s in order to make way for the construction of the hotel. Many of the community activists involved in fighting the New Otani more than thirty years ago have returned to support the hotel workers.

Workers say that the best organizers are the hotel's management. In fact, Local 11 had very little to do with the formation of the core group of prolabor union activists that sprang from the back-of-the-house of one of Los Angeles's luxury hotels. As workers recall the story, the attempt to form a union started in 1993 when the son of a housekeeper who worked in the purchasing office was being harassed and eventually pushed out. A worker explains what occurred in those early days of the union campaign.

> "They were pressuring him. When they want to get rid of you they put on the pressure. They start by increasing your work, and then they continue to criticize what you do, no matter how good of a job you're doing. They stay on top of you and don't let up. They transferred him to dish washing from his office job and cut his hours to only two days a week. And then they gave him one day during the night shift and the other during the day. That's pressure, no?"
>
> She continues. "He asked me and others what he should do. His friend in purchasing said that without a union this is going to keep happening. But we didn't know what union. My brother-in-law worked at the Hilton and was in a union, and the monthly union letter was delivered to my address. I wrote the name of the union down and called. We went to the union and talked to someone named Patricia. She said to gather those interested, but don't tell anyone else, and come back. Then she gave me her card. Carlos's mom called to make an appointment. Six of us showed up. At that time we met with Maria Elena (the president of Local 11) and Jennifer

(the chief of staff). They told us that we had to organize. We had to talk to our *compañeros* and form a leadership committee and work hard at organizing others.

"This happened three and a half years ago. We thought that just by showing up, the union would take over and the problem would be resolved. No, it doesn't work that way. It's been a difficult fight, but we're getting there. We were thinking that we were just going to tell others, and that was that. They told us that it wasn't going to be easy. But if we wanted it, we could do it. They never told us anything different. They are the same people that we met that first day. Maria Elena asked us if we knew who the union is? She answered, 'You are the union. We're only going to represent you.'

"While we were working on the workers, they (the union) began introducing us to Japanese community members, Glen, David, Art. They told us that they had a reason to help us because the construction of the New Otani involved destroying parts of the community significant to them. We met at the cultural center, Jennifer, Beti, and me. We told them why we wanted a union. We wanted better treatment, and we were tired of the injustices. Glen offered to work together with us. He's got determination and commitment. He puts everything into us like he's fighting for himself. We've had a lot of support."

The workers' activities over the next three years following that initial meeting with Local 11 led to the growth of the small group of six into a leadership committee of thirty-five workers who meet every other week at the union hall to plan organizing strategies. Their efforts have been fruitful, and in spite of the aggressive resistance from hotel management, the leadership committee gained the support of the majority of their coworkers. As of November 1995, the majority of the 270 New Otani workers have signed cards pledging their support for the union. The hotel has put up quite a fight against the union, and the very existence of a large vocal group of workers who challenge the hotel on a daily basis is a victory in itself.

The multiethnic picket line, the speakers at the rallies in support of the hotel workers, the working class leadership that meets every other Tuesday at the union hall—all challenge the assumption of the disorganizing role of difference. Theories that focus on the disorganizing effects of difference are particularly critical of the role of citizenship. Michael Piore's (1979) dual labor market thesis suggests that the orientation of immigrants toward their country of origin make them especially willing to cast off the social aspects of work, resist unionism, and to accept lower wages and substandard working conditions (see also Bonacich, 1972). The strategy of capital to make citizenship a factor for wage differentials has led both social theorists and labor unions to condemn the presence of immigrant workers as a source of competition and intraclass conflict (Bonacich, 1972; Olzak, 1992; Waldinger, 1993). The added element of state coercion and the structural constraint that it poses makes the role of citizenship especially problematic for organizing undocumented workers (see Delgado, 1993). Although as Hector Delgado (1992; 1993) demonstrates, citizenship is a contingent variable and not at all determinate. Assumptions about the potential disorganizing role of gender have also provoked further research that has demonstrated the contingent nature of difference (Cobble, 1996; Hochschild, 1983; Milkman, 1987). It is assumed that women are unorganizable because of their family responsibilities, marginal commitment to the labor market, and submission to patriarchy. Again, these various assumptions revolve not only around the impact of structural constraints but also around a reified understanding of the meaning of difference. Thus, the following sections will evaluate both the role of structure and the meaning of difference on solidarity.

THE SOCIAL DIVISION OF LABOR

The division of labor along not only occupational lines but also along gender, ethnic, racial, and citizenship boundaries has long been one of the major challenges for organized labor to overcome. The booming hotel industry with its large diverse workforce appears to be no exception. According to the information obtained from hotel employers throughout the Los Angeles area, the majority of the hotel industry's workforce is concentrated in the back-of-the-house service jobs. Housekeeping makes up the majority of these service jobs. The majority of the housekeepers are Latina immigrants, mostly from Mexico, with a large minority from El Salvador and Guatemala. Immigrant Latinos also fill the remaining back-of-the-house jobs in laundry and the kitchen. Thus, the information from the interviews with employers and with the union suggests that there is a distinct social division of labor along the lines of gender, ethnicity/race, and citizenship status. While Latina immigrants are concentrated in housekeeping and Latino immigrants in the kitchen, native whites tend to occupy the front of the house and managerial positions. Native blacks, however, are the most polarized group, with half of the workers in the service sector, almost 20 percent in managerial positions, and the rest in front of-the-house clerical and support-staff positions.

The New Otani Hotel patterns the dominant trends in the industry, with the added exception of having a large Asian immigrant segment in its workforce. The union estimates that 70 percent of the workers at the New Otani are Latino, with the vast majority of these Latinos being immigrants. Twenty percent are Asian immigrants, the majority being Japanese, with a significant minority from the Philippines. A few of the Asian immigrants are from Korea and other Asian countries. The remaining 10 percent of the workforce is made up of native whites and native blacks. The composition of the New Otani also differs in several respects from other Los Angeles–area hotels, in their employment of African Americans. The management and administrative positions of the majority of the hotels in Los Angeles are occupied by native whites, with a significant representation of native blacks. In contrast, the New Otani has a significant Japanese presence and little black representation in management and administrative positions. The Japanese presence extends to the upscale Thousand Cranes restaurant, where the waitresses are exclusively Japanese women who work in traditional costume, and where the chefs are also of Asian descent. The busboys in the restaurant are immigrant Latinos. In addition, immigrant Filipinos make up almost the entire accounting department. At the New Otani, the few black workers on staff are most likely to be present in service occupations. The majority of service positions—busboys, housekeepers, laundry workers, waiters, and housemen—are Latino and immigrant, a trend consistent with the rest of the industry.

There is little question that historically, wage discrimination consolidated the social division of labor along the lines of race/ethnicity, citizenship, and gender and protected capital from the working-class threat (Bonacich, 1972; Braverman, 1974; Foner, 1955, 1964; Piore, 1979; Thurow, 1975). The theoretical lens used to clarify the structural processes, political motivations, and social relations that shaped these divisions, however, needs adjustment in order to understand the alternative possibilities for the role of difference. It is highly doubtful that at any time, either historically or at present, there has ever been an organizing effort taking place in the presence of difference where these categories did not need to be negotiated. It is precisely the absence of an analysis, from both the theoretical and political levels, of the contingent and the historically specific nature of difference that has distorted our understanding of the role of race in the labor movement in the United States and has often portrayed immigrant Latino laborers as puppets of class structure, rather than progressive actors in the class struggle.

Historically, when not viewed with sheer contempt, both the academic and traditional union organizers viewed difference as either something to combat as divisive or to ignore as irrelevant.

This shortsighted approach, whether rooted in the blackened heart of bigots or the caged minds of well-intended universalists, has undermined the development of a theory that adequately captures the meaning of difference and provides a theoretical base for successful labor organizing. Basically, race/ethnicity, citizenship, and gender are seen as tools for capitalists to manipulate as either a means of increased profit through the greater exploitation of minority, immigrant, or women workers, or as a means of creating distinctions that translate into wage and/or job competition and consequently provide the material incentive for intraclass conflict, and exclusion, and interclass collusion and co-optation. While manipulating difference as a means to undermine labor solidarity represents the dominant tendency historically, the historical record simply by default does not define the role of difference. The weight of history has influenced a reified view of the effects of difference on class formation and overlooks the potential for an evolving historical record where a changing economy, demographic shifts, and the dynamics of political struggles offer new possibilities for working-class solidarity when difference is salient.

The point is not to deny or downplay the divisive role that difference has played in shaping our thin labor history in favor of a romanticized appeal to identity politics. Rather, the goal is to establish and define the structural conditions and political relations that predispose difference toward having particular effects. Clearly, segmented labor markets as a central structural characteristic of industrial capitalism provided capital with an edge in undermining working-class solidarity and led to the concentration of minority, immigrant, and women workers into the secondary sector of the economy, most notably the service sector. Like the segmentation of labor markets, workers within the secondary sector are again stratified along lines of difference into particular job categories that serve to keep workers divided at all levels. While the main source of segmentation during the industrial period that provided a base for today's stratification patterns can be directly traced to employers' manipulation of difference with the intention of controlling labor, in today's global economy several factors influence the shape of contemporary divisions and are central to the understanding of the expanded possibilities for progressive unionism. Since contemporary employers reaped the benefits of the disorganizing strategies of industrial capitalists, they are less concerned and somewhat more constrained in designing social relations specifically to "divide and conquer." In the absence of class conflict, human resources makes profit the main hiring priority and relies on the historical lessons learned in "Exploitation 101" to manipulate inherited distinctions when necessary. In a global economy, particularly in the service industry where image as much as labor power constitutes a commodity to exploit, profit provides the primary motivation to reproduce the racial/ethnic, citizenship, and gender distinctions from the industrial period. The expectation that earlier strategies of manipulating these distinctions to disorganize labor provides an added benefit.

The management of the New Otani invests great effort in manipulating distinctions between workers. However, their efforts are not always fruitful and instead, rather than undermine the organizing campaign, the hotel's miscalculations inadvertently serve to produce resistance. The unintended consequences are not only misjudgments on the part of the hotel; they represent the influence of structural conditions and political relations to give difference new meanings and class formation renewed potential. The class struggle at the New Otani provides insight for evaluating changing structural and political conditions that foster the tendencies that undermine or facilitate working-class solidarity.

SEGMENTS, SPLITS, AND SOLIDARITY

The theoretical analysis of the industrial period, from both a split labor market and a segmented labor market perspective, suggests that segmentation provides the primary condition for undermining working-class solidarity. The split labor market perspective views capitalism as inherently conflictive and points to competition between high- and low-paid workers as the process underlying segmentation. The threat of cheap labor (i.e., minorities, immigrants, and women) that capitalists employ as strikebreakers or to challenge labor resistance provokes the exclusionary political activities of better-paid native white male workers that lead to split labor markets. This view points to the forces of exploitation that produce wage and job competition and intensifies the class struggles as the material conditions for undermining solidarity.

Segmented labor market theory emphasizes the need to control labor to facilitate capital accumulation as the driving force underlying segmentation and working-class disorganization. Michael Piore's (1979) dual labor market theory offers a variation of the segmented labor market theory that focuses on migrant labor and suggests relevant implications for the immigrant workers at the New Otani. According to Piore, both labor and capital suffer from the uncertainty and fluctuations that inhere in modern economies. From the point of view of capital, we would expect that during economic downturns, capitalists would be more than happy to release the variable factors of production. But capital cannot easily do so because certain investments in training and such have made a sector of the skilled working class a quasi-fixed aspect of the production process. In other words, similar to the way that capitalists bear the cost of idle machinery, they also bear the cost of workers in whom they have invested training. Instead of dealing with uncertainty and flux through the turnover of labor, capitalists internalize the factors of production that meet the stable basic demand and externalize the seasonal factors. Native labor remains in the primary sector, and the secondary sector is opened up for temporary workers. The outcome of the separation between stable factors of production and variable ones is the dual labor market.

Piore focuses on the role of migrant workers and thus introduces an additional dimension to the process of segmentation. In contrast to Edna Bonacich's capitalists, who strike a bargain with low-paid, minority, immigrant, or women workers to undermine unions, dual labor market capitalists buy the allegiance of higher-paid, native white male workers with internal labor markets in exchange for their cooperation in maintaining economic stability. An elective affinity between economic organization of the labor market and the orientation of workers determines the alignment between primary sector labor and capital. Aligning with higher-paid labor rather than with the more profitable low-paid labor makes more sense to the goals of capitalists to limit market uncertainties since the orientation of migrant workers as target wage earners makes them less reliable to meet the stable basic aspects of production. This same orientation also influences the stance of secondary sector workers toward labor organization. Their temporary relationship to the labor market provides them with little incentive to engage in potentially long labor disputes. Labor unions have often made this case against women workers as well, in their attempts to exclude female participation. And they have made their case again, against Southern black sharecroppers who migrate in between the planting and harvest seasons.

The points that split and dual labor market theories developed from labor relations during the industrial period are often distorted to fuel the reified assumption that difference undermines labor solidarity. This long-standing belief extends even into the global period as the mass migration of immigrant Latino/as ignites fear among the remnants of traditional unions who question whether they are even organizable (Defreitas, 1993). However, contrary to the conventional wisdom of the unorganizable immigrant workers, activities in Los Angeles show that immigrant workers are organizing. The distorted reality reflects the absence of an analysis in theories of segmentation of the dynamics of difference and their failure to capture the dominance of racial/ethnic, native, and gender ideology that influenced the activities of labor and unions. Common to both theories is the absence of a political dimension to complement structural process. The silence about the independent role of the ideology of difference in both theories reflects the overwhelming impulse to reduce segmentation purely to economic processes and matters of race, gender, and citizenship, exclusive to the material realm. In practice, this dogma captures the tenacity with which traditional labor unions held on to the belief that difference was inherently divisive to solidarity in order to justify their racism, nativism, and sexism. Ironically, it was after labor lost power that the rates of minority, immigrant, and women labor union participation increased. In fact, the greater rates of union participation among blacks and Latinos when compared with whites suggest the missed opportunities during the industrial period for advancing working-class interests resulting from the unidimensional view of difference, not the presence of difference.

Surely immigrants are affected by the same conditions that have undermined the organization of native workers, and like native workers, immigrants may accept below-standard work conditions for all sorts of different reasons. Given the history of nativism in this country and the limited rights for immigrant workers, it is not unusual that immigrant workers in some instances have historically been more compliant than other workers. Historical moments of immigrant-led radical labor activism central to U.S. labor history contrast wildly with the image of the unorganizable immigrant, as do the activities of immigrant workers at the New Otani. In fact the data from the New Otani suggest that unionism holds a strong appeal for immigrant workers. As one worker stated, "Contrary to what others think, in our countries unions exist. We also know what we want. We want respect for our rights, for the rights of all workers. We are organizing for our children who are the future, for other immigrants yet to come. We want the industry organized so that no one is treated badly, and we will continue to organize so that others aren't frightened."

The lack of a political dimension surely challenges the coherence of these theories. But, aside from the validity of the theories even for the industrial period, they do offer several theoretically relevant points about the structural conditions that can be used to develop an understanding for organizing among difference in the contemporary period. Both theories suggest that economic organization determines segmentation and that the processes that sort workers within labor market segments are the same processes involved in undermining solidarity: competition for split labor market and the orientation of workers for dual labor market theory. Thus the main question driving the analysis of the structural context framing the struggles at the New Otani is: What is the relationship between the production process and occupational segmentation at the New Otani? Second, does the process that segments workers into particular jobs also undermine their solidarity? Less relevant, given the theoretical differences that frame the present case from the theoretical views that produced split and dual labor market theories, but somewhat interesting for the present case, what is the impact of competition and the orientation of immigrant workers at the New Otani on solidarity?

THE GLOBAL ERA

In light of the present case, examining the relationship between the production process and stratification proves theoretically significant and requires an analysis of the commodification of images, particularly, racial/ethnic, immigrant, and gender stereotypes, in the sorting of workers. Both split and dual labor market views share the common implication that the division of labor along racial/ethnic, citizenship, and gender lines sorted workers to facilitate the exploitation of workers as workers. In other words, labor, the actual work and commodities produced, constituted the workers' value and motivated distinctions along lines of difference. Thus, this view assumes an equality among workers rooted in their labor, making social distinctions relevant only as a means to facilitate exploitation. Today, with the emergence of service production as the major form of work, image emerges as a dominant commodity and provides the motivation to make distinctions among workers and to sort them into particular jobs.

While it is doubtful that the concentration of racial/ethnic, immigrant, and women workers into the secondary sector was an unintended consequence of economic organization during the industrial period, it is evident that today segmentation has less to do with an affinity between the occupation and the orientation of immigrants, or of prior wage differentials, and more to do with the attitudes and stereotypes of employers. For as has already been argued, the orientation of immigrants—or minorities and women for that matter—is historically and contextually determined and therefore variable, whereas the division of labor and the sorting of groups along lines of difference remain constant, thus suggesting the influence of an autonomous ideological base interacting with material conditions. The evidence from the case study suggests that segmentation is a direct result of the implementation of racial, nativist, and gender ideology rather than simply a product of the process of production.

In the glitz and glamour of a service economy, what sells is not the products of industry but the value of images. It is in the hotel industry where the commodification of the self is taken to new heights and where employers attach the meanings of race/ethnicity, citizenship, and gender to the job. My basic argument is that prior racial/ethnic, nativist, and gender ideology determines the sorting of workers. In the case of the New Otani, the management prefer immigrant Latina/o workers for the back-of-the-house jobs because their status as noncitizens implies subservience, the image desired when the commodity is personal service. For citizenship signifies abstract equality under the law, and it carries cultural connotations about hierarchy that fit well when the product of service is deference and servitude. In this sense, the skills that the employers look for to exploit are not so much a skill that is learned but a meaning that is attached to the image of the immigrant Latino. In addition, employers assume that the immigrant status makes Latino workers more controllable and compliant to the degrading demands of the job than the citizen worker. Lack of citizenship also magnifies prevailing unequal social relations revolving around race and gender that carry implications about status and hierarchy. The profound position of structural inequality in which immigrant Latino workers, particularly women, are situated, make them prime candidates to be exploited for their physical labor. In addition, their lower status as immigrants, Latinos, and sometimes women is often used to package their labor and to sharpen the image of inequality between worker and client.

The notion that back-of-the-house jobs require that workers present a particular image, in this case a subservient image, is similar to what Arlie Hochschild (1983) described as emotional labor in her study of airline stewardesses. According to Hochschild, "this labor requires one to induce or suppress feeling in order to sustain the outward countenance that produces the proper state of mind in others—in this case, the sense of being cared for in a convivial and safe place. This kind of labor calls for a coordination of mind and feeling, and it sometimes draws on a source of self that we honor as deep and integral to our individuality" (7). The demands of the hotel industry on their service workers are similar to what the airline stewardesses experience. Similar to Hochschild's findings, employers emphasize the importance of the style of the workers' interaction as part of the job. Representative of the majority of employers interviewed, one employer stated the need for a certain style of "interaction with people because we're a service industry so we need people with smiles and good attitudes for a harmonious work environment." Hotel workers are not only engaging in the physical labor of cleaning rooms, handling baggage, and waiting on customers, they are also expected to maintain a particular attitude as part of the service. Hotel employers often stressed that in a competitive environment clean rooms are no longer enough, they must also sell service where the customer is "number one." Making the customer feel like number one often translates into putting up with the demands of unreasonable customers. One employer stated the importance of acting skills in doing the job. He states,

> "You almost have to be an actor or actress in the hotel business because you're playing a role to a great extent. You know you had a bad day. But when you go to work you got to leave that at the door and put on this face. You have to put on a face and listen to others who have gripes and complaints. And a lot of times it doesn't have anything to do with you. So to have the ability to diffuse a negative situation is a plus in this business."

The type of "acting" required of service workers in the hotel industry is often thought to come naturally to some folks and not others. For example, in the sexual division of labor, women are relegated to positions that involve nurturing, such as nurses, elementary school teachers, and airline stewardesses, to name a few. The underlying assumption here is that women are "natural" caretakers. In the hotel industry, a similar principal applies, and employers look for employees with hospitality skills, or as one employer puts it, "with the natural inclination to want to please, help, and serve others. Something that you can't train someone to be." The notion that immigrant Latinos are more inclined to serve than to be served, and the expectation that they act accordingly sets the context of oppression that these workers experience. Hochschild makes the important point that "if we can become alienated from goods in a goods-producing society, we can become alienated from service in a service-producing society" (1983, 7).

In the hotel industry where part of the commodity is an abstraction of the self, the alienation of the worker is central to understanding the context of oppression and resistance. The interviews with employers reveal the extent to which immigrant workers are stripped of their real selves and expected to operate as robots, or as one employer described them, as "soldiers." These expectations of immigrant workers and the notion that immigrant workers can be easily controlled appears to be the main motivation behind the preference for immigrant Latinos over native workers. It is the reluctance of native workers to be treated as anything but equals that makes them undesirable workers in the eyes of employers. The reluctance to hire black workers and the racist justifications used demonstrates the employers' desire for workers without the entitlements of citizens. For example, the main complaint employers had about African Americans was that they had a bad attitude and "felt entitled." Employers see African Americans as a less compliant labor force. In a sense, they see them like whites. In this view, the real distinction becomes not a racial one but one between citizens and noncitizens. An employer in one of Los Angeles's most exclusive hotels captures this distinction when she states, "I would not group the blacks with Hispanics; I would group them with whites. They don't have a very high work ethic either." Another employer adds, "Realistically a guy who hops the border is willing to bust his butt. . . . Most of the Hispanics and Asians have a solid work ethic. Can't say that for the natives in this country."

The notion of a work ethic as it is understood in general usage is often distorted to mean the willingness to submit to severe exploitation. The employers' distortion of the notion of work ethic, which in general usage refers to enabling values, becomes more apparent when considering a second theme that runs through the interviews, most notably the assertion that "Immigrants never even find out what America is about. They're happy making $5 an hour." The notion of entitlement suggests that one feels entitled to certain rights encoded in law and culture. In a democracy, political citizenship guarantees one's entitlement. The history of disenfranchisement for African Americans makes it even more likely that they will assert their rights of citizenship when employers attempt to go beyond mere class exploitation and attempt to cast blacks in an image of servitude.

The notion of immigrants as naturally subservient, docile, and maintaining a superior work ethic contrasts remarkably with the notion employers hold of native workers, particularly African Americans. As employers talked about the work ethic of various ethnic/racial groups, it became quite clear that the notion of a work ethic was often conflated with the extent that workers would submit to exploitative work conditions. A downtown Los Angeles employer stated, "My experience is that most Latinos have a much better work ethic than the whites and blacks I've employed here. . . . There is less complaining. More or less tell them what has to be done, and they do it in a rather happy manner." Another employer states, "Immigrants are good workers. They do the job. They are like soldiers— work and go home without knowing what's going on around them." Thus, the main issue for employers is not so much skills and wages, but one of image and control, the image of the happy-go-lucky worker who has the control of a soldier. A black employer at a large airport area hotel expressed the industry's view of immigrants: "I have to say that employers tend to think that they'll be good workers and keep quiet. It is what it is, I have to say. . . . People think that way. Hire them and there won't be no problems." The image of the happy servile worker, which employers sell to clients seeking hospitality, and the need to control the workforce are closely intertwined. For both control of physical labor and control of emotional labor are central to the new service economy, since it is the emotional labor that today adds value to the goods of service. As one employer states, "In the hotel industry we sell service. People come to sleep, and all hotels provide beds. The only thing we can provide them is to come in contact with competent individuals who want to serve them and take care of their needs. A room attendant who does not speak to a guest in the hallway after he requests something is not going to be remembered in a kindly manner. You can teach skills. You cannot teach someone to be pleasant."

The interviews with employers suggest how the changes in the labor process have increased aspects of alienation. While basic requirements like "on-the-job know-how" and "interaction with customers" were ranked as the most important skills for entry-level workers, employers also overwhelmingly emphasized soft skills, particularly attitude. One employer states, "We can train them to do technical tasks. But we cannot train a service attitude." Another employer states, "It's important that they are friendly because we can train to clean." Another employer felt that attitude was everything. As the interviews developed beyond specific questions on skills, it was clear that soft skills such as ability to please, good attitude, and servitude made up key aspects of the work process. While employers were not always blatant about the meanings they attached to these soft skills, workers were quite open as to their interpretation of how their social identity rooted in race/ethnicity and citizenship were used to further degrade them.

The interviews with hotel employers indicate that the stereotypes employers carry guide them in their assessment of the appropriate job for particular groups. This assessment is most pronounced in the attitudes of employers toward immigrant Latinos and Asians and native blacks. The virulent racism against blacks excludes them altogether from segments of the labor market where employers require increased control for the purpose of extra-economic exploitation. Whereas as racist stereotypes of immigrant Latina/os serves to lock them into dead-end jobs. For example, when asked to compare various groups, one employer said of Latinos and blacks, "If I tell him [a black man] to do the job this guy is doing [she pointed outside to a Latino male hauling a hose in the parking lot], he's going to say I'm discriminating. They're lazy. They come here dressed up, and they don't want to get dirty." Of black women, the same employer says, "The women apply for housekeeping jobs, but they are limited in what they will do. They refuse to do certain things. Overall just taking orders, they can't take orders. Black women, they're lazy, miss work, eventually they have children because they can get more on welfare." She states that "immigrants are willing to work and learn. . . . Mexicans are more dedicated, family-oriented, willing to get ahead, and establish roots. They are going to be homeowners." Her view of Central Americans was more tempered, "Central Americans come here with the idea that they're going home someday. They don't look like they contribute to the community. They don't take care of the apartments. They don't have long-range plans." And finally, she says of Asians that they "are quiet, dedicated, hard-working. Have initiative to get ahead."

Given these distinctions, it is not surprising that particular groups fill particular niches and segments within the industry. The "industrious, quite Asian" is segmented into clerical and support staff, the immigrant Latino is given the dirtiest work and made to follow orders, and blacks are not given any work at all in occupational segments that provoke resistance. Similarly, it is probably likely that anyone suspected of carrying union sympathies is tagged as a troublemaker. The general point in all this is that the distinctions and perceptions that employers hold of particular groups are going to determine the positions the workers are given and the way they are treated. As one employers states,

"In some of my interviews with Latinos, I'm asking them about the work ethic. I ask 'is the job a necessity?' And they say, 'yes.' And I say, 'the work is not easy, are you willing to sweat?' And they say, 'yes.' 'But you have to sweat with *ganas*.' And they say, 'yes.' 'Because this job requires that you have *ganas*.' I wouldn't approach it that way with blacks."

The particular views employers hold of diverse groups go far in determining the type of jobs workers get and the way they are treated on the job. Thus, contrary to the view that the structure of the industry determines who fill the slots, the data from employers and from the New Otani suggest the role that continued racial prejudice and discrimination play in the occupational sorting of groups.

SEGMENTATION AND RESISTANCE

It appears that the consequences of racist, nativist, and sexist attitudes have led to the occupational segmentation of groups. But under conditions of a global economy, what is the impact of segmentation for working-class solidarity? The split and dual labor market theories assumed that segmentation sustains working-class disorganization. The structural influence of seasonal production that demanded temporary employees in dual labor markets completed the disorganizing impact of segmentation. But under conditions of globalization and the dominance of a service sector, industries employing immigrants and women demand a stable labor force. The vast majority of employers interviewed cited the need for a stable labor force and praised the low turnover rates of their immigrant employees. Hence, globalization diminishes the key structural influence of instability that underlie the disorganizing impact of segmentation. Thus, what is the decisive role of occupational segmentation at the New Otani for working-class resistance?

The activities of the New Otani Hotel workers demonstrate the role of ethnicity/race and citizenship for understanding class formation. While the structure of exploitation provides the basis for class formation, it is not what motivates workers to come together. Workers experience their exploitation differently, and citizenship and racial/ethnic status inform these experiences. Indeed, the condition of exploitation has worsened in the hotel industry with the intensification of the labor process. The majority of employers reported that the business environment demanded that they get more out of their workers. And while the New Otani management was not among those interviewed, the workers' comments suggest that the same process of increasing the workload is going on at that hotel. A houseman states, "Chuey [the housekeeping manager] has really increased the workload. She calls our attention when we don't finish the work. But the problem is the time. She wants more done for the same amount of time. It's impossible. She increases the amount of work but not the time or money." Housekeepers also complained that the hotel added an extra room to their workload, and large rooms with more than one large bed that used to count as two rooms now only count as one. Similarly, housemen are expected to clean four floors of the public areas, rather than the two floors they were expected to clean in the past.

While the intensification of the labor process was one theme echoed in my interviews with workers, it was not, however, the most dominant theme. In fact, workers made distinctions between good and bad workers similar to those that employers made. After a house visit with a reluctant union supporter, I asked the carload of workers about the man we had just visited. One woman said, "Oh he's a bad worker. He moves so slow. Watching him work is like watching a movie in slow motion." The distinction between good and bad workers was made even about workers who had signed a union card. What the New Otani case reveals is that the issue for workers is not necessarily that they're exploited. Rather they see the problem in terms of how they are exploited, and the notion of rights and respect determine how they will experience their exploitation. For instance, I asked one laundry service worker why she was interested in unionizing the hotel. She answers, "No respect. That's why we need a union. Respect is how we are told to do something. From my point of view you say, 'please do this,' not 'you have to do this.'" This worker points out how the objective condition of exploitation can be experienced in two different ways. It is this combination of feelings of alienation with concrete forms of exploitation that influences class formation.

Understanding how the subjective notion of alienation is constructed, then, is crucial for understanding the process of class formation. In the case of the New Otani workers, alienation is often experienced in response to their citizenship status and ethnicity/race, and working-class resistance is expressed as a product of alienation. When workers talk about their alienation, their struggle for rights and respect, they often couch their work experience in terms of their immigrant or ethnic status rather than in class terms. The fact that employers treat workers according to the immigrant stereotype they hold of them has pushed workers to organize. For example, a Latina worker from Mexico who has been here for nine years says, "If you're a person, regardless of your race or where you're from, you deserve respect. But here they see you're from somewhere else and they disrespect you. They don't care about the worker. They want robots. They don't care how we feel. They intimidate us. They tell us if we're not satisfied with our job there are plenty of others who want it, and then they show us a stack of applications. I rebel when I get treated like that."

The process of coming over to the union side often begins with recognizing one's exploitation based on ethnic/racial and citizenship status. The experience may be more directly related to their class position of powerlessness, but workers perceive it as rooted in racism and/or nationalism. For example, a dominant theme in the union campaign is the capricious manner in which privileges are allotted. There is clearly a culture of favoritism promoted in the hotel that undermines a standard system of designating rewards that workers relate to, such as seniority. Workers often feel that ethnicity/race often plays a role in who receives privileges and rewards. Latina/o workers at the hotel feel that since the New Otani management is Asian, favoritism is directed toward Asian workers. While favoritism is not always clearly based on ethnic/racial grounds, when it is, it serves as a rallying point, and Latino workers incorporate the incident into a list of instances of discrimination and injustices that the hotel imposes on them.

For example, a long-standing pattern among immigrant workers is to return to their country of origin for a vacation or to update their visas. In one instance a Japanese worker and Salvadoran worker both returned home to update their status. Immigration rules had changed, forcing the workers to stay over longer than expected. The Salvadoran worker had his embassy send a letter to the hotel explaining his predicament. On return, the Japanese worker was allowed to keep her job, while the Salvadoran worker was dismissed. The dismissal of the Salvadoran worker prompted a contingent of workers to demand a meeting with the general manager, Kenji Yoshimoto, in hopes of resolving the matter and securing the dismissed worker's job. In addition to the contingency of workers applying pressure, the Salvadoran embassy also attempted to intervene. In the end, Yoshimoto promised to give the worker a job, but failed to keep his word, prompting outrage in the hotel. In an interview with one of the leaders of the organizing effort, she cited this event as one of the major incidents that influenced the workers' receptiveness toward the union. This view is echoed in other interviews and suggests the formation of a collective outlook where the inequalities of ethnicity/race and citizenship are firmly imprinted.

The role of ethnicity/race and citizenship in its reified version that has often been considered disruptive for class formation fails to capture the extent to which ethnicity/race and citizenship inform class relations. The New Otani case, however, suggests that ethnicity/race and citizenship, rather than undermining union organization, often facilitate it. Similar to the oppression they feel as immigrants, workers feel discriminated against based on their ethnic/racial background. And similar to their sense of solidarity based on immigrant status, New Otani workers often talk about their struggle in ethnic terms. In other words, rather than saying, "we need to unite as workers," you more often hear, "we need to unite as Latinos or as immigrants." And while at face value, the notion of organizing based on ethnicity appears antithetical to class formation, the point is that ethnicity is fluid and is often used as a way of experiencing exploitation. For example, a Latina housekeeper explained that when she started working the manager only gave her three days of training and had her cleaning a sixteen-room load by her fourth day. The experience in itself was exploitation that came with the territory of being a worker. However, a week later a Filipina worker was hired. She was given two weeks of training and it was a month before she had to clean sixteen rooms. Now that unequal treatment based on ethnicity and race had entered the picture, her class experience was intensified and she joined the union leadership committee before her probationary period was even over.

One can argue that highlighting ethnic/racial oppression is merely a tactic that plays on the most base of instincts and sidelines the universal experience of class exploitation that brings workers of all backgrounds together. Indeed, raising the issue of racial/ethnic oppression is a strategy on which the union and New Otani leadership rely to recruit workers and to gain community support. The effectiveness of this strategy, however, stems from the fact that race/ethnicity makes up a central part of the working-class experience for the New Otani workers. The prevalence of the relationship between class and ethnicity/race and citizenship is noted in the derogatory comment made by the hotel's general manager about Latino workers. Kenji Yoshimoto the general manager of the New Otani wrote to City Councilman Richard Alatorre that the Latino workers at the hotel "are of Hispanic origin, born in other countries, and not yet as sophisticated perhaps as some others." This view provokes the resistance of workers and community alike and serves to fuel the workers' commitment to organize the hotel. Given the inseparable relationship between ethnicity/race and class, it is not surprising that the passion to fight for one's rights as a worker is often justified in ethnic terms. For example, one worker states, "Unionizing is the only way we're going to gain respect. We fall and get up because it's the only way to get something for our families. It's the way to show Yoshimoto that although we came from different countries, we are not ignorant." The worker continued to explain that

> "after Anna [a vocal union organizer] got fired, Councilman Alatorre sent a letter to him in protest. Yoshimoto wrote back saying we come from unsophisticated countries and that we are ignorant Latinos from unsophisticated countries. Alatorre was very upset. He's also Latino. Those words rather than bringing us down bring us up so that we can demonstrate how wrong he is. They all feel the same way about Latinos, but Yoshimoto actually put it on paper and signed it. . . . In another meeting I asked him what he meant by saying unsophisticated and ignorant. He replied by saying that I misunderstood what his letter said. Alatorre said that this was a double offense. First he insults us and then he says we don't understand the insult."

It is the language of ethnicity/race and citizenship that shapes the collective consciousness of the group and that facilitates a shared basis for solidarity for groups as distinct as Mexicans and Salvadorans. Globalization influences the volume of this discourse in another respect: the political upheavals in Latin America that preceded the migration of the latest wave of immigrant workers provides a foundation for political experiences reminiscent of the politicized European immigrants that ignited labor in the 1930s.

While structural and political changes have transformed the impact of segmentation in some respects, the distance it posed between workers in the past continues to have an effect today. The segmentation at the New Otani has made it difficult to get all workers on board the union campaign. The most significant divisions are between immigrant Latino and Asian workers. The Filipinos in accounting, for example, do not support the union drive. Nor as of spring 1996 had any great progress been made in organizing the Japanese workers who were mostly concentrated in two of the hotel's Japanese-theme restaurants. According to one Local 11 organizer, six out of the approximately twenty-five to thirty Japanese workers supported the union. But only two had actually signed a union card. The general attitude of the Japanese workers toward Local 11 was that "the union is for lazy Mexicans. I work hard, therefore I don't need a union." The attitude of Asian immigrant workers toward the union changes, depending on the distance between the groups. For example, in contrast to the Filipinos who are concentrated in accounting, the Filipinos in housekeeping have signed in support of the union. The distance imposed by occupational segmentation leaves room for the emergence of ethnic/racial stereotyping and for the employers' manipulation of employee attitudes toward their coworkers and thus sets up a basis for intergroup conflict.

The disparities found in segmented labor markets are a product not only of wages and workloads but also of how groups are treated. It is the perception of unequal treatment fostered through segmentation that leads to intergroup hostilities. "Treatment" is somewhat an intangible measure and difficult to isolate. But we can grasp it in the words of workers when they say they are fighting for "dignity and respect." Do some groups of workers get treated with more dignity and respect than others? According to immigrant Latino workers, the hotel treats Asian workers with greater respect. Once a year, workers get the opportunity to determine the attitude of the hotel toward them, when it comes to yearly raises. On the first day of the card-signing drive, several workers pointed to their small or nonexistent raises and compared them to what another worker got as a measure of the bad treatment and favoritism that permeates the workings of the hotel. One black worker who has worked in the laundry room for sixteen years and who arrived at the union to sign a card pointed at the nickel raise he was given as an indication of employer racism toward blacks. This worker also felt that the Asian workers are treated better. Although none of the workers knew for sure if the Asian workers in other departments had received substantial raises, many believed that this was the case. Thus, it is the separation of groups into particular segments of the hotel that reduces the communication and information between groups that lead to suspicion and inaccurate assessment of the other groups' experiences within the hotel.

Instances of favoritism, such as allowing the Japanese workers to park in the hotel lot and get vacations, are generalized to mean that favoritism occurs at every instance. Thus, the perception of unequal treatment is compounded by the segmentation of groups. Very few of the Latino workers see the harsh conditions the Japanese workers face, with the exception of the busboys in the restaurant where the Japanese workers are concentrated. The Latino workers having firsthand experience with Japanese workers see that at times the Japanese workers are treated worse than they themselves are. They are told, "Oh you're such a good worker. Here's more work."

The perception of favoritism influences Latino workers to believe that the perceived greater status of the Japanese worker gives them little reason to rebel against the company. In addition, Latino workers feel that racial/ethnic ties between the hotel management and the Asian workers override class solidarity. Ironically, Latino workers also carry with them stereotypes of the unorganizable Asian immigrant. Latinos say that Asian workers are conformists and attribute perceived conformity as inherent in the Japanese culture. As a result, Latino workers have ignored Japanese workers for the first two years of the campaign. By doing so, they have given the hotel a two-year head start in capturing the support of a crucial segment of the workforce. As one organizer states, "Nobody in their lives were talking about the union. Instead they were bombarded daily with antiunion propaganda. They are told that the union is Mafia, that unions are for lazy Mexican workers, and so on."

According to a Local 11 organizer brought on board specifically to help organize the Asian workers, although Asian workers are much better paid, they are also treated much worse in many respects than the Latino workers and have much less knowledge about workers' rights. The waitresses at the New Otani make at least one hundred dollars a night in tips. But as one organizer who has interviewed six of the Japanese workers suggests, they also dislike the hotel.

"We found out about the atmosphere, what it means to work there. It's hellish being a waitress there. The supervisor has created an atmosphere of competition between older and younger waitresses. Waitresses abuse each other as a result. They get yelled at and even get their hand slapped when they do something wrong. Waitresses often sabotage each other's food. There is a lot of snitching and backstabbing going on between older and newer waitresses. Older workers use these tactics to maintain their seniority. They make tons of money. They get regular schedules. But they hate working there anyway. There is abuse and constant fear. The reason that they stay is because they generalize their experiences and think all Japanese restaurants are like that. Since they make so much money at the New Otani, they might as well stay."

In addition to this sense of disempowerment, Japanese workers have greater reason to fear the hotel. The hotel looms over Little Tokyo and plays a prominent role in the Japanese community in Los Angeles. There are only so many Japanese-theme restaurants in the area, and the workers fear the hotel's influence over the rest of the community. There is also some loyalty to the company, which, as one organizer suggests, is cultural and promoted in Japan. This loyalty, however, reflects the fact that Japan has not experienced the great social dislocations that have occurred in Latin American countries. Thus, the Japanese immigrants do not have the same kinds of prior political experiences that the Latino workers have. In other instances, the hotel has brought some of the workers over from Japan and demands their loyalty in return. After interviewing the six Japanese workers, the organizer believes that the loyalty is tenuous and not as great as the Latino workers believe. She also insists that there is a racialization of fear that is unfounded. In other words, "Fear everyone has. But when the Japanese workers don't fight back, it's attributed to their culture, They're *gente conformista.*"

For now, much of the organizing of the Asian workers is left up to the union. One organizer explains that when progress with the Asian workers is reported in meetings, the Latino workers respond with, "Oh that's great. The Asian organizers are organizing the Asian workers." The organizer explains, "We have to get Latino workers to see themselves doing the organizing with the Japanese workers, to see it as part of their efforts. While the Latino workers maintain the majority without the support of the Asian workers, the role of the Asian workers is crucial for accelerating the campaign. As one organizer suggests, "the day that the Japanese workers get on the picket line, Yoshimoto [the hotel's general manager] will shit bricks."

Ironically, segmentation creates two contradictory situations. On the one hand, perceptions of unequal treatment foster resentment and resistance from a politicized workforce. On the other hand, the perception of unequal treatment generates conflict between workers who logically should be in solidarity. In both these cases, conflict and antagonism are the outcome rather than harmony and stability.

COALITIONS AND COMMUNITY

The union has responded to its commitment to intraethnic organizing and launched an aggressive campaign aimed directly at the Japanese workers. Organizers were brought on to work specifically with Japanese workers, and the union has continued with its community-based strategy to help overcome the barriers that the social division of labor reinforces. Central to this organizing campaign is an effort to gain the support of the local Little Tokyo community. And central to this effort is the work of the New Otani Workers Support Committee, which is made up of local activists with strong ties to the Japanese community. Among the members are prominent clergy, lawyers, professors, students, and local activists. Many of the support committee members were central to the campaign for government reparations to the Japanese interned during World War II. A position statement dated June 9, 1995, and written by Glen Omatsu, a community activist, states,

> For the past year-and-a-half, Asian American community groups and individuals have participated in the New Otani Workers Support Committee. The mission of the support committee is threefold: 1) to build solidarity in the Asian American community for workers' efforts to form a union; 2) to educate the Asian American community about the significance of the workers' campaign, especially relating to inter ethnic relations, protection of immigrants rights, and the community demand for corporate accountability; and 3) to monitor and counteract management's attack on workers. Thus, the support committee defines the Asian American community, especially the local Japanese American community, as directly involved in the workers' campaign. The organization of a union at the hotel will benefit not only workers employed there; it will also raise the quality of life in Little Tokyo.

The formation of coalitions within communities has proven to be an effective strategy whenever the potential for racial and ethnic antagonisms exists (see Horton, 1989). The hope of community activists, workers, and Local 11 is that the prominent community support will undermine the hotel's attempt to write off the struggle at the New Otani as mere racial/ethnic conflict. In the same position piece Omatsu writes,

> The New Otani is managed and owned by Japanese corporations, while the workforce is predominately immigrant Latinos. Thus, conflict regarding unionization at the hotel can easily be perceived as inter ethnic conflict. Asian American community groups are acutely concerned about the state of race relations in Los Angeles in this period following the Los Angeles Uprising. Corporations from Japan often take ac-

tions that inflame racial tensions; unfortunately, local Asian American communities usually become the targets of righteous anger of others upset by the racism of corporations from Japan. Thus, in this period, Asian American community groups have a special responsibility to directly confront corporations from Asia.

Another aspect of the support from the Asian American community comes in the form of obtaining endorsements for the boycott from prominent Asian organizations. At this point, it is not clear how effective the support committee will be in terms of helping to directly organize the Japanese workers. It is clear, however, that without the coalitions formed between workers and the community, the boycott could have never gotten off the ground and the perception of racial/ethnic conflict would have dominated the scene. The important lesson here is that in multiethnic communities, multiethnic coalitions overcome the perception that hostilities are racially based and emphasize the reality of a class-based struggle.

ETHNICITY AND RACE AS RESOURCES

The assumption behind the formation of interethnic coalitions is that race/ethnicity plays an important role in influencing workers about where they should stand. This is not a novel idea. But it is amazing how often the ethnic/racial dimension is ignored, with failure of unionism as an outcome. One example of this failure colors the history of the garment workers' union (ILGWU). In his study on the decline of the ILGWU, John Laslett argues that the failure to organize Latinos led to a reversal of the progress that the ILGWU had made in the post–World War II period. The failure to organize sportswear workers was particularly devastating after the 1950s when this became the fastest-growing segment of the industry. Laslett suggests that racism and sexism on behalf of the white leadership rather than cultural differences undermined the organization of Latinas. In the post–World War II period, ILGWU officials refused to heed the lessons that Rose Pessota's earlier successful efforts to organize Latinas in their own language had produced. While bilingual organizers had volunteered to organize the sportswear industry, their efforts were undermined by ILGWU leadership. This happened either because of condescension of their efforts by the union or because of the ILGWU's refusal to allow for Spanish-speaking locals (Laslett and Tyler, 1989: 64–5). Although these events happened almost fifty years ago, the garment industry is still reeling from the fallout.

It appears that the emerging union leaders, on the national as well as the local level, have learned their historical lessons and are working hard not to make the same mistakes. The lessons are reflected in the composition of the union leadership and frontline organizers as well as in their mode of communication. For not only are unionists organizing immigrant Latinos, they are doing so in Spanish. The important role that language plays in organizing workers is suggested in the comments that workers often make in admiration of the white organizer who did not know any Spanish when she started on the campaign but was almost fluent after three years on the job.

In addition to having ethnic/racial representation in union organizing, the union also learns where ethnic bonds exist and attempts to organize around them. In an interview with the president of Local 11, she explains,

> We try to be very aware of those situations where there are family relations in order to have them help organize. You get the right people that are related to each other, then you get the whole network. That network runs through not only within the hotel, but within the whole industry. That network is there, and we try to uncover the relationships. For example, at the Sheraton Grande Downtown and at the Intercontinental there was some relations between the stewards, the dishwashers, in those two nonunion hotels. They would recruit from their families so that they would make sure that in the union organizing drive they would have the loyalty of their family members. To break through that network is almost impossible.

The role of networks in organizing the New Otani has been of great importance. There is an understanding that the bonds between people are often based on family membership or friendships forged in their native country. It is through these networks that ethnicity plays a role in influencing class formation, and that represents a strong basis for worker loyalty. The understanding of these networks has led to winning over central groups in the hotel. For example, the majority of banquet workers live in Lennox and come from Jicalpan. This group of workers for the longest time was ambivalent toward the union. The union recognized Alfonso's importance within the network and concentrated on recruiting him. They learned that the group met every morning at a neighborhood doughnut shop. One of the union organizers approached him and continued to talk to him about the union. Once Alfonso was won over, the rest of the Jicalpan group also signed in support of the union. This kind of maneuvering is only possible with a real understanding of the dynamics of the immigrant Latino community. It is an understanding that appears to be forged in the union's commitment to go beyond merely organizing the workplace, to being involved in organizing communities.

CONCLUSION

Previous theories on the relationship between difference and working-class solidarity highlight the disorganizing impact of difference. The transformation from a goods-producing to a service-producing economy, demographic shifts, and the emergence of progressive unions provides the context for the reinterpretation of the role of difference on working-class solidarity. In contrast to the views that see labor market and occupational segmentation as unintended consequences of economic organization, the interviews with employers show that the ideology of difference determines the sorting of workers. The alienation that stereotypes create provides the basis for resistance. Although, as in the past, these divisions continue to undermine solidarity across occupational segments. Thus, organizing requires that unions and workers directly address the conflict that segmentation creates. Thus, looking toward the community and building coalitions of difference informs the political practice of unions and demonstrates the importance of political practice in building solidarity.

Local 11 attributes its success in organizing immigrant workers to its reliance on grassroots organizing. Grassroots means having to rely on the rank and file and the community for support. Of course, this reliance demands that the union understand the community it serves. This level of understanding of how particular communities operate is one of the factors that have made Local 11 so successful. Like the CIO of the 1930s, there is a movement to organize groups traditionally ignored by organized labor. And in contrast to what conventional wisdom dictates, immigrants, women, and ethnic minorities are more than willing to organize. The strategies of Local 11 suggest that they understand the strength of the immigrant experience and are willing to move away from reified understandings of race/ethnicity, gender, and citizenship and build a union based on the understanding that the social can be overcome and can even serve to facilitate the organization of workers.

The struggle at the New Otani Hotel has yet to be resolved. There has been no letup since the boycott began in 1996. It is not clear whether the workers will win or lose. The hotel shows no sign of being willing to meet the union at the bargaining table. But optimism prevails, an optimism forged with the continued support and dedication of community groups.

Whether the workers at the New Otani win or lose, they have already made their mark on history. The high-profile case has captured the attention of labor leaders and serves as a model for interethnic organizing. The message the workers at the New Otani send out is clear. Immigrants do organize. Latinos will fight for their rights. Race/ethnicity, citizenship, and gender status do not necessarily undermine the organization of workers. There are still lessons to be learned and obstacles to overcome, but in the end, the process of unionism at the New Otani has paved the way for a more complex understanding of the role of race/ethnicity, gender, and citizenship on the process of class formation.

REFERENCES

Ansell, Phill, Fred Broadwell, Ellen Goodman, Kristen Grimm, Patricia Larsen, Marc Norman and Alice Salinas. "Accidental Tourism: A Critique of the Los Angeles Tourism Industry and Proposals for Change." Master's thesis, University of California, Los Angeles, 1992.

Bodnar, John. *The Transplanted: A History of Immigrants in Urban America*. Bloomington: Indiana University Press, 1985.

Bonacich, Edna. "A Theory of Ethnic Antagonism: The Split Labor Market." *American Sociological Review* 37 (1972): 547–59.

———. "A Theory of Middleman Minorities." *American Sociological Review* 38 (1973): 583–94.

———. "Advanced Capitalism and Black White Relationships." *American Sociological Review* 41 (1976): 34–51.

Borjas, George. *Friends or Strangers: The Impact of Immigrants on the U.S. Economy*. New York: Basic, 1990, chap. 1.

———. "Immigration, Minorities, and Labor Market Competition." *Industrial Labor Relations Review* 40(3) (1987): 382–92.

Braddock, Jomills, and James McPartland. "How Minorities Continue to Be Excluded from Equal Employment Opportunities: Research on Labor Market and Institutional Barriers." *Journal of Social Issues* 43(1) (1987): 5–39.

Braverman, Harry. *Labor and Monopoly Capital*. New York: Monthly Review Press, 1974.

Bukowczyk, John J. "The Transformation of Working Class Ethnicity: Corporate Control, Americanization, and the Polish Immigrant Middle Class in Bayonne, New Jersey 1915–1925." *Labor History* 25(1) (Winter 1984): 53–82.

Cobble, Dorothy Sue. "The Prospects for Unionism in a Service Society." In *Working in the Service Society*, edited by Cameron Lynne Macdonald and Carmen Sirianni, 333–58. Philadelphia: Temple University Press, 1996.

Cobble, Dorothy Sue, and Michael Merrill. "Collective Bargaining in the Hospitality Industry in the 1980's." Unpublished ms., Institute of Management and Labor Relations: Rutgers Labor Education Center, 1994.

Davis, Mike. "Trying to Build a Movement in Los Angeles." *Los Angeles Times* (20 March 1994), M1.

Defreitas, Gregory. "Unionization among Racial and Ethnic Minorities." *Industrial and Labor Relations Review* 46 (1993): 2.

Delgado, Hector L. "IRCA and the Unionization of Mexican and Central American Workers in Los Angeles County." *Policy Studies Review* 11 (1992): 2.

———. *New Immigrants Old Unions: Organizing Undocumented Workers in Los Angeles*. Philadelphia: Temple University Press, 1993.

Doeringer, Peter B., and Michael J. Piore. *Internal Labor Markets and Manpower Analysis*. Lexington, Mass.: Heath, 1971, chap. 1.

Foner, Philip S. *History of the Labor Movement in the United States, Volume II*. New York: International Publishers, 1955.

———. *History of the Labor Movement in the United States, Volume III*. New York: International Publishers, 1964.

Friedlander, Peter. *The Emergence of a UAW Local, 1936–1939: A Study in Class and Culture*. Pittsburgh: University of Pittsburgh Press, 1975.

Goldfield, Michael. *The Decline of Organized Labor in the United States*. Chicago: University of Chicago Press, 1987.

Horton, John. "The Politics of Ethnic Change: Grass-Roots Responses to Economic and Demographic Restructuring in Monterey Park, California." *Urban Geography* 10 (1989): 578–92.

————. "The Politics of Diversity in Monterey Park, California." In *Structuring Diversity: Ethnographic Perspectives on the New Immigration*, edited by Louise Lamphere, 215–45. Chicago: University of Chicago Press, 1992.

Hochschild, Arlie Russell. *The Managed Heart: Commercialization of Human Feeling.* Los Angeles: University of California Press, 1983.

Kang, K. Connie. "L.A. Hilton Owner Will Keep Service Workers." *Los Angeles Times* (20 February 1995), B3.

Kasarda, John. "Urban Industrial Transition and the Underclass." *The Annals of the American Academy of Political and Social Science* 501 (1989): 26–42.

Katznelson, Ira, and Aristide R. Zolberg. *Working Class Formation: Nineteenth-Century Patterns in Western Europe and the United States.* Princeton, N.J.: Princeton University Press, 1986.

Kautsky, Karl. *The Class Struggle.* New York: Norton, 1971.

Kirschenman, Joleen, and Kathryn Neckerman. "We'd Love to Hire Them, But . . .: The Meaning of Race for Employers." In *The Urban Underclass*, edited by Christopher Jenks and Paul E. Peterson, 203–32. Washington, D.C.: The Brookings Institution, 1991.

Laslett, John, and Mary Tyler. *The ILGWU in Los Angeles 1907–1988.* Inglewood, Calif.: Ten Star Press, 1989.

Marx, Karl. *The Eighteenth Brumaire of Louis Bonaparte.* New York: International Publishers, 1987.

Massey, Douglas. *Return to Aztlan: The Social Process of International Migration from Western Mexico.* Berkeley: University of California Press, 1987.

McDonnell, Patrick J. "Hotel Boycott Is a High-Stakes Battle for Union." *Los Angeles Times* (3 February 1996).

Milkman, Ruth. *Gender at Work: The Dynamics of Job Segregation by Sex during World War II.* Urbana: University of Illinois Press, 1987.

Mink, Gwendolyn. *Old Labor and New Immigrants in American Political Development: Union, Party, and State 1875–1920.* Ithaca, N.Y.: Cornell University Press, 1986.

Moss, Philip, and Chris Tilly. "Raised Hurdles for Black Men: Evidence from Interviews with Employers." Unpublished ms., 1991.

Neckerman, Kathryn, and Joleen Kirschenman. "Hiring Strategies, Racial Bias, and Inner City Workers." *Social Problems* 38(4) (1991): 433–7.

Oestreicher, Richard Jules. *Solidarity and Fragmentation: Working People and Class Consciousness in Detroit, 1877–1895.* Ph.D. Dissertation, Michigan State University, 1979.

Olzak, Susan. *The Dynamics of Ethnic Competition and Conflict.* Stanford, Calif.: Stanford University Press, 1992.

Piore, Michael, *Birds of Passage.* New York: Cambridge University Press, 1979.

Ruiz, Vicki L. *Cannery Women, Cannery Lives: Mexican Women, Unionization, and the California Food Processing Industry 1930–1950.* Albuquerque: University of New Mexico Press, 1987.

Silverstein, Stuart. "Going to Work on L.A.: In Its Many Low-Paid Laborers, Unions See Big Potential for Organizing." *Los Angeles Times* (27 February 1996), D1.

Thomas, Robert J. *Citizenship, Gender, and Work: Social Organization of Industrial Agriculture.* Berkeley: University of California Press, 1986.

Thompson, E. P. *The Making of the English Working Class.* New York: Vintage, 1966.

Thurow, Lester. *Generating Inequality: Mechanisms of Distribution in the U.S. Economy.* New York: Basic Books, 1975.

U.S. Department of Labor. *The Effects of Immigration on the U.S. Economy and Labor Market.* Washington, D.C.: Government Printing Office, 1989.

————. *The Labor Market Consequences of U.S. Immigration: A Survey.* Washington, D.C.: Government Printing Office, 1990.

Waldinger, Roger. "Taking Care of the Guests: The Impact of Immigrants on Services— An Industry Case Study." Unpublished ms, University of California, Los Angeles, 1991.

————. "Who Cleans the Rooms? Who Washes the Dishes? Black/Immigrant Job Competition Reassessed." Unpublished ms., 1993.

Wilson, William Julius. *When Work Disappears.* New York: Knopf, 1996.

Wood, Jim. "Labor's L.A. Gains." *Los Angeles Times* (20 February 1995), B7.

Zamudio, Margaret M. "Globalization and the Organization of Immigrant Latina/o Workers: Lessons from the New Labor Movement." In *Transnational Transformations: Reexamining the Politics of Latino Communities in the 1990's,* edited by Anna Sampaio and Carlos Velez-Ibanez. Boulder, Colo.: Rowman & Littlefield, forthcoming.

Zavella, Patricia. *Women's Work and Chicano Families: Cannery Workers of the Santa Clara Valley.* Ithica, N.Y.: Cornell University Press, 1987.

Zieger, Robert H. *American Workers, American Unions, 1920–1985.* Baltimore: Johns Hopkins Press, 1986.

7

Natives and Nations: Identity Formation in Postcolonial Melanesia

Geoffrey M. White

National identities are everywhere beset with competing forces of identification, besieged from within by local and ethnic formations and from without by global flows of capital and popular culture. The ambiguity of the term *nation* — referring at times to the nation–state and at times to a more general sense of cultural commonality — reflects the predicament of the state as a locus of collective identity. One of the most problematic aspects of nation making, it seems, is the task of imagining community in an idiom of *culture*, of shared meaning and value.

Everyone from news media and multinational corporations to NGOs and government ministries now talks about "culture" in contexts of nation making and national development. Despite wide variation in the culture and history of diverse regions, global talk about identity politics tends to proceed in a highly limited and reductive English-language vocabulary, rehearsing a mantra of "national," "ethnic," and "indigenous." The most common context for talk about "ethnicity" in the global media and in the international arena generally are situations of intergroup conflict, represented inevitably as "ethnic" struggles. In these contexts "ethnicity" is most often conceived as a kind of primordial identification that generates intense loyalties and animosities. In these contexts, images of ethnicity evoke related concepts of the "native" and the "tribal" that strongly connote primitive and irrational forces at work in human life.

In this chapter, I draw on observations from the Southwest Pacific to argue that popular conceptions of indigenous identity in global circulation today draw upon longstanding conceptions of "ethnic" and "native" identities. These, in turn, are tightly interconnected, each working to define the other, particularly in the border zones of today's international economic and political transactions. In these contexts, images of the indigenous—of "traditional" or "native" culture—are reproduced in the self-essentializing rhetoric of national governments in concert with global forces of "development" (cf. Gegeo, 1998; Hanlon, 1998). I explore this interaction by considering some of the ways that one Pacific state, the Solomon Islands, projects images of national culture for purposes of tourism and economic growth. The discussion turns up examples of what Arif Dirlik (1990) calls "culturalism"—ideologies of culture that tend to divorce concepts of culture and tradition from historical forces of economic change.

The societies I am concerned with are the mostly rural communities of the newly independent states of the Southwest Pacific region known as Melanesia. As in much of the decolonizing world, discourses of modernization and "development" have been a standard feature of life in this region throughout the latter half of the twentieth century. In its usual form, development is imagined as a process of rationally managed socioeconomic change that transforms traditional subsistence practices into modern cash economies. Insofar as similar concepts of development are found throughout the world's tropic zones, much of what I have to say may be extended to postcolonial situations elsewhere.

The social meanings of development are coded in a series of binary constructs that contrast the "traditional" with the "modern" and the "indigenous" with the "Western." But the value loadings of these terms are not fixed. One of the fundamental changes brought about by decolonization has been the revalorization of the "traditional" and "indigenous" (Jolly and Thomas, 1992; Thomas, 1992; White and Lindstrom, 1993), unsettling the usual equation of "development" with progress and Western style modernization. But this critical consciousness has tended to invert rather than to disturb in any fundamental way the binary opposition of tradition and modernity, leaving intact much of its meaning and power. Despite newly positive images of the "native," earlier European models of evolution from primitive tribes to modern states continue to lurk just behind the scenes, such that concepts of "native" or "indigenous" culture remain nested in a web of associations with "tribal" and "primitive." Collective identities in Melanesia are frequently represented in both news media and in official national representations with images of timeless traditions that displace other ways of representing or knowing Melanesian peoples (cf. Fabian, 1983).

English-language concepts of the "ethnic" and the "native" have complex and overlapping histories. Both are embedded in historical narratives of evolution and modernization, where they emerge in counterpoint with concepts of the "modern." But the "native" is usually conceived as existing outside of (or prior to) Western influence, whereas "ethnicity" typically refers to group differences within modern states. There is even a disciplinary division of labor in studying native and ethnic cultures. While native cultures have been the province of anthropology, ethnicity more often falls within the scope of sociology. The difference, of course, is that anthropology has historically focused most of its attention on small, non-western, nonliterate cultures, while sociology and other social sciences have attended to the culture and politics of contemporary nation–states.

Despite their distinct genealogies, these terms also inform one another in complex ways. For example, when intergroup conflict turns violent it is frequently explained in terms of "ancient" hostilities. Narratives of evolution and modernization create a certain degree of overlap in the meanings of the categories "ethnic" and "native." Ethnicity is often presumed to be rooted "in the blood"—defined in terms of ancestry and a set of "primordial" features, such as language, religion, place, and custom. In this, modern concepts of ethnicity stand between notions of primitive "tribal" identity and modern identity associated with secular states, rationality, and bureaucracy.

To draw a more familiar parallel, the prolonged genocidal conflicts in Bosnia and Rwanda have been widely reported and understood as specifically "ethnic" and "tribal" conflicts. But such characterizations mystify as much as they illuminate, insofar as they direct attention to supposedly primal sentiments rather than the historical conditions under which cultural identities harden into violent political and emotional realities.[1]

This chapter argues that concepts of ethnicity are not so easily transplanted in Oceanic soil (or waters), in part because they carry cultural and historical baggage (cf. Linnekin and Poyer, 1990) and in part because they are displaced by concepts of the "indigenous." To suggest that terms such as *ethnic, ethnicity,* or *ethnic group* are misapplied in this region is not to exoticize Melanesian identity, but to draw attention to problems of interpretation as well as to the constructed nature of local identities. I begin by discussing examples of media representations of "ethnic" conflict in the Pacific, followed by consideration of some of the factors that have historically defined local identities in the Solomon Islands.

In the second part of the chapter I discuss some of the ways that Melanesian governments have featured images of native culture to represent the process of "development," especially in the context of tourism. Melanesian governments have without exception attempted to revise and foreground images of tradition as valued aspects of national culture. These redefinitions, supported by global discourses of the "indigenous," prove useful in a variety of contexts, including tourism promotion. Nonetheless, these images are direct descendants of concepts of the "primitive" that once populated the colonial imagination. As such, they continue to carry many of the same disabling connotations of the "uncivilized" and "irrational" that have bracketed native voices throughout colonial history.

ETHNICITY, *NEW YORK TIMES* VARIETY

The more cultural identity becomes topicalized in global media, the more locally and historically specific identities are rendered as essentialized labels for fixed, homogenous groups. Representations of ethnicity tend to extract social identity from history, opposing ideas about timeless traditions with historical processes of change and modernization. Three varieties of identity discussed in this volume—the national, the ethnic, and the indigenous—may be located along a continuum of culture versus nature, of *primordialness*, such that national identifications are regarded as more abstract and rational and indigenous identities as more natural and rooted in blood and soil.

Ethnicity, perhaps the most frequently used term in the American identity lexicon, serves an important linking function. On the one hand, ethnicity signifies identities that are naturalized by virtue of common ancestry, language, and behavior. On the other hand, ethnic identifications obtain political/legal significance within the bureaucratized institutions of the (pluralistic) state. As many observers have pointed out, concepts of ethnicity slip easily between the language of culture and the biological idiom of *race*, with its logic of natural essences (Dominguez, 1995). Talk of race is powerful because it finds its most common signifiers in physical characteristics that connote immutable traits, given in the body rather than acquired in culture. In the same manner, ascriptions of ethnic identity are politically effective to the extent that they also naturalize the basis for collectivity, locating the authenticity and force of identity in ideas about ancestry and tradition, outside the vicissitudes of politics and history.

It is now almost obligatory when discussing global politics to refer to the rise of ethnicity and ethnic rivalry as a feature of the post–Cold War world. The collapse of bipolar superpower politics created a policy and media vacuum that was rapidly filled with images of local conflicts characterized as specifically *ethnic* in origin. Foreign policy statements and newspaper articles alike declared that the demise of Cold War controls that once kept ethnic tensions in check resulted in an upsurge of ethnic violence. Samuel Huntington achieved infamy for his articulation of a culturalist paradigm of post–Cold War conflict as a "clash of civilizations" (1996; 1993). In point of fact, Huntington's thesis is not original. His 1993 article in *Foreign Affairs* gave scholarly formulation to ideas that were already widespread in popular and academic thinking, substituting talk of a few grand civilizations for numerous and hard-to-keep-track-of "ethnic groups."

By the time Huntington's article appeared, the Western press was already busy highlighting stories about global conflicts as clashes of culture and ethnicity. A good example of this genre is a front-page *New York Times* article that appeared with the headline: AS ETHNIC WARS MULTIPLY, U.S. STRIVES FOR A POLICY (February 1993). The article noted that the United States was "struggling to meet the challenge," quoting Secretary of State Warren Christopher to the effect that new approaches to foreign policy and conflict resolution would have to be devised to meet the complexities of the post-bipolar world. "If we don't find some way that the different ethnic groups can live together in a country, how many countries will we have?" (1) In the more flamboyant words of Patrick Moynihan, "The defining mode of conflict in the era ahead is ethnic conflict. . . .

It promises to be savage. Get ready for 50 new countries in the world in the next 50 years. Most of them will be born in bloodshed" (12).

To document the scope of this new upsurge in ethnic war, the article lists forty-eight specific armed conflicts, grouped in five regions. Under the headline "As Ethnic Wars Multiply . . ." the listing implies that all forty-eight trouble spots are instances of specifically *ethnic* conflicts. I am not sure how journalists and newspaper readers interpret the notion of *ethnic group* or *ethnic war,* but these terms connote identities that are in some way primordial, rooted in ancestral, territorial, linguistic, and religious affiliations that are deep seated and not easily changed. Audiences of the *New York Times* and CNN tend to associate these premodern dispositions with primitive human impulses of aggression and lack of civilizing controls. These connotations were nicely captured in a cartoon about the Bosnia conflict printed in the *Boston Globe* that depicted two cavemen reading a newspaper with the headline, "Serbia/Croatia Ancient Rivalry" and saying "Nice to see them keeping up the old traditions." (Presumably Samuel Huntington's "civilizations" refine and modernize these impulses, equipping them with the latest weapons technology.)

In light of the proliferation of historically specific local conflicts around the world, the *New York Times,* Samuel Huntington, and others interested to represent conflict in terms of a single global paradigm face substantial difficulties. What do such paradigms jettison in order to represent political identities and conflicts in a single worldwide model of "ethnic war" or a "clash of civilizations" compared to the Cold War? Here a closer look at the *New York Times*'s summation of its forty-eight cases, each described in a few sentences, gives some idea of the kinds of obfuscation likely to result.

The article mentions two ethnic conflicts in the Pacific, both in Melanesia: cases 43 and 44, Papua New Guinea and Fiji, respectively.[2] Here is what the *Times* says about these two:

43. PAPUA NEW GUINEA Rebels on the island of Bougainville declared independence in 1990. The Papua New Guinea government subdued the rebellion in 1991 after fighting in which 3,000 died.

44. FIJI Violence erupted after the Indian-dominated Government was elected in 1987. The Government was overthrown and the current Government consolidates ethnic Fijian dominance.

Both of these cases are ongoing, sustained political conflicts that have generated a great deal of commentary and analysis. Space does not permit adequate description of these crises. However, it is safe to say that "ethnicity" has little to do with the Bougainville conflict and has done as much to obscure as illuminate the case of Fiji. In Fiji, the division of the population into two culturally distinct populations of indigenous Fijians and Indo-Fijian descendants of plantation labor brought from India around the turn of the twentieth century, offers an easy analysis in terms of the idiom of ethnicity. Yet most analysts argue that such descriptions are only partial and distract from an adequate understanding of Fiji politics (Lal, 1988, 2000).

As this chapter was being written, the democratically elected government of Fiji was again overthrown in a prolonged drama of hostage taking in the national Parliament. Despite the claims of the stage takers themselves that they acted in the interest of assuring indigenous paramountcy, Fijian scholar Teresia Teaiwa writes that "The problem with prevailing analyses of the political situation in Fiji is the notion that the conflict is between indigenous Fijians and Indo-Fijians. The "race" card is misleading and mischievous." In fact, it has become almost obligatory for recent commentaries on the Fijian crisis to assert that the conflict is not *only* about ethnic conflict. Even a recent op-ed essay by the editor of the *Lonely Planet Guide* to Fiji led with the headline "Fijian turmoil goes beyond racial politics" (Kay 2000).

Reporting such as that in the *New York Times* shows how a paradigm of "ethnic" violence may skew the scripting of a story. The two sentences given to Fiji begin by saying that "Violence erupted after the Indian-dominated Government was elected in 1987." In fact, the violence after the election was quite minimal and easily contained by Fiji's largely indigenous military. The presumption is that ethnic tensions are a violent tinderbox that destabilizes national governments (those old Neanderthal urges depicted in the Bosnia cartoon, perhaps). In point of fact, the major violence occurred when a squad of soldiers raided the Parliament and took the elected prime minister and others into custody. This is not even mentioned in the article, simply that the "Government was overthrown."

The relative absence or silence of Indo-Fijians in the most public aspects of Fijian national political crises is even clearer in the most recent drama. Although the overthrow focused originally on the act of taking an Indo-Fijian prime minister hostage (along with thirty-five others, both Fijian and Indo-Fijian), this was followed by a series of violent clashes between indigenous Fijians, resulting in two deaths from gunfire. While noting the complex lines of conflict running within and across ethnic lines, it is important to note that both crises, especially the 2000 overthrow, served to give form and meaning to conflict as "ethnic" conflict—crystallizing and directing Fijian hostilities toward Indo-Fijians. In other words, the violent overthrow did as much to *cause* ethnic conflict as it was itself a consequence of such tensions.

The case of Bougainville—case number 43—is even more distorted than the Fiji profile (Regan, 1998; Wesley-Smith and Ogan, 1992). In Bougainville, where there is no large nonindigenous group as in Fiji, but rather a patchwork of smaller language groups, the concept of "ethnicity" itself is difficult to apply. That detail aside, almost nothing reported in the two sentences for this case is correct. The article says simply that "rebels" "declared independence in 1990" and that the government "subdued the rebellion in 1991," after fighting in which three thousand died.

First of all, the article says nothing about the cause of the "rebellion," which followed economic and environmental disputes associated with operation of the world's largest open-pit copper mine. These disputes erupted into open conflict with a campaign of sabotage against the mine in 1988. The assertion of "independence" came about in response to the Papua New Guinea government's declaration of an emergency to deal with escalating acts of sabotage that eventually shut down the mine and the country's largest single source of foreign revenue. Finally, far from ending in 1991 when the government "subdued the rebellion," the conflict has continued for years, up to the present, including a failed United Nations–sponsored peace conference in October 1994, when a multinational peace-keeping force monitored one of several rounds of peace negotiations.

Note that in this example there are no references to which "ethnic groups" are involved in this "ethnic war." This is because there aren't any. One side consists of the Papua New Guinea government and its defense force, composed of troops from many of the country's 750+ language groups, while the other is composed of a shifting subset of the twelve or so language groups on Bougainville, some of whom align themselves with the government, while others do not. In light of these ambiguities, the very issue of whether "Bougainville" constitutes an ethnic identity has been a point of contention. For example, a former minister of justice for Papua New Guinea, Bernard Narokobi, testifying before the United Nations Human Rights Commission, declared flatly, "There is no such tribe as Bougainville," in order to challenge the claim that there is a cultural or historical basis for an independent Bougainville (Spriggs, 1992: 269).

Why the difficulty in applying concepts of ethnicity in the context of Bougainville, or, more widely, Papua New Guinea and the Melanesian countries? Certainly anthropologists, sociologists, political scientists, and others have increasingly applied this terminology in recent years (e.g., Chowning, 1986 #1599; Larmour, 1992 #1600; Nash and Ogan, 1990; Schwartz, 1975).

·

CONSTRUCTING DIFFERENCE IN MELANESIA

If one uses the term *ethnic group* simply to refer to sociodemographic groupings recognizable in terms of *some* kind of cultural markers, then Melanesia not only has ethnic groups, but it has more than any other region in the world. It is the world capital of multiculturalism, the heartland of ethnic diversity. In fact, the proliferation of small populations of just a few thousand linguistically distinct people has become one of the hallmarks of the region, a defining characteristic that has lured legions of anthropologists, linguists, and missionaries to the area since the early part of the twentieth century. Papua New Guinea alone, with its population of four million people, is home to over 750 language groups, one-third of the world's total. For the Solomon Islands and its 500 thousand people, the language count is eighty-seven.

If in fact social and political commentators in Melanesia do not regularly employ the language of ethnicity, why not? One reason is that the most common forms of self-identification in Melanesia rarely align the kinds of signifiers commonly associated with ethnicity in pluralistic, industrialized economies. Even the marker of group identity most favored by academic observers — language — is only one of numerous forms of collective self-identification in this region today. Consider some of the complexity typical of Melanesian communities, with examples from the island of Santa Isabel where I have worked periodically over the past twenty years.

The island of Santa Isabel, one of the largest in the Solomon Islands, is home to about 25 thousand people and five major language groups (figure 7.1). About one-half of the population speak a language that is referred to with several different names. When I first began working on the island in 1975 I found this situation confusing, given my expectations of a more orderly one-to-one relationship between language, geographic locale, and group name. Yet in the area where I was living, the most common name used to refer to the language is *Maringe*, a term that refers to both geographic locale and language. Yet, only a portion of the speakers of this language reside in Maringe. Nearly half reside on the other side of the island, where they refer to the language in other ways, including the name for their district, *Hograno*. Maringe and Hograno are the same language, yet the different place-names are commonly used to refer to the language and to the people in these respective regions. Thus, people of Maringe speak the same language as Hograno people on the other side of the island, engage in the same kind of (Anglican) religious practices as people all over the island, and include descent groups that often have closer links to people outside the area than inside.[3]

What, then, *are* the most salient criteria for self-identification in this region? At the most local level, identities that are associated with land, locale, and descent lines are especially meaningful. Orientations to both place and ancestry are indexed by connections with land — connections once marked by ancestral shrines that dotted the landscape. As landowning entities, descent groups are in many ways the foundation for collective identity making, linking both social space and genealogical time. Yet these groupings are small, a fact reflected in the relatively shallow memory for genealogy characteristic of the region. Larger named collectivities are generally associated with place, especially places of residence.

Historically, such regional groupings have existed in a field of exchange relations, where collective identities are expressed most vividly in ritualized transactions between neighboring groups. With changes in exchange practice and the formation of larger villages in the early decades of this century, villages became an important locus of identification. And when the larger islands were made into governmental administrative units in the 1940s and 1950s ("districts," then "provinces"), these began to acquire greater social meaning as well. Today, islands that had no single name prior to European exploration (such as "Santa Isabel") have become significant sites of collective identity.

The most recent large-scale group conflicts in the Solomon Islands involve precisely these forms of island identity — between people from the islands of Malaita

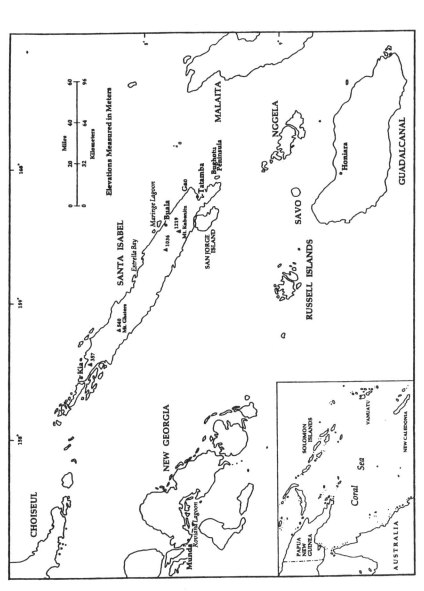

Figure 7.1   Santa Isabel and the western Solomon Islands.

and Guadalcanal, where the national capital, Honiara, is located. In this case, a wide range of unresolved grievances among landowning groups in Guadalcanal, combined with long-simmering conflicts between migrants from Malaita settling in the capital district (frequently in "squatter" settlements), led to increasing acts of violence on Guadalcanal through 1998 and 1999, climaxing in an armed overthrow of the elected government in June 2000.[4] As the conflict escalated, it bred the formation of two armed militias—one (the Isatabu Freedom Movement or IFM) claiming to represent Guadalcanal landowners and the other (the Malaita Eagle Force or MEF) formed in response, claiming to protect Malaitan residents of settlements on Guadalcanal. Initially, the emergence of small groups of militants on Guadalcanal, armed with shotguns, homemade weapons, and even old World War II arms, called themselves the Guadalcanal Liberation Army, modeled after the resistance army inn Bougainville located across the border with Papua New Guinea to the north.[5] By late 1999, the tensions had escalated to a stage where at least fifty people had been killed and more than twenty thousand people (mostly Malaitans) forced out of settlements on Guadalcanal.

Here again, media reporting on these conflicts uses the language of ethnicity and "ethnic war" even though the terms *Malaita* and *Guadalcanal* are island names and not ethnic groups. These names are products of colonial history that gradually have become salient terms for collective identity during the twentieth century. In this instance, the conflicts involve struggles between landowners and urban migrants, settling in large numbers in the capital district to pursue wage labor. The conflict resulted as much from failures of national urban policy and the incapacities of provincial and state governments as from "ethnic hatreds." Yet, true to the paradigm of ethnic war set out by the *New York Times* in 1993, this is the concept that framed global reporting on the Guadalcanal conflict. On June 20, 1999, a front-page article appeared in the *Honolulu Advertiser* under the headline "Civil War Threatens Solomon Islands," with the subtitles "Ethnic Trouble Rises" and "Old Hatreds Boil on Guadalcanal." The second sentence stated, "The main island of the Solomon Islands is in danger of becoming engulfed in an ethnic civil war." Later, after providing useful information about the land and population pressures around the capital, the article gives background on the country by saying, "they are a fiercely divided people with 70 distinct languages. In the old days neighbors seldom got along." The article then goes on to construct the words *Malaita* and *Guadalcanal* as ethnic categories, while noting "it is hard to distinguish a Malaitan from a Guadalcanal" (A9). Here the use of "a Guadalcanal" exposes the attempt of reporters to render the conflict meaningful in terms of ethnicity and ethnic conflict. For conflict to be interpreted as *ethnic* conflict, there must be "ethnic groups" or ethnic identities aligned in antagonistic hostilities. Reporters and their readers can more easily make a good story by appealing to easily understood story lines—those built around characters locked in irrational intergroup (ethnic) antagonisms. If the categories and language do not exist, they will be invented to service the discursive needs of the model. Whereas the term *Malaitan* is widely used (largely in the context of the migrant communities in Guadalcanal and elsewhere), the term *a Guadalcanal* is rarely heard (e.g., "a Guadalcanal" or "the Gaudalcanal"). Other tems such as *Guale*, a shortened name for "person from Guadalcanal" or the name for the Guadalcanal militia, Isatabu Freedom Movement (IFM), are emerging, rendered useful by a conflict that increasingly demands labels for oppositional identities represented on a national scale. Thus, some foreign writers have transformed the made-up term for the Guadalcanal militia, Isatabu Freeedom Movement, into a label for peoplehood: *Isatabus.* For example, a recent CNN article on the suspension of peace talks referred to the earlier expulsion of Malaitans: "Pushing them out were indigenous Guadalcanal residents, known as Isatabus. The well-armed fighters from Malaita have kept control of Honiara while the Isatabus, a ragtag group armed mostly with homemade weapons and often dressed only in loincloths, hold most areas of Guadalcanal outside the city."

Similar to the model advanced in the *New York Times* article discussed earlier, international reporting on the Solomon Islands conflict has consistently represented events there in the language of ethnicity. A particularly clear example is an article of the BBC published on June 7, 2000, reporting the armed coup that took the prime minister hostage and deposed the elected government. The headline, "Ethnic tension behind Solomons coup," was followed by the statement, "Ethnic rivalry is a key factor behind the coup in the Solomon Islands, just as it is in Fiji. The dispute has sprung out of a power struggle and a bitter fight over land and resources between the two ethnic groups from the main islands of Guadalcanal and Malaita." The reference to "the two ethnic groups" is entirely imaginary. The populations of Guadalcanal and Malaita are made up of multiple language groups, some of which are more closely related to each other than to other groups on the same island. Yet, attempting to bolster the "ethnic" story, the article asserts, "Physically, Malaitans look the same as people from Guadalcanal, both groups being Melanesian. But they speak completely different languages and have distinct cultures."

Perhaps the most accurate terms used to describe the protagonists in the current struggle are the names for the two opposed militias: the Malaita Eagle Force (MEF) and the Isatabu Freedom Movement (IFM). The conflict is in fact between armed forces, assembled from a variety of constituencies, not entire "peoples." Initially, the Guadalcanal crisis was a conflict between the state and Guadalcanal militants. However, with the emergence of a Malaita militia (the MEF), the struggle took on more of the characteristics of "ethnic war." With time and the growth of popular support for the militants, the "Guadalcanal Liberation Army" name was dropped in favor of the Isatabu Freedom Movement, reflecting an indigenous sense of place, the "sacred mother" of the land.

As in the case of Fiji, where a national political crisis has worked to further "ethnicize" conflicts there, the current Solomon Islands crisis is also working to define conflicts as "ethnic war." The more the conflict is represented in this way, the more other sources of conflict and hostility are elided. As Solomon Islands scholar Tarcisius Kabutaulaka wrote in the May 2000 *Pacific News Bulletin,*

So far, the public media, government officials and commentators on the crisis have taken the easiest explanation and described it as simply a result of ethnic differences between the peoples of Guadalcanal and Malaita. But while ethnicity should not be completely disregarded, there is a need to situate the crisis within the context of broader socio-economic and political developments rather than as merely a result of "hatred" between the peoples of two islands.

. . .there is a need to look beyond ethnicity as the only cause of the crisis. We must explore the socio-economic and political issues that underlie the issues raised by the various actors in the crisis. . . . Ethnicity is merely the avenue through which people's frustration becomes manifested.

Because of the dense elaboration of cultural and linguistic difference in this region, *inter*cultural relations have long been a feature of social life. In the past, many people were multilingual and developed networks of relations that spanned several linguistic, cultural, and geographic regions. Given these patterns of cultural differentiation, with descent groups, language groups, and regional groupings arrayed in a patchwork of overlapping alliances and animosities, what would it mean to privilege language or any other feature as a fixed determinant of "ethnic" identity? A more interesting question would ask how particular identities acquire significance in the context of national politics.

Even as anthropologists and political scientists ponder the lack of obvious *cultural* bases for national unity in Melanesia's new states (Jourdan, 1995; Lindstrom, 1998), indigenous scholars have suggested a number of answers, including notions of "unity in diversity" and forms of integration that emerge from historical experience (Simet and Iamo, 1992). Recent events have shown that fissiparous forces can easily take a violent turn in Melanesian countries today. Nonetheless, the case of Bougainville is the only sustained separatist movement that has posed a serious threat to national unity. Given the degree of cultural differentiation in the region, why have there not been more conflicts based on specifically "ethnic" divisions?

One of the reasons that the language of ethnicity was slow to come to Melanesia is that its genealogy descends from industrialized states where ethnic identities are associated specifically with *minority* status in the context of minority-majority relations (Gladney, 1998). Much of the discourse of ethnicity in modern nation–states today concerns the bureaucratic codification of minority rights in the face of disparities of population and power characteristic of minority/majority relations. In such contexts, the term *ethnic* is associated with marginality, such that minority cultures are marked as distinctively "ethnic," while unmarked majority forms remain invisible (Dominguez, 1995).

In Melanesia, the proliferation of linguistic and regional differences mitigates against the ethnicization of the state that occurs when a single, dominant cultural group controls the apparatus of government. In the absence of any single dominant culture, it is less likely that ethnic antagonisms will translate into institutionalized forms of dominance and marginalization. This is essentially the argument put forward by Papua New Guinean writer Bernard Narokobi, author of *The Melanesian Way*. In that volume, he writes, "PNG maintained a fine sociological balance based not on large nation states, but on small communal autonomy. Some people call this disunity, anarchy, even chaos. I say it is an aspect of unity, because no one group can claim on the basis of its technology that it is better or superior to another" (1983: 19). What Narokobi is writing *against* here is another unifying force: colonialism.

Narokobi is arguing that cultural proliferation in the absence of marked forms of ethnic domination may even facilitate national unity. To the extent that this might be so, the same logic may be extended even further to supranational formations, such as the regional identity "Melanesian." During the postwar, postcolonial period, the notion of "Melanesian" identity has attained an increasingly visible cultural reality, especially among English-speaking elites in the nations of Papua New Guinea, Solomons Islands, and Vanuatu. It is expressed philosophically in Narokobi's somewhat romanticized "Melanesian way" and politically in a variety of contexts such as the alignment of these nations in a regional interest bloc referred to as the "Melanesian Spearhead Group" (MSG). The MSG has provided a regional forum for establishing trade links and other forms of cooperation, including a common position on the decolonization of New Caledonia and sponsorship of a Melanesian Arts Festival in 1998. Whereas Narokobi sees Melanesian identity as a *prior* cultural unity that was fragmented by the imposition of artificial colonial divisions (1983: 20),[6] it is also possible to see Melanesian identity as a regional formation made possible by colonization and nationalization as they have fostered new rhetorics of commonality.

With the arrival of European explorers, traders, missionaries, and colonial agents, an important shift occurred in the local cultural imaginary. These outsiders used new technologies and cultural practices to establish relations of dominance coded in cultural categories such as European/Native, white/black, 'master'/'boy,' and so forth. These categories cut across and subsumed many of the "ethnic" differences that characterized local group relations. One of the most significant developments in this colonial border zone was the emergence of a regional lingua franca, Melanesian Pidgin, comprehensible in Papua New Guinea, Solomon Islands, and Vanuatu. As a language of convenience that grew up on plantations and ships where Melanesians recruited from different areas found themselves thrown together, Pidgin became a sign of, and vehicle for, common "native" identity.

It is this oppositional relation of foreign and native (or colonizer and colonized) that forms a major fault line in Melanesian national and regional identity making today. Having said this, it is important to note that there are also important forces of identification that crosscut this binary. One of the most significant is Christianity, a potent force for religious and sociopolitical transformation that has been widely influential, obtaining the status of state religion in Fiji, the Solomon Islands, and Vanuatu. Although numerous communities have resisted Christianity, primarily in Papua New Guinea, Christian practices are now widely viewed as an element of indigenous tradition.

More than descent, language, or place, the sense of being indigenous or "native" provides some of the core meanings of national identity in Melanesia today (Foster, 1995; Otto and Thomas, 1997). In local parlance in many parts of Melanesia, native culture is signified with the Pidgin *kastom*, "custom," — a term that refers to local traditions, particularly those that predate European arrival. These include practices such as ancestor worship, sorcery, chiefly leadership, and various technologies and artifacts associated with subsistence activities such as gardening, fishing, and house building. The production of self-conscious ideologies of custom as markers of collective identity has been widely discussed in writings on the politics of tradition and nationalism in the region (e.g., Foster, 1995; Jolly and Thomas, 1992; Keesing and Tonkinson, 1982; Otto and Thomas, 1997; White and Lindstrom, 1993). The next section of this chapter takes a look at some of the images of native culture and traditions that emerge in these national cultural productions in Melanesia today.

FROM "THE TRANSFORMED ISLES" TO "ISLANDS LOST IN TIME"

From the earliest moments of colonization to the present, "tradition" and "custom" have been powerful idioms of collective identity. In postcolonial Melanesia, discourses of tradition may be found inscribed in such official texts as the Preamble to the Papua New Guinea constitution: "We, the people of Papua New Guinea, pay homage to the memory of our ancestors—the source of our strength and origin of our common heritage: acknowledge the worthy customs and traditional wisdoms of our people which have come down to us from generation to generation."

Given the cultural diversity of Papua New Guinea, how does the voice of the national body, the "we" of Papua New Guinea, obtain relevance for ordinary citizens? One answer lies in commonalties that emerge in the context of colonial history. While specific linguistic and cultural practices may vary sharply from one region to the next, the political and economic situation of small-scale indigenous communities caught up in wider systems of colonial power provide a broad story line for shared history. Narratives of transformation from traditional past to modern present have broad resonance across widely disparate regions in Melanesia today (Foster, 1995; Otto and Thomas, 1997). So, for example, many local communities regularly tell stories of conversion to Christianity that constitute a kind of creation mythology representing the origins of today's religious culture (White, 1991). On the surface, such stories often seem to resemble earlier mission narratives of salvation, with their motifs of "heathen darkness" and "Christian light." However, upon closer inspection, local histories of colonization and conversion often tell tales of appropriation and resistance that are as much about transforming Christianity as about changing local traditions.

What happens as local traditions are elevated to the status of national culture, especially in the context of wider flows of culture and capital in the international arena? Consider two examples from the Solomon Islands: a documentary film produced for the purpose of promoting the country as a tourist destination; and a magazine published under the auspices of the Solomon Islands mission to the United Nations for purposes of tourism promotion and introducing the country to foreign investors. In both cases, images of *tradition*, of indigenous culture as it might be imagined prior to European contact, are the central trope for national self-representation. In contrast to the robust forms of blending evident in local appropriations and combinations of custom, modernity, and Christianity, these official constructions present a more purified, static picture of tradition. By implication, the imagined universe of tradition is more readily cast as separate from, and threatened by, forces of modernization and economic change. These national constructions of tradition reflect Arif Dirlik's concept of "hegemonic culturalism," which "abstracts culture from its social and political context in order to present it as an autochthonous attribute of entire groups and people that is exterior to, and independent of, social relationships" (1990: 424).

Like many nations rich in natural and cultural resources, but lacking in the economic infrastructure necessary to build its own industries, the Solomon Islands has been actively seeking to expand its tourism economy. As part of that effort the Tourism Council of the South Pacific, headquartered in Fiji, assisted the national tourist authority in producing a documentary film about the country for tourist markets. The film is titled *Ocean of Dreams, Currents of Change* (1990), and was made by an Australian film team. Overall, this documentary does a remarkable job of packing information about the contemporary Solomons into a visually appealing narrative presenting a geocultural destination worthy of the tourist imagination. As a film made by outside interests for foreign audiences, however, it inevitably reproduces many of the essentialized images of traditional island cultures that have long circulated among curious audiences in foreign lands.

In this case, the (self-)orientalizing of national agencies does not come in the form of *exclusive* images of palm trees, coral seas, and natives in tune with nature, with evidence of the "taint of civilization" edited out. To the contrary, rather than romanticize the Solomons as a tropical idyll untouched by the corrupting influences of civilization, the film presents the nation's traditional culture through its contrast with forces of modernization and development. Visions of national culture emerge in the film's historical narrative. But the history so imagined seems to flow around these islands of tradition, perhaps eroding their metaphorical beaches, but otherwise leaving them distinct and separate from modernizing influences.

The title of the film, *Oceans of Dreams, Currents of Change*, signifies the counterpoint of (natural) tradition versus a more historically contingent process of modernization. This counterpoint is established in the opening scenes of the film with the juxtaposition of tropical paradise-like scenery with scenes of modernization.

The juxtaposition underscores the fragility and value of indigenous culture and sets up the central problematic of national identity as that of pursuing development while maintaining and protecting long-standing traditions.

The film begins with views of tranquil ocean settings accompanied by the kind of romantic commentary one would expect in film scripted for the purposes of tourist promotion:

> The South Pacific Ocean
> The exotic setting for many a dream
> Paradise on Earth

But in the 1980s and 1990s it is difficult to sustain images of "paradise" without an immediate insertion of irony. People everywhere, especially tourists predisposed to find inauthenticity, know that there are no more unspoiled paradises in today's globalized, interconnected world. And, indeed, this film does not attempt to create one. To the contrary, it moves quickly from its opening images of tropical waters to set up a critical tension with modernizing influences ("currents of change"). After a glimpse of Polynesian dancers performing in front of a thatched house with a volcanic mountain backdrop, the film cuts to shots of teenage youth, video games, and a television/VCR playing a Rambo movie. Carrying on its metaphor of "heavenly paradise," the film describes these tokens of familiar popular culture as "earthly challenges":

> [scene: traditional dancers:]
> Certainly there is a heavenly touch about these islands
>
> [scene: teenagers, TV/video:]
> But some very earthly challenges are facing its inhabitants.

The film's narrator characterizes these dual aspects of Solomon Islands life as a "balancing act" between valued traditions and desired economic advancement: "The people of young island states are trying to perform an extremely difficult balancing act: that of bringing about economic development while still maintaining the essence of their traditional cultures and values." These lines are accompanied by more oppositional images, switching from a dock crane to a feathered chief followed by scenes of traditional reef fishing.

The film frames the touristic appeal of the Solomons in images that merge natural beauty with valuable (but threatened) indigenous cultures. In doing so, it intersperses scenes of the natural environment with icons of traditional culture, as in cutting between island scenes and shots of people in native dress performing various kinds of customary activities. The result is a traditional culture that is as natural as it is timeless. Thus, at one point we see a group of paddlers paddling a traditional style "war canoe" with elaborate shell decoration, and the narrator explains, "The first reports to reach Europe about these remote islands were made by the Spanish explorer Alvaro Mendaña who visited the islands in 1568. He described how the inhabitants were using war canoes for their headhunting raids." Without any explanation that the style of canoe shown in film had completely disappeared before several development grants designed to revive traditional culture financed the construction of several new ones, the viewer might be pardoned for inferring that these "headhunting" canoes are part of the continuous stream of tradition that dates back to 1568 and beyond.

As traditional cultural practices have gained more public recognition as a valued resource, they have also been defined in more exclusionary terms as separate from "economic development." One of the consequences of this sort of dichotomization is that narratives of *economic* development are easily rephrased as narratives of *cultural* deterioration. The story line of modernization (or Westernization) threatening vulnerable indigenous cultures is now a common theme everywhere, not only in national self-representations but in global discourse of all kinds. The more that indigenous culture is portrayed as fixed, bounded tradition, the more contemporary influences and "development" are construed as sources of erosion or corruption.

Narratives of decline are by no means new. In fact, they are in many ways descendants of earlier narratives of culture contact and modernization that were also organized around the binary opposition of indigenous tradition and Western modernity. The major difference today, as mentioned earlier, is the revaluation of tradition that inverts this moral polarity. So, for example, where missionary narratives of conversion and salvation once literally demonized indigenous practices as "dark" heathenism, today's discourses of development and tourism have recast traditional practices as an endangered national resource. Today's narratives are about the recovery and revalorization of indigenous practices, rather than about their replacement or modernization.

As a brief illustration, compare the tourist film just discussed with an earlier silent film made in 1920 by the Methodist Missionary Society of Australasia to promote the work of the mission among foreign audiences (see Thomas, 1991). Separated by a span of seventy years, both films originate in the intercultural border zones where the peoples and cultures of the Solomon Islands are represented for distant audiences. Despite the massive sociopolitical transformations that have occurred during the twentieth century, the discourse of the "native" has remained surprisingly stable, reinforced by the same decontextualizing practices that once produced anthropology's "ethnographic present" (Fabian, 1983). One of the most notable examples of the production of images of the "native" in big-screen Hollywood cinema is the recent Academy Award–winning film *The Thin Red Line,* Terrence Malick's production of James Jones's World War II novel set in Guadalcanal. Although accounting for only a few minutes of script time, depictions of native life in a Guadalcanal vilage perform an important symbolic function, framing the film's dream reverie of tropic paradise and subsequent falling from grace. Images of the "native," like "nature," stand in for a kind of idyllic, Rousseauian life not yet caught up in the horrors of war, only to be tainted by the end of the film.

Only thirty minutes in length, the Methodist Mission documentary is an extraordinary example of the early use of (silent) film to project identity images, in this case depicting contrastive images of the "dark," violent life of the past and the "light," peaceful life said to have come with Christianity. The full title of the film captures its message of transformation: *The Transformed Isle: Barbarism to Christianity, a Genuine Portrayal of Yesterday and Today, the Story of Fifteen Years among the Head Hunters of the Island of Vella Lavella*. Here the moral drama of cultural encounter is framed in a manner that maximizes the contrast between indigenous and European.

Lest the film's rhetorical techniques be dismissed as a quaint production of a bygone missionary era, its binary tropes of "darkness and light," of "old ways and new ways," and of "heathenism and Christianity" have been incorporated widely in local historiographies and are reproduced in various ways in today's Christian communities (Burt, 1994; Hereniko, 1994; White, 1991). Indeed, the strong identification with Christianity in many Solomon Islands communities and the narratives of conversion that support that identification provide an important basis for today's positive readings of "development" and desires for education and social change. However, whereas the missionary film builds its narrative on sharply exclusionary images of (violent) custom and (peaceful) Christianity, local accounts of conversion tell a far more complex story of appropriation and incorporation of Christian practice *into* customary practices (White, 1991).

For the purposes and projects of the Methodist Mission in the Solomon Islands at the turn of the twentieth century, it was the exclusionary, sharply binary imagery of "heathen" and "Christian" that was most effective. Although one segment of the film reviews a variety of traditional practices (such as making shell money) in positive terms ("more artistic sense than any other aboriginal race"), the social and moral attributes of the past life are completely subsumed within the narrative of religious conversion and pacification. The film begins with a reenactment of a headhunting raid that, together with its rituals, becomes the signifier of an entire race. The scene is introduced with a caption that summarizes the cultural character of the society in question, Vella Lavella: "The Vella Lavellans were a cruel, crafty, vicious race. They were cannibalistic head hunters and were numbered amongst the most bloodthirsty savages in the Pacific." It then proceeds with a series of portrait shots of renowned cannibal chiefs, such as "Chief Gau — Most fiendish of all South Sea cannibals." This portrait and the scenes of mayhem that follow as canoes full of bloodthirsty headhunters descend on an unsuspecting village set up the ensuing contrast with the peaceful life of the present, depicted at the end of the film. The captions that introduce the final portion of the film continually invoke oppositions of past/present and heathen/Christian to narrate a story of progress. (The narrative is further punctuated with questions such as, "Is it worth it?" implying the need for more funding to expand the work of the mission. For example,

Today the island of Vella Lavella is Christian in character and in social custom throughout the length and breadth of it.

From crafty cruel headhunters of human prey the natives have become a happy industrious Christian people.

As the film continues in this contrapuntal mode, it uses visual contrasts to narrate a story of transformation by juxtaposing a scene of headhunters dancing around a pile of skulls with one of young Christian men dressed in white waistcloths standing at attention outside a church. These scenes are captioned with the proclamation:

> YESTERDAY—A CANNIBAL
> HEAD HUNTER.
> TODAY—A CHRISTIAN
> GENTLEMAN.

Motifs of darkness and light typify a vast amount of colonial discourse of the "native" and the civilizing effects of colonization. Over time, they have also been incorporated in local histories that often formulate Christianity as a feature of *indigenous* identity (White, 1991).[7] In the next section of this chapter, I argue that representations of national culture that rely on essentializing rhetorics of the "native" have significant consequences for imagined scenarios of change and "development."

In 1994, the Solomon Islands, through its United Nations mission, contracted a publishing company to publish a special issue of its magazine, *U.S. World Journal*, profiling the social and economic situation of the Solomon Islands. The company concerned, U.S. World Journal Publishing and Printing Enterprises, describes itself as "a diversified, international communications company specializing in Emerging Nations–Third World magazine publishing & information news network services, promotional printing, private sector development liaison services." The Solomon Islands issue probably typifies formats used to represent nonwestern ("Third World") societies for foreign investment audiences in many areas. The Solomon Islands ambassador to the United Nations summed up the aim of the publication as follows:

> To the more adventurous traveler, Solomon Islands offers a unique, untouched alternative destination to the South Pacific. To the prospective investor, this magazine introduces the potential opportunities that exist on an island environment like the Solomons. . . . With its beautiful tropical environment, peaceful and friendly people, stable political and business climate, Solomon Islands promises an exotic magical place for both tourists and business investors. The Permanent Mission of Solomon Islands to the United Nations will be pleased to assist anyone with a serious interest in the country.

Following this introduction, the magazine goes on to lay out a wide variety of information about the Solomon Islands, interspersing sections on culture and history with sections on economic outlook and conditions for investment. The magazine devotes somewhat less space to representing present-day economic opportunities than to social and cultural aspects of the Solomon Islands. "Culture" in this publication is presented narrowly as *traditional* culture, suggesting that it is the indigenous or the traditional that has currency when national identities are constructed for purposes of international consumption.

In focusing on *traditional* culture, the magazine highlights pre-European artifacts, styles, and practices to the exclusion of Christianity, sports, popular music, and other innovations that are central elements of cultural life today. The dominant message that the Solomon Islands is home to interesting *native* cultures is carried especially forcefully in the magazine's many color photographs. Its cover is emblazoned with four photos arranged in a geometric diamond shape showing traditional body decoration (two of these), a traditional carving, and a young man in a canoe holding a fish he has caught. The captions for these photos read as follows:

"Proud looking Santa Cruz Chief in traditional tribal costume, Temotu Province"

"Young Malaitan girl wearing shell money, part of her traditional ceremonial dress"

"Elaborately wood carved, seashell inlaid nguzu-nguzu, Western Province. Sacrifices were made to the nguzu nguzu before raids on neighboring islands"

"Deep sea fishing and world class diving abound in lush tropical waters around Guadalcanal at idyllic Tambea, Tavanipupu and Vulelua Resorts"

The dissonance between these characterizations of Solomon Islands people and the interests of the presumed audience for the magazine is evident in the inscription that appears just below the title: "Southwest Pacific Export/Investment Gateway into Emerging Asian Pacific Rim Markets." The same contrast is evident as one flips from the front cover with its visual depiction of traditional decorative objects to the back cover with its map of airline routes for the national airline, Solomon Airlines, connecting Solomon Islands with Australia, New Zealand, and other Pacific countries.

The counterpoint of images of pre-European tradition, on the one hand, and the country's modern economic infrastructure, on the other, continues throughout the magazine. Immediately following messages from the Solomon Islands U.N. ambassador and prime minister, the text begins its substantive presentation with a colorful page titled "Historical-Cultural Kaleidoscope View of Solomon Islands: Ancient Indigenous Historical Heritage; Vibrant Traditional Cultural Life."[8] Turning from this page with its traditional dancers dressed in leaves and loincloths, one flips to a section on "Solomon Islands Economic Perspective" illustrated with black-and-white photos of a satellite dish, wharf facilities, and a tuna-processing factory. There is, however, little connection between these tradi-

tionalist and modernist iconographies. The depiction of *people* throughout is rigorously traditionalist, presented consistently in images of cultural practices that
derive from the indigenous past.

One of the reasons for emphasizing the culturally different or exotic is to appeal to a certain kind of tourist market, specifically tourists interested in ecotourism and cultural tourism. This market has been clearly identified in national
development plans and is addressed explicitly in this magazine. In a two-page lay-
out titled "'Pearl of the Pacific': Solomon Islands Touristic Overview: Conserva-
tion/Eco-Tourism and Cultural Tourism," the magazine reviews the opportunities for eco- and cultural tourism. Titled "Islands Lost in Time," the essay states,

> This truly beautiful archipelago is a little known environmentally and culturally un-
> spoiled corner of our planet. Solomon Islands is for a special breed of sophisticated
> traveler. . . .
>   The Solomons may well be the last unspoiled tourist destination in the world, and
> in the hands of a caring Government determined to keep it unspoiled for visitors and
> for her own people. (14)

This section is illustrated with five black-and-white portrait photographs taken at
the turn of the twentieth century of Solomon Islands natives posing in traditional
finery. Even though these photos were taken one hundred years ago, they can easily be interpreted as black-and-white versions of the color photos of present-day
Solomon Islanders who appear, decorated with traditional regalia, on other pages.
Even though the photos are dated 1900 and 1906, the connection is not left to
the imagination. The caption of one shot showing four rather fierce-looking men
reads "Proud Chiefs of Graciosa Bay. Their cultural legacy is actively maintained
today in the Solomons" (15).

The magazine's approach to cultural representation fits comfortably within the
marketing strategies of travel magazines and tourist brochures. The value of culture for tourist markets increases in proportion to its distance from the familiar.
Not surprisingly, then, Solomon Islands national culture is consistently depicted
in images from the pre-Christian past, underlining the message that authentic
culture equals pre-European traditions. The trope of timeless tradition sets up an
inevitable undercurrent of dissonance with those portions of the essay that refer
to sociohistorical transformations. The story of *transformation* once trumpeted by
the Methodist Missionary Society of Australasia is present, but muted. The magazine notes, almost in passing that "About 95% of the population is Christian"
(15). But the cultural significance of this fact is reduced to a kind of "minimal"
impact on customs and traditions: "Customs and traditions are still a major part
of everyday life, even though somewhat minimized by Christianity" (22).

The magazine's historical sketch of changes in Solomon Islands society focuses
primarily on the actions and influences of foreigners, as in a prominent section on
World War II (World War II veterans are a significant but declining sector of the
tourism market). But these historical events do little to alter the magazine's message

of *timeless* culture. References to historical events and changes serve more as a backdrop to heighten the image of tradition as something that persists (even if endangered) in the face of change. Under "Socio-Cultural Notes" the magazine reports that,

> The introduction of a cash economy onto a subsistence economy is causing a number of substantial changes, but the Solomon Islands' way of life, in many ways, remains much that same as it has for hundreds of years. The majority of people continue to live a subsistence way of life, adhering to the extended family system. Most know little about the world outside their own village or island, the majority seldom, if ever, seeing a white person. . . . Few Europeans have had much impact on them. . . . Anthropologists have been regarded with amusement and perhaps slight irritation rather than anything else, the more credulous among them being led to believe all sorts of absurd and untrue tales.
>
> Ages old customs shrouded in mythology, mystery, fear and respect are handed down from one generation to the next, allegedly from the ancestral spirits themselves, to form the cultural values that distinguish Solomon Islands. . . . Customs and traditions are still a major part of everyday life, even though somewhat minimized by Christianity, drift of young people to urban centers and other contemporary influences.
>
> While ancient traditions and customary practices have tended to slowly wane, with the inevitable encroachment of modernity and socio-economic development, the Solomon Islands has steadfastly maintained a vibrant dynamic cultural way of life. Solomon Islanders are keenly aware of their special cultural heritage and traditional Pacific island environment, determined to coexist their customary life in balance with the inherent changes of the modern world. (22)

National interest in constructing cultural identity for global audiences is reflected in the kinds of ministries that have been created to deal with "culture." Typical of many such configurations throughout the postcolonial world, departments of culture in the Melanesian countries became departments of culture and tourism in the 1980s. Papua New Guinea created first the Department of Civil Aviation, Culture and Tourism and then the Department of Culture and Tourism. In Solomon Islands "culture" moved from the Ministry of Education and Culture to the Ministry of Culture, Tourism and Aviation.

The responsibilities bundled together in these departments make it clear that, in the agenda of Melanesian states today, national culture acquires much of its significance in the context of international flows of capital and people. In Papua New Guinea (PNG), anthropologist Wari Iamo has described the emphases of national cultural policy as folklorizing its approach to culture by emphasizing only artistic artifacts and performances to the exclusion of other dimensions. Referring to a Five Year Cultural Development Plan (1990–94) put together by the Department of Culture and Tourism, Iamo writes that, when the PNG government placed responsibility for cultural policy under the "commercially oriented" Tourism Corporation, culture was identified "as performing arts, visual arts, crafts and national heritage, and omits a wide variety of areas, such as religious systems, rituals and magic, architecture, prehistoric sites, food/agriculture, customs and traditions, laws and social organization" (Iamo and Simet, 1998: 201). When the Solomon Islands Ministry published a three-year "Programme of Action" in 1995 it listed eleven points. The first four were concerned with the country's airline—a large investment, which is dependent on filling seats with foreign travelers.

In the dichotomous world created in these representations of tradition, one need only turn the prism through which Westerners view island cultures, and the "traditional" easily becomes simply the "impoverished" or "underdeveloped." For example, an article on the front page of the *Los Angeles Times* in 1995 (reprinted in the *Honolulu Advertiser,* 19 March 1995 under the banner headline "HEART OF PACIFIC AWASH IN POVERTY: Island States Caught in a Vicious Cycle" [with a sidebar titled "Troubles in Paradise"]) describes the plight of small island states plagued with stagnant economies and rapid population growth. With brief mention of colonial history, the article locates the cause of contemporary economic problems in poor education and governmental mismanagement.

It is likely that the readers who pay attention to such articles retain only the barest impressions of tiny Third World nations in trouble. In all likelihood, the photograph that accompanied the article in the Honolulu paper left more of an impression than the article itself. The photo is the same type as those used throughout the U.S. *World Journal* magazine discussed previously, showing a young girl adorned with shell money decoration. The caption read simply, "A 15-year old Solomon Island girl is decorated in traditional shell money and coral jewelry." This might seem a curious choice to illustrate an article that discusses rapacious logging, illiteracy, bureaucratic corruption, and "doomsday" economic scenarios. However, as an icon of "timeless traditions" set in opposition to rational economic development, the photo offers its own subtext, possibly even an explanation: given the radical separation of culture and modern economic practice, one might surmise that economic failure somehow follows from deep cultural differences.

Here the risks of projecting essentialized images of tradition in contexts of global economic transactions are obvious. Land policies connected with economic development tend to divorce "customary" practices from the needs of a rational market economy. In 1994 the Bank of Hawaii announced that it had acquired 51 percent interest in the National Bank of Solomon Islands, extending its presence in the "neighborhood" of the Pacific Islands. In the fall of 1994 the bank released a report titled "Economic Assessment of the Solomon Islands," in which it reviewed various sectors of economic activity, including agriculture, fishing, logging, and tourism. It concluded with comments on the local system of land tenure (one of the core tenants of local "custom") and the need to make changes if development is to make progress in the future. The report contrasts the "communal system" (that does not allow alienation of land and frequently involves conflicting claims of ownership) with the need to acquire or lease land for development ("economic change and growth"):

Concern over land preservation as a source of sustenance is both legitimate and understandable in the Solomon Islands. As in other small island countries, land and the surrounding ocean are virtually the community's only resources. . . . Access and title to these lands (desirable for "higher and better" uses) should play a critical role in the development of alternative sources of income, both in and outside tourism. . . .

To the extent that doing nearly anything to generate new income requires secure and certain access to land in the Solomon Islands, it will be essential to find a practical solution to the problem of uncertain land titles. The principle advantages of a market-like land system would be both efficiency and certainty that would aid the process of economic change and growth. (Bank of Hawaii, 1994: 16)

Here prevailing conceptions of culture lie just beneath the surface, tending to disconnect local cultural practices from assessments of economic change. The image of customary land, enmeshed in traditions separated from the institutions of modern-day development, sets up the inference that modern economic growth will depend upon setting aside the uncertain and conflicting claims to land titles, to allow for an efficient process of "economic change and growth." The same kinds of images of "custom" that attract tourists to see an "unchanging" world "lost in time" augur for an approach to large-scale development (logging, mining, hotel construction, plantations) that brackets serious engagement with indigenous practices. Despite the difficulties of obtaining "certain" access to land for economic development, the logging industry in the Solomon Islands has developed at such a fast pace that some estimates project that the archipelago will be completely depleted of primary forests by 2010.

Whereas earlier mission and government agents of colonization once represented the transition from traditional past to modern (Christian) present as a narrative of enlightenment made possible by education and modernization, today's discourse of "development" is more contested, clouded by ambivalent readings of modernity with its failed promises of steady economic improvement. In this context, references to the "traditional," "tribal," and "native" have obtained new, more positive readings, projected in national discourses of tradition that have been used constructively for a variety of purposes, including education and tourism development. But the essentializing practices evident in these national productions also set disabling limits on the kinds of social, political, and economic relationship that can emerge between local constituencies, state agencies, and international flows of global capital.

As a final consideration of the ways persistent discourses of the "native" continue to inform representations of today's political crises in the Solomons, consider an example of reporting from one of the major regional news sources, the *Sydney Morning Herald.* Just two weeks after the elected government was ousted by armed militia in June 2000, at the very moment when the Solomon Islands government had collapsed and the political fabric was being torn apart by violent struggles, the *Herald* ran a lead story titled, "Centuries-old culture confronts a strange modern world" (anonymous 2000). The article said almost nothing about the ongoing crisis, but instead focused on (timeless?) cultural practices of the last remaining non-Christian groups located in the remote mountains of Malaita Island. Reproducing a centuries-old fascination with headhunting, the article noted that "In the old days, they used to take enemy heads and keep them in bamboo containers or wrapped in bark," adding (erroneously) that "Headhunting was practised until the 1940s." When the article did, briefly, make reference to the current crisis, it did so by extending its images of (uncivilized) native culture, explaining that "The dispute on Guadalcanal, where Honiara is, centres on political manoeuvrings that exploit the remnants of what were once warrior cultures and highly emotional attachments to land." In this manner, Solomon Islands political and economic conflicts, like Bosnia or Rwanda, are rendered explicable through models of ethnicity—in this case indigenous or "native" ethnicity—that have informed the (Western) imagination for centuries.

NOTES

1. Numerous writers have suggested that we should think skeptically about the characterization of the conflicts in Bosnia and Rwanda as simply the modern, lethal expression of ancient ethnic animosities. For Rwanda, anthropologist Alex de Waal writes,

> Rwanda has long been known as a true nation in Africa, containing three groups: Twa, Hutu, and Tutsi. . . . The truth is that they were three different strata of the same group, differentiated by occupational and political status. There is some analogy with the Indian caste system, though individuals could and did move between the categories. . . .
>
> Speaking the same language, sharing the same culture and religion, living in the same places, they are in no sense "tribes" nor even distinct "ethnic groups".
>
> Two things enable one to identify an individual as Twa, Hutu or Tutsi: knowledge of the person's ancestry, and the possession of an identity card which, since 1926, has by law specified which group he or she belongs to. The latter is a legacy of Belgian rule: those with ten or more cows were classified as Tutsi, those with less as Hutu. (*Anthropology Today* 10(3) (June 1994) : 1–2)

In the case of Bosnia, Michael Ignatieff writes about the region's religions in much the way de Waal describes ethnicity in Rwanda, noting "traditions of syncretism" which "had developed, over the centuries between the religious traditions in Bosnia. Even in the twentieth century Christian peasants often went to the local mosque, and Muslims took to wearing Christian amulets. . . . the shift from folk Christianity to folk Islam was not very great." Far from being a fatal frontier between the two antithetical civilizations—Christendom and Islam—Bosnia was the place where the two had learned, over five centuries, to understand each other and to coexist.

2. A problem in typology is immediately evident, however, as both of these are listed under the regional grouping for "Asia." Presumably, "Oceania," with its two candidate cases isn't big enough for its own section, so Papua New Guinea and Fiji are part of "Asia." And the one long-running political struggle in the non-English-speaking Pacific, New Caledonia, is not mentioned, even though a large portion of its indigenous population has pursued a vigorous international campaign for independence from France.

3. Of course, as an anthropologist I was eager to standardize these names, disciplining an unruly situation so that it could more easily be coded and communicated in the conventions of anthropological discourse. Fieldwork studies ought to focus on a "culture" or "group" and be generalizable to some bounded social or territorial universe. Regularizing the language name was the first step, even if it meant adopting one that was not at the time in common usage. Eventually, *local choice* of language name was mandated by a church group working on Bible translation, and the place-neutral name of *Cheke Holo* was chosen, a choice that conveniently provided the title for my own dictionary labors—another project that required new forms of authoritative labeling and standardization (White, Kokhonigita, and Pulomana, 1988). To what extent this now enjoys common usage, I am not sure, but anthropologists and linguists now have something to cite as the definitive name for yet another "ethnic group" in Melanesia.

4. Ironically, efforts at international mediation of these conflicts in 1999 were led by former Fijian Prime Minister Sitiveni Rabuka, the very individual who led the armed coups that overthrew the Fiji government in 1987. These efforts, along with numerous other peace negotiations and "summits," failed to resolve the conflicts that culminated in the armed overthrow in 2000.

5. There is a direct link between the war that had been unfolding in Bougainville since 1988 and the events in Guadalcanal a decade later. Specifically, as the killing and death from disease spread on Bougainville, thousands fled into the Solomons, where they generally found sympathetic refuge. It is estimated that up to nine thousand Bougainvillean refugees have moved into the Solomons, mostly to Guadalcanal (Kabutaulaka 2000). The first name chosen for a Guadalcanal militia, the Guadalcanal Liberation Army, reflects their influence on Solomon Island thinking.

6. In this way, Narokobi argued against the Indonesian takeover of the western half of the island of New Guinea as well as against the aspirations of Papuan separatists who sought to retain affiliation with Australia at the time of Papua New Guinea independence in 1975.

7. Consider Narokobi's comments to a church conference that "if Christ were born in Melanesia, he would have said, 'I come not to destroy your customs and values but to make them more perfect'" (1983: 29).

8. Here, the brief text that accompanies photos of more traditional decoration, dancing, and carving slips briefly from its bright promotional language to an earlier European discourse that relied on darker images of difference, saying that the term *Melanesia* "means 'black islands', possibly because of the dark brooding jungles" (4).

REFERENCES

Anonymous. "Ethnic tension behind Solomons coup." BBC news online service. http://
     news6.thdo.bbc.co.uk/hi/english/world/asia%2Dpacific/newsid%5F781000/781735
     .stm. Wednesday, June 7, 2000.
Anonymous. "Centuries-old culture confronts a strange modern world." *Sydney Morning
     Herald.* http://www.smh.com.au/news/. Saturday, 24 June 2000.
Anonymous. "Talks suspended on Solomon Islands cease-fire." http://www.cnn.com/2000/
     ASIANOW/australasia/07/21/solomon.islands.ap/. July 21, 2000.

Bank of Hawaii. "Economic Assessment of the Solomon Islands." Honolulu: Bank of Hawaii, 1994.

Burt, Ben. *Tradition and Christianity: The Colonial Transformation of a Solomon Islands Society*. Chur, Switzerland: Harwood Academic Publishers, 1994.

Chowning, Ann. "The Development of Ethnic Identity and Ethnic Stereotypes on Papua New Guinea Plantations." *Journal de la Societé des Oceanistes* 42 (1986): 153–62.

Dirlik, Arif. "Culturalism as Hegemonic Ideology and Liberating Practice." In *The Nature and Context of Minority Discourse*, edited by D. Lloyd and A. Jan Mohamed. Oxford: Oxford University Press, 1990, 394–431.

Dominguez, Virginia. "Invoking Racism in the Public Sphere." *Identities* 1(4) (1995): 325–46.

Fabian, Johannes. *Time and the Other: How Anthropology Makes Its Object*. New York: Columbia University Press, 1983.

Foster, Robert, ed. *Nation-Making: Emergent Identities in Postcolonial Melanesia*. Ann Arbor: University of Michigan Press, 1995.

Gegeo, David. "Indigenous Knowledge and Empowerment: Rural Development Examined from Within." *The Contemporary Pacific* 10(2) (1998): 289–315.

Gladney, Dru. *Making Majorities: Constituting the Nation in Japan, Korea, China, Malaysia, Fiji, Turkey, and the United States*. Stanford: Stanford University Press, 1998.

Hanlon, David. *Remaking Micronesia: Discourses over Development in a Pacific Territory, 1944–1982*. Honolulu: University of Hawaii Press, 1998.

Hereniko, Vilsoni. "Representations of Cultural Identities." In *Tides of History: The Pacific Islands in the Twentieth Century*, edited by K. Howe, R. Kiste, and B. Lal. Honolulu: University of Hawaii Press, 1994, 406–34.

Huntington, Samuel. *The Clash of Civilizations and the Remaking of World Order*. New York: Simon & Schuster, 1996.

Huntington, Samuel P. "The Clash of Civilizations?" *Foreign Affairs* 72(3) (1993): 22–49.

Iamo, Wari, and Jacob Simet. "Cultural Diversity and Identity in Papua New Guinea: A Second Look." In *From Beijing to Port Moresby: The Politics of National Identity in Cultural Policies*, edited by V. Dominguez and D. Wu. Amsterdam: Gordon and Breach, 1998, 189–204.

Jolly, Margaret, and Nicholas Thomas. "The Politics of Tradition in the Pacific." *Oceania*, Special Issue 62(4) (1992).

Jourdan, Christine. "Stepping-Stones to National Consciousness: The Solomon Islands Case." In *Nation-Making: Emergent Identities in Postcolonial Melanesia*, edited by R. J. Foster. Ann Arbor: University of Michigan Press, 1995, 127–49.

Kabutaulaka, Tarcisius Tara. "Beyond Ethnicity: Understanding the Crisis in the Solomon Islands." Suva: *Pacific News Bulletin:* the monthly magazine of the Nuclear Free and Independent Pacific movement, May 2000.

Kay, Robert. "Fijian Turmoil Goes beyond Racial Politics." *The Honolulu Advertiser*, 16 July 2000, B-1.

Keesing, Roger, and Robert Tonkinson, eds. "Reinventing Traditional Culture: The Politics of Kastom in Island Melanesia." *Mankind*, Special Issue (1982).

Lal, Brij V. *Power and Prejudice: The Making of the Fiji Crisis*. Wellington, New Zealand: Institute of International Affairs, 1988.

———. "Fiji: Damaged Democracy." www.fijilive.com/ May 25, 2000.

Lindstrom, Lamont. "Pasin Tumbuna: Culture and Nationalism in Papua New Guinea." In *From Beijing to Port Moresby*, 141–88.

Linnekin, Jocelyn, and Lin Poyer, eds. *Cultural Identity and Ethnicity in the Pacific*. Honolulu: University of Hawaii Press, 1990.

Narokobi, Bernard. *The Melanesian Way*. Port Moresby: Institute of Papua New Guinea Studies, 1983.

Nash, Jill, and Eugene Ogan. "The Red and the Black: Bougainvillean Perceptions of Other Papua New Guineans." *Pacific Studies* 13(2) (1990):1–17.

Otto, Ton, and Nicholar Thomas, eds. *Narratives of Nation in the South Pacific*. London: Harwood Academic Publishers, 1997.

Regan, Anthony. "Current Developments in the Pacific: Causes and Course of the Bougainville Conflict." *The Journal of Pacific History* 33(3) (1998):269–85.

Schwartz, Theodore. "Cultural Totemism: Ethnic Identity, Primitive and Modern." In *Ethnic Identity: Cultural Continuities and Change*, edited by G. D. Vos and L. Romanucci-Ross. Chicago: University of Chicago Press, 1975, 106–131.

Simet, Jacob, and Wari Iamo. *Cultural Diversity and the United Papua New Guinea*. Boroko, Papua New Guinea: National Research Institute, 1992.

Spriggs, Matthew. "Alternative Prehistories for Bougainville: Regional, National, or Micronational." *The Contemporary Pacific* 4 (1992):269–98.

Teresia Teaiwa. "An analysis of the current political crisis in Fiji." http://pidp.ewc. hawaii.edu/PIReport/2000/May/05–22-up2.htm. May 22, 2000.

Thomas, Nicholas. "Religious and Secular Colonial Discourse: The Methodists in the Solomons, c. 1902–1915." Paper given at meetings of the Association for Social Anthropology in Oceania, 1991.

———. "The Inversion of Tradition." *American Ethnologist* 19 (1992):213–32.

Wesley-Smith, Terence, and Eugene Ogan, eds. "A Legacy of Development: Three Years of Crisis in Bougainville." *The Contemporary Pacific*, Special Issue 4(2) (1992).

White, Geoffrey M. *Identity through History: Living Stories in a Solomon Islands Society*. Cambridge: Cambridge University Press, 1991.

White, Geoffrey M., Francis Kokhonigita, and Hugo Pulomana. *Cheke Holo (Maringe/Hograno) Dictionary*. Volume 97. Canberra: Australian National University, 1988.

White, Geoffrey M., and Lamont Lindstrom. "Custom Today." *Anthropological Forum*, Special Issue 6(4) (1993).

White, Geoffrey M., and Lamont Lindstrom, eds. *Chiefs Today: Traditional Pacific Leadership and the Postcolonial State*. Stanford: Stanford University Press, 1997.

8

The Indigenization of Ethnicity

Elizabeth Rata

INTRODUCTION

The intrusion of global capitalism into local economies and the interaction between the intruding forces and responding local movements have resulted in the
establishment of localized postfordist modes of regulation that structure the capital-labor relationship within the reified communal relations of revivalist social
movements. This chapter discusses the subversion of the local with reference to
the New Zealand experience of the past three decades.

Within the transformation of ethnic social movements in that country, the local response has been subverted by glocal capitalism to the extent that the local
now provides nondemocratic modes of regulation that organize the capital-labor
relation in the depoliticized sites of community. Furthermore, the class exploitative relation between capital and labor, and its nondemocratic regulation outside
the state, are concealed through the neotraditionalist ideology of communality
and revivalism.

The extent of global capitalist intrusion appears to be modified by the very character and strength of local "people power" movements. Certainly, new social movements do appear to have, if not actually triumphed over global intrusion, at least re-
created the global into local versions that seem to maintain both community forms
of social life and the texture of local histories and cultures. However, the New
Zealand experience shows that the revival of communality and tradition may not be
what it seems. Despite the appearance of a revived Maori society, the meaning of
social relations, between people as well as between people and place, has been qual-
itatively altered. Processes that enabled the capitalization of traditional resources,
the use of these resources for commodity production, and the structuring of the relations of production outside the contradictory democratic-capitalist state into
neotribal capitalist modes of regulation have altered the meaning of social relations
and of place in fundamental, though concealed, ways.

I have argued elsewhere (Rata, 1996a, 1999b, 1999c) that the recent Maori re-tribalization movement that developed out of the 1970s' pan-Maori ethnification has led to the emergence of a new form of tribal structure and social organization that is fundamentally different from the traditional tribal form. This emergent regime is conceptualized as a neotribal capital regime of accumulation, resulting both from the capitalization of the traditional means of production, and also from the production of commodities within the new tribal modes of regulation. Neotribal capitalism is characterized by class relations of production concealed by the reified communality of neotraditionalist ideology.

The capitalization mechanisms have been: first, the juridification of the tribes as the owners of traditional lands, waters, and knowledge; second, the brokerage of these traditional resources into the institutions of the capitalist state; third, the subsequent inclusion of these capitalized economic resources into the national and international sphere of wealth circulation; fourth, the exclusive and privileg-ing relationship of a section of Maori (a comprador bourgeoisie) to the capital-ized means of production; and finally, the exclusion and dispossession of detrib-alized ethnic Maori from ownership of the means of production.

The use of the newly capitalized lands, waters, and knowledge for commodity production has resulted in the emergence of exploitative class relations between a new bourgeoisie, located in sites of power and control in the corporate tribal reg-ulatory structures, and a proletarianized worker-in-community class. While com-modity fetishization and surplus-value appropriation common to all capitalist regimes results in division and exploitation, the dual status of the tribal worker, as both wage earner and shareholder in neotribal capitalism, provides a double con-cealment of the exploitative relation of commodity production and its conceal-ment in the reification of communal social relations.

In New Zealand, the response to global intrusion and the resultant emergence of neotribal capitalism has taken an indigenous form. Both Maori and Pakeha[1] sought solutions to the disruptions resulting from the post-1960s capitalist crisis in constructions of indigeneity. The imagining of the ethnic subject as the Maori indigene, or as an ethnic subject (a Pakeha) in relation to the indigene, was to de-fine a new relationship between Maori and Pakeha, and between each group and its geographic and historical place.

Maori and Pakeha exist as ethnic categories in relation to each other.[2] A shared history, structured by nineteenth-century colonization and twentieth-century as-similation, has shaped the identity of each to the other. The most recent expres-sion of reflected identity construction is the indigenization of ethnicity, a new de-velopment in the relationship in which difference rather than similarity is emphasized, particularly difference in relation to place, though still embedded within the older historical self-other construction.

In this new repositioning structured by the concept of indigeneity, Maori were to be both the driving force and the referent. Indeed for a brief period in the 1980s, the term *tangata whenua*, or people of the land, became synonymous with the word

Maori, as the indigenous referent became accepted and used, not only by Maori re-vivalists, but also by Pakeha biculturalists. During this intense, although short-lived, period of commonality of reference, which I refer to as the bicultural project (Rata, 1996c), significant numbers of Maori and Pakeha shared aspirations of a new and more equitable relationship based on the concept of indigeneity. The status of Maori was to shift from that of a subordinate colonized and assimilated group to that of tangata whenua, with the associated rights of priority to place.

Pakeha were to establish their relationship to the land through their relation-ship to Maori. This new repositioning, with Maori as tangata whenua and Pakeha as tangata tirili (people of the treaty), placed Maori in the senior position, as the tuakana, or elder, and Pakeha, the more recent arrival, as the teina, or junior.[3] From the 1975 Treaty of Waitangi Act, the honoring of the 1840 Treaty of Wait-angi[4] through legislative inclusion of the principles of the treaty in government statutes became the structuring principle of the relationship. The Treaty of Wait-angi, within the bicultural period of commonality, was perceived to legitimate the right of Pakeha to occupy New Zealand in a defined relationship with Maori.

This use of the concept of indigeneity to establish belonging to place is a local solution to the destablizing processes and psychological uncertainties that char-acterize globalization. In a world that was rapidly shedding the remnants of old colonial ties and the economic certainties[5] that those ties have provided, Pakeha sought to establish their identity as a people with a particular history and culture through a redefining of their relation to geographical place. For their part, Maori responded to the new economic order with a redefining of their history and ge-ography. The increasing impoverishment of a diminishing and disempowered working class (a class they had recently entered in large numbers during the post-war migration from tribal areas to the rapidly expanding industrializing cities) and the likely future of generational unemployment within the new and growing un-derclass created during New Zealand's free fall into neoclassicist ideological "pu-rity,"[6] initiated a response that empowered and liberated.

The Maori solution was to be the revival of a past identity, the revival of a tribal people with power over their lands, waters, forests, and knowledge and in control of their past and their future. It was to be the rejection of the disempowerment of a colonial heritage and the establishment of a revived society secured within the treaty partnership with Pakeha. The defining of their relation to geographical place was to be the legitimation of that self-determination. Ironically, that process required the recognition of the Pakeha dominant group, who, in turn, required an identity grounded in place and attainable through the new relationship to Maori. The process of a new form of mutual recognition and interdependence became the bicultural project of the 1980s, a project notable for the vigor and commitment of its adherents in its early stages and for the rapidity and silence of its demise in the early 1990s.

Despite the briefness of this period of commonality, the bicultural project is a watershed in New Zealand history. Out of the enabling processes accompanying the political recognition of indigeneity emerged a neotribal capitalist regime of accumulation, a regime characterized by the incorporation of traditional Maori lands, waters, and knowledge into the global economy, by the emergence of new class relations between people and these traditional means of production, and by the concealment of these new class relations of production in the neotraditionalist ideology of communality.

Out of the identity redefining processes emerged a Pakeha bourgeoisie secured by a cultural grounding and a class identity that could then reject the interdependence with Maori. The bicultural project had served purposes very different from those intended by its original adherents. The next section looks at the biculturalists. Who were they? What were their original motives and intentions? How did new structural forms of social organization emerge out of the channeling processes of the juridification and institutionalization of the tribes established by the bicultural project? What was the character of these new tribal modes of regulation? And importantly, why has the ideal of biculturalism based on treaty partnership failed? The second section turns to the Maori identity redefinition in response to changing material conditions; to ethnification, indigenization and retribalization in order to discuss the ways in which these local solutions to global intrusion became reshaped in their enactment, emerging as the modes of regulation of neotribal capitalism. Finally, the concept of the indigenization of ethnicity is demonstrated in a discussion of a research study into a Maori family's revival and retribalization.

THE BICULTURAL PROJECT

Localization in New Zealand cannot be understood outside the particular Maori-Pakeha interdependence of the past three decades. The ways in which Pakeha responded to global capitalism included a reorientation of Pakeha to Maori, with a redefining of the relationship through the establishment of a bicultural project. In turn, the Maori response to global forces was enabled in large measure by the new form of the interdependence. The bicultural project enabled the institutionalization and juridification of Maori indigeneity. This process resulted in the capitalization of the traditional means of production and the recognition of the reviving tribes as the legitimate inheritors of these capitalized economic resources.

The bicultural partnership project was articulated by the phrase *one nation, two peoples*. Within the unity of cultural dualism, Maori were to occupy a special position as the indigenous people of the land. "Maori people are the tangata whenua, the indigenous people of Aotearoa/New Zealand. Their language and culture provide the distinctive character of New Zealand life" (*Tihe Mauri Ora*, 1990: 8). The 1840 Treaty of Waitangi became the emblem of Maori revivalism and Pakeha support for this revivalism. Its guarantee of the rights and privileges of British citizenship to Maori, together with guarantees of continued Maori control of autochthonous lands and other treasures, appeared to offer a structural framework for the ideal of biculturalism. The treaty linked two partners, each to the other, in an agreed unity. Pakeha may indeed have failed to observe the treaty, but this was to be addressed as a necessary part of the bicultural project. Importantly, the guilt was not to be based in the historical reality of conquest and oppression. Instead that status of conqueror, antipathetical to the Pakeha new class's intellectual and democratic heritage, was transferred to a redeemable location in the fulfillment of treaty obligations, albeit a century and a half later.

A nation originating in military conquest and colonial oppression was unacceptable as an explanation for the foundation of nationhood and cultural identity. The bicultural project was to be the solution to this moral dilemma. Pakeha control of New Zealand sovereignty was to be located in treaty agreement. Maori grievances were to be understood as the result of the failure to honor the Treaty of Waitangi, a situation that was to be addressed through specific policies, and not as the result of conquest. This provided the political means for the resolution of the Pakeha new class's guilt, a guilt arising from its intellectual idealism and incorporated into the composition of the new class through the paradox of knowledge as its cultural base and also as its capital commodity.

The atonement of this guilt was the bicultural partnership ideal of the 1980s. It was designed to correct the wrongs of a colonial past and point the way to the "good" society based on "the principles of justice, equity and partnership" (Clark, 1995). Maori people were to be included fully in the life of New Zealand society. In the imagery of the new class's mainly Protestant heritage, the expiation of guilt requires acknowledgment and correction. From such atonement would come the "goodness" that would justify the righteousness. From righteousness would come the legitimation of power. The concept of righteousness provides the link between the dualities of the goodness-power paradox and evokes notions of the "worthiness" that underlies the new class's claims to be the universal class. It is not without significance that the word *atone* is to be found in the apology and acknowledgment of guilt in the Tainui Settlement, "the Crown seeks on behalf of all New Zealanders to atone for these acknowledged injustices" (Article 6, Tainui Settlement).

Emerging out of the Maori cultural renaissance of the 1960s the political development of ethnic revivalism, increasingly textured by the politics of indigenization, had its most significant "moment" in the 1975 Treaty of Waitangi Act. This was the first of many legislative mechanisms for the inclusion of Maori into the structures of the state. Ranginui Walker (1990: 265) refers to the "remarkable elevation in the status of the Treaty in a few years from a 'simple nullity'" to the level of a constitutional instrument in the renegotiation of the relationship between Maori and Pakeha." This inclusion enabled the change from a more generalized demand for the recognition of the cultural distinctiveness of a marginalized and impoverished ethnic group, to demands for the juridification of the tribal structures of social organization. It enabled the recognition of the tribes as the legitimate inheritors of traditional lands, waters, and knowledge and the capitalization of those resources within the sphere of circulation of national and international capitalism. In other words, the repositioning of Maori and Pakeha established the conditions that led to the emergence of neotribal capitalism.

The bicultural project had many faces. The structural inclusion of ethnic Maori, and later tribal Maori, into state institutions at every level of government activity ranged widely across all areas of New Zealand life. Along with the pervasive inclusion of the principles of the treaty into parliamentary legislation and government statutes, there were other broadband approaches, such as the establishment of Maori programs in the national education curriculum. Schools and universities established *marae*—open spaces in a village for meetings. Maori language classes flourished, government departments adopted Maori names, and the new Maori-Pakeha relationship became the subject of heated debate in middle-class homes throughout New Zealand. In hospitals, *whanau* (family) rooms were allocated for Maori extended families to stay overnight. The Maori greeting "kia ora" became commonplace, and many public occasions were marked by the inclusion of Maori speeches from local Maori elders. The discourse of the bicultural project became popularized from the mid-1970s with slogans such as "honor the treaty" and a range of key words: whanau, iwi, tangata whenua, bicultural, partnership, taha Maori, kaumatua, the treaty, and te reo[7] became part of everyday speech for many New Zealanders.

By the 1985 Treaty of Waitangi Amendment Act, which backdated Maori land grievance claims to 1840 and endorsed the Waitangi Tribunal as the institution for the recognition of indigeneity, New Zealand society appeared to be committed to biculturalism. Yet a decade later, biculturalism had been replaced as a societal ideal by retribalization on the Maori side, and an "embourgeoisiement" and class closure by many of the Pakeha new professional class. To understand the initial vigor and the rather hasty demise of the bicultural project requires an understanding of the contradictory motives and actions of the constituent features of its participants and the ways in which these features interacted.

The Pakeha biculturalists were idealistic and radicalized people belonging, in the main, to that section of the new middle class employed in the "creative and welfare professions such as social work, teaching, medical services, the church and journalism" (Parkin, 1968: 179). Their commitment to universalist projects, such as the anti-Vietnam War, the peace movement, New Zealand's antinuclear position, various green programs, and the antiracist movement is characterized by a liberal guilt grounded in the contradictions of an intellectual universalism-economic particularity antinomy. Alvin Gouldner (1979: 36) refers to the way in which this class "conveys that it can solve the fundamental requisites of the universal grammar of societal rationality: to reunite both power and goodness" through its universalistic social-political projects, emerging only through the expression of the generalized liberal guilt that tends to characterize these projects.

During the prosperous postwar period, the welfare and creative professions provided "acceptable sanctuaries" (Parkin, 1968: 192) enabling middle-class radicals "to avoid direct involvement in capitalist enterprises by affording outlets for the exercise of their talents which entail no compromise of (their radical) political ideals." However, such "protection" from the realities of class location disappeared in the erosion of the prosperity that had enabled the humanists of the new class to appear as the "legitimate defenders of the common good" (Kellner and Heuberger, 1992: 11). The new middle class were forced to confront the particularity of their class interests as the increasing insecurity of public service employment, the massification of higher education, and the rejection of universalism made their economic position less stable and less protective.

According to Hunter and Fessenden (in Kellner and Heuberger, 1992: 159), the new class has resolved the tensions of the idealistic universality-economic particularity antinomy by merging its culture of idealistic universalism and its economic interests within the "wider context of the expansion and transformation of capitalism." "New cultural trends," carried by these professionals, "open up new markets for the economy." Knowledge, the very basis of the new class's existence, has become increasingly more valuable in its information form within the global capitalist market. Those with control of the crucial productive forces of knowledge and information, now "the principal form of property," occupy new structural positions within the market relations of capitalism.

This movement of the new class toward an overt expression of its economic interests indicates a consolidation within the middle-class structure of capitalism and a movement away from the previous adversarial relationship into a "historic compromise" with the old bourgeoisie (Kellner and Heuberger, 1992: 19). A reconstituted and repositioned middle class has emerged, supporting and benefiting from neoclassicist wealth redistributive taxation and state spending policies. By securing its location within the middle class and abandoning its political identification with, and championing of, the working class, the new class has resolved its contradictory social position. This process of middle-class consolidation has effectively ended the more or less egalitarian distribution of wealth that had characterized New Zealand's relatively homogeneous society since the "social contract" days of the 1935 Labour government.

By the early 1990s many (although not all) of the Pakeha new class had retreated into the self-interested narcissistic consumerism and cultural aestheticism that characterize embourgeoisiement in late capitalism. Style and form rather than function have become important in determining ways of living. Idealistic universality (the ideal of social cohesion) has been replaced by the marriage of cultural aestheticism and economic opportunity as many of the radical humanists have joined other sections of the new class in the narcissistic consumerism of "liberation markets" (Kellner and Heuberger, 1992: 19). These "burgeoning niche markets created by feminism . . . or environmentalism" together with markets for health foods and fitness, for designer lifestyles in the homes and gardens of high-priced locations, and for expensive and fashionable children's activities, have become visible signs of the new class's separation from its social and political universalism.

The bicultural project collapsed under the weight of conflicting ideologies as well as the consolidation of separate economic interests. Universalistic idealism, an idealism that incorporated a collective sense of historical guilt arising out of the new class's tendency toward self-reflection and intellectual objectivity, was rejected as latent imperialism by the Maori participants who moved from this new form of mainstreaming inclusion for their own ethnically prescribed particularity. Although the bicultural project was a universalistic project, it was simultaneously a vehicle for fragmentation. The inclusion of the other involved the recognition of the other. The new class Pakeha humanist could not mainstream Maori without first recognizing a distinctive ethnicity and, in the process, setting up a romanticized traditional-modern duality.

A widening ideological rift emerged in the bicultural project between a primordialist neotraditionalist ideology and a historical modernity over such fundamental differences as the relationship between the group and the individual, the location of authority, rules controlling conduct according to gender and seniority, the criteria for group belonging, and the relationship of people to place. For the Pakeha new class intellectual, caught in the double paradox of intellectual liberty producing the rationality of political correctness and emotional control producing the isolation of the solitary individual, Maori cultural forms of the self-social relation had seemed to provide a solution. It appeared that these forms united the political-intellectual dimension and the personal-emotional dimension, enabling the "personal is political" to be more than a slogan. However, Maori cultural forms of the emotional dimension were not based upon the individualism of the Pakeha new class. Emotional belonging could only be secured at the expense of the autonomous self, that nonnegotiable element fundamental to the very concept of the Western individual. The psychological security of particularism could only be attained at the expense of the universalism so crucial to the new class's righteousness.

Biculturalism had offered the possibility that the Pakeha new class could solve the dilemma of identity by gaining access to the "security of place" through its association with Maori. In traditionalism lies the mythology of place with which to counter the universalizing machine of rationality. David Harvey (1989: 273) has described the "ideological labour of inventing tradition" as a "facet of modernisation," that is, as a means of establishing geographical security. Ideologies of place were central to the Maori revival and emerged in concepts of indigenous status and tribal belonging. However it did not take long for the Pakeha new class to realize that a bicultural identity did not entitle them to such status. Eligibility for tribal membership was through genealogical links only. The Maori tribe was not a Western group to which membership was conferred according to various criteria such as interest, commitment, or through marriage. Belonging to a tribe was a birthright and was located in concepts of place, time, and ancestral ties that excluded the autonomous individual of the Pakeha new class.

The quiet abandonment of the bicultural project was the consequence of both its success and its failure. Biculturalism had succeeded in repositioning Maori and Pakeha in order for each group to respond to global intrusion in its separate ways. By locating itself within the global new professional class, many Pakeha with bicultural aspirations had resolved the issue of identity of place. Rather than maintaining and developing a new position in relation to Maori as the structuring principle of identity, the new middle class has fixed its identity as a class identity, structured by the global-local relationship. In their turn, Maori have moved on from the earlier ethnification and indigenization movements of the 1970s and 1980s to the retribalization processes of the 1990s.

THE-ZATION OF ETHNICITY

Wini Breines's (1980: 421) "prefigurative" and "strategic" concepts of the different approaches used by groups in subordinate power relations to change those relations serve as a useful means of distinguishing the Maori groups that concentrated upon identity formation and reformation from those concerned more with the expression of that identity in relation to the other. On the one hand, the "prefigurative" traditionalist project indicted both capitalism and Pakeha society as its exponents and sought a return to the precapitalist social relations of the precontact era. On the other hand, exponents of the "strategic" project sought to establish a concordat with capitalist Pakeha society based on the assumption that a capitalist economy could be made compatible with Maori political and cultural autonomy.

However, neither project, "prefigurative" traditionalism nor the "strategic march through the institutions of capitalism," achieved the objective of tino rangatiratanga (Maori for sovereignty). Irrespective of approach, Maori ethnification, indigenization, and retribalization became reshaped and reconstituted by the conditions that made the movements possible and that shaped them in decisive ways. These tino rangatiratanga movements emerged from the institutional channels enabled by Pakeha bicultural idealists and given substance by the Waitangi Tribunal as a neotribal-capitalist regime of accumulation characterized by exploitative class relations and reified communal relations. The dialectical interaction of agency and structure, which transformed the projects, became a reconstituting and shaping mechanism of change, transforming the ethnification and indigenization movements into the new class formations of neotribal capitalism and also constituting the class fractions that define the regime.

As the intrusive global force subverts the local in the dialectically conceptualized moment of interaction, reified communal relations of neotraditionalist forms of capitalism, such as neotribal capitalism, become part of the conditions of existence of the postfordist regime. New modes of regulation, situated within local social structures such as the tribe, enable the depoliticization of the capital-labor antagonism. Two main mechanisms enable this process of depoliticization to occur. First, the labor-capital relationship is resited outside the capitalist state into communities that lack structural recognition of class contestation. Second, the class consciousness of the worker and the opportunity for the expression of its antagonistic relationship to capital within the contradictory capitalist-democratic state are replaced in the re-creation of subjectivity or identity formation.

Self-consciousness (that is, how one learns to know one's self in complex processes of imaging and recognition in the self-other interaction) develops as the consciousness of the ethnic self as the subject. Social relations that are, in reality, structured by material conditions are reified as teleologically and ideologically determined. The subject as the ethnic self is structured into kinship vertically through genealogy as well as horizontally through present-day family relationships. This placement within three dimensions of time, the past and future as well as the present, expands subjectivity as the ethnic subject is conscious of him- or herself within social relations outside of the living. This otherworldly belonging strengthens the consciousness of the self as an ethnic subject and of kinship as the structuring principle of subjectivity. It is a double reification that makes class-consciousness a limited temporal self-constructing principle in comparison. This explains the pervasive strength of ethnicity in identity formation (Rata, 1999c).

It is not surprising that the Maori ethnification movement was the revival of kinship relations in the temporal world. As importantly, indeed more so, was the revival of genealogy, the mechanism that establishes ethnic continuity across time. Genealogy provides the historical dimension to ethnic self-definition. It enables the shift from an identity formation based on ethnicity alone to an identity constructed within the discourse of an ethnic indigeneity.

The reasons for the rapid shift from the Maori pan-ethnification movement of the 1960s and early 1970s to an indigenization movement in the 1980s are to be found in the new politics of recognition between Maori and Pakeha that was the bicultural project. Initially Pakeha had recognized the distinctive ethnicity of Maori within the liberal tradition of universalism,[8] which, paradoxically, involves the recognition of the other's distinctiveness. However, the search by Pakeha for a self-defining postcolonial history and geography meant the recognition of Maori history and geography. Indigeneity moved to a central position in the political relationship between Maori and Pakeha because it established Maori as the referent of place. This enabled Pakeha to relate to the referent in their own path toward geographic positioning.

The intention of the proponents of indigenization, both Maori and the supporting Pakeha biculturalists, was to change the colonial-based dominant-subordinate relationship between Maori and Pakeha and establish a new political positioning in which Maori social and economic aspirations could be realized. However, despite the emancipatory intentions driving this project, the outcome has been the creation of wealthy corporate tribes and the double dispossession of urban Maori. Those ethnic Maori who are unable to establish identification with a tribe are excluded from the settlement of the historical injustices. Ironically it was these injustices that led to their impoverishment and loss of identification in the first place.

It is in the shift from the pan-Maori indigenization movement to retribalization that urban Maori have become dispossessed. Returning to the past for the components of indigenous identity construction, such as the Maori language, family genealogy, and kinship revival, also involved reviving the concept of the tribe as the structure of social organization. However, the revived contemporary tribe, juridified within the state as the legitimate inheritor of a traditional communal society, was not the same societal structure of that previous historical period. Fundamental differences, such as the capitalization of traditional lands and waters, the use of those resources to produce commodities for profit within the national and international sphere of capitalism, and the emergence of class relations of production in relation to those capitalized resources, ensured that the outcome of retribalization was not the revival of the traditional tribe but the emergence of the mode of regulation of neotribal capitalism.

The replacement of communal relations by class relations and the change in the meaning of the lands and waters have been concealed by the neotraditionalist ideology of communality. The contemporary tribe has been juridified as the legitimate inheritor of the traditional lands and as the legitimate social structure of the indigenous people. To be indigenous has become defined as being tribal. Urbanized ethnic Maori who are not tribalized, now exist as a separate group and are excluded from the benefits of indigenization. The result is dispossession from the return of lands, waters, and reparation payments made by the New Zealand government during the past decade as compensation for historical injustices. Ethnic Maori have been joined by another group who are only now emerging as dispossessed. These are the tribes who were either too late, too powerless, too scattered, or too poor, to claim indigeneity to a particular area. For a variety of reasons, these groups lacked the components of indigeneity, that is the new histories, at the crucial time of the juridification of the tribes in the decade following the 1985 Treaty of Waitangi Amendment Act.

Indigenization emerged as a concept of historical and geographical definition in order for Maori to achieve a political recognition intended to result in improved material conditions for all Maori. However, it became transformed within the retribalization process to become an important concept within the neotraditionalist ideology of the new tribes. Indigeneity became the concept of historical continuity. The traditional tribe of the past became linked to the contemporary tribe within a historical continuum despite the fundamental difference between the traditional and contemporary tribe. Indigeneity was the link between past, present, and future. Whoever could define themselves as indigenous could claim this historical continuity and claim ownership of traditional lands and waters.

Indigenization was a positioning of relationship to place across time. The revival of kinship links, researching genealogy, and establishing histories that conceptualized the tribe as indigenous, were important tasks for many Maori during the 1980s. Identifying the self as the ethnic self, with an identity positioned in time and place though claims of indigeneity, was the task of those Maori who sought an identity that would be recognized by the Pakeha protagonist. Out of the recognition of identity (first, Maori recognizing themselves in ethnic, indigenous terms) then having that self-recognition accepted by Pakeha, emerged a new power relation. Both Maori and Pakeha claimed political rights based on their relation to geographical place. Pakeha had become willing to recognize Maori identity in terms of place at this particular historical point because they, too, in their response to globalization forces, were constructing their own identity as a particular people with a particular relation to New Zealand.

Just as the ethnic self was conceptualized as an indigenous self, so too was the tribe conceptualized within a historical continuum, forming the indigenous self as a tribal self. Reparation claims to the Waitangi Tribunal for the settlement of historical grievances were based upon evidence that demonstrated this continuity between the tribal claimants and the historical tribe. Considerable research was undertaken to establish the historical claim. The issue here is not the authenticity of the historical evidence. Lands had been taken illegally, the tribes had been dispossessed and displaced over a 150-year period. That is not in question. The issue is rather who are the inheritors of those processes of dispossession and displacement? Where is the real continuity between that past and the present?

Despite the appearance of continuity, the contemporary tribes are a new structure. Their capture of the settlements has resulted in a double dispossession of the very people for whom the settlement process was designed to compensate. Access to the benefits of the grievance settlements is through the tribes only. Many ethnic Maori, unable to establish their tribal genealogy and gain access to the settlements, are dispossessed from these reparations as a direct consequence of the thoroughness of their displacement. A more just criteria of entitlement to the settlement benefits based on continuity with the past would recognize tribal displacement rather than tribal identification. After all, contemporary Maori poverty is the consequence of the historical displacement and dispossession.

Given the reparative purpose of the grievance settlement process, it is a harsh irony that those most entitled to reparations are those who will not only be excluded from these settlements but will be permanently placed within a newly created impoverished underclass as a consequence of the settlement benefits going elsewhere. There is now no possibility of inclusion. The emergence of neotribal capitalism, from out of the intended liberating settlement process of the bicultural project, has established permanent class divisions, including that of an excluded underclass of ethnic Maori.

Indigeneity is not a concrete thing. It is the concept of the meaning that we give to belonging to place in time. The new contemporary meaning of indigeneity is a meaning possible only within the historical period in which it has emerged. Previously it wasn't important to be indigenous. In order for the concept to emerge, it had to mean something to those using the word. The meaning had to be recognized and shared by those able to provide that recognition. Indigeneity emerged as a way of relating Maori ethnicity to Pakeha. Without the Maori-Pakeha relationship, the concept of Maori as indigenous is merely descriptive. But within that relationship indigeneity became the means of differentiating the two ethnic groups geographically and historically. The relationship between the two differentiated groups is a power relation mediated by indigeneity.

The concept of indigeneity is a political construct of historical and geographical placement. Referring to "indigeneity" as a construct does not mean that Maori did not occupy New Zealand before Pakeha, or that they are not "indigenous." Of course they are. It does mean, however, that the meaning of indigeneity has changed within the political repositioning of the bicultural project. For their own reasons, Maori claimed indigenous recognition. In turn, for their own reasons, Pakeha recognized that claim in concrete material ways through the establishment of historical grievance settlements. The claim and its recognition established a shared meaning of the concept of indigeneity, a meaning mediating the power relation between the two groups. Once recognized by those in power, the indigenous claim brings political benefits, its disallowing results in exclusion and dispossession. The claim for indigeneity recognition was made by the tribes and recognized by the state as the crucial time when the settlement process was being established. This early recognition enabled the tribes to become the legitimate claimants, and ethnic Maori, outside the legitimated tribal identity, to be excluded. The fact that the Treaty of Waitangi was signed by the tribal chiefs supported this position of tribal legitimacy.

The rapidity of the movement in tribal definition from the social structure of a traditional people to the mode of regulation of a neotribal capitalist regime of accumulation is demonstrated by the speed with which retribalizing groups had to move in order to stake their claim for indigeneity, and therefore their status as the legitimate inheritors of traditional resources.[9] The juridification of the tribes occurred in the first half of the 1990s. Those with histories in place, those with the means to establish a history, were recognized. Urban Maori had already been excluded by the decision to recognize the tribes as the legitimate inheritors of the traditional resources. The years since 1992 have been marked by urban Maori fighting a rearguard action to have that legitimacy extended to urban collectivities as "new" tribes (not to individual urban Maori).

KINSHIP REVIVAL AND RETRIBALIZATION

The next discussion refers to a research study of a Maori family's revival and retribalization to show the concrete ways in which indigeneity became constructed, as families and tribes developed histories and self-definitions located within a historical and geographical consciousness.

The extent and determination of the Maori prefigurative movement of kinship and tribal revival is exemplified in the story of the Rimu whanau.[10] Not only did this family restore kinship ties lost during the tribal diaspora of the 1930s and 1940s, but important cultural practices concerning land, birth and death were revived, family and tribal history and genealogy were researched, the Maori language was revived by some whanau members and used with young children as their first language, family claims to tribal lands and waters were revived with the return of some of the family to the ancestral homelands, and finally, a marine farm was established on these tribal lands. These were enormous accomplishments, which attests to the determination of the whanau to reject the impoverishment of life in the cities for the potential of a return to a traditional way of life. That these tasks were accomplished within a decade makes the feat more impressive.

Family revival and tribal identification were two sides of one coin for the Rimu whanau. Access to traditional resources depended upon genealogical knowledge, and that depended upon the extent of family disintegration that had occurred in the previous two to three generations during the migration to the industrial cities. As with many Maori families in the 1970s and 1980s, considerable effort was made to research family genealogy. The reconstituted Rimu whanau was made up of two contributing nuclear families who had been unknown to each other until the death of one of the fathers in 1987 was recorded in the regional newspaper. In accordance with the revivalist aspirations of the Pawhau family, the death notice was in the Maori language and gave genealogical information that alerted a family in another city to their close kinship ties with the dead man.

During the previous decade the Pawhau family had been totally committed to reviving traditional Maori ways. A second marriage and family enabled the Maori father, known in the research study of his life as "Pia," to reject the Pakeha working-class lifestyle of his adult urban years. Pia began using the Maori language again, he talked incessantly and obsessively to his wife, Elizabeth, about his childhood spent on tribal lands. Stories were told about the illegal and volatile alcohol brewed in kerosene tins hidden away from the vigilant eyes of the marae committee in secret locations on the gumfields. He talked about the violence generated by this explosive brew and the time, as just a young boy of five or so, he saw a man kicked to death during one terrible night of drunkenness and rage.

He spoke of the anger and humiliation felt by the entire village, and still remembered vividly by the adult man, when Department of Health officials arrived along the rough and rugged dirt road that led down to this most northern and isolated New Zealand settlement, with brand new corrugated iron toilets. He recalled the mixture of languages that existed in that space before Maori was replaced by English. The descendants of the gumdiggers from the Austrian Empire who had settled in the wopwops of northern New Zealand around the turn of the twentieth century were known as Tararas, onomatopoeically echoing their Maori-

Dalmatian patois. Humorous examples of Maori-English were recalled with accompanying stories of the old people who had never quite grasped English but enjoyed playing with the sounds, making such neologisms to amuse the children as "santapoos" for sandshoes.

Frequent references to tangi (three-day death ceremonies) evoked the poverty of those 1930s Depression times. Pia vaguely remembered his mother giving birth to twin boys, who died in infancy, but he never knew whether or not this event had really occurred. It was only after his own death that the genealogical research revealed the veracity of his memory as a two-year-old. Twin boys had in fact lived for several months, and, like many other infants, had died of "mate Maori" or Maori sickness. Perhaps the high infant death rate, attested to by the headstones in the hilltop cemetery, was linked to the poor water supply (the village had been a nomadic settlement in previous centuries) and could explain the arrival of the "flash" and offending "Pakeha" toilets.

The migration from tribal lands, the frequency of early death in the family, alcoholism, and violence—those illnesses of poverty—and the continual biting angst of loss drove Pia and his wife to a single-minded determination to fill the empty spaces for the sake of their children. Genealogy was to be the base. From genealogical research would come the knowledge of kinship, the means of tribal identification, the link with history, and the certainty of belonging to place. However Pia, like so many other displaced Maori, had little to begin with and few to ask. The name of only one grandparent was known and that had been anglicized—from what exactly? Even the memory of his father, killed in a farm accident many years previously, had faded into brief childhood recollections of a thin man with one arm, vigorously playing the fiddle, his stump gripping the bow, head bent in effort at concentration.

The search for genealogy also included a search for the grave of this one-armed man. An essential task in the return to Pia's Maori sense of self was to find his father's burial place and erect a headstone. However, the mother too had died at a relatively young age. After several years of unsuccessful research, made difficult by the fact that the father had been buried in the lands of his mother's people, it was a great sadness to Pia that he became ill and died[11] without finding his father's burial place. The task was entrusted to his widow who eventually found one old man with memories of Pia's father's burial so long ago in 1944.

That location of the father's grave became important for the next generation's tribal identification. With the juridification of the tribes as the owners of traditional lands, waters, and knowledge, and the subsequent capitalization of these resources and their inclusion in the capitalist sphere of accumulation, retribalization changed in fundamental ways. Tribal identification became economically, as well as culturally, significant. Genealogical identification with one or more tribe began to mean access to a share in the historical grievance settlements and the tribes' material wealth. During the 1990s indigeneity shifted from its role in providing ethnic definition to become the means of settlement claim.

Throughout New Zealand, tribes developed histories that established their claim to be the indigenous people of a particular area. In the Chatham Islands, to the east of New Zealand's South Island, the indigenous Maori, or tchakat henu Mori-ori, have challenged descendants of the nineteenth-century invading South Island tribe for legal recognition as the owners of extensive fisheries stretching two hundred miles out into the Pacific Ocean.

And in October 1998, national television news juxtaposed two revealing shots. The first showed the jubilation of the large Ngai Tahu tribe celebrating their historic signing of the Settlement Deed on the steps of the Parliament buildings. The return of lands, of the waters containing the prized greenstone that Te Wai Pounamu, or the South Island, is named after, of extensive fisheries, of monetary compensation for historical injustices will establish Ngai Tahu as a major corporation in the New Zealand economy. The second shot was of the subdued group, whose bid for recognition as the legitimate historical owner of some of these returned resources had been rejected. This group identify as Waitaha and claim an indigeneity preceding that of Maori by a thousand years, despite the absence of any supporting archaeological, genealogical, and historical evidence (Anderson, 1998).

The politics of the historical justification of indigeneity is illustrated in the story of the Pawhau family's search for its tribe. Pia had grown up secure in very little, but absolutely sure that his family belonged to the Te Aupouri tribe. He knew of the tribe's migration into the far northern peninsula of New Zealand's North Island during the eighteenth century and took pride in discovering his direct descent from the eponymous ancestor of Te Aupouri. The family's tribal research during the late 1970s supported the identification with Te Aupouri and confirmed the status of Te Aupouri as the tribe of the Te Aupouri peninsula, that long tail of the fish sweeping out to divide the Tasman Sea from the Pacific Ocean. Indeed an important Maori Land Court Hearing in 1975, attended by the elders of the peninsula had declared Te Aupouri to be the tribe of the area. Although references to the Ngati Kuri tribe had surfaced in a grandfather's death certificate and in an occasional verbal reference, Pia regarded Te Aupouri as the family's tribe and wondered if Ngati Kuri was perhaps a subtribe of Te Aupouri.

The rise of the Ngati Kuri tribe between 1986, when the tribe first entered the political arena as a claimant in the Muriwhenua Claim for the restoration of historical grievances, and 1996, when the a tribal historian (Norman, W. in Kawharu, 1989: 195) could refer to Ngati Kuri as the original people of New Zealand, predating the canoe arrivals of many of the tribes, is a fascinating story of emergence from historical "invisibility." Indeed Te Aupouri, after a hundred years as the recognized tribe of the peninsula, have recently been referred to as a migrant tribe, a newcomer whose claim to belong to the now renamed Muriwhenua peninsula and subsequent claim for a share in the ownership of the traditional resources and reparatory payments soon to be returned to tribal ownership with the settlement of the Muriwhenua Claim, is disputed. How did Ngati

Kuri regain its historical existence, and how did Te Aupouri go from its recognized position as the tribe of the peninsula to the ignominy of outsider status in just one decade? And importantly, why did the people of the tribe, such as the retribalizing Pawhau family, support this turn of events? Indeed, by the 1996 census, the Pawhau children were able to state Ngati Kuri as their main tribe.

Indigeneity had a new meaning. To be indigenous was to be eligible to claim reparation for historical injustices. History reclaiming had become more than the means of cultural identification. History had become the means to material wealth. Whoever could claim the history could claim the reparations. The historical defining of indigeneity enabled a group to claim ownership of considerable traditional resources and reparation payments that could be used to establish an economic base for wealth generation. Those in the tiny settlement of Te Hapua, the most northern settlement in New Zealand, the settlement left by Pia and many others in search of a better life many decades ago, had endured generations of poverty. A subsistence existence, living off the land and off the pristine waters of the Parengarenga harbor, was to be further decimated by a 1983 change to New Zealand's fishing legislation, a change that would license the large fishing interests at the expense of the small part-time fisherman.

The possibility of the destruction of the only cash economy left to the people of Te Hapua fueled a resistance, which, associated with the indigenization and re-tribalization movements occurring simultaneously, produced a localized movement of indigeneity. The people of the Parengarenga harbor saw, in their indigeneity to the local area, the means to challenge the proposed legislation and, even more significantly, the means to regain control of their lands and waters. A tribal self-definition, which secured them historically to the area, was required to legitimate the political fight for recognition and for reparation.

This was the basis of the new history of Ngati Kuri.[12] A self-defining entity, distinguished from other groups in the region, located in the past, and were able to assert the rights of indigeneity in order to acquire the material wealth for tribal economic development. Ngat Kuri came back into history because it was needed. It was not that the tribe had never existed. It had. It still existed as a memory in the consciousness of the local people. The name surfaced in the occasional historical document, death certificate, and oral narrative. But as a history of a people, a patterned organized narrative of names and events, Ngati Kuri had become invisible. Its disappearance from historical consciousness had many interdependent causes. Defeat by the migrating Te Aupouri in the eighteenth century meant that a very early map of the tribes (one that fed into other authoritative maps for the next two centuries) contained the name Te Aupouri but not Ngati Kuri. The few official references to Ngati Kuri at the beginning of the nineteenth century ended when the combined Ngati Kuri/Te Aupouri group was defeated and enslaved by a southern tribe, Te Rarawa. The forced migration south from their ancestral land occurred at the same time that Pakeha were moving into the area so that, when small groups of Ngati Kuri/Te Aupouri began making their way back into the peninsula, much of the land had new occupiers. The previous traditional mode of production was replaced with a mixture of subsistence farming and fishing, and with a small cash economy based on gumdigging and road building.[13]

The peninsula itself and its people were known in the official discourse by the appellation Te Aupouri. It was not until 1986 that an older history, reemerging through the genealogical research undertaken by hundreds of Maori families such as the Pawhau family, became the way of claiming that past, and with that claim, securing the future. Genealogical lines showed the generations of Ngati Kuri who had occupied Muriwhenua before the intermarriage with the Te Aupouri migrants in the eighteenth century. The new history of Ngati Kuri made visible a people who had lost their self-definition. It was a process of self-consciousness that had to occur before recognition by others was possible. The crucial "event" of self-definition was the compilation of the Muriwhenua Report to the Waitangi Tribunal, claiming the return of ancestral lands and waters, and asking for reparations for historical injustices. This document established the history of Ngati Kuri. It was compiled from the oral reports of elders, the collective memories of people, and stories of events handed down through generations, from the genealogical information researched by many families, and from the paucity of written material available.

The term *new history* does not mean a fictitious account. Genealogical evidence establishes Ngati Kuri as the original people of the far north with a distinctive entity before the assimilation into Te Aupouri. However, the contemporary consciousness of this previous self-defining entity has arisen out of current material circumstances. This is not a matter of authenticity or inauthenticity. It is a matter of the circumstances that allow a degree of self-consciousness of identity. History is not the past. It is the story, told in the present, of the events and people known to have existed in the past. It is the circumstances of the present that determine how the story is told, how those people and events are arranged in the telling, who is edited in or edited out in the compilation, and how meaning is constructed.

The people of Te Hapua needed to reestablish a self-defining identity, located in a specific place, in order to take up a political position. Their material survival was threatened. The new history of Ngati Kuri is, like all histories, a statement of identity through the ordering and patterning of existence so that shared meaning or a collective consciousness is created. What mattered in the changing material circumstances of the 1980s was the establishment of an indigenous identity in order to take up a political position within the bicultural project's recognition of indigeneity. Because Pakeha now recognized indigeneity, because indigeneity now had currency within that recognition, it had acquired a value not there in the past. Identification with Te Aupouri did not provide the depth of indigeneity that Ngati Kuri identity could offer. The genealogy of Ngati Kuri goes back to precanoe[14] settlement period, to the people of the area known as Te Ngaki or Te Kahui o Ngo/Ngu or Karitehe. The later entry of the canoe names, the eighteenth-century entry of Te Aupouri names, the early-nineteenth-century entry of the conquering Te Rarawa people, and the late-nineteenth- and twentieth-century entries of Pakeha names is clearly recognizable in family genealogies.

Establishing tribal connections to place in order to claim historical continuity to the past and into the future is illustrated by the choice of burial sites for Pia and later, for his brother and sister. Traditionally, claims to belonging had been secured by the burial of the placenta and later, the dead person's burial, on tribal lands. These practices symbolically linked the generations, each to the other, and each generation to the ancestral place. The urban migration of the mid-century had broken these connections, although a number of Maori families had used the practice of returning a family member for the tangihanga and burial, to maintain links with their tribes. An important part of retribalization was the return of the living, but a way needed to be found for those buried outside their tribal lands to be included. The fact that these people were dead made no difference. In traditional terms their retribalization was as important as that for the living.

Retribalizing families have dealt with the issue of "retribalizing" the dead in different ways. Some have accepted the fact of urban burial, while others have kept the person "alive" in the tribe by ritual discussions of possible reinterment on tribal lands (even if this will never occur), or have indeed carried out that task. Others have ensured that the person has been buried in a Maori cemetery in the city and regular visits are made to the site. Pia's family dealt with the issue of family members buried outside tribal lands in an ingenious way. His father had been buried at Ounuwhao, several hundred miles south of Ngati Kuri lands. His mother was buried even farther south, at a Maori cemetery in Auckland. In turn the deaths of three of their children (also in mid-adulthood) provided the opportunity to symbolically reunite the parents with their tribe. Pia was buried with his mother in Auckland. This meant that she would not remain alone. Pia's brother was returned to Te Hapua so that one of that generation would "represent" the family on Ngati Kuri lands. The sister was buried with the father so that he too, would remain connected to his descendants. The presence of father and daughter at Ounuwhao would also serve an important tribal purpose. A hundred years previously, a marriage with a woman from the Ngati Whatua tribe at Ounuwhao had established a tribal connection that was revived by the mid- and late-twentieth-century burials at Ounuwhao. Through the burials of Pia and his siblings, three places were linked to the main tribal site in the far north. And it was to this location that the efforts of the reviving families were directed.

Through the genealogical research Ngati Kuri had been established in the minds of the whanau as their main tribe. This tribal identification provided the access to the lands and waters of their ancestors. Through the need to secure their survival the people of Ngati Kuri had established their history as the tangata whenua of the far north. Through the revival of kinship bonds the reconstituted Rimu whanau had returned to tribal lands and established a marine farm in order to provide the material base for their tribal life. Ironically, however, the result for this family, as for many others pursuing the same dream, was the failure of that dream, a failure resulting from its very success.

The establishment of the marine farm, the means of economic survival and prosperity, was also the means of family disharmony and disintegration. The genealogical research and the restoration of kinship ties to the family's tribe had provided access to the traditional lands and waters and to rights to use these resources for economic production. Yet the operation of an economic enterprise designed to support those restored kin relations led to disputes about the very nature of that kinship. Issues of worker–management relations, of ownership of the plant and product, of profit allocation and wage payments, raised deeper questions of eligibility to the fruits of the enterprise.

Questions were raised about who was kin and who wasn't. How was family membership to be decided? Was it a question of descent from the eponymous ancestor selected at the beginning of the family's restoration as the symbol of kinship unity? Was membership to be determined by commitment to the family, by the provision of the manual skills or management abilities, or by financial contributions to the farm? What about those members who, for various reasons such as caring for young children, were not yet in a position to offer direct assistance to the farm project but who wanted future involvement? What was the relationship of each member to the land and waters? Who were to be considered owners of the farm, and who must settle for an indirect connection via a direct-decent member? What did "ownership" mean? Were family members who had married into or out of the family, or who were Pakeha or from another tribe, entitled to the rights of ownership (including profits) in the same way as family members descended from the eponymous ancestor? Just as the meaning of the lands and waters has changed in fundamental ways, so too has the meaning of kinship. It is now a concept that enables access to place, but that relationship to place is no longer mediated through the communal relations of production of a traditional society. Instead class relations have emerged in the production of the Maori families' material conditions on their historical lands.

A tribal history was created in order to overturn the invisibility of two centuries and to ensure the juridification of Ngati Kuri as the owners of the lands and waters of the far north. Access to the material benefits of the bicultural project grievance settlements is now available only through tribal association. To secure this entitlement, first the tribe must exist as an indigenous group in relation to the lands and waters. Second, individuals and families must have the knowledge with which to link to the tribe. Those tribes who missed the claim for indigeneity recognition during the tribal juridification period between 1985 and 1995, and those individuals without the knowledge to link to a tribe are dispossessed.

The ideals of the earlier pan-Maori indigenization movements of the 1970s and 1980s had been to use the recognition of indigeneity in the creation of a new political relation between the dominant Pakeha and the subordinate Maori in order to improve the material conditions of Maori. Yet the process of the repositioning has resulted in the emergence of a neotribalcapitalist regime in which disinheritance and dispossession may well have been made permanent. Urban Maori, who make up the majority of the new underclass of New Zealand's increasingly class-divided society, are excluded both from Pakeha society and from tribal society. They are an impoverished ethnic group unable to claim the position and benefits of indigeneity. Those have gone to the new tribal corporations of the neotribal capitalist regime. From its initial concept as the means by which dispossessed ethnic groups could establish new power relations within the idealism of emancipation, indigeneity has become a part of the mechanisms of dispossession and disenfranchisement.

NOTES

1. The two main ethnic groups in New Zealand are Maori and Pakeha. *Maori* is the generic term for the descendants of the tribal Polynesian people who settled New Zealand in the first millennium. During colonization by British settlers (known as Pakeha) in the nineteenth century, the Maori population declined rapidly. Maori now comprise about 15 percent of the total population of three and a half million. Other ethnic groups comprise immigrants, and the descendants of immigrants, from the Pacific, Asia, and Europe.

2. Renata Tamakihikurangi to the Settlers of Hawkes Bay, November 1860: "Just as you are all English, though one is a Bishop, and another a soldier, and another a settler; so we (Natives) are all one; Maori is my name: though one man builds houses, and another provides food, and another makes canoes, and some (thanks to you!) are fighting now." Cited in Caselberg, 1975: 83.

3. The concept of the tuakana/teina (elder/younger, senior/junior) is central to Maori kinship and is used widely to express a status principle. Tuakana may refer to the older siblings, to a senior genealogical descent line, or to the pedagogical concept of the older caring for the younger in return for authority recognition.

4. The 1840 Treaty of Waitangi was signed between the majority of Maori tribes and the British Crown to establish colonial rule on New Zealand. Despite the Treaty articles guaranteeing continued Maori possession of their lands, most of the land was alienated from Maori hands during the 1860s' land wars and by subsequent legislation. The campaign to honor the Treaty and redress its neglect was a basic platform in the bicultural project of the 1970s and 1980s.

5. New Zealand enjoyed a close cultural and economic relationship with its "mother country" Britain, until the early 1970s. The loss of special trading privileges forced New Zealand to reorient its position away from Europe toward the Pacific Rim and to reconsider its cultural identity in terms of its geographical position as a nation at the bottom of the South Pacific.

6. New Zealand's new rightist governments of the past fifteen years have based their policies on the then fashionable neoclassicist ideology that captured a group of influential Treasury officials, businesspeople, and politicians during the early 1980s. Despite assurances that policies of state deregulation, privatization, and marketization would bring increased prosperity, New Zealand is now characterized by decreased prosperity, greater

wealth inequalities, increased poverty, the appearance of Third World diseases such as TB, and social fragmentation. The mythical reified "market" of the neoclassicists as been unable to maintain an organized society that provides benefits to all its citizens, although it has increased the wealth of its adherents. A recent "hikoi of hope," or march from one end of the country to the other by the poor and excluded, sought to bring to the attention of the enriched middle class the less pleasant consequences of wealth redistribution for others in the society.

7. Whanau means family, iwi, tribe/people, tangata whenua, people of the land, taha Maori, the Maori dimension, kaumatua, elder, and te reo, the Maori language.

8. Throughout the modern period liberal universalism has been the ideology of global capitalism. However, its tendency to include other groups politically, as well as economically through assimilationist policies, has enabled groups to demand political rights based on those very principles of inclusion, and thus, to become increasingly distinctive.

9. Legal proceedings are under way between urban Maori and tribal Maori for the right to claim access to the large fisheries resources that have been returned to Maori ownership during the grievance settlements of the past decade. The tribes claim exclusive ownership on the basis that they are the legitimate inheritors of the traditional means of production. Urban Maori argue that the fisheries belong to all Maori and that the inability to make genealogical links to a tribe dispossesses large numbers of Maori from their rightful inheritance. No one has yet disputed the definition of the tribes as the revived traditional tribe in these prolonged legal battles. Refer to Rata (1996a, b, c and1999a, b, c) for the argument that the tribes are the mode of regulation of a neotribal capitalist regime of accumulation characterized by the capitalization of traditional resources, class relations of production, and a neotraditionalist ideology of communality and are therefore no more the legitimate inheritors of those resources than are urban Maori. It may be argued that the intention of the biculturalists who established the grievance settlement process was to bring all Maori "in from the margins" and that the dispossession of large numbers is in contradiction to the purpose of the process of establishing historical justice. The final outcome of these lengthy legal proceedings will affect not only the fisheries resource but the wealth generated by the return of large areas of land, confiscated since 1840, and the right of Maori groups, tribal or urban, to access government funding through the provision of social, economic, health, and education services to Maori. The stakes of legal recognition are very high.

10. Refer to Rata (1996a, 1996b, 1996c, and 1999a) for a full account of the Rimu whanau's revival and retribalization and also for the research studies of the prefigurative movement of kura kaupapa Maori, a separate Maori education system.

11. One of the many consequences of the high incidence of illness and premature death among Maori in comparison with Pakeha is the familiarity of young Maori with experiences associated with illness and death. Such familiarity tends to encourage a fatalist acceptance of lifestyle illnesses, such as lung cancer and heart disease. The premature death of Maori adults means that more Maori children and young people than Pakeha experience their childhood years without grandparents or indeed without a parent. Illness and death become significant factors in the socialization process.

12. An elaborated version of the reemergence of Ngati Kuri is available in Rata, 1996a and 1999a.

13. For a critique of the concept of an articulation between a traditional mode of production and the introduced capitalist mode, refer to Rata, 1996a and 1999a.

14. New Zealand's settlement by the Polynesian ancestors of contemporary Maori occurred over several centuries from near the beginning of this millennium. While the circumstances of the first arrivals are unknown, the later part of the settlement process is recounted in the canoe traditions of many tribes. Names from the Kurahaupo canoe begin to appear seventeen generations ago in the Pawhau family's Ngati Kuri genealogy. Those generations preceding the canoe names begin in mythical times and include names from the Hawaiki, or pre-New Zealand, period, with eighteen generations from Ngo, who may have lived in New Zealand given the reference to the people of the far north as Te Kahui o Ngo/Ngu, to Pohurihanga of the Kurahaupo canoe

REFERENCES

Anderson, Atholl. *The Welcome of Strangers: An Ethnohistory of Southern Maori A.D. 1650–1859.* Dunedin, New Zealand: University of Otago Press/Dunedin City Council, 1998.

Breines, Wini, "Community and Organization: The New Left and Michel's 'Iron Law.'" *Social Problems* 27(4) (April 1980).

Caselberg, John, ed. *Maori Is My Name.* Dunedin, New Zealand: John McIndoe, 1975.

Clark, Helen. *New Zealand Herald* (27 January 1995).

Gouldner, Alvin. *The Future of Intellectuals and the Rise of the New Class.* London: Macmillan, 1979.

Harvey, David. *The Condition of Postmodernity.* Cambridge, Mass.: Basil Blackwell, 1989.

Kawharu, Hugh, ed. *Waitangi, Maori and Pakeha Perspectives of the Treaty of Waitangi.* Oxford: Oxford University Press, 1989.

Kellner, Hansfried, and Frank W. Heuberger, eds. *Hidden Technocrats: The New Class and New Capitalism.* New Brunswick, N.J.: Transaction, 1992.

Ministry of Education. *Tihe Mauri Ora, Maori Language Junior Classes to Form 2, Syllabus for Schools.* Wellington, New Zealand: Learning Media, 1990.

Parkin, Frank. *Middle Class Radicalism.* Manchester, Engl.: Manchester University Press, 1968.

Rata, Elizabeth. *Global Capitalism and the Rise of Ethnic Traditionalism: The Emergence of Tribal-Capitalism.* Auckland, New Zealand: University of Auckland. Unpublished Ph.D. thesis, 1996a.

———. "Whanau Revival and Retribalisation." *Sites* 32 (Fall 1996b).

———. "'Goodness and Power' The Sociology of Liberal Guilt." *New Zealand Sociology* 11(2) (November 1996c).

———. *A Political Economy of Neotribal Capitalism.* Lanham, Md.: Lexington, 1999a.

———. "A Theory of Neotribal Capitalism." *Review* 22 (1999b): 3.

———. *The Self's Identity.* (In preparation, 1999c).

Walker, Ranginui. *Ka Whawhai Tonu, Struggle without End.* Auckland, New Zealand: Penguin, 1990.

Part III

Contra Developmentalism: The Political Ecology of Indigenism

9

Place, Economy, and Culture in a Post-Development Era

Arturo Escobar

INTRODUCTION: POSTDEVELOPMENT AND THE POLITICS OF PLACE

The question of development remains unresolved in any modern social or epistemological order. By this I mean not only "our" (modern expert knowledge and policy-making apparatus) inability to deal with situations in Asia, Africa, and Latin America in ways that lead to lasting improvement—socially, culturally, economically, environmentally—but that the constructs on which we rely for explanation and prescription no longer enable satisfactory questions, let alone answers. Moreover, the crisis of development puts in evidence the obsolescence of the functional domains with which modernity has equipped us to enunciate our social and political concerns—the domains of nature, society, economy, polity, and culture. Societies are not the organic wholes with structures and laws that we thought them to be until recently, but fluid entities stretched on all sides by migrations, border crossings, and transnational economic forces; cultures are no longer bounded, discrete, and localized but deterritorialized and subjected to multiple hybridizations; similarly, nature can no longer be seen as an essential principle and foundational category, an independent domain of intrinsic value and truth, but as the object of constant reinventions, especially by unprecedented forms of technoscience; and, finally, nobody really knows where the economy begins and ends, even if economists, in the midst of neoliberal frenzy and seemingly overpowering globalization, steadfastly adhere to their attempt to reduce it to every aspect of social reality, thus extending the shadow that economics casts on life and history.

The deconstruction of development, nature, and culture effected in recent years by poststructuralist analyses have gone a long way toward showing both the historicity of these notions and the need to clear the space for imagining alternatives.

This exercise of the imagination, however, has met with much more limited success. At the root of this limitation are on the one hand, dominant social processes and practices that continuously renew themselves, keeping established orders in place—in the guise of neoliberalism today; and, on the other hand, entrenched habits of thinking in Western social sciences that shelter certain notions of individual, society, and economy that subvert our best efforts at thinking reality differently. It is paradoxical, as we shall see, that emerging theories of globalization that purport precisely to transcend modern frameworks of capital, culture, and society nevertheless continue to preclude the development of new ways of thinking—making the relationship between globalization and neoliberalism, and neoliberalism's impact on the Third World, invisible along the way (Slater, 1995). Entrenched concepts of culture, space, and modernity continue to construct capitalism as the central referent of development, globalization, and the economy.

A handful of recent works try to move beyond this paradox by working through some of the epistemological traps that constrain theories of globalization. At the same time, they provide elements that lead to thinking beyond development—that is, for a conceptualization of postdevelopment that is more conducive to the creation of new types of languages, understanding, and action. Novel debates on economy and place seem particularly useful in this regard. In these works, place is asserted against the dominance of space, and noncapitalism against the dominance of capitalism as an imaginary of social life. The argument I shall make in this chapter is that theories of postdevelopment are a hopeful arena in which to introduce a place-based dimension and the idea of manifold forms of economy in discussions of globalization. Reconceived in this fashion, postdevelopment would facilitate the incorporation of place-based practices, modes of knowledge, and models of the social and the economic into the process of outlining alternative orders. Said differently, a reassertion of place, noncapitalism, and local culture against the dominance of space, capital, and modernity that are central to globalization discourse should result in a theory of postdevelopment that makes visible possibilities for reconceiving and reconstructing the world from the perspective of place-based cultural and economic practices. This, in the last instance, is the goal of the present chapter. In what ways do our frameworks allow us or not to visualize actual or potential ways of reconceiving and reconstructing the world embodied in manifold localities? Which new forms of "the global" can be imagined from this perspective?

While the answer to these questions might be clearer today in the domain of ecological practices—and we shall illustrate the argument by drawing on recent works on the anthropology of nature—the argument is by no means restricted to this area. Similarly, while the chapter is largely centered on debates on what is still known as the Third World—and, more particularly, Latin America—this geographic focus is not exclusive. In the long run, what we aim at is to shift our understanding of the process through which discourses of development and modernity have imperialized the wishes and worldviews of ruling groups and, consequently, how we ought to think about alternative social orders. Can we explain today's world in ways that do not reproduce the centrality of Western ways of creating the world? Can we elevate place-based imaginaries to the language of social theory and project their potential onto novel types of globality so that they can appear as "alternative" ways of organizing social life? In sum, to what extent can we reinvent both thought and the world according to the logic of place-based cultures? Is it possible to think about alternatives to capitalism and development? How would theory and social life emerge after this exercise of the imagination?

The first part of the chapter summarizes succinctly the poststructuralist critiques of development and the emergence of postdevelopment as a heuristic device for clearing the space for new perceptions. Next, I introduce recent critiques of notions of space and economy—particularly as they are used in globalization discourse—and how these critiques shift the grounds of social theory in their attempt at rescuing other locations, voices, and concepts from their theoretical marginalization. More particularly, critiques of capitalocentrism and of spatial thinking in much contemporary theory are reviewed in terms of their contribution to recovering for social theory and ethnographic research notions of "noncapitalism" and place-based consciousness, respectively. Next I illustrate the argument with examples of discourses and practices of ecological difference that are being used by rainforest social movements for alternative social and economic projects. The defense of territory by social movements is seen as enacting a relation between place, culture, nature, and economy that has important lessons for how we think about "alternatives." In the conclusion, I return to postdevelopment as a research program for both deepening the desconstruction of the economy and suggesting steps to alternative conceptualizations.

FROM "DEVELOPMENT ALTERNATIVES" TO POSTDEVELOPMENT

Since its inception, "development" has been considered to exist in reality, "out there," solid and material. Development has been taken to be a true descriptor of reality, a neutral language that can be used harmlessly and put to different ends according to the political and epistemological orientation of those waging it. Whether in political science or sociology, economics or political economy, development has been debated without questioning its ontological status. From modernization theory to dependency or world systems; from "market-friendly development" to self-directed, sustainable, or ecodevelopment, the qualifiers of the term have multiplied without the term itself having been rendered radically problematic. This seemingly uncritical tendency has held throughout the development decades despite the fact that "as an arena of study and practice, one of the fundamental impulses of those who write development is a desire to define, categorize and bring order to a heterogeneous and constantly multiplying field of meaning" (Crush, 1995: 2). No matter that the term's meaning has been hotly contested; what remained unchallenged was the very basic idea of development itself, development as a central organizing principle for social life, the fact that Asia, Africa, and Latin America can undoubtedly be defined as underdeveloped and that their communities ineluctably need "development"—in whatever guise or garb.

The naturalization of development began to crumble in the late 1980s in critical development studies, particularly those inspired by poststructuralist theories of discourse and power. While the tension between political economy and discursive approaches continues, the poststructuralist contribution is more commonly appreciated today in critical development studies. A recent collection on languages of development, for instance, takes on the challenge of analyzing the "texts and words" of development, while rejecting "that language is all there is" (Crush, 1995: 5). "Many of the authors in this volume"—writes the editor in his introduction—"come out of a political economy tradition that argues that politics and economics have a real existence that is not reducible to the text that describe them and represent them" (6). He finds, nevertheless, that the textual turn, postcolonial, and feminist theories, and critiques of the dominance of Western knowledge systems provide crucial ways for understanding development, "new ways of understanding what development is and does, and why it seems so difficult to think beyond it" (4). These new ways have been openly discussed by authors embracing the analysis of development as discourse since the late 1980s. It is important to review succinctly what these analyses accomplished, before addressing the question of "thinking beyond" development.

The poststructuralist analyses of development start by suggesting that if we want to understand development, we need to examine how development has been understood historically, according to what perspectives, with what principles of authority, and with what consequences for what groups of people. What regimes of truth and what silences did the language of development bring into place? It is not so much a question, then, of providing new grounds for doing development better, or differently, but to examine the very grounds on which development could emerge as an object of thought and practice. The aim? To destabilize those grounds in order to modify the social order that regulates the language production process. Poststructuralism also provides tools for fulfilling a task that was always at the heart of anthropology, even if seldom realized: to defamiliarize the familiar. As Jonathan Crush puts it, "the *discourse* of development, the form in which it makes its arguments and establishes its authority, the manner in which it constructs the world, are usually seen as self-evident and unworthy of attention. The [discursive analysis's] primary intention is to try and make the self-evident problematic" (1995, "Introduction," 3). Another set of authors, more wedded to this defamiliarizing task, have sought to render the language of development unspeakable, to turn the basic constructs of the development discourse—markets, needs, population, participation, environment, planning, and the like—into "toxic words" that experts could not use with such impunity as they have until now (Sachs, 1992).

Building upon related critiques of Western representations of non-European cultures—such as those by Edward Said (1979) and V.Y. Mudimbe (1988)—the discursive analysis of development took off in the late 1980s and has continued throughout the 1990s. They have offered "new ways of understanding what development is and does" (Crush, "Introduction," 1995: 4), particularly the following:[1]

1. To begin with, a different way of posing "the question of development" itself. How did the language of development emerge? In what ways was the "Third World" constituted as a reality for modern expert knowledge? What was the order of knowledge—the regime of representation—that came into existence with the language of development? To what extent has this language colonized social reality? These questions could not be asked by relying on the realist paradigms of the past, those that took for granted development as a descriptor of reality. James Ferguson framed the poststructuralist formulation in its most general way: "Like 'civilization' in the nineteenth century, 'development' is the name not only for a value, but also for a dominant problematic or interpretive grid through which the impoverished regions of the world are known to us. Within this interpretive grid, a host of everyday observations are rendered intelligible and meaningful" (1990: xiii).

2. A view of development as invention, that is, as a historically singular experience that was neither natural nor inevitable, but very much the product of identifiable historical processes. Even if its roots extend back to the development of capitalism and modernity (Watts, 1995; Porter, 1995)—and in this sense it cannot be claimed that development was an invention of the post–World War II period—the late 1940s and the 1950s brought with them a globalization of development and an explosion of institutions, organizations, and forms of knowledge "whose *raison d'etre* was the lodestar of development" (Watts, 1995: 55). To say that development was an invention does not mean that it is a lie, a myth, or a conspiracy; it is to assert its strictly historical character and, in traditional anthropological fashion, to diagnose it as a exotic cultural form embedded in a set of practices that can be studied ethnographically. The view of development as invention also suggests that the invention can be unmade or reinvented in multiple ways.

3. A "map" of the discursive regime of development, that is, a view of the apparatus of expert knowledge forms and institutions that organized the production of forms of knowledge and types of power, linking one to the other in a systematic manner, as a diagram of power. This is the central insight of the poststructuralist analysis of discourse in general: the organization of the production of knowledge and power. As Ferguson (1990) put it, mapping the apparatus of knowledge-power made visible those "doing the developing" and their role as culture producers. The gaze of the analyst thus shifted from the so-called beneficiaries or targets of development to the allegedly neutral

social technicians of the development apparatus. What are they actually doing? Are they not producing culture, ways of seeing, transforming social relations? Far from neutral, the work of the apparatus is precisely intended to achieve very particular goals: the etatization and governmentalization of social life; the depoliticization of issues; and the transformation of the cultural fabric of communities along the lines of modern principles of individuality, rationality, economy, and the like (the conquering of place, as we shall see).

4. Also important for these analyses was to provide a view of how the development discourse has changed throughout the decades—from its emphasis on economic growth and industrialization of the 1950s to the focus on sustainable development of the 1990s—managing, nevertheless, to maintain a certain core of elements and relations intact. As the apparatus incorporated new domains into its scope, it certainly changed, yet its basic orientation went unchallenged. Whatever modifier was attached to it, the fact of development itself was not place under radical questioning.

5. Less explored have been the forms of subjectivity fostered by the development discourse, in both the Third and First Worlds. In what ways has this discourse contributed to shaping subjectivities and identities among people everywhere? What differences can be detected among classes, genders, ethnicities, and places in this respect? For the Third World, this investigation was outlined by Ashis Nandy through his notion of the "intimate enemy" (1983), but much remains to be done. Recent works on cultural hybridization can also be interpreted in this light (García Canclini, 1990). Another aspect of the question of subjectivity that has attracted some attention is the investigation of the circulation of concepts of development and modernity in Third World settings. How are these concepts used and transformed? What are their effects and modes of operation once they enter a Third World locality? What is their relationship to local histories and global processes alike? How are global conditions processed at the local level, including those of development and modernity (Pred and Watts, 1992)? In what concrete ways do people use them to negotiate their identities? (Dahl and Rabo, 1992; Pigg, 1992).

It should be clear from the preceding analysis that the poststructuralist critiques aim at something more than the provision of "development alternatives." For some, what is at stake is imagining something more radical, namely, alternatives to development. As I mentioned in the introduction to this chapter, this task has met with very limited success. However, attention is being given to other issues that have emerged out of the poststructuralist critique.[2] It should also be noted that to the extent that the poststructuralist analyses have succeeded in defamiliarizing development descriptions, they have contributed to two other processes: to reassert the value of alternative experiences and ways of knowing (an important item of research in political ecology and the anthropology of local knowledge, for instance, to be discussed) and to unveil the sites and mechanisms of knowledge production and this latter as inherently political—that is, as linked to the exercise of power and the creation of lifeworlds—and, concomitantly, to ask whether knowledge can be produced otherwise. The poststructuralist analyses, in this way, have given renewed poignancy to the politics of knowledge production. How should we behave as knowledge producers, acknowledging that expert knowledge is central to the exercise of power, to putting the world together in certain ways at the exclusion of others?

Perhaps the most useful notion to emerge from the analyses just reviewed, from the perspective of our interest in alternatives to capitalism and development, is that of "postdevelopment"; postdevelopment has become a heuristic for relearning to see and reassess the reality of communities in Asia, Africa, and Latin America. Is it possible to lessen the dominance of development representations when we approach this reality? Indeed, what happens when we do not look at that reality through development agendas? As Jonathan Crush put it, "is there a way of writing (speaking and thinking) beyond the language of development?" Let us say for now that postdevelopment is a way to signal this possibility, an attempt to carve out a clearing for thinking other thoughts, seeing other things, writing in other languages.

THE END OF DEVELOPMENT (AS WE KNEW IT): NONCAPITALISM AND DISCOURSES OF DIFFERENCE

One of the most constructive critiques of the poststructuralist development literature has been made recently by two Marxist geographers who engaged themselves in a poststructuralist critique of economic narratives. For these authors, even the notion of postdevelopment is, like most conventional or left economic discourse, "capitalocentric." "Capitalocentrism in this context involves situating capitalism at the center of development narratives, thus tending to devalue or marginalize possibilities of noncapitalist development" (Gibson-Graham, 1996: 41). This is so despite the fact that the "postdevelopment literature militates against the economic essentialism of both mainstream and left development theories and practices" and that "in the postdevelopment literature, anti-economism and anti-eurocentrism work in tandem to displace monolithic images of the future and to bring into visibility cultural and social differences, resistances to hegemony, local power, dynamism, and subjectivity" (p. 42). It is instructive to review in some detail the argument these authors make, to further release alternative ways for thinking about the Third World and for releasing the Third World from the grip of economism (see also Gibson, Graham, and Ruccio, forthcoming).[3]

In *The End of Capitalism (as we knew it)*, Julie Graham and Katherine Gibson (Gibson-Graham, 1996) present a powerful case against the claim, shared by mainstream and left theorists alike, that capitalism is the hegemonic, even the only, present form of economy and that it will continue to be so in the foresee-able future. Capitalism has been endowed with such an overpowering domi-nance and hegemony, that it has become impossible to think social reality differ-ently, let alone imagine capitalism's suppression. Building on poststructuralist marxism, feminism, and queer theory, these authors seek to demolish the "straw man" of capitalocentrism and to create the space for the production of discourses of economic difference; these discourses, they argue, could enable theorists not only to resist reducing every aspect of social reality to a single principle of (capi-talist) determination, but to reintroduce a principle of multiplicity and alterity in our view of reality and the struggles around it. By demonstrating how capitalism has become a "an absolute presence," Gibson, Graham, and Ruccio lay down the basis for an antiessentialist critique of capitalocentric discourses, in which capi-talist practices would appear as overdetermined, contingent, and specific rather than necessary. What emerges from this critique is a notion of the economy as "a complexly structured social totality made up of relations irreducibly multiple and various, without a center or origin, existing as a fabric, and articulation of rela-tively autonomous and specific relations, overdetermining one another" (Gibson-Graham, 1996: 29). The question thus becomes: What are the constitutive rela-tions that account for the economy? How can discourses of difference be articulated so that they do not reduce the multiplicity of the economy to a single overarching process of overdetermination?

At issue is the production of noneconomic and noncapitalist economic imagi-naries in which noncapitalist forms are not seen as the same in relation to capital-ism (as in the notion of independent commodity producers, or petty commodity producers in the informal sector), or as opposite (as when they are seen as primitive, traditional, or marginal) or complementary to it (as in the articulation of modes of production discourse), or as located inside of capitalism itself (for instance, in analy-sis of cooperatives or local initiatives). Transcending capitalocentrism means learn-ing how to see these forms as sources of life and alternative practices in and of them-selves. Certain class processes, market transactions, independent commodity production, household and family production and reproduction, informal economies, resistances to globalization, economic practices of immigrants in the North, and so on are reinterpreted to reveal important instances of noncapitalism. Even new forms of feudal, independent, and communal class processes—the result of the demise of older forms—have partial logics and modes of self-generation that cannot be reduced to those of capitalism; neither can a variety of household and community structures that become visible once we shift our gaze from the usual sites of farms, factories, and offices to other domains.

Women wage earners, for instance, are often able to disrupt exploitation pat-terns in the hands of husbands, elders, and bosses, propitiating in some cases in-dependent or communal class processes. In these cases, a class process in which a man appropriates the surplus labor from his female partner might give way to other forms of appropriation of surplus labor by women, more communal perhaps, as recent studies in feminist economics suggest. As capitalism develops in some sites, forms of noncapitalism might be emerging in others. To these examples we should add others such as the noncapitalist class processes exhibited by cooperatives, even those who sell for external markets. Communal kitchens, self-help organizations, collective household structures, barter economies, and certain types of rural and urban cooperatives, in sum, might represent noncapitalist ways of organizing the production of surplus labor (Gibson, Graham, and Ruccio, forthcoming).

What allows these authors to engage in this reinterpretation is an antiessentialist conception of class in which the classes constituted by capitalism are not the only ones defining the economy. Following Stephen Resnick and Rick Wolff's (1987) reinterpretation of Althusser, Gibson and Graham define class in terms of the processes of producing, appropriating, and distributing surplus labor. Defined in this way, the economy exhibits a diversity of class processes, and development must consequently be seen as the source of various noncapitalist class processes, including some of those mentioned previously. The focus on how producers individually or collectively appropriate their own surplus labor thus enables a different view of the economy. Whether the critique of capitalocentrism entails a displacement of the economy from the center position that it has been given in modern history and its forms of analysis—besides and beyond the decentering of capitalism—remains to be seen. As Karl Polanyi (1957)—and, more recently, poststructuralist analysts such as Giovanna Procacci (1991)—have argued, this would be a more far-reaching project, and more difficult to accomplish. It is one, I believe, that is essential to the task at hand, namely, thinking about alternatives to capitalism and development, which in some important ways depend on displacing the economy from the center of social life.[4]

The consequences of the redefinition of class along antiessentialist lines, however, have important implications for analyses of globalization and their critique, which Gibson and Graham make explicit. In particular, this reinterpretation challenges the inevitability of capitalist "penetration" that is assumed in much of the literature on globalization. By making an analogy with constructions of rape that represent women as always already raped or rapeable—thus making inevitable a politics of fear and subjection for women—they problematize mainstream and left views of globalization as inevitable:

> In the globalization script . . . only capitalism has the ability to spread and invade. Capitalism is presented as inherently spatial and as naturally stronger than the forms of noncapitalist economy (traditional economies, "Third World" economies, socialist economies, communal experiments) because of its presumed capacity to universalize the market for capitalist commodities. . . . Globalization according to this script involves the *violation* and eventual death of "other" noncapitalist forms of economy. . . . All forms of noncapitalism become damaged, violated, fallen, subordinated to capitalism. . . . How can we challenge the similar representation of globalization as capable of "taking" the life from noncapitalist sites, particularly the "Third World"? (1996: 125, 130)

Not everything that emerges from globalization can be said to conform to the capitalist script—not even all forms of economic practice or development can be reduced to capitalist practices or development. In fact, globalization and development might propitiate a variety of economic development paths, which could be theorized in terms of postdevelopment so that "the naturalness of capitalist identity as the template of all economic identity can be called into question" (Gibson-Graham, 1996: 146). But do we know what is there "on the ground" after centuries of capitalism and five decades of development? Do we even know how to look at social reality in ways that might allow us to detect elements of difference that are not reducible to the constructs of capitalism and modernity and that, moreover, could serve as nuclei for the articulation of alternative social and economic practices? And, finally, even if we could engage in such an exercise of alternative vision, how could alternative practices be fostered?

The role of ethnography can be particularly important in this respect, and there are some trends that point in this direction. In the 1980s, a number of ethnographies focused on documenting resistance to capitalism and modernity in various settings, thus starting the task of making visible practices and processes that revealed that development itself was being actively resisted in manifold ways.[5] Resistance by itself, however, is only suggestive of what was going on in many communities, stopping short of showing how people have actively continued to create and reconstruct their lifeworlds. Successive works characterized the local models of the economy and the natural environment that have been maintained by peasants and indigenous communities, in part embedded in local knowledge and practices that ethnographers have begun to explore in depth.[6] Other works, already mentioned, focused on the circulation of concepts and markers of development and modernity in local settings (Dahl and Rabo, 1992; Pigg, 1992). The attention paid, particularly in Latin American anthropology, to cultural hybridization can be seen as an attempt to make visible the dynamic encounter of practices originating in many cultural and temporal matrices, and the extent to which local groups, far from being passive receivers of transnational conditions, actively shape the process of constructing identities, social relations, and economic practice.[7]

Ethnographic research of this sort—which will certainly go on for a number of years—has been important in illuminating discourses of cultural, social, and economic difference among Third World communities in contexts of globalization and development. Although much remains to be done in this respect, this research already suggests ways in which discourses and practices of difference could be used as the basis for alternative social and economic projects. This line of thinking has advanced the most perhaps in connection with the rethinking of the relation between environment and development, and I will return to this literature in the next section. Before doing so, however, it is important to bring into consideration a question that in important ways underlies discussions of both economy and ethnography, namely, the question of place. If the goal of Graham and Gibson is to provide an alternative language—a new class language in particular—for addressing the economic meaning of local practices, and if the goal of the postdevelopment literature is similarly to make visible practices of cultural difference that could serve as the basis for alternatives, it is necessary to acknowledge that these goals are inextricably linked to conceptions of locality, place, and place-based consciousness. Place, to begin with—like local culture—can be said to be "the other" of globalization, so that a discussion of place should also afford an important perspective toward rethinking globalization and its relation to the question of alternatives to capitalism and modernity.

As Arif Dirlik points out in his contribution to this volume, place and place-based consciousness have dropped out of sight in debates on the local and the global. This is doubly regrettable because, on the one hand, place is central to issues of development, culture, and social relations and is equally essential, on the other, for imagining other contexts for thinking about the construction of politics, knowledge, and identity. The erasure of place is a reflection of the asymmetry that exists between the global and the local in much of contemporary literature on globalization, in which the global is associated with space, capital, history, and agency, while the local, conversely, is linked to place, labor, and stasis—as well as with women, minorities, the poor, and, one might add, local cultures. While some feminist geographers have attempted to correct this asymmetry by arguing that place can also lead to articulations across space—for instance through networks of various kinds (Chernaik, 1996)—they do not discuss the relation between place and concrete locations; place—as ecological conceptions of territory to be discussed make patently clear—continues to be a grounded experience with some sort of boundaries, however porous and intersected with the global. Other critiques of modernity and the global in terms of networks, such as Bruno Latour's (1993), while restoring some symmetry to global/local debates, are however blind to the historicity of power and difference.

Discussions of the local appropriation of the global by anthropologists and geographers, in Dirlik's account, also fail to move away from globalocentric logic. More fundamental perhaps in Dirlik's analysis is that the neglect of place in current conceptions of the categories of social theory such as class, gender, and race makes such categories susceptible of becoming instruments of hegemony. To the extent that they are significantly sundered from place in the "globalization craze" of "deterritorialized identities"—and in much discourse that privileges traveling, mobility, displacement, and diaspora—contemporary notions of culture do not manage to escape this predicament. This is because in all of these cases the existence of a global power structure—in relation to which cultures (hybrid or otherwise), traveling, and the delinking of place from identity are supposed to play an oppositional role—is assumed and naturalized. For Dirlik, this is also a reflection of the privilege accorded in Western theory to abstract (disembodied and disembedded, one might add) knowledge, as opposed to referential (embodied, experiential) knowledge of place.[8]

Is it possible to launch a defense of place in which place and the local do not derive their meaning from their juxtaposition with the global? Who speaks for "place"? Who defends it? Dirlik highlights several domains in which the reassertion of place is being worked out, including the work of certain geographers and ecologists (below), to which I should add a brief note on phenomenological notions of place in political ecology and the anthropology of experience. As a first step in resisting the marginalization of place, Dirlik summons Henri Lefebvre's distinction between space and place (between first and second space, in Lefebvre's work), particularly his notion of place as a form of lived and grounded space and the reappropriation of which must be part of any radical political agenda against capitalism and spaceless and timeless globalization. Politics, in other words, is also located in place, not only in the supralevels of capital and space. Place, one might add, is the location of a multiplicity of forms of cultural politics, that is, of the cultural-becoming-political, as we shall see in our discussion of rainforest social movements.

Lefebvre's distinction has been taken up recently by Edward Soja as a way to suggest ways to move beyond the binarism of much social theory and to reinfuse politics with considerations of place. Building upon the work of Lefebvre and of feminist and postcolonial theorists like bell hooks, Gloria Anzaldúa, and Hommi Bhabha, Soja suggests a notion of Thirdspace that transcends the binarism of the first space (material space) of positivist science (geography, planning, etc.) and the second space (the conceived space of theory and design) of interpretive theories. By contrast, Thirdspace involves both the material and the symbolic; it is closest to "space as directly lived, with all its intractability intact . . . the space of 'inhabitants' and 'users' (1996: 67). The three spaces, needless to say, are moments in the generation of overall social space. What is important to realize is that to the trialectic of spatiality, historicality, and sociality corresponds a trialectic of lived, perceived, and conceived spaces, which, on the one hand, is essential to transcending the binarism of the real and the imagined, subjectivity and objectivity, into a new complex totality of sorts and, on the other, constitutes the grounds for an strategic political choice in defense of lived space.[9]

That lived space can also be seen as the essential feature of place is highlighted by phenomenological accounts of nature and space. In these accounts, places are not purely empirical and external entities defined, say, by geographical or geometric features, but lived entities endowed with meaning and significance. For phenomenologists, we "dwell" in the world (from Heidegger), and dwelling involves a unit of human beings with their environment, a lack of distance between people and things, and an engagement with the world that is not articulated in discourse but which arises out of using the world (Thomas, 1993). This position resonates with the literature on local models of nature, to be discussed shortly, in which local knowledge is seen as embedded in practices, and with trends in the philosophy of technology that reverse the assumed primacy of theoretical over practical knowledge and that locate the crafting of knowledge and identities not in abstract reflection but in the engagement with tools and the world in general. From the perspective of the anthropology of experience, "use, not logic, conditions belief" (Jackson, 1996: 12). Finally, from phenomenological biology we learn that cognition is always embodied experience that takes place in a historical background and that must be theorized from the perspective of the "unbroken coincidence of our being, our doing, and our knowing" (Maturana and Varela, 1987: 25). In refusing to separate knowing from doing and these from existence, these biologists—as well as the phenomenologists of landscape and place—provide us with a language with which to question radically the dualisms and asymmetries of nature and culture, space and place, theory and practice.

Can place be reconceived as a project? For this to happen, we need a new language. To return to Dirlik, "glocal," for instance, constitutes a first approximation that suggests the localization of the global and the globalization of the local. The concrete forms in which this two-way traffic takes place is not so easily conceptualized. Even the local of social movements against capital and modern natures are globalized in some ways, for instance, to the extent that they borrow metropolitan discourses of identity and the environment. Conversely, many forms of the local are offered for global consumption, from kinship to crafts and ecotourism. The point here would be to distinguish those forms of globalization of the local that become effective political forces in defense of place and place-based identities, as well as those forms of localization of the global that locals can use to their own ends. The notion of "hybridity" has been used in some ways as a shorthand for this two-way traffic between the local and the global, but this notion, for Dirlik, is not only insufficient but dangerous in this regard. Unlike the notion of Thirdspace, which "does not eliminate the other two spaces but enriches and complicates choice," hybridity "is a static resolution of the problem of difference in naturalized boundaries, that does not recognize the contradictions produced by hybridity, the way in which hybridity produces its own structural contexts" (chapter 2, this text).[10]

A more satisfactory way to repoliticize debates on globalization and alternatives to capitalism, for Dirlik, is found in the reassertion of place. To construct place as a project, to turn place-based imaginations into a radical critique of power, and to align social theory with a critique of power by place requires that we venture into other terrains. This proposal resonates with, and moves a step beyond, Jane Jacobs's idea that "by attending to the local, by taking the local seriously, it is possible to see how the grand ideas of empire become unstable technologies of power with reach across time and space" (1996: 158). In what follows, I attempt to give concrete presence to this possibility by focusing on the ecological domain. In this domain, we will find clues for addressing Dirlik's call to rethink the world according to the logic of place. To reconceive the world according to the categories of life, nature, and economy still at play in places throughout the world is an ambitious project to say the least. Let us look first at the current historical and ethnographic research that might suggest ways for thinking about this project before moving to a consideration of the individual and collective processes required to advance it socially in the last part of the chapter.

To construct place as project, finally, does not entail seeing places as unconstructed or unconnected to larger circuits of patriarchy, capital, and modernity. Places are surely characterized by their own forms of power and have often been the site of domination of women and ethnic minorities. Places, then, must be reimagined without feminizing them, naturalizing, or locating them outside of history. It is important to imagine their defense, moreover, from the perspective of constructing other possible relations between place, on the one hand, and gender, culture, and space, on the other (Massey, 1994). A "progressive concept of place" starts by positing a conception of place as process, rather than as a static entity; concomitantly, it needs to examine the ways in the identity of place is constituted through multiple social relations, without denying its uniqueness and specificity. A "global sense of place" thus moves back and forth between the insertion of place in the global and its local specificity (Massey, 1993). It is out of this specificity that ideas for the reconstruction of local and regional worlds can be imagined.

POLITICAL ECOLOGY, SOCIAL MOVEMENTS, AND
THE DEFENSE OF PLACE

As anthropologists, geographers, and political ecologists have begun to demonstrate with increasing clarity, it is often the case that rural communities in the Third World "construct" nature in strikingly different ways from prevalent modern forms. In other words, many Third World communities signify—and, thus, use—their natural environments in ways quite different from modern ways and uses. These different systems of meanings-uses of nature, some authors have begun to argue, should be the basis for sustainable development proposals, instead of the managerial and rationalist recipes promoted by the ecodevelopment establishment. The incorporation of this type of ecological and cultural difference, and the political struggles to which it is giving rise, into a theory of postdevelopment—let alone a political theory of nature (Escobar, 1999) is far from accomplished. The above discussions on noncapitalism and the reassertion of place have much to contribute to this task, and vice versa.

Anthropological studies unveil a significantly different set of practices of thinking about, relating to, constructing, and experiencing the biological and the natural in many Third World communities. In a classic article on the subject, Marilyn Strathern (1980) made the case that we cannot interpret native (nonmodern) mappings of the social and the biological in terms of our concepts of nature, culture, and society. For many indigenous and rural groups, "'culture' does not provide a distinctive set of objects with which one manipulates 'nature' . . . nature is not 'manipulated'" (174, 175). Instead, the anthropology of local knowledge of nature suggests that, unlike modern constructions with their strict separation between biophysical, human, and spiritual worlds, local Third World constructions of nature are often predicated on links of continuity between the three spheres. This continuity is culturally established through symbols, rituals, and practices and is embedded in particular social relations that also differ from the modern, capitalist type.[11]

A local model of nature could thus exhibit features such as the following, which may or may not correspond to the parameters of modern nature, or only partially: categorizations of human, social, and biological entities (for instance, what is human and what is not, what is planted and what is not, the domestic and the wild, what is produced by humans and what is produced by forests, what is innate or what emerges from human action, what pertains to spirits and what pertains to humans, etc.); boundary settings (differentiating, say, humans from animals, forest from settlement, men from women, or among various parts of the forest); systematic classification of animals, plants, and spirits; and so on. It may also contain mechanisms for maintaining the good order and balance in the biophysical, human, and spiritual circuits; or circular (not linear) views of time and of biological and social life, ultimately validated by Providence, gods or goddesses; or a theory of how all beings in the universe are "raised" or "nurtured" out of similar principles, since in many nonmodern cultures the entire universe is conceived of as a living being with no strict separation between humans and nature, individual and community, community and the gods.

While specific formulas for arranging all of these factors vary greatly from group to group, they tend to have certain features in common: they reveal a complex image of social life that is not necessarily opposed to nature (in other words, one in which the natural world is integral to the social world), and that can be thought about in terms of relations such as kinship, extended kindred, and vernacular or analogic gender. Local models also evidence a particular attachment to a territory conceived of as a multidimensional entity that results from many types of practices and relations; and they also establish relations between symbolic/cultural systems and productive relations that can be highly complex. What is most important about these models from the perspective of postdevelopment is that they could be said to constitute ensembles of meanings-uses that, while existing in contexts of power that increasingly include transnational forces, cannot be reduced to modern meanings and uses.[12]

This brief reinterpretation of the literature on local knowledge of nature suggests that it is possible to articulate a discourse of ecological difference of cultural origin. This task is actually being advanced by two separate, but increasingly interrelated, social actors: political ecology theorists attempting to articulate an alternative theory of ecological rationality and sustainable development; and social movement activists in a variety of communities, such as those of rainforest peoples. Briefly, for the former, faced with the evidence presented previously, the question becomes: Is it possible to elaborate a new paradigm of production that incorporates—for any given ecosystem and social group—cultural, ecological, and technoeconomic factors into a strategy that is culturally and ecologically sustainable? If each ensemble of meanings-uses is held together by particular cultural constructions, social relations, and ecological practices—each with its particular productivity—is it possible to articulate an alternative productive rationality that respects and builds upon the respective productivities? In sum, how can we weave together the cultural, the ecological, and the technoeconomic into a different theory of production that is not subordinated to the economized production of commodities for profit and the rationality of managers and planners? (Leff, 1993; Escobar, 1999).

Social movements of the rain forest invariably emphasize four fundamental rights: to their identity, their territory, political autonomy, and to their own vision of development. Most of these movements are explicitly conceived in terms of cultural difference and of the ecological difference that this difference makes. They are not movements for development and the satisfaction of needs, even if of course economic and material improvements are important for them. They are movements of cultural and ecological attachment to a territory. For them, the right to exist is a cultural, political, and ecological question. They are necessarily open to certain forms of the commodity, market exchange, and technoscience (for instance, through engagement with biodiversity conservation strategies), while resisting capitalist and scientific valorization of nature. They can thus be seen as advancing through their political strategy a tactics of postdevelopment, to the extent that they forcefully voice and defend discourses and practices of cultural, ecological, and economic difference.[13]

How do place and noncapitalism figure in this strategy? As Dirlik (this volume) mentions, place consciousness offers a way for recentering both theory and people into a new articulation (nondivisibility even?) of humans and nonhumans (or, in the biologists' terms, in the continuum of being, doing, and knowing). The notion of territory being worked out by social movement activists and political ecologists, like the notion of landscape of phenomenological ecologists and unlike the modern concept of "land," can be said to enact a relation between place, culture, and nature. In a similar vein, the activists' definition of biodiversity as "territory plus culture" is another example of place-based consciousness—moreover, of place and culture becoming a source of political facts. Similarly, the local models of nature can also be reinterpreted—as Stephen Gudeman and Alberto Rivera (1990) have done with peasant models of the economy in the Andes—as constitutive of a variety of noncapitalist practices—many of them ecological. Some of these ensembles of meanings-uses of the natural can be seen, for purposes of the present analysis, as endowed with noncapitalist economic meaning. Whether they can be thought about in terms of alternative forms of appropriating and distributing surplus, as Gibson and Graham would have it, is another question.

Can we say, in the spirit of Gibson and Graham, that together local models of nature and the economy, and the social movements linked to them, adumbrate a postdevelopment era and "the end of development (as we knew it)"—that is, as a hegemonic and overpowering organizing principle of social life, an overarching principle of determination to which all aspects of social reality are subordinated? Needless to say, the requirements for this to happen are immense and complex, well beyond the social movements and critiques of development just discussed. In the conclusion of their book on capitalocentrism, Gibson and Graham ask a provocative question that serves as intuitive entry into this issue. "Why can feminists have revolution now, while Marxists have to wait?" (1996: 251). Their aim is not to erase the links between Marxism and feminism, but to highlight, despite the "flippancy and falsifications" of the question the fact that, while some feminisms envisage certain social transformations—the idea of gender as always under re/construction, of certain social transformation always taking place at the interpersonal and societal levels—by contrast "Marxism seems quite distant from both personal and social transformation" (251). "Why can't my Marxism have as its object something that I am involved in (re)constructing every day?," they go on to ask. "Where is my lived project of socialist construction?" (251).

These suggestive questions point again at the logic of capitalocentrism: the fact that what Marxism has been called upon to transform is this impossibly large monster that cannot be transformed, a capitalism that is immune to radical reconceptualization and the position of which seems to get further entrenched in the very act of critique, a capitalism with no outside, something nobody can escape. But is it possible to see it otherwise? "What if we theorize capitalism not as something large and embracing but as something partial, as one social constituent among many? . . . What if capitalism were a set of different practices scattered over the landscape that are (for convenience and in violation of difference) often seen as the same? If categories like subjectivity and society can undergo a radical rethinking, producing a crisis of individual and social identity where a presumed fixity previously existed, can't we give Capitalism an identity crisis as well?" (260, 261).

Similarly with space and development in the analyses we have recounted—that is, they are given an identity crisis in such analyses. Moreover, are not social movements of the rainforests, for instance, saying loud and clear that the world according to the development discourse is not all there is? Are not a multiplicity of communities in the Third World making equally clear through their practices that capitalism and development—despite their strong and perhaps growing presence in the same communities—have not succeeded in reshaping completely their identities and models of nature and the economy? Is it possible, then, to accept that postdevelopment is already (and has always been) under continuous (re)construction? That places are always being defended and re-created, and noncapitalisms always on the rise? To dare giving serious consideration to these questions certainly supposes a different politics of reading on our part as analysts, with the concomitant need to contribute to a different politics of representation of reality.

In the field of alternative development, a lot of experimentation is indeed taking place in many localities, in terms of trying out combinations of knowledge and power, truth and practice that incorporate local groups actively as knowledge producers. How is local knowledge to be translated into power, and this knowledge-power into concrete projects and programs? How can local knowledge-power constellations build bridges with expert forms of knowledge when necessary or convenient, and how can they widen their social space of influence when confronted, as is most often the case, with detrimental local, regional, national, and transnational conditions?[14] An anthropology of globalization predicated on the need to identify socially significant discourses of difference (cultural, social, economic, political)—and the ways in which they can operate as discourses of articulation of alternatives—would examine the manifold ways of constructing culture and identities today, as well as the production of differences through historicospatial processes that are not solely the product of global forces—whether capitalism, new technologies, market integration, or what have you—but also linked to places and their defense. It is important to make visible the manifold local logics of production of cultures and identities, economic and ecological practices, that are ceaselessly emerging from communities worldwide. To what extent do they pose important, and perhaps original, challenges to capitalism and Eurocentered modernities? Moreover, once visible, what would be the conditions that would enable place-based practices to create alternative structures that give them a chance to survive, let alone grow and flourish?

This last aspect of "the question of alternatives" remains largely intractable. For Dirlik, the survival of place-based cultures will be ensured when the globalization of the local compensates for the localization of the global—that is, when symmetry between the local and the global is reintroduced in social and conceptual terms and, we need to add, when noncapitalism and different cultural practices are similarly rendered into centers of analysis and strategies for action. Such a symmetry requires a parallel one between modern abstractions and everyday life, and consideration of context, history, and structure. In the last instance, however, the imagination and realization of significantly different orders demands "the projection of places into spaces to create new structures of power . . . in ways that incorporate places into their very constitution" (Dirlik, chapter 2, this text), the release of noncapitalist imaginaries into the constitution of economies and economic structures (including social classes), and the defense of local cultures from their normalization by modern mechanisms so that they can become effective political and life forces. For this to happen, places—with their forms of noncapitalism and particular form of cultural practices and ecological rationalities— must "project themselves into the spaces that are presently the domains of capital and modernity" (Dirlik, chapter 2, this text). Again, we can say that some social movements are pointing the way with their redefinition of the relation between nature and society, the cultural and the political.

This in no way entails reifying places, local cultures, and forms of noncapitalism as "untouched" or outside of history. To give attention to place and cultures is to destabilize "the surer spaces of power and difference marked by geopolitical or political economy perspectives" (Jacobs, 1996: 15). As Jane Jacobs adds, "the dichotomy of the authentically local and the appropriative global has its own problematic nostalgia. At best, the residual category of the local provides the hope for resistance. At worst, the local is seen as succumbing to the global, a compromised space of accommodation" (36). To restore symmetry to our forms of analysis, to speak about activating local places, cultures, and knowledge against the imperializing tendencies of space, capitalism, and modernity is not a deus ex machina operation, but a way to move beyond the chronic realism fostered by established modes of analysis. Surely places and localities are brought into the politics of commodification and cultural massification, but the knowledge of place and identity contributes to produce different meanings—of, say, economy, nature, each other—within the conditions of capitalism and modernity that surround it. New cultural, economic, and ecological opportunities might be opened up in this way against the imperial ecologies of nature and identity of capitalist modernity.

As social analysts, we must learn to see the defense of place, noncapitalism, and culture in the practices of those with whom we might work. Our analyses, perhaps despite our best wishes, continue to enact a defense of the global, an erasure of place. Perhaps we can say, paraphrasing Ranajit Guha (1988), that we too are complicit with "the prose of counterinsurgency," with representations of space, culture, and globalization that reduce place-based practices to the logic of something else, allegedly superior. What redefinitions of meanings and practices of the economy, nature, and social relations are necessary to advance this project of imagining alternatives? What types of research (historical and ethnographic, for instance) and what political practices by intellectuals, social movements, and communities are required to give social force to such a project?

These are important questions for poststructuralist strategies of knowledge production that self-consciously problematize disciplinary boundaries and that seek to theorize, as an integral part of their practice, their own contribution to making visible and possible subaltern, marginal, dissident, or emerging constructions of identity and lifeworlds. Malaysian anthropologist Wazir Jahan Karim put it bluntly in an inspired piece on anthropology, development, and globalization, and we can fittingly end this section with her words. Anthropology needs to concern itself with projects of social transformation, lest we become, she aptly says, "symbolically dissociated from local processes of cultural reconstruction and invention" (1996: 24). This dissociation is, we can now see, linked to the translation of place into space, of local economies into unreformed languages of political economy and globalization. Karim offers an alternative to this type of translation along the lines I have suggested here. For her, "the future of local knowledge is contextually dependent on its globalistic potential to generate new sources of knowledge from within" (128), and anthropologists have a role to play in this process, which also demands from us "a differentiated concept of who is who in the global and the local" because "whose definitions one may use becomes important" (135). Otherwise, anthropology will continue to be a largely irrelevant and provincial conversation among academics in the language of social theory.

CONCLUSION

That whose definitions of the local and the global, of place, culture, and economy one uses is, indeed, crucial can be said to be the main argument of this chapter and of some of the literature on which it is based. The critique of the privilege of space over place, of capitalism over noncapitalism, of global cultures over local ones is not so much—or not only—a critique of our understanding of the world but of the social theories on which we rely to derive such understanding. Whether these critiques are also an attempt to bring social theory into line with the views of the world and political strategies of those who exist on the side of place, noncapitalism, and local knowledge—an effort to which anthropologists are usually committed—it is too early to say. If it is true that "postdevelopments" and "noncapitalisms" are always under construction, there is hope that they could get to constitute new grounds for existence and significant rearticulations of subjectivity and alterity in their economic, cultural, and ecological dimensions. In many parts of the world, we are witnessing an unprecedented historical movement of economic, cultural, and biological life. It is necessary to think about the political and economic transformations that could make such movement a hopeful turn of events in the social history of cultures, economies, and ecologies.

In the last instance—suggested at least by a utopian imagination as the critique of the current hegemonies—the question becomes: Can the world be reconceived and reconstructed according to the logic of local cultures, practices, natures, and economies? Which forms of "the global" can be imagined from other, multiple local perspectives? Which counterstructures can be set into place to make them viable and productive? What notions of "politics," "democracy," and "economy" are needed to release the effectivity of the local, in all of their multiplicity and contradictions? What role will various social actors—including technologies old and new—have to play in order to create the networks on which manifold forms of the local can rely in their encounter with the multiple manifestations of the global? Some of these questions will have to be given serious consideration in our efforts to give shape to the imagination of alternatives to the current order of things.

NOTES

1. Among the "first wave" of book-length works contributing to the analysis of development as discourse are: Mueller (1987); Ferguson (1990); Apffel-Marglin and Marglin (1990); Sachs (1992); Dahl and Rabo (1992); Escobar (1995); and Crush (1995). For a

more complete bibliography on the subject, see Escobar (1995). These analyses are branching out in many directions, as will be discussed.

2. Attention is being paid to the following aspects: the historical predecessors of development, particularly the transition from the colonial to the development encounter; ethnographies of particular development institutions (from the World Bank to progressive NGOs), languages, and subfields; investigation of the contestation and resistances to development interventions; and critical biographies and autobiographies of development practitioners. These investigations are producing a more nuanced view of the nature and modes of operation of development discourses than analyses of the 1980s and early 1990s at first suggested.

3. From this perspective, the postdevelopment literature is capitalocentric because it endowed the development discourse with a similar dominance, linking this dominance to the spread of capitalism in the Third World. While it can be argued that this feature of the discursive critique was inevitable in the late 1980s—this was, indeed, the moment of emergence of critical development studies of poststructuralist orientation, and the argument perhaps needed to be made with a certain discursive excess—it is time to move beyond this moment and start the process of theorizing the existence of social, cultural, and economic difference in the Third World on antiessentialist grounds. I will enlist the notions of different class processes and place-based consciousness to this end.

4. The relation among capitalism, modernity, and the economy is not clear in the work of Gibson, Graham, and Ruccio. It is not true either that in the postdevelopment literature "the economy" is accepted as "real" (Gibson, Graham, and Ruccio, forthcoming: 9). For an analysis of economics as culture, see Gudeman (1986), Gudeman and Rivera (1990), and Escobar (1995: chap. 3).

5. The most important were those of Taussig (1980), Scott (1985), and Ong (1987). Fox and Starn, (1997) moved beyond everyday forms of resistance to consider those forms of mobilization and protest that take place "between resistance and revolution." For a review of some of this literature, see Escobar (1995), chap. 4.

6. The literature on local knowledge is vast. See Hobart (1993); Milton (1993). For an important discussion on peasant models of the economy, see Gudeman and Rivera (1990). This literature is reviewed in Escobar (1999).

7. The literature of hybridization and its relevance to postdevelopment is assessed in Escobar (1995), chap. 6.

8. It is true that anthropologists have recently celebrated the end of the notion of culture as bounded in time and space, even if warning against seeing culture as completely independent of place (Gupta and Ferguson, 1992). It could be said that today culture needs to be seen simultaneously as deterritorialized and place-based, even if not place-bound. It can also be argued that if it is true that by moving away from conventional, bounded definitions of culture the native has been released from the "incarceration" to which it has been subjected (Appadurai, 1986), "the local" has been reincarcerated in asymmetric discourses of globalization.

9. Soja's attempt, to be sure, succeeds only partially and can be seen as an illustration of the difficulties faced by poststructuralism in its efforts at transcending the binarisms of conventional social theory. Hall (1992) has equally referred to this problem in cultural studies. In this field, the tension between the ideal and the material, the textual and that which underlies it, representation and its grounding, etc., continues to be problematic and perhaps cannot be resolved in the terrain of theory. Some anthropologists have taken a hopeful turn in their ethnographic accounts of systems of production and signification,

meanings and practices, as inextricably bound (Comaroff and Comaroff, 1991). For an analysis of these efforts from the perspective of the cultural politics of social movements, see Alvarez, Dagnino, and Escobar (1998).

10. It is perhaps the case that the time has come to abandon the concept of hybridity, which was always a provisional one. I should point out, however, that in the Latin American discussion on the subject, hybridization (a process, not a state) is conceived as embodying forms of opposition and resistance and as a means of cultural affirmation, not of the negation or disappearance of difference. The new forms—perhaps as the new forms of noncapitalism visualized by Gibson and Graham—are neither entirely new (completely detached from long-standing cultural practices) nor necessarily "determined by" the dominant forms. Hybridization, in this way, might provide new spaces for the dynamic elaboration of tradition, for renegotiating forms of power predicated on (class, gender, race) difference, and—more importantly—for constructing political strategies geared to the reassertion of difference and identity. Whether this notion of hybridization can—or even should—be salvaged by infusing it with a keener sense of history, contradiction, and structure remains to be seen.

11. The argument of this section is developed more fully in Escobar (1999), including a review of the literature on local constructions of nature—whether informed by structuralism, ecosystems ecology, landscape ethnography, or the anthropology of local knowledge. For a state-of-the-art statement on some of this literature, see Descola and Pálsson (1996).

12. Is it necessary to say that not all local practices of nature are environmentally benign and that not all social relations that articulate them are nonexploitative? The extent to which local knowledge and practices of nature are "sustainable" or not is an empirical question. Dahl has perhaps best summarized this point: "All people of necessity maintain ideas about, and of necessity act on, their natural environment. This does not necessarily mean that those who live as direct producers have great systematic insights, although on the whole subsistence producers have detailed knowledge about the working of many small aspects of their biological environment. Much of this knowledge has from experience proved to be true and efficient, some is misconceived and counterproductive, and some is incorrect but still functions well enough" (Dahl, 1993: 6).

13. The cultural politics of biodiversity is discussed in Escobar (1997) with a focus on the Pacific Coast rain forest of Colombia. The development of a significant black movement of ethnocultural and ecological orientation in the same region is chronicled and analyzed in Grueso, Rosero, and Escobar (1998).

14. Again, it is necessary to point out that "local knowledge" is no panacea. Local knowledge is not "pure" or free of domination; it is historical and connected to the wider world through relations of power, and in many ways determined by them. The defense of local knowledge proposed here is both political and epistemological, arising out of the commitment to a discourse of difference. Against those who always think that to highlight local knowledge is undeniably "romantic," one could say, with Jacobs (1996: 161) that "it is a form of imperial nostalgia, a desire for the 'untouched Native', which presumes that such encounters [between local and global] only ever mark yet another phase of imperialism."

REFERENCES

Alvarez, Sonia, Evelina Dagnino, and Arturo Escobar, eds. *Cultures of Politics/Politics of Cultures: Revisioning Latin American Social Movements.* Boulder: Westview, 1998.

Apffel-Marglin, Frédérique, and Stephen Marglin, eds. *Dominating Knowledge: Development, Culture and Resistance.* Oxford: Clarendon, 1990.

Appadurai, Arjun. "Theory in Anthropology: Center and Periphery." *Comparative Studies in Society and History* 28(1) (1986): 356–61.

Chernaik, Laura. "Spatial Displacements: Transnationalism and the New Social Movements." *Gender, Place and Culture* 3(3) (1996): 251–75.

Comaroff, Jean, and John Comaroff. *Of Revelation and Revolution.* Chicago: University of Chicago Press, 1991.

Crush, Jonathan. "Introduction: Imagining Development." In *Power of Development,* edited by J. Crush. New York: Routledge, 1995, 1–26.

Crush, Jonathan, ed. *Power of Development.* New York: Routledge, 1995.

Dahl, Gudrun, ed. *Green Arguments for Local Subsistence.* Stockholm: Stockholm Studies in Social Anthropology, 1993.

Dahl, Gudrun, and Anika Rabo, eds. *Kam-ap or Take-Off: Local Notions of Development.* Stockholm: Stockholm Studies in Social Anthropology, 1992.

Descola, Philippe, and Gísli Pálsson, eds. *Nature and Society: Anthropological Perspectives.* London: Routledge, 1996.

Escobar, Arturo. *Encountering Development. The Making and Unmaking of the Third World.* Princeton, N.J.: Princeton University Press, 1995.

———. "Cultural Politics and Biological Diversity: State, Capital and Social Movements in the Pacific Coast of Colombia." In *Between Resistance and Revolution: Culture and Social Protest,* edited by O. Starn and R. Fox. New Brunswick, N.J.: Rutgers University Press, 1997, 40–61.

———. "After Nature: Steps to an Anti-Essentialist Political Ecology." *Current Anthropology* 40(1) (1999): 1–30.

Ferguson, James. *The Anti-Politics Machine: Development, Depoliticization and Bureaucratic Power in Lesotho.* Cambridge: Cambridge University Press, 1990.

Fox, Richard, and Orin Starn, eds. *Between Resistance and Revolution: Culture and Social Protest.* New Brunswick, N.J.: Rutgers University Press, 1997.

García Canclini, Néstor. *Culturas Híbridas: Estrategias para Entrar y Salir de la Modernidad.* México, D.F.: Grijalbo, 1990.

Gibson, Katherine, Julie Graham, and David Ruccio. "'After' Development: Negotiating the Place of Class." In *Class: The Next Postmodern Frontier,* edited by J. K. Gibson-Graham, S. Resnick, and R. Wolf. Oxford: Blackwell, forthcoming.

Gibson-Graham, J.K. *The End of Capitalism (as we knew it).* Oxford: Basil Backwell, 1996.

Grueso, Libia, Carlos Rosero, and Arturo Escobar. "The Process of Black Community Organizing in the Southern Pacific Coast of Colombia." In *Cultures of Politics/Politics of Culture: Revisioning Latin American Social Movements,* edited by S. Alvarez, E. Dagnino, and A. Escobar. Boulder: Westview, 1998, 196–219.

Gudeman, Stephen. *Economics as Culture.* New York: Routledge, 1986.

Gudeman, Stephen, and Alberto Rivera. *Conversations in Colombia: The Domestic Economy in Life and Text.* Cambridge: Cambridge University Press, 1990.

Guha, Ranajit. "The Prose of Counter-Insurgency." In *Selected Subaltern Studies,* edited by R. Guha and G. Spivak. Delhi, India: Oxford University Press, 1988, 37–44.

Gupta, Akhil, and James Ferguson. "Beyond 'Culture': Space, Identity, and the Politics of Difference." *Cultural Anthropology* 7(1) (1992): 6–23.

Hall, Stuart. "Cultural Studies and Its Theoretical Legacies." In *Cultural Studies,* edited by L. Grossberg, C. Nelson, and P. Treichler. London: Routledge, 1992, 277–94.

Hobart, Mark, ed. *An Anthropological Critique of Development*. London: Routledge, 1993.

Jacobs, Jane. *Edge of Empire: Postcolonialism and the City*. London: Routledge, 1996.

Jackson, Michael, ed. *Things as They Are: New Directions in Phenomenological Anthropology*. Bloomington: Indiana University Press, 1996.

Karim, Wazir Jahan. "Anthropology without Tears: How a 'Local' Sees the 'Local' and the 'Global'." In *The Future of Anthropological Knowledge*, edited by H. Moore. London: Routledge, 1996, 115–38.

Leff, Enrique. "Marxism and the Environmental Question." *Capitalism, Nature, Socialism* 4(1) (1993): 44–66.

Latour, Bruno. *We Have Never Been Modern*. Cambridge, Mass.: Harvard University Press, 1993.

Leff, Enrique. "Marxism and the Environmental Question." *Capitalism, Nature, Socialism* 4(1) (1993): 44–66.

Massey, Doreen. "A Global Sense of Place." In *Studying Culture*, edited by A. Gray and J. McGuigan. London: E. Arnold, 1993, 232–40.

———. *Space, Place and Gender*. Minneapolis: University of Minnesota Press, 1994.

Maturana, Humberto, and Francisco Varela. *The Tree of Knowledge*. Boston: Shambhala, 1987.

Milton, Kay, ed. *Environmentalism: The View from Anthropology*. London: Routledge, 1993.

Mudimbe, V.Y. *The Invention of Africa*. Bloomington: Indiana University Press, 1988.

Mueller, Adele. *Peasants and Professionals: The Social Organization of Women in Development Knowledge*. Ph.D. dissertation, Ontario Institute for Studies in Education, 1987.

Nandy, Ashis. *The Intimate Enemy*. Delhi, India: Oxford University Press, 1983.

Ong, Aihwa. *Spirits of Resistance and Capitalist Discipline*. Albany: SUNY Press, 1987.

Pigg, Stacy. "Constructing Social Categories through Place: Social Representations and Development in Nepal." *Comparative Studies in Society and History* 34(3) (1992): 491–513.

Polanyi, Karl. *The Great Transformation*. Boston: Beacon Press, 1957.

Porter, Doug. "Scenes from Childhood: The Homesickness of Development Discourses." In *Power of Development*, edited by J. Crush. London: Routledge, 1995, 63–86.

Pred, Alan, and Michael Watts. *Reworking Modernity*. New Brunswick, N.J.: Rutgers University Press, 1992.

Procacci, Giovanna. "Social Economy and the Government of Poverty." In *The Foucault Effect*, edited by Graham Burchell, et al. Chicago: University of Chicago Press, 1991, 151–68.

Resnick, Stephen, and Rick Wolff. *Knowledge and Class: A Marxian Critique of Political Economy*. Chicago: University of Chicago Press, 1987.

Sachs, Wolfgang, ed. *The Development Dictionary*. London: Zed, 1992.

Said, Edward. *Orientalism*. New York: Vintage, 1979.

Scott, James. *Weapons of the Weak*. New Haven, Conn.: Yale University Press, 1985.

Slater, David. "Challenging Western Notions of the Global: The Geopolitics of Theory and North-South Relations." *The European Journal of Development Research* 7 (1995): 366–88.

Soja, Edward. *Thirdspace*. Oxford: Basil Blackwell, 1996.

Strathern, Marilyn. "No Nature, No Culture: The Hagen Case." In *Nature, Culture and*

Gender, edited by C. MacCormack and M. Strathern. Cambridge: Cambridge University Press, 1980, 174–219.

Taussig, Michael. *The Devil and Commodity Fetishism in South America*. Chapel Hill: University of North Carolina Press, 1980.

Thomas, Julian. "The Politics of Vision and the Archaeologies of Landscape." In *Landscape: Politics and Perspective*, edited by Barbara Bender. Oxford: Berg, 1993, 19–48.

Watts, Michael. "'A New Deal in Emotions': Theory and Practice and the Crisis of Development." In *Power of Development*, edited by J. Crush,. New York: Routledge, 1995, 27–43.

10

Globalization and Environmental Resistance Politics

James H. Mittelman

Not all types of environmental degradation are of recent origin or global in scope—some are long established and local.[1] Even so, unsustainable transformation of the environment under globalization differs from environmental harm in previous epochs. Although contemporary environmental abuses have their antecedents in earlier periods of history, globalization coincides with new environmental problems such as global warming, depletion of the ozone layer, acute loss of biodiversity, and forms of transborder pollution (e.g., acid rain). These problems have emerged not singly, but together. Moreover, some ecological problems are clearly the result of global cross-border flows, as with certain kinds of groundwater contamination, leaching, and long-term health threats traceable to importing hazardous wastes.

Large-scale growth in world economic output since the 1970s has not only quickened the breakdown of the global resource base; it has upset the planet's regenerative system, including its equilibrium among different forms of life and their support structures. A large part of the explanation is that deregulation and liberalization mean more global pressure to lower environmental standards, albeit there are, of course, counterpressures to shift from environmentally destructive activities to cleaner technologies. In the absence of stringent regulations and effective enforcement mechanisms, fear and insecurity about the planet's future are on the rise.

With hypercompetition for profits, the market is trespassing nature's limits (Shiva, 1992: 211, 216). Yet nature's protest, its signals of breakdown, provide an opening. Rather than reify the environment, it is important to resist the ontological distinction between humans and nature, a dualism rooted in modern thought since Descartes. If so, humankind and nature may be viewed interactively as "a single causal stream" (Rosenau, 1997: 190–1; also Goldblatt, 1996). The environment may then be understood as political space, a critical venue where civil society is voicing its concerns. As such, the environment represents a marker where, to varying degrees, popular resistance to globalization is manifest. Slicing across party, class, religion, gender, race, and ethnicity, environmental politics offers a useful entry point for assessing counterglobalization.

Accordingly, the questions that frame this chapter are: What are the specific sites of environmental resistance to globalization? Who are the agents of resistance? What strategies are adopted? And to what extent are they localized or regionalized and globalized? In other words, is there evidence to demonstrate the stirrings of counterglobalization?

In attempting to answer these questions, I will show the complex layering of different modes of resistance politics. My chief concern is organized environmental responses to globalization, though not to the exclusion of other types of resistance. For reasons that will be elaborated in the next section, I am especially interested in direct environmental initiatives—solid patterns and cumulative action—but also in the soft, or latent, forms of protest that may or may not sufficiently harden so as eventually to challenge global structures. Attention will be given to submerged forms of resistance insofar as they are emerging into networks. Networks are important here because they may serve as venues for resistance, and also because global capitalism is not at all singular (Yearley, 1996; Heng, 1997; Hefner, 1998). Rather, capitalism is organized in multiple ways. For example, "network capitalism" is widely recognized in the Japanese and transnational Chinese forms of ties originating at universities and continuing in professional circles, information exchange, and government-business collaboration.

A major goal of this chapter, then, is to present evidence for exploring the politics of resistance (in view of theoretical propositions developed in Mittelman, 1996, and Chin and Mittelman, 1997) and to bring to light the diversity of environmental politics in encounters with globalizing processes. The evidential material adduced here centers on transboundary problems, illustrates the myriad ways that environmental groups operate, and offers fresh and original examples of the emerging and varying consciousness of resistance.[2] For the purposes of academic research, it would be desirable to separate the domain of resistance to globalization from resistance to other forms of hierarchical power relations, but they cannot be neatly divided. Rather, spheres of resistance surrounding the environment, labor standards, women's issues, human rights, and the like merge and interpenetrate. One can, however, identify certain emphases in consciousness and action as a basis for analyzing potential transformations in world order (Mittelman, 1997).

This chapter considers but in no way romanticizes the voices of the subjects of globalization who are engaged in environmental resistance politics. Not limited to perceptual evidence, it draws on both documentary research and seventy-five separate interviews (some for attribution and others on condition of anonymity) that I conducted in Eastern (i.e., East plus Southeast) Asia and Southern Africa. I say "separate" because in some cases, and to my pleasant surprise, more than one member of an organization unexpectedly turned up for an appointment with a single interviewee and participated in what became a group interview. The interviewees were selected with reference to the categories deemed theoretically central, discussed later. In carrying out research in countries where civil society is of recent origin and relatively thin, I sought out leading activists who are pursuing environmental objectives (though they may also mobilize around other causes pertaining to social justice) and challenging global structures either directly or indirectly. Of course, the proximate issues vary from one case to another—for example, from deforestation to toxic waste—but in all instances involve transboundary problems.

It was of course impossible to hold interviews or do other types of fieldwork in all the countries in the two subregions, but this project did entail research of varied duration and intensity in Japan, Malaysia, the Philippines, Singapore, and Vietnam, as well as in Botswana, Mozambique, South Africa, and Zimbabwe. I attended meetings of environmental resistance groups, accompanied them on their campaigns, including to a toxic waste dump (Holfontein, South Africa, July 20, 1996), visited lands contested as *ancestral domain* (a term used to underline the relationship between the issues of land rights and social justice), and queried ministers and a high court justice. Thus, I had ample opportunity to talk formally and informally with people in international and indigenous nongovernmental organizations (NGOs)—including what are known as people's organizations (POs) in the Philippines and community-based organizations (CBOs) in South Africa—businesses, state agencies, universities, and the media. With most of the interviewees, it immediately became apparent that the architecture of globalization is too huge to perceive as a whole, but if one moves to a finer scale, the structures become discernible.

To enter the crucible of resistance politics, I first explore the characteristics of environmental resistance politics. The next section turns to the sources of popular resistance, followed by a discussion of the agents challenging macrostructures. Inquiry then focuses on the sites of resistance and, finally, weighs the efficacy of multilayered strategies.

CHARACTERISTICS OF ENVIRONMENTAL RESISTANCE POLITICS

The environment is not a single phenomenon and, as implied previously, may be viewed through different prisms: a series of interactions between the physical and human worlds, a site of resistance, and a social construction that is contested. In terms of the latter approach, attitudes toward nature are always changing, are linked to time and place, and initially reflect the dominant culture. In fact, the relationship between nature and culture has been rapidly and variously transformed around the world. This is not new, but technological innovations and hypercompetition accelerate the trend. Moreover, a hallmark of globalization is the explosion of cultural pluralism, and some cultural conflicts tied to imbalances in power relations find expression in environmental ideologies, understood as systems of representation of a definite group or class.

A graphic example of the social construction of the environment is the Eurocentric conservation ideology that developed in Southern Africa. In the mid–twentieth century, there emerged an extension of the colonial paradigm, a conservation ideology based on a wildlife-centered, preservationist approach that buttressed white privilege and power in the subcontinent (Khan, 1994). The story of game and nature reserves in Southern Africa is embedded in the mythology surrounding Kruger National Park and symbolized by the portrayal of Paul Kruger as a visionary who championed wildlife protection. Environmental historians have deconstructed this romantic myth, showing that Kruger actually opposed stricter game protection laws and supported the legal right of whites to continue to hunt. But the icon of "Paul Kruger's dream" was appropriated by the purveyors of an emergent Afrikaner nationalism and manipulated to gain the support of poor whites; it helped to unite opposed factions and classes in Afrikaner society in the post–World War I period. After 1948, the apartheid regime revived the Kruger wildlife, protectionist myth in an attempt not only to rouse patriotism but also to gain international respectability for the pariah state among its critics overseas (Carruthers, 1995; Khan, 1990).

Racial discrimination in the application of conservation policies, such as stock culling, forged anticonservation attitudes. The marginalization of blacks generated a negative attitude toward government decisions concerning the environment, which were seen as imposed by an unjust system that denied meaningful representation or participation to people who believed that they had a rightful claim to the land. Africans engaged in poaching, withheld their services, and lived clandestinely in the game reserves—all expressions of freedom of action. Popular resistance gave rise to initiatives such as the Native Farmers Association (NFA), the first black organization in South Africa to record a formal environmental ethic and thereby contribute to a counterideology opposed to the culture of the park as being white, pristine, and scientistic. The NFA, in fact, called for a paradigmatic shift toward socially responsive policies (Khan, 1994). What many white South Africans and Westerners came to regard as a science—conservation and park, or more generally, environmental management—others came to interpret as a disguised form of resource control.

This illustration indicates that the environment may be construed as a set of alternative moral forces forming ideological representations. It demonstrates that submerged responses to environmental use (or abuse) may in turn be transformed into organized political resistance that props up its counterideologies. It also implicates the basic categories of analysis used by the master theorists of resistance—Antonio Gramsci (1971), Karl Polanyi (1957), and James C. Scott (1976, 1985, 1990)—discussed in Christine Chin and James Mittelman (1997). At this juncture, I will not revisit what was said there, but want to position myself within this triad so as to forge a link to environmental resistance politics.

Needless to say, all three frameworks advanced by these authors have great explanatory power. Their merits do not require elaboration in this chapter, but a few critical comments are in order. A Marxist who subscribed to the view that class conflict is the motor of history, Gramsci differed from Marx in allowing considerable autonomy for consciousness, which helps to understand the cultural dimensions of resistance. Nonetheless, a drawback to Gramsci's two-pronged conceptualization of wars of movement and position is that in both cases, the objective is to take control of state power. With globalization, however, resistance may or may not target the state. If one of the roles of the state today is to provide the domestic economy with greater access to global capital, then the state is a part of the whole matrix of globalization. To rotate the holders of state power may not alleviate the problems that ignited resistance in the first place. Accordingly, Gramsci's conceptualization must be stretched to include a range of other actors and different spaces in which, at the turn of the millennium, consciousness develops.

Like Gramsci, Scott turns attention to the culture of resistance. His emphasis on "infrapolitical" activities offers a subtle way to probe everyday responses to globalizing processes. Indeed, there are valuable empirical studies documenting the microrelations of encounters between local and global conditions. For example, Aihwa Ong (1987) details spirit possession episodes, when Malay factory women become violent and scream abuses as a symptom of their loss of autonomy at work. Nevertheless, the limitation to Scott's probing of covert acts is that the wide gamut of forms of resistance he suggests is a catchall. Not only are they highly diffuse, but they also may make little overall impact on power relations. This problem in Scott's framework is revealed in the very first line of his 1990 book. The aphorism he selects to open it is an Ethiopian proverb: "When the great lord passes the wise peasant bows deeply and farts." Yet how much political impact does farting really have? How much effect do foot-dragging, squatting, gossip, and other forms of uncoordinated resistance actually have on environmental problems such as global warming and deterioration of the ozone layer? Where is the evidence to demonstrate that countless microscopic activities will ultimately amount to a shift in macrostructures?[3]

Although, as Scott cautions, these acts, even when multiplied, may not topple regimes, they often signal weaknesses in a regime's legitimacy and can help undermine faith in authority. Indeed, it might be argued that numerous subversive measures do add up, for they are cumulative. But it seems fair to ask, If the consequences are fully felt only in the *longue durée*, how long will that be? As the eruption of multiple environmental crises patently shows, nature is already vetoing its subordination to the market economy (Harries-Jones, Rotstein, and Timmerman 1992).[4] By all indications, it will not wait for the *longue durée* to resolve the matter. Whereas it is right to be alert to the subtexts of resistance, and thus the seeds of potential transformation, the question is: How and under what conditions, do submerged forms of resistance coalesce and genuinely contest globalizing structures? Conversely, it is important to specify the conditions that prevent the crystallization of resistance politics. What factors facilitate and hinder the stiffening of resistance?

Few contemporary scholars (with notable exceptions, including Walker, 1994; Shaw, 1994; Murphy, 1994; Sklair, 1994; 1997; Smith, Chatfield, and Pagnucco, 1997; and Keck and Sikkink, 1998) have attempted to theorize the connections between social movements and world politics. It should be recalled that master thinkers such as Gramsci and Polanyi offered traces of a finely grained analysis of the emergence of social movements within the global political economy of their times. Turning attention to the Owenites and Chartists of his day, Polanyi underlined that "both movements comprised hundreds of thousands of craftsmen and artisans, laborers and working people, and with their vast following ranked among the biggest *social movements* in modern history" (1957: 167; emphasis added). It was Polanyi's insight that the dialectic of movement and countermovement advances understanding of resistance but only if concrete political, economic, and social institutions are brought into an analysis of historical transformation. Polanyi was, above all, concerned with the specific institutional arrangements by which particular societies ensure their livelihood. Following from Polanyi's contribution, an area of inquiry that needs to be extended is: As societies try to protect themselves against the traumatic effects of the market, including what he regarded as "the disintegration of the cultural environment" (1957: 157), how do submerged expressions of resistance solidify and actually take shape as countermovements? In this vein, a Polanyian framework may be readily applied to the relationship between political economy and ecology (Bernard, 1997). In fact, writing more than a half century ago, Karl Polanyi ([1944] 1957) himself registered grave concern over the disembeddedness of markets not only from society, but also from nature.

An ecological reading of Polanyi requires a grasp of his critique of classical political economy and liberalism. In opposition to Adam Smith's emphasis on individual economic gains over an appreciation for embeddedness in social relations, and in contrast to Smith's response to the Physiocrats' proclivity for agriculture, Polanyi held that it is an error to exclude nature from political economy. Similarly, he pronounced Ricardo guilty of the commodity fiction of treating land as only a factor of production and detaching it from social institutions. Karl Marx, too, came under fire for one-sidedly judging the character of an economy in terms of the labor process. According to Polanyi, always the economic historian and anthropologist, nineteenth-century society differed from its forerunners in the way that economic gain became preeminent in organizing, or reorganizing, human life. For Polanyi, both Marxism and liberalism erroneously posited that the dominant pattern in their societies was dominant throughout history (Block and Somers, 1984: 63). Adopting a wider, historical frame, Polanyi delimited forms of integration of humans and nature in premarket society and showed that the economy had been governed by basic institutions of society, and not vice versa. The institutional mechanisms had included reciprocity, redistribution, and household relations (Polanyi, 1968).

To extrapolate from Polanyi, the error of economic rationalism is to vest an economistic culture with an economistic logic. A science of economics subordinates the science of nature. This relationship turns on one's understanding of the "economic," which cannot be taken for granted. One definition commonly used is formal and centers on scarcity. It is to be distinguished from a second, the substantive sense, which involves "the fundamental fact that human beings, like all other living things, cannot exist for any length of time without a physical environment that sustains them; this is the origin of the substantive definition of *economic*" (Polanyi, 1977: 19; emphasis in original). The interactions between humans and their natural surroundings thus carry "meanings," and there may be counteracting forces at work.

For a condition in which economics subordinates both nature and society, and hence creates market society, the antidote is reembedding. But in practice, what does it really mean to reground economics in nature and social relations? Posing this question underscores the elemental dilemma in resistance politics today. The challenge is even greater than in Polanyi's time—and requires an extension of his framework—because of the increasing integration of national economies. The search for a formula for reembedding has clearly given rise to different political projects, and is a contested issue. To examine these projects, let us first identify *forms* and sources of popular environmental resistance so that we can then delineate the work of *agents* for change, especially the politically organized wings of civil society, the *sites* at which they operate, and the principal *strategies* of resistance. What must then be taken into account is whether these wings of resistance fall into any sort of formation.

FORMS AND SOURCES OF POPULAR ENVIRONMENTAL RESISTANCE

Forms of environmental degradation are diverse and have several root causes. The main problems pertain to the home environment, the workplace, and nature, and are to be found in different sectors of the economy, especially energy, agriculture, mining, and manufacturing. The sources have both objective and subjective dimensions and may be mapped as a combination of factors:

- Hypercompetition
- Social inequality and poverty
- Unsustainable levels of exploitation of resources
- Occupation of land and its conversion into commercial and industrial projects
- Migration and overcrowding
- Fears of displacement
- Debt structures, which in turn further resource exploitation
- Criminalizing the customary use of resources (or a perception thereof) and a lack of accountability

Rather than speak only of a list of discrete sources, one must also trace distinctive historical trajectories culminating in environmental abuse. These constitute interactive webs of social relations. Some of the sources noted originated in the preglobalization periods, but globalization intensifies these processes. There are also new forms of age-old problems, such as debt. Consider, for example, the environmental impact of structural adjustment programs. Greater austerity at home, coupled with the need to meet heightened interest payments required by international financial institutions, often result in more emphasis on the export of natural resources to earn foreign exchange. The exploitation of resources and big projects, such as the construction of dams, displace people. Most often, it is poor people who become internal migrants (Freedom from Debt Coalition, 1996). On Mindanao, the southernmost island in the Philippines, transnational corporations (TNCs)—for instance, big pineapple concerns such as Dole—have gained possession of lowlands, eroding the soil and driving peasant farmers upland. Amid a sharp conflict between lowlanders and uplanders, indigenous peoples—"tribal groups"—battle to protect their cultural integrity and "ancestral domain."

While not a mountainous terrain, the landscape of eastern Zimbabwe straddling the Mozambican border is the scene of a similar form of encounter. With Cargill, a transnational food processing conglomerate, controlling large tracts of land, and with the erosion of the soil, internal migration is on the rise. Ethnic groups, or subdivisions of them, are competing for resources and coming into conflict with one another. In this case, it is difficult to distinguish internal from international migration, for local peoples regularly cross the border with impunity. They do so partly to evade laws—for example, Zimbabwean rural dwellers drive elephants, which destroy crops, over the border into Mozambique and kill them there. The attitude among these peasant farmers is that borders are a nuisance that interfere with both their livelihood and relations with kin, redound to the advantage of the well-to-do, and are another way in which the political authorities seek to impose control. In this instance, the state is seen as constraining cross-border flows—of fish, ivory, meat, marijuana, and spirits—rooted in culture and economy. From this perspective, borders are instruments of coercion and sites of conflict. Such visions are underpinned by divisions of labor and power at the national, regional, and global levels. In both the Philippines and Zimbabwe, not only are there pressures on poor people to become migrants, but to survive, they must also destroy resources.

Hence, the targets of environmental resistance may be direct and take on a tangible form, or be indirect in the sense of process. The issue, at bottom, is control: control of land, species, forests, marine life, labor, and ideology. These aspects of control may be inscribed in law and enforced by the state. The resisters are ultimately motivated by the desire for access, and in varied measures, react against layers of structural power. One aspect of such opposition, increasingly apparent among different power positions, is the disjuncture between environmental ideologies (Nazarea-Sandoval, 1995). Evident under varied guises in both Eastern

Asia and Southern Africa is a clash between advocates of a modern-day, neoliberal variant of the trickle-down approach, which holds that the first task is to grow the economy; then, one can attend to distribution and equity, and proponents of alternatives that stress the need for community-based development and the linkage between economic reform and social policy (e.g., "social forestry"). In other words, access to resources is reinforced or challenged by different ideologies; but the dominant one is reform, understood as growth before equity. Although from one interview to another, my interviewees' terminology differed, this same point was made several times over. In a joint interview that centered on forestry, an interviewee punctuated his remarks by proclaiming: "The root causes [of environmental abuse] are in social structures reinforced by the development paradigm. The paradigm is the villain" (del Castillo, 1996; Rebugio, 1996).

The resisters adopt time and space perspectives consonant with their own sense of dignity and interests, which at present is a matter of sheer survival for many. The specific forms that reactions take turn on the type and degree of environmental abuse, as well as the strategies available to the resisters (Peluso, 1992: 13; Scott, 1985). The recourse may be outward in the sense of striking at an external phenomenon, inward in taking on local forms of control, or both inasmuch as layers of outsiders and insiders become so interwoven that structures of resistance seek to break both down (Peluso, 1992: 13, 16–17; Scott, 1985). This then begs the question: What are the sites at which agents resist globalizing structures and craft alternative strategies?

SITES OF RESISTANCE

Aside from self-help societies and local charities, a dense web of private, associational life was not available as a site of resistance—it did not exist in Japan and most other areas outside the West—before the 1960s and 1970s. In fact, it is generally absent in Vietnam today, where environmentalists work with a ministry but do not find a scope for private initiatives outside the state. There are only a handful of Vietnamese environmental NGOs, each one small, based in Hanoi, and lacking autonomy. Environmental groups also face severe constraints in Singapore and Malaysia, but the conditions differ and beget a distinctive mix of strategies.

There have been tentative attempts by Singaporean environmentalists, a multiclass group but mainly professionals, administrators, and managers, to open up political space and test the state's rhetoric about tolerance. Most notably, the Nature Society of Singapore (NSS), founded more than thirty years ago as the Singapore branch of the Malayan Nature Society, has contested government policy within stringent parameters. Inasmuch as NGOs in Singapore are subject to restraining legislation, such as the Societies Act and deregistration, which effectively bans their operations, as well as court proceedings, the NSS has represented its actions as "constructive dialogue." Composed of about two thousand members, the NSS has engaged in letter-writing campaigns, designed a master plan for conservation, and commissioned its own environmental impact assessments (Ho, 1997b). The NSS also takes the initiative and submits proposals to the government, even though most of them—99 percent—are rejected. The most extreme move involved enlisting up to twenty-five thousand signatures for a petition and submitting it to the appropriate authority. A major constraint is that the NSS and Singapore's few other environmental groups, which are mainly involved in school activities, risk losing credibility with the state—and thus facing sanctions—if they work with NGOs in other countries. Apart from sharing information, there is little transnational collaboration. Even so, tussles over environmental projects have contributed to important changes in land use: converting eighty-seven hectares zoned for an agro-technology park to a bird sanctuary at Sungei Buloh, shelving plans for a golf course at the Lower Pierce reserve catchment area, and the diversion of a proposed mass rapid transit line so that it would not disrupt the natural habitat of bird life in Senoko (Ho, 1997a; Rodan, 1996: 106–7; Kong, 1994). Notwithstanding coercive rule and co-optation wrought by a postcolonial transformation from poverty to economic well-being, and despite a culture that values "consensus," not dissent, clearly there are fledgling attempts to expand civil society and, however tenuously, to foster resistance.

As in Singapore, civil society in Malaysia is constrained by economic co-optation, draconian laws such as the Internal Security Act (a relic of colonialism that permits detention without trial), and intimidation against environmental activism, including Prime Minister Mahathir Mohamad's rhetoric about "green imperialism." So, too, the state requires NGO registration, controls access to the media, and is dominated by one party, which not only penetrates deeply into society, but also is extremely shrewd in mixing coercion and consent (as emphasized, the ingredients of hegemony so long as the latter is the main component). The holders of state power have nipped off elements of checks and balances—for example, by eroding the prerogatives of farmers associations and other semiautonomous structures in the rural areas. Ideological representations—issues of race, language, and religion—have deflected attention from critical problems, including environmental degradation. Nevertheless, there have been bottom-up actions by environmentalists—mobilization in *kampung* (villages) around acid pollution, protests over radioactive waste, residence issues concerning trees in Cheras, and logging blockades in Sarawak (Gurmit, 1997). A handful of environmental organizations—including the Environmental Protection Society; the Malayan Nature Society; Sahabat Alam Malaysia; and the Centre for Environment, Technology, and Development, Malaysia—as well as various consumer associations—have established space for low-key agitation and "critical collaboration" with the government.

In contrast, a robust civil society has developed in countries such as the Philippines and South Africa, and there are vibrant activities elsewhere—for example, in Thailand and South Korea. Highly politicized Philippine and South African civil societies emerged in the context of mobilization: in one case, through armed struggles against Spanish colonialism, U.S. domination, and martial rule, while, in the other, against the apartheid regime. Among the different kinds of civil society activities illustrated above, countries such as Zimbabwe are in an intermediate position: Environmentalists and other activists push the limits but are ever mindful of the consequences of not respecting them. In all instances, the concrete institutions of civil society, specific to countries and regions, are crucial.

THE AGENTS

The spectrum of environmental institutions does not form a continuum running left and right. Rather, the environmental movement may be likened to a broad tree with many branches and shoots of varying degrees of maturity. The thickness changes from the roots to the different sides and levels. With the thickening of civil society, its tree-like growth may still be a matter more of twigs than boughs.

In practice, this structure consists of several institutions such as churches, trade unions, the business sector, peasant associations, and student groups that have participated, and often joined together, in rallying around environmental issues. All these institutions are part of civil society. It is civil society that is the main vector in environmental resistance. Within civil society, there appear to be five layers of environmental resistance to globalization. Without underestimating the silent struggle of poaching, killing animals, cutting fences, burning fields, and so on, it is direct and organized action at these five levels that seems to have the greatest impact and bears the most potential for gaining momentum.

First, there are a host of international environmental organizations, such as Greenpeace, Friends of the Earth, and the World Wildlife Fund, that work closely with indigenous groups or have local affiliates under their aegis (see Wapner, 1996). Most of the former are based in the West, and may or may not have the same agenda as their partners in the Third World (Brosius, 1997; Eccleston, 1996). In some cases, those on the ground express reservations about the discrepant priorities of external bodies and, at times, seek to fuse indigenous values with Western environmental concerns (Lee and So, 1999: 291). At the second level of generality come national coalitions or networks, such as the Caucus of Development NGO Networks, an umbrella organization of fourteen major NGO networks in the Philippines. Its objective is to serve as a network of networks (Songco, 1996). Together, these coalitions encompass nearly three thousand individual organizations. An important research need is to map these coalition structures. Essentially, this is a weblike realm of functionally specialized organizations that link many NGOs, associations, societies, and so on, as well as share a common agenda and set of priorities.

Third, individual NGOs at a national level play multiple roles. They are catalysts that strive to facilitate action, often by advocacy, mobilizing resources, and providing expertise: skills in local administration, legal drafting, accounting, and other forms of training, as well as research on specific issues. Swept up in transformations of their livelihoods and modes of existence, leaders of civil society are searching for an understanding of these conditions. In honing their mission and carrying out research, NGOs require, and indeed seek, analytical paradigms. Notions such as trickle-down economics, participatory development, and community organizing are all born out of paradigms. Yet, with globalization, more compelling explanations are sought, especially to help generate means of action.

Next, although the idiom varies from one region and country to another, grassroots organizations are engaged in the actual implementation of projects. POs and CBOs are grassroots organizations involved in collective action. They may or may not seek the assistance of NGOs. Finally, civil society also includes a large swath of unheard masses who are unorganized but not unconcerned citizens, for they too are stakeholders. They can be mobilized around issues of severe environmental degradation and have been incited to join campaigns to block activities such as illegal logging and the dumping of toxic wastes. Religious leaders, from Catholic bishops to the mufti, have indeed implored their followers to stop ecological destruction. The influence of Buddhism, Christianity, Confucianism, Islam, Judaism, and other religions runs deep in environmental resistance politics, but extends farther down in some contexts than in others.

The Catholic Church, for example, sometimes serves as an alternative power structure or helps to establish one. Hence, in 1988, the Catholic Bishops Conference of the Philippines issued a signed pastoral letter that lamented the damage done to the forests, rivers, and corals attributable to "human greed and relentless drive of our plunder economy." The bishops also praised the efforts of the local people of Bukidnon and Zamboanga del Sur, who "defended what remains of their forest with their own bodies," and urged the people to "organize around local ecological issues" (as quoted in Magno, 1993: 15). Through their sermons, parish priests have rallied the masses to self-organize and take action such as blocking illegal logging in the Philippine countryside. They have made moral and practical appeals, explaining that "God created the trees, but the trees are being cut down." One priest even called on the people to revive their tradition of headhunting, and this threat was used against the loggers and their collaborators in local government (de Guzman, 1996; Dacumos, 1996). Similarly, Zimbabwean environmentalists draw on ancestral rights as well as entreat church goers for consideration of the fact that if one cuts a tree, one is cutting the body of Jesus Christ; and if one plants a tree, one is healing the body of Jesus Christ (Matowanyika, 1996).

In South Africa, Earthlife Africa has catalyzed protests by unemployed and working-class people against the building of toxic waste dumps adjacent to black townships by arranging for blacks, many in these communities unemployed and with little formal education, to visit residents of other such townships near toxic dumps (Earthlife Africa, Toxics Group, 1996). Not restricted to instances of environmental racism, which places a disproportionate burden on the most marginalized sector of the population, such cross-visits are used in the face of various environmental abuses in other poverty-stricken communities as well.

Drawing on different support bases of privileged and underprivileged elements, civil society crosscuts class structures, but the roots of the contemporary environmental movement, at least in the more economically advanced areas, are implanted in the privileged sector. Again, it is important to underscore the wide variation from one context to another. In Japan, for example, lawyers, some of them doing pro bono work in other countries in Eastern Asia, as well as intellectuals, have played a leading role in the environmental movement, although the middle classes and many working-class people have mobilized around consumer issues. In some other Eastern Asian countries and throughout Southern Africa, environmental politics for the many is linked to matters of livelihood and, thus, social justice, not ecocentric causes—conserving nature for its own sake—as in parts of what is known as the developed world (although eco-*dhamma*, or Green Buddhism, in Thailand may be an exception).

Nowhere in my research was the link, or the impediments to linkage, between the environmental movement and class structure more apparent than in interviews with working-class black South Africans. Pelelo Magane (1996), a union organizer, noted that although the black community faces multiple problems, such as consumer waste, toxins, pollution, and safety issues, there is a stigma to organizing around environmental issues: "The environment is looked at as a liberal phenomenon that doesn't interest working-class people." In the wake of the anti-apartheid mobilizations around race, an implication of this statement is that the environment is the concern of those who can afford the luxury. Similarly, in the black townships adjacent to Cape Town, respondents stressed the class barriers to organizing around the environment, given the dire need for jobs, housing, health care, and protection against crime. In Langa township, whose residents migrated there as a result of forced removals (a feature of the Group Areas Act), Tsoga, an environmental movement, encounters the perception that the environment is "a white thing." Hence, in the view of its director, local people see but two worlds—"the advantaged and the disadvantaged" (Dilima, 1996).

A power structure has emerged within the environmental movement. Groups are arrayed according to size of staff, as well as the number of projects undertaken; scope and type of activities; and human and financial resources. In terms of access to resources in both Eastern Asia and Southern Africa, the organs of civil society have little connection to regional international organizations. An exception, perhaps, is the convening of workshops on matters of environmental concern and the building of a wildlife college—to be sure, not a grassroots activity, but a registered Southern African Development Community (SADC) project funded by Germany and a consortium of local donors. Such forms of regionalism, some of them under a SADC unit, Environment and Land Management Systems (ELMS), are only beginning to emerge. ELMS is mainly donor-driven, and has established some NGO focal points in various countries. Formed as a defense against apartheid, SADC remains a loose organization without much capacity vested in it. For the most part, the formal regional infrastructure to support civil society projects is weak.

Both SADC and the Association of Southeast Asian Nations (ASEAN) are largely remote from the day-to-day activities of civil society. Part of the explanation is that different political coalitions are operative in each country and embrace diverse paradigms, some of which discourage the development of civil society. Another factor is the power relationship between North and South. In civil society in Eastern Asia and Southern Africa, ties to Northern governmental and nongovernmental institutions are stronger than links within the subregions themselves. Surely, regional and subregional international organizations have not developed clear environmental policies, and the United Nations Environmental Programme has had little capacity to connect to civil society.

In the practice of environmental resistance politics, several problems have arisen. A large NGO bureaucracy has mushroomed, and individual NGOs have established a sense of territoriality. There is no formal code of ethics that governs or mitigates competition among NGOs. More conversation among different institutions in civil society is a good thing, but can there be too much diversity? Sometimes schisms emerge—for example, between the conservationists and those who stress the link between environment and development—over fundamental aims or resources. Bilateral and multilateral donors generally offer an environmental package. Implementation of their projects on the ground produces an island effect: isolated initiatives that are not effectively interrelated. Embeddedness in the local social structure is often lacking. Nationally based NGOs can serve as proxies for international agencies, with little or no organic connection to the roots of society. Frequently, there is a "pizza" effect as well: Environmental programs are spread on top of one another without any overall design (Braganza, 1996). In fact, some of the institutions in civil society are not really civil-society-driven, but corporate- or state-driven, for they are held accountable to their sponsors and have little autonomy.

Closely related is the question of co-optation. Under what conditions do or should grassroots movements accept or rebuff funding, and who is setting the agenda? In a proposed reversal of the classical dependency syndrome built into aid packages and structural adjustment programs, some organs of civil society have proposed systematically monitoring international agencies and other donors. There is also the ethical dilemma, anticipated by Gramsci more than half a century ago, of whether to contest elections in government and become part of the state, rather than serve as a countervailing source of pressure and perhaps as a social conscience that raises ethical issues. Even if leaders of civil society do not take government posts, the dangers of state substitution and parallelism arise. Government agencies and interstate organizations are essentially subcontracting some of their work to NGOs. The institutions of civil society thus perform certain functions normally executed by the state, and sometimes carry them out more efficiently than do the politicians and bureaucrats.

To mitigate these tensions, techniques of negotiation within civil society are, of course, used to solve problems. Forums such as the Environment Liaison Forum, formally launched in Zimbabwe in 1996, and the Consultative National Environmental Policy Process in South Africa, set in motion by the postapartheid government in collaboration with the myriad institutions of civil society, are bringing diverse stakeholders together in an ongoing process of attempting to find common ground. Nonetheless, there are serious differences over strategies appropriate for contesting globalization, a wide variety of which have been deployed.

CORE STRATEGIES OF RESISTANCE

The resistance employs both old and new strategies. There is nothing new about counterbalancing state power; plying symbols such as placards, posters, and leaflets; relying on the residual power to refuse; or networking in order to galvanize the efforts of different groups up against a variety of forms of environmental degradation, as occurred at the 1992 United Nations Conference on Environment and Development in Rio de Janeiro. These tested strategies remain important, and as Robin Broad points out: "[N]o unified strategy on how to build a sustainable alternative has yet emerged" (1993: 146). There is not one single model of resistance.

Yet globalization is transforming the parameters, redefining the constraints, and upping the environmental ante, especially for future generations. Innovative strategies specifically crafted to resist globalization are not merely stabs in the dark at an amorphous phenomenon. Some—but by no means all—groups that are self-organizing have engaged in self-conscious strategizing about countering globalization. These resisters have thought out the question, What kind of political interventions can be adopted to subject neoliberal globalization, often mediated by national and local programs, to social control? Five core strategies seem most important and are being employed individually or in combination.

First is a social compact devised to curb such abuses as the destruction and erosion of watershed areas, frequently through "legal" or illegal activities carried out by transnational corporations, as in North-Central Mindanao, which includes the Autonomous Region of Muslim Mindanao, as well as the Cagayan de Oro-Iligan Growth Corridor. A social compact is a formal understanding among all concerned parties about objectives and methods. It entails a public pledge and commitment among the signatories for the attainment of the common social good. It is based on consensual solutions and cooperation among people of different faiths (Albaran, 1996). In other words, in the teeth of top-down globalization, the concept of a social compact is designed to promote democratic control from the bottom in localities. It requires technical capacity in the form of a monitoring body to ensure that all parties abide by the agreement.

Inasmuch as globalization embraces, and is facilitated by, technological advances, resistance involves developing new knowledge structures. Simply put, a precondition for resisting globalization is to understand it. Hence the importance of the chain of education-research-information. In the view of Zukiswa Shibane, a Zimbabwean activist: "Desperate people won't fight globalization unless they are educated" (Environmental Justice Networking Forum [EJNF], 1996: 17). What some educators are striving to reclaim and transmit is indigenous and traditional knowledge about the environment, which is seen as but one part of building research capacity through networks in an effort to comprehend the dynamics of globalization. The objective of environmental education is to generate information for action, share it with the public, and channel it to the media in order to challenge globalizing forces that jeopardize the public interest. Not only is this an aspiration but one with broader implications: providing access to information regarding municipal zoning and the risks encountered with toxic materials clearly affected the mobilization of a number of communities around Chloorkop, South Africa. In a rich case study of Chloorkop, a researcher observes: "[I]mportant is the fact that the development of an environmental consciousness, a precursor to environmental mobilisation, stemmed from both organisational activity and access to information" (Buchler, 1995: 72). In short, an appreciation of the strategic importance of knowledge generation is not new, but what is novel are the linkages suggested in knowledge production and diffusion, as well as perhaps the method to point toward an alternative paradigm. If only in a very preliminary way, it may be possible to piece together a method of developing knowledge for resistance politics: deciphering the codes of domination, exposing the fault lines of power structures, identifying the pressure points for action, and fashioning images for counteridentification (Zawiah, 1994: 16–18).

The third core strategy is scaling up: an increase in the scope of operations. More specifically, it is a process whereby groups within civil society broaden their impact by building links with other sectors and extending their reach beyond the local area. Asked what scaling up means in practice, two leaders in civil society, interviewed jointly, stressed "expanding the level of operations in the field" and "having a strong voice at the policy level to influence government" (Morales, 1996; Serrano, 1996). Another activist explained scaling-up resistance in terms of the different time horizons of globalization. Unlike the resistance that seeks to strike immediately at concrete manifestations of globalization, scaling up takes a longer span of time. It involves synergizing different skills and capacities, as well as building spaces to contest globalization (dela Torre, 1996; for a concrete illustration and analysis, see Kelly, 1997).

Translated into practice, scaling up can entail establishing multisectoral forums beyond the *barangay*, the basic unit in the Philippines, or coordinating among several sectors in order to paralyze a city or stop plans for, say, opening casinos. Operationally, however, it seems that when resisters try to scale up, the parametric transformation wrought by globalization, especially the ideology of neo-liberalism, obfuscates its dynamics. Insofar as globalization's architecture is perceived as too big for local life, it causes disorientation. In some cases, the ambiguity rendered by globalizing structures precipitates a paradoxical reaction, which is not to scale up but to scale down. This backlash is an attempt to erect a fortress around the community, to localize rather than to engage the forces of globalization. Indeed, there is good reason to try to assert local control, particularly in places and spheres of activity where globalization involves the most acute forms of loss of control. To be sure, the more local groups extend to the global arena, the greater the temptation to conform to global norms. Nonetheless, the quickening speed of environmental degradation, its irreversibility in some cases, and its transnational reach suggest that by itself, scaling down is not a sufficient means to protect nature's endowment.

Fourth, resisters seek to thrust out in order to gain wider latitude for direct voluntary action. Earlier, reference was made to top-down forms of market-driven and state-led regionalism. In response, regionalism at the base may be either bilateral or multilateral among organizations and movements and may thrust globally to forge links with civil societies in other regions as well. Although sometimes circumspect about "going regional" or "going global" because of fear of being eclipsed or losing control, especially to large Northern partners, Southern NGOs are increasingly aware of the potential advantages of transnational collaboration (Eccleston, 1996: 82). Earthlife Africa, for example, now has branches not only in South Africa, but also in Namibia and Uganda. And trade unions in the region share information and mount joint educational workshops to provide training. In Eastern Asia, the strategy of thrusting out draws significantly on the experience of the Philippines, given the density and relative maturity of civil society there. Its NGO sector has been invited to share experiences with its counterparts in other countries. In dialogue with the representatives of civil society elsewhere, Philippine NGOs have also been involved in monitoring international financial institutions such as the Asian Development Bank and the World Bank, with the goal of fashioning sustainable and alternative policies.

Noteworthy among attempts to define alternatives to neoliberal regionalism is the People's Plan of the Twenty-First Century (PP21), a process that began in Japan in 1989. A coalition of grassroots movements and action groups brought together 360 activists from various countries to meet with thousands of members of Japanese civil society. They sought to establish goals and strategies based on modeling alternative social relations, not direct struggle with state structures. Following a meeting with representatives from six Central American countries, a second PP21 forum was held in Thailand in 1992, and basic concepts were hammered out. Efforts are under way to breathe life into the idea of "transborder participatory democracy," and consideration is being given to the implications of living according to the strictures of a "single, global division of labor," a hierarchy that spawns "inter-people conflicts and antagonism." As well as conferences, workshops, and electronic communication, the PP21 process includes a secretariat based in Tokyo and a quarterly review, AMPO (Muto, 1994; 1996; Inoue, 1996).

Engaging regional processes is a space that popular movements in Eastern Asia have sought to establish. For example, environmental organizations in Indonesia, Malaysia, and the Philippines have set up the Climate Action Network, with its own secretariat. In 1995–96, environmental NGOs requested observer status in ASEAN and were rebuffed on the ground that there was no such mechanism. When this bid was scotched, the NGOs argued that inasmuch as other international institutions, including the UN, provide access for people's organizations, ASEAN should do so too. Then in 1997, the members of the Climate Action Network wrote to the ministers of the environment in their respective countries asking for the opportunity to address them, but were told that the officials did not have time for a hearing (Gurmit, 1997).

Popular movements in Eastern Asia have also targeted the APEC process of summitry and its agenda of deepening and broadening liberalization policies. Working across borders, people's movements took aim at the 1996 APEC summit in Manila. First, they held a preparatory meeting in Kyoto and mounted parallel NGO forums in various countries, yielding specific resolutions and action points designed to oppose member governments' trade and investment regimes that damage the environment and transgress people's rights. Preparations entailed presummit fact-finding missions to various locales so that delegates themselves could study precisely how forms of integration affect communities and their modes of livelihood. The documentation included a critique of "the breakneck pace and unilateral character" of blanket liberalization, especially in terms of its impact on the most vulnerable sectors and the environment, and took issue with the way that the APEC provisions "dissociate economic issues from their social implications and effects" ("Proposed Philippine PO-NGO Position," 1996). Women have contested "APEC opportunities that will fast track our rapidly shifting economic environment" (National Council of Women of the Philippines, 1996). In light of a labor market structured along gender lines and the consequences for women and children, delegates called for, among other things, government financing for "a social welfare agenda to soften globalization's adverse effects" (Women's Forum, 1996). Although probably unintentional, the presummit forum's message seemed to bear shrill—hardly modulated—overtones of a Polanyian analysis; it assailed APEC for its "anti-democratic, unaccountable and untransparent" free trade practices and stressed the need to protect the people from "the ravages of market forces" (Manila People's Forum on APEC, 1996).

Without exaggerating the importance of the above-mentioned instance—amplified in a forum of NGOs, known as the Asia Pacific Peoples' Assembly, at the 1998 APEC meeting in Kuala Lumpur—there are important lessons to be derived. The Asia-Pacific Economic Cooperation forum, a market-driven, state-led process, has catalyzed intercourse among resistance movements in different countries, and grassroots organizations have set a regional agenda, one very different from that of state power holders. For example, in contrast to the latter's thrust, grassroots groups emphasize the need to link trade and investment on the one hand and social policy on the other. Additionally, this process of resistance not only ties the substate level to the state level, but also elucidates key relationships between regionalism and globalization.

In Southern Africa, the impetus for thrusting out at the regional level and beyond comes from different pressure points, but the program of one environmental movement stands out for its level of resistance activities, especially those that highlight the contradictions between professed policies and the lack of implementation. Its green stance implicitly contests economic policy as well. The Environmental Justice Networking Forum includes more than 550 organizations that embrace common values, and largely represents the underprivileged sector of society. It seeks to identify spurs to regionalization, and engages in bridge building with other movements (Albertyn and Coworkers, 1996).

Landmark resistance activities have centered on chemicals. The case of Thor Chemicals, a British-based corporation that imports waste from the U.S. company called Cyanamid, came to the fore in 1990, when large concentrations of highly toxic mercury were found in the Umgeweni River not far from its Cato Ridge plant near Durban. Earthlife Africa (a member of EJNF), the Chemical Workers Industrial Union, local residents under their chief, and white commercial farmers pursued the question, Why did Thor build the world's largest toxic mercury recycling plant in a remote location in South Africa? An alliance of trade unions, rural peasants, and green groups from different countries mounted demonstrations at Thor and at Cyanamid's plant in the United States. This joint action within civil society put pressure on the Department of Water Affairs, which ordered Thor Chemicals to suspend its operations (Crompton and Erwin, 1991).

The toxic waste issue, however, did not go away. Rather, South Africa's Department of Trade and Industry was reluctant to endorse a ban on movements of toxic waste among African, Caribbean, and Pacific (ACP) countries. It became apparent that there is a regional trade, a thriving industry, in toxic waste. The EJNF expressed outrage at the revelations that postapartheid South Africa imported waste for recycling from several African countries and that Pretoria feared losing the income if it were to sign Article 39 of the Lomé Convention, which stipulates that "the ACP States shall prohibit the direct or indirect import into their territory of such waste from the Community or from any other country" (Fourth ACP-EEC Convention, 1990: 1). The government agreed to sign the Basel Convention on the Transboundary Movements of Hazardous Waste and Their Disposal, adopted by sixty-five countries in 1989 and implemented in 1992. This international accord bans all movement of hazardous waste from industrial to developing countries from January 1998, but does not apply to traffic in toxins within Southern Africa. Hence, EJNF exposed a possible backdoor route for bringing in lucrative materials through neighboring countries (Koch, 1996a;

1996b; 1996c). It became evident that state officials were trading off the regime's progressive agenda against neoliberal economic pressures. Resistance to the government's original policy contributed to the decision to reverse its position and include Article 39 of the Lomé Convention in its final trade and development agreement with the European Union. Gathering information and access to the media were important aspects of the resistance strategy. A strategy of thrusting out involved developing links with the transnational green movement so that vital information could flow back to South Africa. Again, illuminating the specific links between the regional issue and globalization was crucial.

Another strategy of resistance builds innovative relationships between social movements in order to directly engage the market and establish an alternative, sustainable ecological system. In 1986, farmers from Negros Island in the Philippines and Japanese consumer cooperatives, large organizations whose members sought a substitute for the chemically laden products sold on the market, began to trade with one another. Negros grassroots communities sought a basis to transform the island's sugar-monoculture plantation economy into an integrated system of agriculture, industry, and finance. They have fundamentally attempted to remake the economy through the mutual exchange of products and services in a cyclic manner. This project includes a transborder North-South trading system, whereby an autonomous association of small farmers delivers chemical-free bananas to Japanese consumer associations of nearly one million people. The Negros growers have developed organic agriculture and set the price of bananas three times higher than the market price of bananas produced by TNCs on Mindanao Island. The elevated price, which consumers gladly pay for chemical-free products, amounts to a reverse transfer of value from the North to the South (Hotta, 1996; Muto and Kothari, undated).

At a Tokyo meeting of representatives of the two organizations, I was struck by their class membership—small farmers from Negros, Japanese workers (many of them in the service sector), and mostly the lower reaches of the middle class. Together, these groups have sought to resist not the market economy, but market society. They have established an alternative circuit of capital under social control—what Polanyi regarded as reembedding the market in society and nature. This project includes cross-visits between the two communities so that social and political ties are generalized beyond trading relations. The strategy is a transboundary initiative that breaks out of the cage of the nation–state, and so do other initiatives by risk takers who strive to build social capital.

Community forestry is another example of movement-to-movement relationships that are meant to offer a sustainable alternative to the conventional market system. To substitute nontimber products such as rattan, vines, and river resources for wood, links are being forged between corporations, NGOs, and associations of direct producers (Tengco, 1996). Without going into more detail, it is apparent that collective resistance is intensifying, giving rise to multilayering strategies employed according to the varied ways that globalizing trends affect individual countries and regions. Such efforts may be suggestive in terms of alternative means of governing the environment.

FLEDGLING TENDENCIES

The research findings show that, in ways that I had not anticipated before undertaking this fieldwork, the three analytical frames—those of Gramsci, Polanyi, and Scott—overlap, deepen understanding of environmental resistance politics, and may be integrated. Yes, Polanyi provides an overall theoretical thrust for exploring resistance to globalization in the environmental realm. Approaching resistance in a Polanyian manner as an attempt to reembed the economy in society *and* nature is extremely valuable, and the probings of Gramsci and Scott enhance this inquiry. For example, fieldwork on strategies of resistance led to the notion of "deciphering codes of domination," and here, Scott's concept of infrapolitics provides the most explanatory power. Gramsci's insights on environmental ideology as a means to secure consent so as to lessen reliance on more costly forms of coercion are also a strong tool for understanding resistance politics. The concrete evidence drawn from Eastern Asia and Southern Africa demonstrates how the three frames are integral to understanding environmental resistance, and this in turn helps to sharpen the theoretical perspective.

By all indications, the data indicate an expansion of space for resistance to neoliberal globalization, but thus far, resistant nonstate politics has had a limited impact. Within civil society, one of the reasons for forming coalitions and networks is to foster more democratic politics. However, upscaling and linking these associations does not, of course, solve the problem of hierarchical power relations integral to top-down globalization. As a political vehicle countering globalization, environmental resistance movements run on many engines. They can both follow and lead the state.

On the basis of the foregoing research findings, it is possible to identify five trends, all microcounterglobalizing tendencies: (1) In light of the diversity of experiences and contexts, many environmental initiatives are issue-oriented and subject-specific. At present, most environmental struggles are localized. (2) Nonetheless, there is a putting together of modest resistance activities based on the forging of overlapping alliances and networks within and between regions. (3) Environmental movements have implicitly adopted a policy of parallelism—that is, replicating in one context resistance strategies that have proven successful elsewhere. (4) The core strategies are positive, not a negation, in the sense of engagement; they do not evade—delink from—either the market or the state. (5) The resistance is accumulating critical venues, such as cultural integrity and ancestral domain, and finding more openings.

Clearly, it would be wrong to celebrate these Polanyian counterforces. One might even call them what Polanyi regarded as a "move" rather than movements to indicate the protoforms by which social forces "waxed and waned" before ultimately giving birth to a political organization that begot a transformation of a particular type (Polanyi, 1957: 239). Although some of them are federating, today's environmental counterforces are anything but coherent. Perhaps a high level of coherence is a desideratum that should be balanced against another consideration, namely, that civil society feeds on diversity. Also, given the impediments to organizing, regional and interregional solidarity from below is a way off. Regional and global civil society are, at best, nascent and highly uneven.

At bottom, the impetus for resistance politics is not only material or technological but also decidedly intertwined with the environmental ethic of protecting people and their diverse ways of life against quickening market forces. The words of a Jesuit priest engaged in environmental struggles in the Philippines give pause: "Spirituality is associated with suffering. This landscape bleeds. This is a suffering landscape" (Walpole, 1996). The force of this message drives a powerful spiritual question in the path of globalization: Must the environment be experienced negatively, as a constraint, in terms of destruction, rather than as beauty to be relished and preserved? Posing the dilemma in this way raises the political issue of who should be entrusted, or empowered, to look after the public good.

NOTES

1. Preliminary versions of this chapter appeared in *Third World Quarterly* 19(5) (December 1998): 847–72; and *Globalisation and the Asia-Pacific: Contested Territories*, edited by Kris Olds et al. (London: Routledge, 1999), pp. 72–87. The editorial team for that book—Kris Olds, Peter Dicken, Philip Kelly, Lily Kong, and Henry Wai-chung Yeung—contributed importantly to this work. In substantially revised form, the chapter is based on James H. Mittelman, *The Globalization Syndrome: Transformation and Resistance* (Princeton, N.J.: Princeton University Press, 2000).

2. An irony in completing the empirical research for this chapter and recording my findings is that I did so in Hanoi, where I temporarily became an environmental refugee, escaping the effects of choking haze that blanketed six countries and reached "hazardous" levels on the official air pollution index in 1997. Ostensibly caused by uncontrolled forest fires in Indonesia, drought brought about by El Niño patterns in the oceans, and winds that swept the smoke into neighboring countries, including Malaysia, where I was living, the problem of course had other causes: the slash-and-burn techniques practiced by transnational agribusiness, the lack of a political will to deal with some of the domestic sources of pollution in countries engaged in high-speed economic growth, and ways that special interests outside and inside the state stymie strong remedial action. The immediate impact of the environmental crisis was deaths linked to respiratory illnesses, a welter of ancillary health problems overcrowding the hospitals, accidents attributable to poor visibility, and enormous direct economic costs, especially in tourism, agriculture, education, and industries that had to cut back. Plainly, the magnitude of this crisis reached major regional and global proportions. A salutary

effect of the haze was that it alerted the public to the systemic consequences of unbridled economic growth and of looking exclusively or primarily to government for solutions.

3. In this vein, Adas concludes his research findings on peasant resistance with a helpful formulation: "Avoidance protest in its many forms can protect, win specific concessions or exact revenge, but it cannot reform in major ways or transform unjust socio-political systems. Only modes of confrontational protest can achieve the latter" (1986: 83).

4. This phrasing embodies a departure from the dualism contained in the distinction between humankind and nature.

REFERENCES

Adas, Michael. "From Footdragging to Flight: The Evasive History of Peasant Avoidance Protest in South and South-east Asia." *Journal of Peasant Studies* 13(7) (January 1986): 64–86.

Albaran, Francisco T. Agriculturalist, MUCARD. Interview by author. Cagayan de Oro City, Mindanao, Philippines, March 4, 1996.

Albertyn, Chris, and Coworkers. National coordinator, Environmental Justice Networking Forum. Interview by author. Braamfontein, South Africa, August 2, 1996.

Bernard, Mitchell. "Ecology, Political Economy and the Counter-movement: Karl Polanyi and the Second Great Transformation." In *Innovation and Transformation in International Studies*, edited by Stephen Gill and James H. Mittelman. Cambridge: Cambridge University Press, 1997, 75–89.

Block, Fred, and Margaret R. Somers. "Beyond the Economistic Fallacy: The Holistic Social Science of Karl Polanyi." In *Vision and Method in Historical Sociology*, edited by Theda Skocopl. Cambridge: Cambridge University Press, 1984, 47–84.

Braganza, Braggy. Research scientist, Environmental Research Division of the Institute of Environmental Science for Social Change (formerly the Manila Observatory). Interview by author. Quezon City, Philippines, March 2, 1996.

Broad, Robin, with John Cavanagh. *Plundering Paradise: The Struggle for the Environment in the Philippines.* Berkeley: University of California Press, 1993.

Brosius, J. Peter. "Endangered Forest, Endangered People: Environmentalist Representations of Indigenous Knowledge." *Human Ecology* 25(1) (March 1997): 47–69.

Buchler, Michelle. "Community-Based Environmentalism in Transitional South Africa: Social Movements and the Development of Local Democracy." Master's thesis, Department of Sociology, University of the Witwatersrand, Johannesburg, 1995.

Carruthers, Jane. *The Kruger National Park: A Social and Political History.* Pietermaritzburg, South Africa: University of Natal Press, 1995.

Chin, Christine B.N., and James H. Mittelman. "Conceptualizing Resistance to Globalization." *New Political Economy* 2(1) (March 1997): 25–37.

Crompton, Rod, and Alec Erwin. "Reds and Greens: Labour and the Environment." In *Going Green*, edited by Jacklyn Cock. Oxford: Oxford University Press, 1991, 78–91.

Dacumos, Victor. Chairman, Guardians of the Environment for the Future of Youth. Interview by author. Gabaldon, Nueve Ecija, Philippines, March 9, 1996.

de Guzman, Apollo. Parish priest and president, Confederation of Nueva Ecijanons for the Environment and Social Order, Inc. Interview by author. Cabanatuan City, Nueva Ecija, Luzon, Philippines, March 9, 1996.

del Castillo, Romulo A. Professor of Forest Resources and director, University of the Philippines, Los Banos Agroforestry Program. Interview by author. Los Banos, Laguna, Philippines, March 11, 1996.

dela Torre, Edicio. President, Folk Philippine-Danish School. Interview by author. Quezon City, Philippines, March 12, 1996.

Dilima, Nomtha. Director, Tsoga Environmental Centre. Interview by author. Langa, Cape Town, South Africa, July 23, 1996.

Earthlife Africa, Toxics Group. Meeting, Brixton, Johannesburg, South Africa, July 15, 1996.

Eccleston, Bernard. "Does North-South Collaboration Enhance NGO Influence on Deforestation Policies in Malaysia and Indonesia?" *Journal of Commonwealth and Comparative Politics* 34(1) (March 1996): 66–89.

Environmental Justice Networking Forum. "Proceedings of the Conference on Regional Cooperation in Environmental Governance." Broederstroom, South Africa, November 1996.

Fourth ACP-EEC Convention. *Internationales Umweltrecht—Multilaterale Verträge* BZUB7/I.92, 989: 93/11, (1990).

Freedom from Debt Coalition, Women's Committee. Interview by author. Manila, Philippines, March 13, 1996.

Goldblatt, David. *Social Theory and the Environment*. Boulder, Colo.: Westview, 1996.

Gramsci, Antonio. *Selections from the Prison Notebooks*. Translated and edited by Quintin Hoare and Geoffrey Nowell Smith. London: Lawrence and Wishart, 1971.

Gurmit Singh, K. S. Executive director, Centre for Environment, Technology and Development, Malaysia. Interview by author. Petaling Jaya, Malaysia, November 15, 1997.

Harries-Jones, Peter, Abraham Rotstein, and Peter Timmerman. "Nature's Veto: UNCED and the Debate over the Earth." Unpublished ms., 1992.

Hefner, Robert W., ed. *Market Cultures: Society and Values in the New Asian Capitalisms*. Boulder, Colo.: Westview, 1998.

Heng Pek Koon. "Robert Kuok and the Chinese Business Network in Eastern Asia: A Study in Sino-Capitalism." In *Culture and Economy: The Shaping of Capitalism in Eastern Asia*, edited by Timothy Brook and Hy V. Luong. Ann Arbor: University of Michigan Press, 1997.

Ho Hua Chow. "A Value Orientation for Nature Preservation in Singapore." *Environmental Monitoring and Assessment* 44 (1997a): 91–107.

———. Senior lecturer, Department of Philosophy, National University of Singapore. Interview by author. Singapore, December 5, 1997b.

Hotta, Masahiko. President, Alter Trade Japan, Inc. Interview by author. Tokyo, February 25, 1996.

Inoue, Reiko. Director, Pacific Asia Resource Center, 1996. Interview by author. Tokyo, Japan, February 24, 1996.

Keck, Margaret E., and Kathryn Sikkink. *Activists beyond Borders: Advocacy Networks in International Politics*. Ithaca, N.Y.: Cornell University Press, 1998.

Kelly, Philip F. "Globalization, Power and the Politics of Scale in the Philippines." *Geoforum* 28(2) (May 1997): 151–71.

Khan, Farieda. "Beyond the White Rhino: Confronting the South African Land Question." *African Wildlife* 44(6) (November/December 1990): 321–24.

———. "Rewriting South Africa's Conservation History—The Role of the Native Farmers Association." *Journal of Southern African Studies* 20(4) (December 1994): 499–516.

Koch, Eddie. "SA Still under Fire for Toxic Waste Policy." *Mail & Guardian* (5–11 July 1996a).

———. Environmental editor, *Mail & Guardian*. Interview by author. Braamfontein, South Africa, July 19, 1996b.

———. "SA Still in the Waste Business." *Mail & Guardian* (26 July–1 August 1996c).

Kong, Lily. "'Environment' as a Social Concern: Democratizing Public Arenas in Singapore?" *Sojourn* 9(2) (1994): 277–87.

Lee Yok-shiu F., and Alvin S. So. "Conclusion." In *Asia's Environmental Movements: Comparative Perspectives*, edited by Yok-shiu F., Lee and Alvin Y. So. Armonk, N.Y.: M. E. Sharpe, 1999, 287–308.

Magane, Pelelo. Organizer, Chemical Workers Industrial Union. Interview by author. Johannesburg, South Africa, July 30, 1996.

Magno, Francisco A. "The Growth of Philippine Environmentalism." *Kasarinlan* 9(1) (3rd quarter 1993): 7–18.

Manila People's Forum on APEC 1996. "Hidden Costs of Free Trade: Statement of the Philippine PO-NGO Summit on the APEC." Quezon City, Philippines, July 6, 1996. Unpublished ms., 1996.

Matowanyika, Joseph Z.Z. Director, ZERO. Interview by author. Harare, Zimbabwe, July 11, 1996.

Mittelman, James H., ed. *Globalization: Critical Reflections.* Boulder, Colo.: Lynne Rienner, 1996.

———. 1997. "Rethinking Innovation in International Studies: Global Transformation at the Turn of the Millennium." In *Innovation and Transformation in International Studies*, edited by Stephen Gill and James H. Mittelman. Cambridge: Cambridge University Press, 1997b, 248–63.

Mittelman, James H., and Mustapha Kamal Pasha. *Out from Underdevelopment Revisited: Changing Global Structures and the Remaking of the Third World.* London: Macmillan, and New York: St. Martin's, 1997.

Morales, Horacio "Boy." President, Philippine Rural Reconstruction Movement. Interview by author. Quezon City, Philippines, March 13, 1996.

Murphy, Craig N. *International Organization and Industrial Change: Global Governance since 1850.* New York: Oxford University Press, 1994.

Muto, Ichiyo. "PP21: A Step in a Process." *AMPO Japan-Asia Quarterly Review* 25(2) (1994): 47–53.

———. Pacific Asia Resource Center. Interview by author. Tokyo, Japan, February 25, 1996.

Muto, Ichiyo, and Smitu Kothari. "Towards Sustainable Systems." Tokyo, Japan, discussion paper for PP21, n.d.

National Council of Women of the Philippines (NCWP). "APEC and the Women: Catching the Next Wave." GO-NGO Forum on Women, July 16, 1996. Unpublished ms.

Nazarea-Sandoval, Virginia D. *Local Knowledge and Agricultural Decision Making in the Philippines: Class, Gender, and Resistance.* Ithaca, N.Y.: Cornell University Press, 1995.

Ong, Aihwa. *Spirits of Resistance and Capitalist Discipline: Factory Women in Malaysia.* Albany: State University of New York Press, 1987.

Peluso, Nancy Lee. *Rich Forests, Poor People: Resource Control and Resistance in Java.* Berkeley: University of California Press, 1992.

"Pointers." *Jane's Foreign Report* 2448 (May 22, 1997).

Polanyi, Karl. *The Great Transformation: The Political and Economic Origins of Our Time.* Boston: Beacon Press, 1957.

———. *Primitive, Archaic and Modern Economies: Essays of Karl Polanyi.* New York: Anchor, 1968.

———. *The Livelihood of Man,* edited by Harry W. Pearson. New York: Academic Press, 1977.

"Proposed Philippine PO-NGO Position." Executive Summary. Manila People's Forum (MPF) on APEC 1996. Manila, Philippines, 1996.

Rebugio, Lucrecio L. Professor and dean, College of Forestry, University of the Philippines Los Banos. Interview by author. Los Banos, Laguna, Philippines, March 11, 1996.

Rodan, Garry. "Theorising Political Opposition in East and Southeast Asia." In *Political Oppositions in Industrialising Asia,* edited by Garry Rodan. London: Routledge, 1996, 1–39.

Rosenau, James N. *Along the Domestic-Foreign Frontier: Exploring Governance in a Turbulent World.* Cambridge: Cambridge University Press, 1997.

Scott, James C. *The Moral Economy of the Peasant: Rebellion and Subsistence in Southeast Asia.* New Haven, Conn.: Yale University Press, 1976.

———. *Weapons of the Weak: Everyday Forms of Peasant Resistance.* New Haven, Conn.: Yale University Press, 1985.

———. *Domination and the Arts of Resistance: Hidden Transcripts.* New Haven, Conn.: Yale University Press, 1990.

Serrano, Isagani R. Vice president, Philippine Rural Reconstruction Movement. Interview by author. Quezon City, Philippines, March 13, 1996.

Shaw, Martin. "Civil Society and Global Politics: Beyond a Social Movements Approach." *Millennium: Journal of International Studies* 23(3) (Winter 1994): 647–67.

Shiva, Vandana. "Resources." In *The Development Dictionary: A Guide to Knowledge as Power,* edited by Wolfgang Sachs. London: Zed, 1992, 206–18.

Sklair, Leslie. "Global Sociology and Global Environmental Change." In *Social Theory and the Global Environment,* edited by M. Redclift and T. Benton. London: Routledge, 1994, 205–17.

———. "Social Movements and Global Capitalism: The Transnational Capitalist Class in Action." *Review of International Political Economy* 4(3) (Fall 1997): 514–38.

Smith, Jackie, Charles Chatfield, and Ron Pagnucco, eds. *Transnational Social Movements and Global Politics: Solidarity beyond the State.* Syracuse, N.Y.: Syracuse University Press, 1997.

Songco, Danilo A. National coordinator, CODE-NGO. Interview by author. Quezon City, Philippines, March 13, 1996.

Tengco, Gary James C. Project coordinator, Institute of Environmental Science for Social Change (formerly Environmental Research Division of the Manila Observatory). Interview by author. Cabanatuan City, Nueva Ecija, Luzon, Philippines, March 9, 1996.

Walker, R. B. J. "Social Movements/World Politics." *Millennium: Journal of International Studies* 23(3) (Winter 1994): 669–700.

Walpole, Peter W., S.J. Executive director, Institute of Environmental Science for Social

Change (formerly Environmental Research Division of the Manila Observatory). Interview by author. Quezon City, Philippines, March 12, 1996.

Wapner, Paul. *Environmental Activism and World Civic Politics*. Albany: State University of New York Press, 1996.

Women's Forum. "Women's Forum for the APEC Manila Process." Manila People's Forum on APEC. Manila, July 3, 1996.

Yearley, Steven. *Sociology, Environmentalism, Globalization: Reinventing the Globe*. London: Sage, 1996.

Zawiah Yahya. *Resisting Colonialist Discourse*. Bangi, Malaysia: Penerbit Universiti Kebangsaan Malaysia (National University of Malaysia Press), 1994.

11

Political Organizing in the Land of the Great Spirit, Tunkashila: A Conversation with Joann Tall

Roxann Prazniak

Over several days in early August 1995, I met with Joann Tall at her home near the Black Hills on Lakota Sioux Lands [Porcupine, Pine Ridge Reservation, South Dakota]. Our conversation focused on issues of environmental protection and indigenous cultures, themes on which Joann spoke briefly at the April 1995 Duke University Symposium on "Asia-Pacific Identities: Culture and Identity Formation in the Age of Global Capital." Ms. Tall has been involved in community issues in the Lakota area since the 1973 events at Wounded Knee, in which she was a participant. She cofounded the Indigenous Environmental Network in 1991, and in 1993 received the Goldman Award for North America in the area of environmental work. The following dialogue is based on tapes made during our conversations and has been reviewed for accuracy by Joann.

COMMITMENT AND INSPIRATION: SOURCES OF SUSTAINABLE ACTIVISM

Roxann: Joann, you said in your remarks at the symposium last spring that spirituality is a very important part of your work. When we were speaking informally just now, you said you wanted to start this conversation with that topic.

Joann: Yes. In my short presentation I made at the symposium about my organizing on different issues, I said a few things about the spirituality of my whole involvement and commitment. I shared that I had dreams actually since I was a little girl, but I didn't come to interpret those dreams until I was much older. I'd like to tell you about another dream I had in February of 1988.

This dream happened here in my house. In the dream I had left my home, my land, a number of times. I think I went off to work or to college somewhere away from the reservation. Then when I came home, as I was coming through the gate, coming home to my land, I saw my land was confiscated; there were tons of people here and these people were represented in two ways. One group had black robes and white collars; they must have been like the Catholic Church. The other group of people that were involved in land confiscation were the cowboy type of people; they reminded me of the mixed-blood, half-breed people here on the reservation who have always been in power with our tribal government, put in place by the IRA [Indian Reorganization Act issued by the United States government in 1934]. Those people have been in control here, and the other arm that they represent is the Bureau of Indian Affairs, which sits over our land. They lease our land out to non-Indians, and a lot of times our land goes through a lot of abuse. But anyway, in this dream those were the two entities that confiscated my land, and as I came back to my home, they even confiscated my home, inside my home, and all over my land. This is 160 acres that I sit on out here where my home is.

In this dream I was just real angry that this happened, so even though I was alone in this dream, I fought everybody physically. I got them out of my home, and I locked the backdoor. Then as I was coming down the stairway here, this long stairway here, out of the darkness in this part midway through the stairway, a real nice looking Indian man came out, and he was looking at me and smiling, and he was reaching out and telling me to come toward him. He looked nice from the outside, but there was something real evil about him in this dream, I felt it. So I just pushed him away, but it was almost like enticing me because of the attraction, but I pushed him away. As I was pushing him away here at this front door, I heard the clickity-clank of a shotgun. I came down the stairway, and I came and opened my front door down here like that, and here's three Indian guides. One had braids with a red headband and army fatigue jacket. He had the gun. The other guys were also long-haired, one had a ponytail, and one wore his hair loose, and I got real happy. I thought, all right, my brothers are here to help me, and I was real happy. I smiled at them and stuff, and I came out the door to that first guy, and he had like a real smile. It wasn't a very good smile, but it was a smile he had on his face. When I came here by the window just west of the house, then he smiled and pointed that gun at me, and he actually pulled the trigger of that shotgun and it blew a hole in my chest. The impact blew me over there at the corner of the house, and I had this gaping wound, and it was like I went into shock because I thought it was my brothers that came here to help me get these people off my land. I was shocked and hurt that these people that I trusted and thought they came to help me out. They did me in, you know.

So something was telling me that as long as I have a breath left in me, to get up and run and help myself as long as I had a breath left in me. I went around the house here, west of the house, and just kind of northwest of the house was a hill that goes down from my log cabin, and as I start going down there, something was telling me I need to get to where that little water brook was. As I was running down the hill, not only was it not enough that everybody had done to me in this dream, but they were still trying to get at me. These entities, the black coats, the cowboy types, and mixed-blood people, and the Indian guys with the long hair and stuff, they were chasing me trying to still get at me and prevent me from getting over to where that water was, and this man that looked nice and was trying to entice me earlier in my dream, he was nowhere around to defend me or help me, you know, and so as I was going down this hill, the scenery started changing and started changing to like how the Black Hills looked. The high mountains and the beautiful trees and the pines and everything was turning that way and then all of a sudden there was a little footpath over the bridge over the brook of water and somehow I was dependent on my life to get there to that bridge. And so I barely got across, and got to there, and I looked across the water and over the bridge, and there was two big boulders that were on the other side, and all of a sudden they turned into human forms, into like warriors, and as I was barely getting across I could hardly breathe, and then, so they started running toward me to help me across and here out of the trees and the blades, even the smallest blades of grass and bushes there were big people Indian people and small people, itty-bitty Indian people peeking out at me and stuff. As soon as the guys came over they grabbed me on each side of my arms, and they took me across, and they started running with me toward the hills, and somebody was hollering, telling us to go, and all these people, big and small, that were peeking out of the bushes and trees at me, they came beside me, behind me, and they were all supporting me and running with me, and all of these different people that wanted to get at me and the guy that shot at me, they couldn't cross over, they couldn't cross over. That was the end of my dream.

I had made it, and I was running toward the Black Hills. The dream has so many meanings to it. I came to my own interpretation, which is that we have to always be vigilant concerning our home and our land because somebody, the United States government, the BIA, even our tribal government, all the churches, somebody is always there to try to confiscate our land, and we always have to be vigilant. The dream also showed me that I no longer have a fear of authority, that I will risk my life to act on the commitment I made to protect our land, even though I may be alone. Organizers who have committed themselves to a cause a lot of times find themselves alone. You have your own personal things that you go through, and a lot of times when you get to the top of dealing with corporations, entities, or even with your own organization, sometimes you stand alone because of your strong belief in what you are doing, and you can't get bought off by playing into all the games. You don't know who your allies are. Like in that dream, the Indian guys with the long hair and headbands, I thought they were my brothers that came to help me, to help me deal with this, my land confiscation, but they were there in disguises, the ones that shot me.

And the other part of the meaning of the dream is that man that entered from the shadow. I look at him as different ways of getting me sidetracked from my commitments, and I think it was like a seduction, and the seduction is not only man and woman but the corporations, how they pay off. They use their money to pay you off and get you off from your issue. He was Indian, but I think he represented enticements of all kinds.

Roxann: The fact that he was handsome, is there a male/female issue in any of this?

Joann: I think that what it is, is that like in our way, Lakota way, sometimes they have medicine and stuff that people try to use. Those medicines get you sidetracked, but it is not natural. It's almost like a, I don't know how to explain it in contemporary terms, like a drug or something, but it is a medicine that can take you in and fill your mind and all of that. Anyway, maybe that is not what it represents, but that is what I see in it, and it might just be with my own personal history too. The thing that gave me hope in this fight, being alone, getting shot at, having home and land confiscated, was that as long as I have one last breath left in me, I'm still going to do what I have to save my land, my home, and myself. I am going to fight for what I believe in. I fight for my people and maybe that's the thing that younger people need to know. I start to look at myself like an elder, I'm forty-three, but those are things that we need to leave with our kids. That they need those things to listen to, to learn from, you know.

And another part is that people are always going to try to get the best of you. No matter how down you are, they are even going to try to bring you down even more. Even though I was barely making it in my dream, it wasn't enough what they had done, they still had to just get at me. Hope and the powers of our spirituality are in crossing over that bridge and looking into the natural world. The land is the power, and our strength comes from the natural world, the natural environment. And that's who showed themselves and that's who came to my rescue. Those were the warriors, the spirits from the spirit world that came to help me get back to the Black Hills. So that's the significance of that dream and kind of like my own interpretation of what I came to from that dream.

Roxann: Has any of your environmental work been directly connected with the Black Hills area?

Joann: Yes. The whole Black Hills area is a sacred area, it's a special place, I hope we can go there while you are here. Our medicine grows up there, a real powerful place, and it's real sad to see the desecration, you know, that is going on with the mining up in Lee Bedwood area. The gold mining. In 1987 I was in the forefront of a campaign to stop Honeywell from testing munitions in the Hells Canyon[1] area of the Black Hills. That was really a learning experience because my involvement in that was through ceremony. I wanted to be sure that my involvement, my pull to it, was because I needed to be there, not just that I wanted to be there for egotistical reasons. I wanted a real confirmation of my motives, so I went into a sweat lodge ceremony with one of my uncles to give me that direction. My uncle just told me, "You have had those dreams since you were little," and he said, "you are going to turn it around, but it's going to be hard, and there will be sacrifices." One time I went in to ask for directions because it was taking long and it was hard and stuff. The spirit of Crazy Horse came into the sweat lodge ceremony and he told me, "Little girl, I want to tell you that my spirit still covers the Black Hills. Remember that I defended my people, that I loved my Black Hills, and my spirit is still covering the Black Hills. Tell your people to remember that." That was at the time of the '87 campaign. I wondered how this could be. But I just took it, you know, that it was part of the whole help that I was getting during that time to take on the Honeywell corporation. It was a long fight, but we were successful. We set up a resistance camp. One of my uncles, June Little, he was a Vietnam veteran, and a bunch of kids, we set up this resistance camp just on the outer ridge of Hells Canyon[2] where Honeywell corporation was proposing to do munitions testing.[3] That's in the southern Black Hills, that's a real sacred canyon to us as Lakota people.

Each campaign is a learning experience for me in terms of the way the spiritual and the political work together. I have always learned as I was going along working on a campaign or an issue. Just like in the southern Black Hills in the '87 campaign against the munitions testing. There were some drawings on the southern canyon wall of seven elk, each thousands of years old. Prior to going into the canyon on July 18, in June, the month before I participated in the sundance ceremony. That's four days of fasting and dancing, daybreak to sunset, praying to the Great Spirit, Tunkashila, which means Grandfather, giving thanks and stating why you are there that year. That year I went to pray for help in stopping the munitions testing. So here I was dancing and praying and out of the sun's rays, when I faced to the east direction, I saw these elk appear. There were two of them, adult females, and underneath, two smaller ones. I went on dancing and praying and asking for help to stop the munitions testing and gazing at this vision. Then I looked to each side at the women who were dancing by me to see if they saw it, but they didn't, and when I looked back it was gone. That was June. On July 18 when we went into the canyon to place prayer flags, afterwards we went to see these ancient drawings. The ones I had seen coming out of the sunrays were the same as the drawings that were on the canyon walls. There were seven of them. The first one was the largest, and I went down inside, and on the seventh one the drawing was real small and pitiful. Even the antlers were real small, and there was no more after that. But they say that all of us have that sacred knowledge or ancient knowledge, then when I looked at that drawing nobody had to tell me what it was. It was symbolism of that is the beginning of our people and also where we were at that time in the generation, then there was the smallest and real pitiful one, and there was no more after that. Because for some reason in our history, that we were at a time where we had a heavy responsibility of holding the destiny of our people in our hands. But what it symbolizes is that we have to strengthen ourselves as the people whether we are Indian or non-Indian, it didn't matter. But that's the message I got—to strengthen ourselves and our values, our morals, our traditions, our languages. As a people we need to strengthen all facets of ourselves. Otherwise, if we don't do it in this generation then we will lose it all. And there will be no more for the next generation coming. That's what the ancient drawings on the canyon wall represent to me. So now they take the kids every spring and summer from the reservation schools to visit the ancient drawings, so that they will have that connection and know their responsibilities of carrying on. As a people we learn something everyday in that way, till we die, we will continue learning new things, new knowledge, different things from the past.

A lot of times I feel that people, organizers, Indian and non-Indian are destined to be involved in these different things. I knew that it was major to stop the munitions testing, but it really came home to me after the Persian Gulf War when I was watching *Nightline* on TV a few years ago. All of these people from our military were talking about all the different illnesses, strange illnesses, they were getting after serving in the Gulf War. What came to me was that the new kinds of weaponry and munitions Honeywell wanted to test in the Black Hills, they had tested in the Gulf War. Not only had the weapons affected the enemy, but they had affected their own. I thought the Great Spirit really has us involved in these things. We often don't know at the time of the great responsibility that's laid on us, but we just do it because we believe in what we are doing. We are committed to preventing and stopping these kinds of catastrophes against our people. One of the munitions they were proposing to test in the Black Hills was a highly radioactive uranium tip munitions. That was one of them that they used in the Persian Gulf War.

Roxann: One of the things that is so important in what you just said is that you have to have information on what particular corporations are planning to do before you can even begin to understand the consequences and respond in a publicly organized way. What sources do you rely on for such information?

Joann: Usually somehow the information always filters in. Somebody sends in something, just like in the '87 campaign against Honeywell. We worked with non-Indian landowners and ranchers in the southern Black Hills that were against having what was coming. They would attend the town meetings that the corporations were having in their area. We didn't have that access here. I think they came into this area first in February of 1987. But the only hearing we ever had here on the reservation was in May, end of May 1987. But those ranchers attended hearings in their area, so they kind of knew, and I think through information, the Freedom of Information Act, they had access to materials.

Roxann: You mentioned in connection with another action that Greenpeace was very helpful.

Joann: Yes, Greenpeace was very helpful with information back in June 26, 27 of 1990. They sponsored financially the first Indian environmental conference down in the southwest of Dilkon, Arizona, on a Navaho reservation. Our area, Pine Ridge Indian Reservation, was being targeted by a waste dump company from Torrington, Connecticut, around that time. We learned about this through a rumor. After we got ahold of plans for the project from a district official here in Porcupine, we realized the rumors were true. Torrington was proposing a five thousand-acre waste dump in the Badlands area of the reservation. They wanted to bring in outside waste. So, armed with this information and the invitation we got from Greenpeace, we went down to the

Dilkon meeting. When we got there, we were thinking we were alone in our area, our Indian country being targeted by a waste company, and we found out that many other Indian tribes were also being targeted for a waste dump or incinerator site. That is when we came together and were able to get help through Greenpeace. They gave us all kinds of information, including technical information that helped us understand the contracts and how bad these contracts were that were written up by the corporations. With this information we went back to the tribal council, which met around the middle part of the next month in July of 1990. Armed with that information then we were able to knock it in the head. In our area a lot of our council people, they speak and understand Lakota, or the Sioux language, and so we were able to use our own language and explain to them the damage this kind of waste dump could do to our land and our water and air and everything.

Roxann: Where does your understanding of Lakota identity and your feeling for the land come from? Was there any one person or situation you consider most important to your outlook?

Joann: I and my children, we are really grounded in our spirituality, and I think that is a major part of our whole life. Not just once a year we practice different ceremonies, but every day of our life it helps us. In return that helps my kids in what they do, so it is a real strong foundation for us, but also in the past it has really been strong in my work over the last twenty-two years. As I have done organizing and educating on various issues, it has been a real vital part.

Roxann: Is the spirituality something you learned, or did you come to it some other way?

Joann: I think for me, probably, it was always there. I was raised strongly in the Episcopalian Church by my grandmother, because here on the reservation a lot of our grandparents were forced into boarding schools, and Christianity was really forced on them as part of a move for them to assimilate. So a lot of families didn't really practice traditional ceremonies. The ceremonies went underground.

POLITICAL CULTURE IN TRANSFORMATION:
THE AMERICAN INDIAN MOVEMENT

Roxann: That's what I'm wondering, Joann. How did you recover a knowledge of those traditions once they were underground? You have also said that many of your dreams you came to interpret and understand only long after the actual dreams. Were there specific experiences that brought these ceremonies above ground again and gave political meaning to your dreams?

Joann: Yes. In the late '60s early '70s the American Indian Movement formed in the Twin Cities area around issues of police brutality and other things. It was like a new Indian warriors society for our people. In '72 they came here to the reservation after one of my stepmother's relatives, Uncle Raymond Yellow Thunder was brutally murdered by two non-Indians right across the border in Gordon, Nebraska. That woke a lot of people up. The Bureau of Indian Affairs and the tribal government would not help our family at all during that time. It woke me up and made me want to stand up and say no more. We are not going to take this anymore. The American Indian Movement was called in by our family to look into the issue, and they did. They went in and shut the town of Gordon, Nebraska. They took over city hall, closed down shops, and said that the Indian people are standing up saying this is not going to happen. This murder needs to be looked into. And finally it was like someone was there to back us up and to support us and help us, a strong organization. And they also brought with them new information, kind of like a renewal. They brought back a strong Indian identity. Be proud. Wear your hair long. Be proud of your tradition and all that. In school as a kid I remember that there was hardly anything written in the textbooks about the Indian people. If there was anything it was always negative. One of the things that really made an impression on me was when I was in grade school. In our social studies book it told about the government building dams across the country. There was a picture on one page of an Indian man. He was from North Dakota. He wore a suit, and he had just signed away a large portion of Indian land. He was weeping, but he had been compelled to sign anyway. That really stuck in my mind. It made me angry. Now our Indian identity began to come back. Old people, including my grandmother, who had been quiet for so long, began to tell me and my bothers and sisters stories from the past that she felt it was important to pass along. It was always there, but it was underground, forced underground by the United States government.

Roxann: So recovering a sense of those traditions involved your participation in the American Indian Movement. Did this involve your trying to find people who knew the old ceremonies, who could speak out, who had been silenced for so long by other circumstances?

Joann: Well, for me it was like a new identity. I was proud of who I am. It brought pride into myself as a Lakota woman. Hey, I am somebody, I am going to be heard. I don't have to be afraid anymore. Other people felt that too. They could speak about their knowledge, their ways that had gone underground. Many people felt there is a group that's coming behind us that's going to stand up for us and help us. I felt that very strongly.

Roxann: I remember you telling me something about that experience. Maybe we should recall that.

Joann: Yes. That was during that time in '72 when I finally started standing up and getting involved, but it took the brutal murder of one of my relatives to wake me up. It's like reservation days and stuff. Our people here, Lakota people, have really been repressed and controlled by the government. You know, it was really in our minds that we had to behave ourselves, be quiet and all of that or the government is going to come in. And so we did.

In '73 there was a lot of tribal corruption here on Pine Ridge Reservation. A vigilante group was organized to suppress us. They were Indian people sent by the tribal government. During that time I was away going to college in junior college, Indian junior college in Muskogee, Oklahoma, when the occupation happened February 27, 1973. It was kind of a forced occupation. The people were just going to Wounded Knee to look into issues of a trading post that was ripping off a lot of our people. But as the people came into Wounded Knee along with their supporters from the American Indian Movement, the situation changed. The Oglala Civil Rights Committee, the GOON they called it, Guardians of the Oglala Nation, it was a vigilante group, they put up roadblocks and locked our people in Wounded Knee. That forced them into the seventy-one-day occupation. Then the United States marshals and the FBI were called in. So they came in with their armaments during that time. They talked about tribal corruption and about the way the United States government had used this to their advantage many times in the past, but especially in 1868 when they violated specific treaty agreements. It was an education for me just before going into Wounded Knee. That's where I first got hooked into organizing food packs and medical supplies. It just came natural to me, and I was good at it. So that was probably my first organizing effort that actually came into place, and people were looking to me to help them do all these different things. And then finally in March, the second week of March, we went into Wounded Knee.[4] There were twenty-five of us. I was the only woman who walked into Wounded Knee with this group of men. During that time going in, it was like a regular war. There were government flares that lit up the sky at night, so the Feds could to see where we were walking and everything. As we were getting closer to Wounded Knee, it was getting more and more like that. And so this was a time for me to really check myself on my commitment and my fear of government authority. I had to deal with those issues going in. Finally, I was just crawling on the ground, you know, and when the flares were going up, it just made me think. I had a backpack on, and I was carrying a load of stuff to take in. And I thought, why should I be crawling around like this? This is my land, you know, and I have every right to be here. It was dealing with that fear of losing your life and fear of the authority of the government that I had to come to terms with. But during that time going into Wounded Knee, I did come to terms with it. Once I had done that, then I was okay.

Roxann: How important was this experience to you?

Joann: It was a major turning point. I would say that in my whole career, all my twenty-two years of being a leader and organizer on all kinds of issues, that was the one experience that strengthened me for all the other struggles. I lost my fear there. I no longer had any fear when I stood up before corporations, government bodies, congress, hearings of all sorts. I no longer had a fear of speaking out. It started there at Wounded Knee.

Roxann: You said you were the only woman out of twenty-five who carried supplies into Wounded Knee. Do you feel that you had any special role as a woman? Was there anything about being a woman that was a part of your identity or approach as an organizer?

Joann: I think that we are destined to be involved in these things and to do these things. During that time I looked at myself as a woman that really believes in what I'm doing regardless of what the consequences might be. And I made a commitment in '73 at that time that I would always stand up for my people, that I would always fight for my people and do what I can, even if it is laying my life on the line for my people. That is how much I believe in appreciating the identity that was given back to me, the identity that I got back in my growing spirituality. This is the Lakota way of thought. Our belief that when you are given something you always give back to the people. That's just how it is.

Roxann: After the '73 experience, when was your next opportunity to get involved?

Joann: Well, after that and it was just being on the run, having to be on the run from the government, from the FBI, from the Feds. I think in the official document it said that when we went in, the twenty-five of us, that we took in arms, even though it was actually medical and food supplies. Through an FBI informant, they said we took in arms into Wounded Knee. So after Wounded Knee, they were desperately hunting down people that were involved. Our names were given to them by various informants. Anybody they could pin a charge on, they did. Somehow through my involvement with going into Wounded Knee, they associated me with arms they said were taken in.

Roxann: What happened in your life then?

Joann: I left. I fled. In the fall of 1973 I went underground and went into Canada, and I stayed in Canada until January 1974. But while I was in Canada, I fled to some traditional people they call the Long House people, the Mohawk people that live up beside Montreal on Indian reservations called Caugnawaga. So I and my old man then, who was from Canada, we spent time with the Long House people. We stayed with them there. They were involved in planning to take some land back in upper state New York in the Adirondacks. It was land that belonged to them by treaty agreements, but it was confiscated. We were asked to be part of that land takeover that was being planned. The Mohawks actually took the land over on May 11, 1974. I wasn't involved but my old man was. I came back into Colorado and started working under the Manpower program. That's when there was big money for Manpower training positions by the government. I needed to make some money so I had something to live on in Canada and so I could help out with things there. Eventually I got busted by the FBI August of 1974. I was expecting during that time. I was surprised it took them that long to find me. I had all those months from May of '74 to the first week of August '74 to make some money before they busted me. They had photographs that were taken inside of Wounded Knee. I saw my own photograph. I could also see how the FBI tried to manipulate me by saying they talked to my family members. They named three of my family members, my grandmother, my older sister, and older brother, and they said they had talked to each of them about my involvement. I knew that wasn't true. I flat refused to talk to them. I told them I needed to talk to an attorney. So they gave me one week to get in touch with them. The trials of some of the leaders who were involved in Wounded Knee were already going on in St. Paul, Minnesota. They said was if I didn't get in touch with them in that week, then they would subpoena me to testify at the trials. So I called a Legal Aid representative in Denver, Bill Hazelton, and asked him. I told him I just got busted and what the Feds were proposing. He said my options were to go ahead and let them subpoena me and take me in. A legal defense team could meet me and coach me on what I should say and what my rights were. The other option was I could run. So I never told him what I was going to do. I just thanked him for his information, and I fled the next day. In a couple of days I was in upper state New York in a Mohawk land takeover. I was kind of forced to cut work short, and then I fled. I knew I would be protected once I got to their land, and they would no way let anyone try to arrest me, or anything, you know.

My baby was due about the second week of November, so when I got there, after the end of the first week of August, then I got involved. I didn't really have time to rest. Some parents wanted to start an alternative school, you know, and also there was a plan to include their Mohawk culture into the education of the kids. I helped put together this alternative school within the community. The community was called Ganiekeh in Mohawk. The English translation means "Land of the Flint," the rock, or the stone. Trouble, however, never seems to be very far away. At the end of October there was a shooting. Some non-Indian hunters shot into our camp. Our security people retaliated, and they shot one person, a child who the hunters had with them. He was wounded in the spine, but luckily the child didn't die. We heard that the state troopers were going to break into the camp, set up road blocks, and they wanted us to give up two people for that shooting during that time. During all that chaos, I went into early labor. On October 29, 1974, my son, Flint, was born.

After that, we went through the justice department of the government, and the investigation that followed showed that the hunters were the ones that started the shooting. After that I went into public relations for the community, dispelling rumors surrounding the shooting, talking to groups about why we wanted this alternative community and self-sufficiency for our children. I did a lot of speaking, and I got invited to different universities, church organizations, and stuff. The money I made went back into the community to buy basic things that were needed, food and different things.

VISION QUEST: RETURNING HOME TO LAKOTA LANDS

Roxann: You were up in Ganiekeh until '75?

Joann: Yes, May of 1975 because, while I was there during that time, I started having dreams, short dreams of myself going into this lodge. The lodge was all covered, a small hut-like looking lodge. In this dream I see myself go into the hut. In the spring, it finally dawned on me that I needed to go home. That hut represented a kind of purification, a sweat lodge ceremony. Historically, you see, our people, the Lakota people, when they went into war and came back they went into that sweat lodge ceremony to cleanse themselves of war and fighting and set themselves on the path to peace. After Wounded Knee I never did. For myself I didn't participate in that particular ceremony, I wanted to be able to understand more about what it was and then to really commit myself before I participated in that. In the dream it showed me that's what I needed to do to get to the next level of where I needed to be.

Roxann: In terms of the rituals and so forth, you said you weren't raised with them, that your grandparents were pushed to assimilate through an Episcopalian congregation. You said the other traditions were here, but underground. There were people who still knew the stories and the rituals. Did you at some point start to know these other people, or had you known them all along and you began to talk about things in a different way?

Joann: When I was in Canada I found that they were more assimilated than what we were here. Because we still had a lot of our traditions and language. A lot of the Ojibwa in the Toronto area where I had been had lost their ways. But I also knew when I was out in the Ganiekeh area in upstate New York that it was time for me to go home. I knew that the searching and all the answers, what I needed to know, were at home. I needed to go through that purification ceremony to help me get to the next step. I knew that I didn't have to run anymore. The trials were pretty much over, and it was found that the government was in violation during that time, so I could safely return home. They formally dropped all charges.

I returned to Pine Ridge in 1976. Actually, I first went to St. Paul, where I ended up going to a survival school they call Red School. It was an alternative school founded by the American Indian Movement. That's where I found some elders. One of them was the principal of the school during that time. They were the ones that invited me to that purification ceremony. I wasn't even with my own people when I went into that purification ceremony. But I went in with them, I guess that's how I look back at it now, that it was meant to be, you know. I stayed there one year, and I worked for the school as a reading teacher aid. Then finally June of 1976 I made it back home here to the Pine Ridge Indian Reservation.

When I came home, I found the people I needed to help me, to come back to my ways, and do the vision quest and eventually the sundance, because I dreamed about both of those ceremonies and knew I needed to go through them. I dreamed them first, and then it all happened.

I didn't have very much time to settle, when I got home. You know how people come and visit who you haven't seen for a long time. They tell you their problems. Tell you what's going on on the res. And one of the stories that I heard over and over again was that a lot of our children were being ripped off, being stolen, placed off the reservation into foster homes, being adopted out through the state welfare agencies. A lot of times parents, weren't even given representation or help. The majority of the time, I think, the cases were due to neglect. Kids were taken off due to alcoholism, or the kids were dirty and weren't taken care of. Based on those kinds of things, they just whisked the kids off, and the parents did not get fair hearings. By that time one of my cousins who was on a relocation program in California felt the need to come home. One of my aunties who went years ago on relocation out to the West Coast, she came home too, all about the same time. So I think by October of 1976 we already formed an organization called Crisis Center. It was a group of women from different districts on the reservation that we formed this crisis organization, and we started documenting cases, actual cases of these children being taken off of the reservation. The parents were not getting due process. And from 1976 it took us not quite a year to establish ourselves through the tribal government where we got ourselves chartered, recognized by the tribal government, and actually formed an office. Manpower programs were still here on the reservation. So I got funded from that government program to organize and get this together. That's how I lived and supported myself. At first I got employed by an alcohol and drug abuse program called Project Recovery, but I felt that my philosophy and stuff didn't connect with the twelve-step program. I needed the money, but I just felt that I couldn't be in a position that I really didn't identify with. I felt it wasn't fair to the client, you know, not to have the same ideas or philosophy as the program. So I removed myself from that, and they transferred the position to the Crisis Center so that I could do the work. From 1977 to 1982 we worked. We brought a lot of kids home, and we were also involved in giving testimony to Congress on the Indian tribal welfare act.

Roxann: How many children do you think you found?

Joann: Maybe a couple of hundred. Some were successful replacements to their families, and some weren't back in the family. Here on the reservation they have a large extended family system that's in place. So a child always went to a relative or to a Lakota family here on the res. The parents got whatever help they needed then through our program. We monitored the families, getting them the help they needed. Not only that but we advocated for them in the court system and the child welfare networks. That was successful, but we got too successful, because the social service of the Bureau of Indian Affairs and the state welfare agencies were threatened because we were allocated some of their money. Eventually our funding got axed, and BIA got it. But by that time we had already had a position put in the court system as a trial advocate for the parents. It is still in existence to this day. It was a permanent victory. Now parents can stand up for themselves. This almost reminds me of that *Forrest Gump* movie, "Oh, I was here at this time and that happened, and then I went there, and that happened!"

Roxann: And then where were you and what happened? No, let's put it another way. Were you doing any other organizing at the time?

Joann: Yes, there was a lot of work organizing against uranium mining in the southern Black Hills. That would have to be right around '78. I was not involved until early '80. By '79 I was involved in the planning stages to build a local radio station just up the road. We held meetings in Porcupine to talk about having a community communication network so there would be no more Wounded Knees and people on Pine Ridge would know what was going on, you know. The KILI station 90.1 FM came out of those meetings. In Lakota "Kili" means "great significance" or "it's really great." By the winter of 1980 we had a working group, and on February 15, 1983, we went on the air. It's been on ever since. There is no tribal government control, no BIA, Bureau of Indian Affairs control, it is a community-based, public-owned station. It broadcasts to two reservations in addition to Pine Ridge. In the beginning they did a lot of programs on political issues, but since a few years ago, it is more like a service station with information on tribal programs. But it is still available for issues information.

Around this time a group called the Black Hills Alliance began to get organized to oppose uranium mining in the southern Black Hills area. Indians and non-Indians came together in that organization, not just from this area. There were a bunch of idealistic young non-Indian people that came from out east and different parts of the country to meet at Rapid City. Some of them were researchers, lawyers, and people interested in alternative energy and the environmental issues. In 1980 there was a big survival gathering just on the other side of Ellsworth Air Force Base on Marv Kammer's land. He was a rancher. We had a weeklong gathering of people from all over, internationally too, to talk about alternative energy and opposition to uranium mining. The Black Hills Alliance was mostly informational. They had some hearings on the uranium issue in Edgemont, I think, with Union Carbide. The Black Hills Alliance was good in their campaigning. They kept the mining out. They wanted someone from the reservation on their board of directors, so that's how I got involved in 1980.

About the same time in the early '80s, the United States Geographical Survey (USGS) unit based in Denver, Colorado, came into the area to take samples of zeolite[5] from the Eagle Nest district, on the eastern part of the reservation. Nick Raymond was in charge of the USGS operation, and the Bureau of Indian Affairs and the tribal council here cooperated with him. One of the ranchers contacted some of us, and we went to take pictures of the guys from Denver taking out the zeolite without having any clearance from the landowners. There was some concern because we suspected, based on some research done by Lorieli Decora in the early 1980s, that the zeolite was cancer-causing when it was airborne, which it would be in the mining process.[6] But the tribal government argued that the local zeolite was not a cancer-causing variety of zeolite. The issue died down until '88 when a new tribal government wanted to promote economic development to raise revenue for local administration, so they revived the possibility of mining zeolite on the reservation. That's when we started the Native Resource Coalition in Porcupine district along with some of the ranchers and community members from Eagle Nest district.

When the people of Eagle Nest district asked for an informational meeting with Native Resource Coalition, they also invited USGS representative from Denver, Nick Raymond, and Frank Marshall, who was head of the mineral studies program. These two came into the hearing and filled the whole table with documents. They even had a piece of rock with zeolite in it to show how harmless it was. I was sitting there thinking, "God, how am I going to come up against all these experts from the government with all of those documents?" I knew I would just have to say what was in my heart. I said a really fast, short prayer to Tunkashila, the Great Spirit, in my language. I asked him to help me say what I needed to say for the people and not for the government representatives, because the government people already had their minds made up. I figured the tribal government would give the government people a lot of time to speak, but they gave them just ten minutes. Before I knew it, I was asked to get up and speak from the grassroots point of view. I looked at all those documents, and didn't know how I was going to do it. Then I heard a voice speak my name as I got up to go to the front. I looked behind me but nobody was there. The people next to me heard it too. That's when I thought it must be a sign in answer to my prayer. I knew I was heard. When I got up to speak, I didn't know at that time what I was actually going to say. But I knew I should speak from my heart, from a mother's point of view in protecting her children and from the point of view of Mother Earth protecting her children. So I spoke on that, and they gave me all the time I needed to speak. That night the district council and voted against zeolite mining in their district. They also voted against the removal of any more zeolite samples.

NETWORKS AND ALLIANCES: OVERCOMING DEMORALIZATION

Roxann: What would you say is the most important thing you have learned in your organizational activities? Many people today feel profoundly demoralized in the face of powerful international corporate and governmental alliances. What would you want to convey to people who are involved in these kinds of organizing efforts?

Joann: The way I feel about this is that even in my dream that I shared earlier, even when I have almost the last breath left in me, in all our organizing and our work sometimes we get to real desperate measures and almost to the point where there is no hope, but somehow there is a light, and you have to have that, even a glimpse of that dream and that hope that you are going to win, you are going to defeat this. Because if you don't, then you almost defeat yourself right from the beginning. So you need to have that energy, that commitment to see this through and to believe in yourself and believe in what you are doing.

Roxann: In the community-based networks which address local issues, do you find that different groups use the Lakota traditions differently?

Joann: Sometimes groups pull in different directions. Those that are based off the reservation can really rip people off. There was one called American Relief. They said they had raised millions of dollars on our behalf, but most of the funds went to overhead, like salaries. Very little of it came down to our people. But that group is gone now. I think they moved to the Navaho reservation to do their stuff, their dirty deeds. You need to really check them out.

One of the organizations I helped cofound works well and is now a nationally based group called the Indigenous Environmental Network. Their main office is in Bemidji, Minnesota. Tom Goldtooth is the director of that. Every year they do a big "Protect Mother Earth" conference. This next year it will be in North Carolina on Cherokee lands. Different indigenous groups from all over the country come and do workshops on environmental issues. It is a big success. It grew out of that meeting that Greenpeace sponsored at Dilkon, Arizona, in 1990 that I mentioned before. I am also a boardmember of Seventh Generation, a funding organization based in Arcata, California. Together Greenpeace and the Seventh Generation Foundation continue to sponsor the IEN's annual conferences, which help promote local self-sufficiency among indigenous peoples.

Roxann: Do you think Lakota identity works as a base for resistance? Or does this identity tend to get misused and become a source of division?

Joann: I think if you are clear on your goals, protection of the land and community well-being, you can have some differences on how to see things and still be able to tell when some group is misusing the intent of the tradition.

Roxann: Can you give me an example?

Joann: In the spring of 1990 here on the res, there were rumors about a toxic waste dump that Amcor Corporation wanted to locate on Lakota lands. Our tribal government was invited on June 21 by Amcor to meet with them at the Hilton in Rapid City. The night before, someone called me to tell me about the meeting. There was also a rumor that the corporation had written an agreement for our tribal government and that the council just had to sign it. So I took my daughter Kimberly and went to the meeting. I didn't know exactly what was going on, but it didn't sound right.

At the hotel, the room was set up to receive the tribal council. The tables were set with little gifts—fancy cups, glasses, and baseball caps. A big meal with T-bone steaks was laid out for them too. I just looked at it all and thought it was like years ago when our people got bought off in the treaties and stuff with whiskey. So I crashed the meeting after the dinner and started asking questions. I and one of the past district chairmen were the only ones asking questions. Our tribal council people didn't even ask questions that needed to be asked. From that meeting I got the impression that none of them had even read the proposal they were prepared to sign.

One of the tribal councilwomen got angry and told the past district chairman and me to sit down. She said we were being disrespectful. "Look at all this food they provided for us. You are not being Lakota to be so ungrateful."

So I just told her to sit down. I said, "It is because of people like you who don't know what you're signing that people like me have to ask questions. You'd sell us down the river, you know, because you don't read what's being proposed. A long time ago it was whiskey that bought our people off, now it is wining and dining by these corporations. But now we have the right to speak and research these things, and it is pretty clear that you have not."

The meeting ended after that. The woman just slammed her briefcase shut and walked out. My daughter Kimberly was ten or eleven at the time. As we left she said, "Mom, you need cups at home. Yours are all broken. Everyone just left these." So she took four of them.

Roxann: So in the name of Lakota culture two different political views were expressed.

Joann: Yes, but only one spoke for the protection of the land, and that was the more true position. You always have to be wary of the real egotistical people that try to infiltrate or even get into key positions in local organizations. It is an ongoing thing. There are always jealousies within an organization. The corporations like to play on those jealousies. The government is good at that too. They have always tried to divide and conquer. Whether it was the American Indian Movement or the Indigenous Environmental Network, both of which do good work, people just don't learn to work without jealousies. IEN works well, though, because it is a technical information group and people from different parts of the country work on their own local projects. I think that is a good model. In other cases, people who are controlling tend to take over and others tend to sit back. When that happens, I just figure it is time to pull out and move on. I've done what I could do. But collaboration from local bases does work in the best cases. It's what you have to hope for.

Roxann: What do you do with the tremendous amount of anger it is possible to feel for the devastation indigenous groups have experienced and which continues to be directed toward them with the efforts to locate nuclear waste dumps and other toxic sites on their lands?

Joann: I don't know how other people deal with it, but I use it. I use it as a tool to give me energy. The idea of enemies kind of diverts you as well. There are just people you can't get through to. They do you harm. You have to put your energy where you can be the most productive. That's the best way to battle enemies. Maybe it was a little bit of that anger that helped me to stand up and not feel afraid of the corporations and the government. Anger and prayer. I relied on my prayers to help me through the difficult times.

Roxann: What kind of prayers do you say?

Joann: No special prayers, just prayer from the heart. Lots of New Age people talk about the spirituality of Native Americans. I don't like the rip-offs, and I don't like the exploitation by the New Age people. I know that some of our tribal members are responsible for doing the sweat lodge ceremony with non-Indian people, exploiting our ways for profit. I'm strong within my beliefs now, but it took me many years to get to where I am at. The way I see it, whatever ethnic background we come from, we each have the power of prayer. And you should stay with and develop your own. That's important. There are so many distractions, so many things in this life that take you away from what you are working on, and that's why you need to stay focused on what your commitment is and stay on that path.

Roxann: Two or three hundred years ago, Lakota traditions were very different from what they are today. How do you recover that culture today, especially after all of the loss and disruption?

Joann: Yes, they are very different today. It is just like anything, you know, things change with time, but some of the sacred knowledge, ancient knowledge still comes back to us in dreams and the vision quest. We are going through changes and reviving and strengthening our traditions for the present and the future. You just have to work on the issues facing you wherever you are. You have to do what works for you in your region and your tribe. It's got to come from you in your area. Not I or anybody else from the outside can come in and do it all for you.

Roxann: Have there been personal costs for your social work?

Joann: Yes. I don't think people realize how much personal loss and sacrifice there is in being an activist. Sometimes the choices you make are not acceptable to other people and the way they think things should be. In 1987 I made a choice to stay here and finish the campaign against munitions testing. My husband wanted to move to the Twin Cities to start a business. It was painful, and I was seen as the bad guy for breaking up my family, but I knew I had to stay. I made a commitment to stay here and work on local issues. I would not compromise that. But it was painful.

Roxann: Are you working on any particular issue now, Joann?

Joann: After twenty-two years of being really busy with local issues, I have had to slow down because of my rheumatoid arthritis. These days I work mostly over the phone. This past month, for example, students from Columbia University came and spent a few hours with me. They were camped out on the buffalo reserves east of here learning about the plant species in the area and talking to people on the res. I guess you could say I am working in education now. But that has always been part of what I've done.

AFTERWORD

As this interview goes to press, the issue of zeolite mining on Lakota lands near the Badlands is once again creating conflict. Newly elected members of the Pine Ridge Tribal Council may attempt a legal maneuver that would place these lands under "immanent domain," allowing the council to grant mining rights on Lakota lands to specific tribal groups without a referendum requiring general voter approval. Various Lakota Land Associations on the Pine Ridge Reservation have begun to take action that could counter this move. The Interior Department would have to approve the council's request for immanent domain status, but some fear that corruption at the tribal council and government agency levels might collude to undermine local land protection efforts. As anyone knows who has traveled through the Badlands, this region is breathtakingly beautiful and environmentally fragile. Extensive mining would destroy the vulnerable ecology of the area and create health hazards for the immediate areas and beyond, the potentials of which are currently unknown because of inconclusive studies on the relationship between lung cancer and zeolite.

NOTES

1. Cindy Reed has been very helpful with information on the 1987 campaign against the Honeywell munitions testing plan. A rancher in the Hot Springs area of South Dakota and a leader of the Alliance, Reed was clear at the time that the main issue was "a land-based ethic versus a profit-oriented motive" (*Los Angeles Times*, 30 August 1987). When I spoke with her after visiting Joann, Cindy wanted to stress in addition that the issue of racism ran alongside the land and profit issues. Reed thought that the "media appeal" of the "Cowboy and Indian Alliance" was a major factor in the movement's success, which was extremely costly. Many financial debts assumed by herself and other supporters were never recouped. The tremendous cost to local people with limited resources in a struggle with a major corporation like Honeywell, even when the campaign was successful, was clearly a long-term organizing issue.

2. Hells Canyon, Thunder Eagle Canyon, to the Sioux people, is "an isolated, sheer-walled chasm cut by the Cheyenne River ten miles from Hot Springs" (*Minneapolis Star and Tribune*, 5 August 1987).

3. It was almost impossible to get a clear idea from Honeywell spokespersons as to exactly what kind of testing would be done in the Black Hills site. One representative for Honeywell said, "most of the tests would involve firing shells as small as 20 millimeters and as large as 155 millimeters down a 1.8-mile range on the canyon floor into a sand-and-cement catch basin." There were concerns that sophisticated munitions, including antitank shells tipped with armor-piercing depleted uranium would also be tested at the site and could pollute both the water table and the atmosphere. To which a Honeywell spokesperson responded that, "few tests at the facility would involve the substance, which emits low radiation levels." But the spokesperson acknowledged that the "weapons mix could change if government standards or testing requirements were revised in the future" (*Los Angeles Times*, 30 August 1987).

4. For additional accounts of the 1973 events at Wounded Knee see Peter Matthiessen, *In the Spirit of Crazy Horse* (New York: Viking, 1983), 58–82; also see Ward Churchill and Jim Vander Wall, *Agents of Repression: The FBI's Secret Wars against the Black Panther Party and the American Indian Movement* (Boston: South End Press, 1990), 141–97; Russell Means with Marvin J. Wolf, *Where White Men Fear to Tread* (New York: St. Martin's, 1995), 257–73.

5. Zeolite is a rare mineral found in only a couple locations in the world. It is valuable for cleaning up nuclear materials.

6. Loreili Decora of the Indian Health Services on neighboring Rosebud Reservation shared with me her findings in a report she compiled in 1984 on studies that had investigated the possible health hazards of zeolite.

12

Beyond Unity: Transcommunal Roots of Coordination in the Haudenosaunee (Iroquois) Model of Cooperation and Diversity

John Brown Childs

So [the Peace Maker] passed from settlement to settlement finding that men desired peace and would practice it if they knew for certainty that others would practice it, too.

But first, after leaving the hunters [the Peace Maker] sought the house of a certain woman who lived by the warriors' path which passed be between East and West.

When [the Peace Maker] arrived, the woman placed food before him, and after he had eaten, asked him his message.

"I carry the Mind of the Master of Life," he replied, "and my message will bring an end to the wars between east and west."

"The word that I bring," he said, "is that all peoples shall love one another and live together in peace. . . ."

"Thy message is good," said the woman, "but a word is nothing until it is given form, and set to work in the world. What form shall this message take when it comes to dwell among men?"

—From the story of the founding of the Haudenosaunee (People of the Long House, or "Iroquois") Native American League of Nations concerning the meeting of the Peace Maker with the woman who came to be called "the Mother of Nations," (circa A.D. fourteenth/early fifteenth centuries).

—Paul A. W. Wallace (ToRiWaWaKon) The White Roots of Peace.

The closer one moves to theoretical unity . . . the ultimate unity proves to be an empty
. . . content. . . . What underlies . . . unity . . . is not a principle as a starting point, but
the fact of an actual acknowledgement of one's own participation . . . this fact cannot
be adequately expressed in theoretical terms, but can only be described and partici-
patively experienced.

—*Mikhail B. Bakhtin, Toward a Philosophy of the Act.*

Talk won't grow corn.

—*Lenni Lanape Native American saying, from Evan T. Pritchard,*
The Way of the Wabanaki.

INTRODUCTION

In 1989, the house of a family that had recently moved to Los Angeles from
Mexico was firebombed. The attacker was an African American man. The
resulting fire caused death and serious injuries to several members of the family. Another African American man, seeing the flames rushed inside to help. He
was shot and seriously wounded by a family member who mistook him for
the firebomber.

Given the lack of general interaction among different racial and ethnic communities, including among Chicanos and African Americans, and given the prejudices and stereotypes that many in these communities have about other groups,
this tragic incident could have led to massive Chicano versus African American
conflict. Indeed, when news of the incident reached the prisons tensions began
to mount among African American and Chicano inmates. In other parts of the
country, such as Miami, Washington, D.C., and Detroit, and in numerous school-
yards and prison yards, ethnic conflict, erupting after incidents in which a person
from one community harms another, are common stories.

But such conflict did not take place in Los Angeles. And it did not occur precisely because of the long-standing cooperative relationship that two groups—the
Chicano Pinto Union and the Black Awareness Community Development Organization (BACDO)—have forged with each other. Both of these groups, consisting of men formerly incarcerated in the California prison system, work with issue of inmate rights and directly with youth to steer them away from prison-bound
trajectories. Each group is rooted and respected in its own community. Simultaneously, the Chicano Pinto Union and BACDO worked cooperatively with each
other. Through that work they established track records of interpersonal trust,
based on the common task of ending inner city violence and the devastation of
massive incarceration.

So it was these two organizations, tied together through common concerns and mutual relations of trust and respect, that came together to assist the family whose home had been firebombed. Both groups worked to raise money for the family. When the African American man who had tried to help and had been wounded recovered, both groups facilitated his visit to the family. With their thick ties to their communities and their strong track records of mutual cooperation, the Chicano Pinto Union and BACDO were not only to avert a catastrophic ethnic/racial conflict, but they further strengthened positive relationships among Chicanos and African Americans.

BACDO and the Chicano Pinto Union are important examples of constructive relations across group lines that accentuate ethnic/racial identity while also being open to cooperation with others. They exemplify a particular form of cooperation that I call "Transcommunality." I believe that this form of cooperation offers hope for social justice among diverse peoples in an age of increasing economic inequality and crisis. It is to the understanding of Transcommunality that this chapter is focused.

By Transcommunality I mean the constructive and developmental interaction occurring among members of distinct groups, cutting across race/ethnic and organizational lines, while maintaining the integrity of these different vantage points. This cooperation, with its emphasis on coordinated heterogeneity across ethnic, race, national, and organizational lines entails nothing less than a changed way of thinking, a paradigm shift, that moves beyond the usual progressive emphasis on homogenizing "unity." Simultaneously, Transcommunality also escapes from a "postmodern" multiculturalism that is debilitated and confused by its emphasis on "diversity" that lacks a method for creating cohesive linkages among heterogenous peoples. Transcommunality recognizes that a wide variety of diverse vantage points are the basic reality of global human existence. As such they cannot be wished away, and as history shows, they cannot be crushed, no matter how powerful the force used. In contrast to such negative and hostile approaches to diversity, Transcommunality emphasizes the way in which multitudinous perspectives must be and can be coordinated to create broad-ranging social justice action.

Certainly, Transcommunal cooperation is a vital necessity in this era of crisis that sees increasing numbers of people ejected from the economic mainstream and from social hope as global cooperations cut back through automation and transfer of production while being aided by political decisions that protect such moves. Both in the United States and around the world, millions of people are facing tremendous insecurity because of job loss. Meanwhile others, who have jobs, are forced by poverty to labor under increasingly brutal and degrading nineteenth-century-style conditions, perilous to their very physical well-being. So across the globe millions of people are being negatively impacted by the global economic order. Simultaneously, the elites who pump large investments into, and direct, giant corporate enterprises are continuing to make increasing profits. In short, there is a fundamental uncoupling of economic growth from the social well-being of millions of people. This is not a depression. Big business is doing quite well, while blue-collar working people, and those in middle-class managerial levels, become more and more insecure, if not already over the edge of financial disaster. "Downsized" companies that eject workers are also the "leaner and meaner" companies beloved by Wall Street.

In such times of stress there is a great danger that people will follow along existing social fault lines of racial/ethnic prejudice and miscomprehension. Consequently, diverse communities are blaming, and will increasingly blame, each other for the problems they face. Such division, based on inaccurate senses of the sources of the crisis, will lead to more racial and ethnic conflict both within the United States and elsewhere, unless we learn to cooperate with greater effectiveness. Such cooperation is necessary not only to avoid and end conflict but also to increase the progressive strength of those who are now compartmentalized at best, and hostile at worst. It is toward such cooperation, that contributes to a broadening social justice movement among diverse communities, that Transcommunality is aimed.

Transcommunality, as we shall see, is a method that incorporates fusion and fission, structure and fluidity. It allows for a high degree of diversity, autonomy, and coordination of its participants. Transcommunality accordingly avoids the dangers of homogenizing top-down centralized organization that requires obliteration of heterogenous outlooks. Simultaneously, Transcommunality also overcomes the weakness of that multiculturalism that lacks any method for constructive interaction among distinct communities.

This supple Transcommunality involves a particular form of dialogue that, in the sense described by Tzvetan Todorov, is "animated by the idea of a possible progression in the discussion; it does not consist in the juxtaposition of several voices but in their interaction" (1993: 52). Through such interaction there is mutual learning and transformation. Consequently, Transcommunality does not negate the communities from which interacting participants emerge. Rather, it involves a form of call-and-response in which the participants' mutual awareness of each other is enhanced and modified. Consequently, *Transcommunality entails a process of self-transformation among its participants as they interact and communicate with one another.*

Such progressive transformation of distinct interacting participants in common projects does not require a melting pot's boiling down of distinctions into a single homogenized whole. *Rather, the mutual learning and transformation are only possible precisely because there really are different vantage points based on distinctive experiences.* As Mikhail Bakhtin points out, none of us can engage in such a pure empathy with another that we loose our own identities in the process. Bakhtin says, "If I actually lost myself in the other instead of two participants there would be one." This would be an "impoverishment of being" (1993: 16). In contrast to such "impoverishment," Transcommunal interaction offers an *enrichment* of social being through its emphasis on distinctly autonomous participants, whose interaction reaffirms their community roots while also nourishing shared identity among them. The glue holding these Transcommunal ties together is that of face-to-face interpersonal relationships of mutual trust, built up through what I will discuss as "shared practical action," in which people from different communities and organizations work together around some key shared tasks and objectives.

The openness to working with a wide range of allies is enhanced by this pragmatic task-focused aspect of Transcommunality. Unhindered by rigid ideological dogma and dedicated to accomplishing the task that it sets forth, the Transcommunal organization is willing and able to work with mutual respect with those who share some degree of common concerns. So, Transcommunality grows from a multiplicity of rooted group locations, involves direct personal action with others aimed at addressing particular tasks, and through these actions emerges a widening scope of affiliations. At the same time as Transcommunal action is pragmatic it is also propelled by broad visionary spirit of social justice, equality, and peace.

In practice, Transcommunality offers a methodology for widening inclusionary interaction among diverse communities and organizations. This open systems approach, emphasizes the creation of shared structures and outlooks through negotiations among diverse participants, rather than being a priori and imposed from one source. Diversity is not a barrier to the development of such shared structures and outlooks. Rather different organizations, rooted in their own distinctive community and institutional settings, form the foundations for interaction. To build a bridge across water requires solid ground on each side. It is the solid ground of cultural, social, philosophical, and organizational identities that allows for the Transcommunal bridges to be built.

In its focus on combining rooted vantage points of different communities and its emphasis on ever widening coordination among those positions, Transcommunality is related to the "triad of movements" that the Czechoslovak philosopher Jan Patocka wrote about before his 1977 death while in police custody. Patocka suggests three stages of cooperation consisting of:

1. the movement of sinking roots, of anchoring
2. the movement of self-extension . . . a movement that takes place in the regions of human work
3. the movement [that] by seeking to give these preceding realms rhythms . . . a global meaning (1989: 274).

Significantly for our purposes here, Patocka emphasizes the "sinking" of "roots" as a preliminary stage of creating a globally embracing movement that consist, not of one small group, but rather of what he calls a "multiplicity of [equally rooted] movements." In this same vein, Simone Weil argued that:

> To be rooted is perhaps the most important and least recognized need of the human soul. . . . A human being has roots by virtue of his real, active, and natural participation

in the life of a community, which preserves in living shape certain particular treasures
of the past and certain particular expectations for the future (1952: 43).

Such communities, said Weil, need not be closed. To the contrary their distinctive identities depend on openness to outside influences: "a given environment
should not receive an outside influence as something additional to itself, but as a
stimulant intensifying its own particular way of life . . . [this] should apply to various communities" (1952: 43).[1]

In Transcommunality, the dynamic movement toward ever greater coordinated
action is grounded in the diverse standpoints of varied individuals from multiple
communities. In this sense, Transcommunality is spiritually akin to the proposal
suggested by Pier Cesare Bori, in which the task is "not that of constructing" a single dominant "metalanguage," to which all must adhere, but is rather one of,
"drawing attention to the plurality of languages and cultures, to their translata-
bility, to the historic continuities which link them, and to their potential universality" (1994: 15).

Transcommunality is a process, rather than a magic goal to be reached. As Tzvetan Todorov points out, we must distinguish "end-point universalism" that requires a map, drawn by one group of cartographers who demand that all others
follow its routes, from "universalism of the itinerary," or journey, in which commonality is worked out along the way by the travelers involved. Transcommunality involves the communicative creation of shared outlooks, values, and methods
through the process of common voyaging by diverse participants. Unlike the pre-
drawn map of elite direction, which has an a priori completeness to it, the
Transcommunal journey is not closed. Rather it entails what Todorov describes
as constant "back and forth movement between others and oneself" (1984: 84).
Such mobile universalism is, says Todorov, not "set forth as dogma" from above,
but rather is created by "comparison and compromise" among an ever expanding circle of diverse participants (1984: 84). Such Transcommunally dynamic
features of mutually developing understanding are akin to what Italian writer Antonio Labriola called "that rhythmic movement of understanding" (Soloman,
1979: 90).

To act Transcommunally requires the shift, already mentioned, from monocen-
tric homogenized top-down organization and from an uncoordinated compartmentalized multiculturalism. But this shift is only "new" in comparison with these
two counterproductive tendencies. Those who are interested in adopting
Transcommunal methods have the advantage of drawing from both its historic existence and its living, ongoing forms. The Native American Haudenosaunee Confederacy (People of the Longhouse), also known as "the Iroquois League," brilliantly
constructed a social system with highly autonomous levels of household, clan, and
tribal-nation, all coordinated into the larger federated society that was essentially
Transcommunal from its starting date sometime in the fourteenth/fifteenth centuries through the present.[2] The French underground resistance to the Nazi occu-

pation had many Transcommunal elements that involved high degrees of autonomy for the participant groups, along with coordination of their actions through
shared structures and objectives. Martin Luther King Jr.'s later work was laced with
Transcommunalistic elements. In *Where Do We Go From Here: Chaos or Community*, he pushed for greater African American unity that would bring the middle
class, which had "forgotten their roots" back to the overall community. Simultaneously he advised that such group unity would have to be outwardly focused in its
concern for others. For example, he wrote that African Americans must:

> be mindful of enlarging the whole society. . . we must not overlook the fact that mil-
> lions of Puerto Ricans, Mexican Americans, Indians and Appalachian whites are also
> poverty-stricken. Any serious war against poverty must of necessity include them. (156)

By illuminating and analyzing the key elements of previous and contemporary
forms of Transcommunality, we can better make constructive use of it in the fight
for egalitarian social justice. Such illumination is necessary because there are
powerful stumbling blocks standing in the way of cooperation among groups with
different histories, cultures, ideologies, and objectives, even if at heart, they all
share a certain primary concern with justice.

THE GENIUS OF HAUDENOSAUNEE ORGANIZATION

There are many important examples of Transcommunalistic action from which
we can learn. Here I will focus on the Haudenosaunee confederation. The Haudenosaunee achievement offers important guidelines for Transcommunal outlooks and methods. It is possible and desirable to draw insights and inspiration
from the key elements in such actual examples of Transcommunality. This ex-
tractive-elemental approach draws out key features, rather than trying to vainly
emulate an entire mode of thought of "another" culture or historical moment.
Such an approach is necessary because, as Robert Holub argues, "the appropriation and understanding" of entire systems of theory across cultural divides (even
the comparatively short historical distance between Europe and North America)
is "bound to context" despite "the universal principles that all theoretical en-
deavors share" (1992: ix). So, in drawing inspiration from a wide range of examples we should avoid the tendency to achieve the obvious near-impossibility of trying to "know what it feels like to be a person from that culture." Instead we can
benefit from the much more practical and achievable objective of learning from
one or more key elements in a variety of cultures.

The Haudenosaunee embody a spirit and mode of organization that I believe is
very close to Transcommunality.[3] My focus here is on the Haudenosaunee model,
but much of that model is related to what Georges E. Sioui, of the Department of
Indian Studies at Saskatchewan Indian Federated College at the University of

Regina, calls, "the universality of Amerindian values" that runs like a great current through many indigenous cultures of the Americas (1992: 23). In his prologue to Paul Wallace's book on the Iroquois, *White Roots of Peace*, Haudenosaunee writer and American studies professor John Mohawk advises us that "The political thought of the Haudenosaunee deserves to be judged on its own merits, not as an artifact of the past. We should investigate it today, question it, expand on it, learn from it just as would from any doctrine of political thought" (xv). Similarly, Lumbee Indian writer and law professor Robert Williams argues that "in our search for law and peace in today's multicultural world we can derive value from efforts to reconstruct this important moment in the history of North American indigenous and political thought" (1994: 2).

Indeed, the Haudenosaunee are a significant example of interaction that accepts and celebrates autonomy of distinct communities within it while being open to growth through cooperation with still other groups. Such elements are fundamentally Transcommunal in their nature. Obviously every culture has its unique features and linkages that cannot be duplicated elsewhere. And no human group has ever created the perfect society that meets all of the ideals. But insofar as the Haudenosaunee creatively and constructively addressed key problems related to unity and diversity, without centralized top-down domination by one group, their achievement is of relevance here to the development of Transcommunal action and outlooks.

There is a vast amount of material on the Haudenosaunee, and I will not attempt to survey it here.[4] Essentially theirs is the story of a people who, early in their history, overcame a period of conflict and violence to create a community of cooperation among five distinct sovereign nations, the Seneca, Cayuga, Oneida, Onondaga, and Mohawk. This "League of Nations" date of origin is disputed, but it clearly emerged before the arrival of the Europeans. Significantly, the league developed in direct response to what John Mohawk describes as "a time of great sorrow and terror for the Haudenosaunee. All order and safety had broken down completely." There was, he says, a "spiral of vengeance and reprisal which found assassins stalking the Northeastern woodlands in a never ending senseless bloodletting" (Wallace, 1946: xvi).

Similarly, Tehanetorens notes, this was a time in which, "although related by blood, the five nations became enemies of each other. They forgot the ways of the Creator, and fought among themselves and with others, bringing sorrow, destruction and death to each nation" (1976: 8).

In the midst of this terrible time appeared a man who became known as the "Peacemaker." The Peacemaker, as John Mohawk says, "sought out the most remarkable survivors of this random and undeclared war and he in initiated discussions with them." In these discussions he, "offered the idea that all human beings possess the power of rational thought and that in the belief in rational thought is to be found the power to create peace" (Wallace, 1946: xvi). The Peacemaker asserted that "in the area of negotiations between nations, the most desirable goal would be not only a cessation of violence but the active interactions which could create a better world for everyone" (xvii).

The Peacemaker went from "village to village and nation to nation." He and his coworker Alionwentha, or "Hiawatha,"[5] met with both support and resistance. But in time their work bore fruit in the cessation of hostilities, in the breaking of the cycles of vengeance. And most importantly the Great Law of Peace offered by the Peacemaker was aimed not only at ending violence but, as John Mohawk says, at creating "active interactions which could create a better world for everyone" (xvii). The Great Law of Peace, as Paul Wallace points out, "is not a defensive instrument dealing solely with safeguards against oppression and war. It is a positive thing, giving expression to the Five Nations way of life" (1946: 34). It is this Great Law of Peace and its implementation in Iroquois society that tells us so much about the possibilities and approaches to Transcommunal action.

A key image in the Great Law of Peace is the "clasping of hands" or the "linking of arms" of different peoples. Those clasped hands indicated an acceptance of shared rights and obligations that tied diverse peoples together. Wallace in the *White Roots of Peace* points out that the Great Law expresses the great principle of unity in diversity, a principle that gives its peculiar strength to the confederacy (39). Each separate nation, with its individual customs and local pride, knew that its chief assurance of essential independence lay in union. And Wallace notes:

> To the outside world the spirit of the League might seem to be expressed in the Latin motto, E Pluribus Unum [out of many, comes one]. But to the nations within the League its spirit might have seemed better expressed in the words Ex Uno Plura. The strength of the whole made safe the individual differences of the members. (1946: 34)

The league offered security to distinct multiple layers of group identities, rather than requiring each nation, clan, and household to simply assimilate into a homogenous larger unit. In this sense, the very identity of the league was that of cooperative diversity among many different but coordinated groups, rather than a reductionist homogenizing unification that jams everyone into a single mold. Important symbols of the league were used to emphasize the importance of both coordination and autonomy among its participating communities. As Onondaga firekeeper and State University of New York American studies professor Oren Lyons says, the ideology of the league "was complex," but its "symbols were easy to grasp" (1992: 39).

In this vein Paul Wallace notes the message of the Peacemaker to the five nations that, "We shall have one dish, . . . and we shall have a co-equal right to it" (1946, 34–5). Similarly, the framing image of the League geographically is that of the longhouse in which there are many distinct compartments. Geographically, from the Seneca in the West to the Mohawks in the East constituted the longhouse of the Iroquois. This longhouse was one structure, but it consisted, as the Peacemaker said, of "the Five Council Fires . . . that shall continue to burn as before" (Wallace, 1946: 34). Moreover, a longhouse can be added to, and made longer. New compartments can be created; room can be made for others. So, its overall structure of identity is not one of closure but of potential openness to an ever-larger population of people willing to live within the message of peace. Yet another key image of this openness to the world emphasized a rooted unity, that of "the Tree, under the shelter of which the Five Nations gathered." The Tree "was growing its Roots were extending" as were its branches, and so was open to a potentially ever wider range of nations (Wallace, 1946: 37).

The writer Tehanetorens, in *Tales of the Iroquois*, describes how the Peacemaker reminded the people "that other nations are to be invited to take shelter beneath the Tree" (vol II, 36). While the ever-growing branches provided shelter to many, peace was always the prominent concern. Under the "white roots" of the Tree of Peace would be "buried all weapons of war" (Mohawk Nation/Akwasasne, n.d.: 13).

The Haudenosaunee spiritual center has its historic roots among the Onondaga, in the very center of the geographic/cultural longhouse that symbolized the international linkages of these diverse peoples. "[The Peacemaker] and the civil chiefs planted a great Tree of Peace at Onondaga, the settlement of Thadodaho now designated as the Firekeeper. The evergreen 'Tree of the Great Long Leaves' (great white pine) sheltered the League" (Denis, 1993: 94). Meetings of the great council of the league took place at Onondaga. Today, Onondaga is still a vibrant element of the Haudenousaunee. In this sense the Onondaga habitat was indeed central to the confederacy. But Onondaga is not a "capital" of a centralized hierarchical system that issued orders to subordinate units. To the contrary, it is the place for discussion and agreement. It is, as Denis observes, the place for debate in "a measured, respectful, courteous manner" (95). As museum curator Lynne Williamson, of Mohawk-Missasagua kinship, notes, "disagreement was handled by allowing different opinions to be openly debated although in a rational way" (personal communication). Moreover, writes Williamson:

> Public speech provided a key dynamic within Haudenosaunee governance. Taking place when all are present in council in the longhouse, the recitation of the Great Law is spoken by leaders from memory in the original languages. . . . The beauty and power of the oratory, its ability to persuade and the evocative quality of the metaphors used, reinforce a sense of Haudenosaunee identity by narrating a common history of the people who are listening and participating. Even while we may be disagreeing or in debate, the essence of the words links us through archetypal principles. (1993: 285–6)

So the complex supple diversity-as-unity of the Haudenosaunee is constantly reinforced by direct interpersonal contacts, structured through complex ceremonies and protocols. In its classic formulation the Great Council of the League met "not less than once a year, and being called by runners at short notice whenever important business arose" (Denis, 43). Commonly recognized rules of conduct that contributed to clearheaded discussion and restraint of anger and violence are essential to the discourse of the diverse participants. "When you administer the Law," said the Peacemaker, "your skins must be seven thumbs thick. . . . Carry no anger and hold no grudges. Think not of yourselves, O chiefs, nor of your own generation. Think of continuing generations of our families, think of our grandchildren and of those yet unborn, whose faces are coming from beneath the ground" (Denis, 43). Through the various expectations of actual interpersonal conduct the maintenance of a common identity among its diverse peoples is made tangible rather than abstract. As Denis notes, with the direct and daily use of the, "symbols and metaphors and the institutions and ritual practices bequeathed by the Peacemaker to the Five Nations. . . . Peace was never abstract or simply ideological; it was concrete and experiential" (108).

Moreover the league was built on the solid rock of local strengths, including those of the household, and this in turn added to the respect accorded women in that society. Denis continues, "The Five Nations conceived of peace and enacted it in terms of domestic harmony—within households, [or] owachiras, and villages. . . . The household [owachira] was a domain controlled by women in the complementary relationship with men . . . women commanded great prestige and authority" (108–9). With the women-centered household as an essential model, the Haudenosaunee "extended the mechanism of domestic harmony" to maintain peace throughout the league (109).

Simultaneously, the classic mode of Haudenosaunee organization emphasizes many different levels of freedom and autonomy even while they act effectively in concert with each other. Oren Lyons writes that "Each of the communities of the Haudenosaunee controlled its internal affairs independently of the Confederacy Council while the Confederacy Council was restricted to controlling affairs of a national or international character" (1992: 39). But in its classic form even "national or international" affairs does not necessarily have to be agreed to by every community, family, or individual. Rather, social life is constantly infused with a high degree of freedom to make decisions that could diverge from those arrived at by the council. Lyons continues:

> Among the Haudenosaunee participatory democracy meant that on some level every individual had a right to voice an opinion and to agree or disagree on actions to be taken In fact, the Confederacy Council had no coercive power whatsoever over its people. There was no permanent army, no police force, no insane asylums, and no jails. This meant that communities were free to disagree with the decisions of the Confederacy Council especially on trade issues. (39)

Similarly, Denis points out that local communities "enjoyed considerable autonomy." Moreover, the essential unity of the league grew upward and outward from the many local grass roots, rather than being arbitrarily imposed by a central elite above. Denis continues:

> The decisions or nondecisions of the confederacy were the product of discussions in households, villages, and tribes throughout Iroquoia. These were the deliberations of

ordinary men and women rather than specialized elites; the discourse of the League council was, then, only a reflection of the considered debates that characterized owachira, clan, town, and nation. (96)

Many Europeans, habituated to authoritarian male-dominated societies with top-down central governments, were often baffled by this grassroots democratic system in which women played a key decision-making role and that emphasized multiple levels of autonomy, was devoid of a ruling elite, and was open to other nations and peoples while strenuously seeking to avoid anger and violence by emphasizing compassion, clear-headedness, and consensus. And, when consensus was impossible, the Iroquois constitution required that no decision be reached, rather than imposing one, all in the interest of maintaining a profound sense of cohesiveness.

Of course, as already suggested, there are distinctive features of Haudenosaunee culture and history that cannot be duplicated or simply imitated by outsiders. For example, the significance of kinship ties is not something that could be used to tie together African American and Latino inner city organizations. As Robert Williams says, "The intricate system of clans and lineages provided the Iroquois with a ready-made structure for maintaining . . . cohesion of their multi-tribal confederacy" (1994: 28).

It is worth noting that the Haudenosaunee were devoid of notions of exclusionary "racial purity" so common in Western culture. They often adopted many people from different Native American nations and from among the Europeans. The Tuscarora people, driven out of North Carolina by colonialists, became the "sixth compartment" of the longhouse in 1722. Some of my Native ancestors, the remnants of an Algonquin nation known as the Massachusett, after being decimated by European-introduced smallpox and land loss, found sanctuary among the Oneida Iroquois in 1775.[6] So, Haudenosaunee kinship can be extended in varying ways to a wide variety of "outsiders," assuming their willingness to live by the Great Law of Peace. Such flexibility offers guidelines for those of us who are not Haudenosaunee that can assist in the development of open, rather than closed, forms of collective identity.

More than five hundred years ago, the Haudenosaunee brilliantly created a highly flexible and coherently open social system of great strength. In this system they produced a supple and complex unity out of and celebratory of diversity, while achieving an essentially egalitarian multinational society that lives on today. From such examples we can glean a set of key organizational elements that constitute Transcommunal action.

ELEMENTS OF TRANSCOMMUNALITY

Drawing from the previous discussion we can delineate key elements of Transcommunality as follows:

Task-focused Transcommunal Outlooks

Transcommunal action is necessarily task-focused. Those who come from different group locations do so in order to work together with others in order to address some basic problem or dilemma. The Haudenosaunee began with a very practical concern of ending violence and creating a cooperative body among previously hostile peoples. Similarly, groups being formed among Asian American, African American, and Latino organizations to end youth violence in the cities have that pressing need as a primary task to accomplish.

Shared Practical Action

As they work to achieve these tasks, the members of the Transcommunal group engage in shared practical action. The design and carrying out of tactics and strategies to achieve the tasks at hand results in cooperative work with pragmatic real-time aspects. While carrying out this work, the interacting participants learn more about each other, they rely on each other, and develop a commonly held body of knowledge based on their task-oriented actions/interactions. Common experience is developed through the process of the work. The actual act of coming together becomes, for the Haudenosaunee, a foundation for continuing and growing interaction. Similarly, Riva Kastoryano, writing about alliances among immigrants in France, points to their common "battle against racial and ethnic discrimination." Based on this task-focused shared practical action, these groups' objective is to create "a veritable new exploration of political representation." out of such concerns come multicultural alliances, as in Marseille, where, "Radio-Gazelle of the local ethnic North African radio station Radio-Gazelle works to alleviate 'conflicts among different communities' regardless of their religious or geographical points of reference" (1994: 171).

Constructive Disputing

Shared practical action will inevitably lead to arguments and clashes within the association. Differences of approach and outlook, emerging out of distinct cultural backgrounds are unavoidable if the association is to be truly Transcommunal. Indeed, constructive disputing is part of the growth of mutual knowledge of the individuals participating in the association. Such disputing is part of what John Dewey, in *The Quest for Certainty*, calls a form of knowing directly related to that which is "securely experienced" (293). Such disputes are actually necessary to the well-being and the continued growth of the Transcommunal association. Disputing is necessary because it will often be the only densely concentrated way in which important distinctive features of the members' way of operating become clear.

Moreover, disputing is inevitable once we move beyond the abstractions of "unity" and "community" into the grit of everyday action. Through that action we expose how different we are to one another. And such exposure is vital if we are to really bridge the gaps between groups. This bridging cannot be built on the thin air of generalities but must be constructed on the concreteness of meaningful events that expand our mutual awareness of one another in the association. The issue here is not simply one of tolerance of different views and procedures. Rather it is recognizing that they exist first and foremost. Disputing can shed a great deal of light on that reality. In fact, constructive disputing can perform a vital function of making problems evident. Too often the embrace of "progressive idioms" such as "solidarity" smother real tensions. In such cases the problem is not that there is conflict, but that the sources of conflict are hidden. As Ivan Illich points out, a "convivial society" must recognize "the legitimacy of conflicting interests" (1973: 106).

There is much that can be learned here from Haudenosaunee protocols for discussion. John Mohawk, Matthew Denis, Paul Wallace, Robert Williams, and others provide usefully detailed discussions on these methods. Denis, for example writes,

> Chiefs were cautioned to take no offense at anything said against them, or for any wrongdoing they might suffer. "Their hearts shall be full of peace and goodwill, their spirits yearning for the good of their people. Long suffering in carrying out their duties, [their] firmness shall be tempered with tenderness. The spirit of anger and fury shall find no lodgement in them, and in all they say and do [they] shall exercise calmness. . . . The League chiefs epitomized the Iroquois ideal of peace and harmony and provided examples of how every Iroquois should live. (96–7)

Nor were such culturally systematic expectations to quote from the Haudenosaunee "Mother of Nations," simply, "words without form and impact in the world." Although no one would expect any culture to fully live up to all its founding principles, the Haudenosaunee ideals are clearly practical and everyday in their essence, rather than abstract, and unattainably remote. A few alert European observers could detect the distinctiveness of this approach that fused inner peace with social calmness. Denis records the French Jesuit, Father Joseph-Francois Lafitau's comments on the Haudenosaunee to the effect that: "Respect for human beings which is the mainspring of their actions serves no little to keep up their union. Each one, regarding others as masters of their own actions, lets them conduct themselves as they wish and judges only himself" (111). This system of containing disputes employed respect for the existence of different individual and group perspectives, an emphasis on leading by example in the use of "calmness" and a constant reminding that the overall good of the society depended on continued cooperation in the midst of difference.

Constructive disputing allows diverse and even competing/conflicting concerns to be confronted and recognized without being suppressed. Constructive disputing breaks out of the negative circle of competition/conflict by reacting with an Iroquoian set of responses that included "sensitivity, condolence, atonement, forgiveness, restraint, circumspection, calmness, and peace" (Denis, 111). Transcommunalists seek to integrate the various elements from various, even competing, vantage points that are mutually assimilable, while avoiding damaging retribution against those who differ from their outlooks.

Of course, constructive *disputing* can degenerate into a disruptive *conflict*. Unmanaged dispute pushes the Transcommunally inclined people toward fission rather than fusion. To avoid fundamentally disruptive conflict, it is vital that the constructive function of disputing be clear to everyone; that there be constant mutual respect shown for the distinctiveness and intensity of different positions; and that everyone be deeply invested in the potential of making some degree of mutual accommodation to these positions while being ready to transform them to some extent also. But the avoidance of corrosive conflict should not be confused with a suffocating imposition of artificial harmony demanded in the name of "unity."

This Transcommunal receptivity to some degree of dispute as positive, requires an organizational willingness to be a melange of colliding positions. Some might consider this to be a postmodern outlook. To the contrary, it is a practical outlook engendered by the very necessity of Transcommunality both old and new.

This acceptance of a mix of distinct, even contentious, outlooks is akin to the African outlook described by Hecht and Simone, in which fluidity "may be according to many African cosmologies the very thing that offers them their only protection. African traditional societies, far from embedding individuals in stolid norms and procedures, generate their own highly plural and contradictory forms, engaging different peoples and activities over a broad landscape" (110). Similarly, in his introduction to Wole Soyinka's *Art, Dialogue, and Outrage,* Biodun Jeyifo points to description of a positive and dynamic "African world" that is "a nexus of dynamically disparate and contradiction ridden matrices, paradigms, tropes, and significations (xv).

The Transcommunalists, engaged in constructive disputing and focused on common tasks enact the larger Transcommunal approach of maintaining distinct positions as they interactively bump into and so learn more about one another. This constant process of unification springing out of instructional contradiction and tension occurs through the shared practical action of the participant activists. In turn, shared practical action is possible precisely because the Transcommunalists thread together the tensions of their different, sometimes conflicting, positions with the common goals of peace, justice, and equality. Soyinka in his essay "Language as Boundary" describes a process very much like this when he writes of, "an awareness" that, "rediscovers eternal causes for human association and proceeds to build new entities held together [through a] a recognizable identity of goals" (*Art, Dialogue, and Outrage,* 87). For our purposes we can recognize these "new entities" as Transcommunal associations created through interactive diverse participants who maintain their roots while linking up with one another.

Given that differences and some dispute are inevitable and moreover are necessary for further construction of the Transcommunality itself, we must learn how to benefit rather than be disrupted by it. Moreover, in this area especially, much can be learned from relevant Native American and African modes of thought.

The Necessity of Interpersonal Relations

Commonly developed experience, such as that involved in constructive disputing, entails deepening the level of *interpersonal relations*. Face-to-face contacts develop into long-term relationships, even friendships, from this shared activity. Interpersonal relations, within which the participants build an increasing sense of trust and predictability with each other, are the glue upon which these small groups form and upon which larger groups will depend. The Haudenosaunee constantly emphasized in complex ways the importance of face-to-face contact. Their Condolence Ceremony for bereaved relatives of the different league nations entailed a richly organized protocol for renewing ties and buffering people against pain and loss. The gatherings of the league at the Onondaga, where the central fire of the Haudenosaunee burned, reaffirmed solidarity through direct interpersonal contacts of warmth and understanding. As John Dewey pointed out, the term *society* goes hand in hand with "the intimacies . . . such as friendship"(1930: 86). In this vein, the Hawaiian sovereignty proponent Haunani-Kay Trask points out that those non-Hawaiians able to work in coalition with the independence movement are trusted by Hawaiian activists precisely because their behavior over the years speaks louder than any sympathetic public statements on their part ever could (1993: 251). As Simone Weil observed, for fundamental cooperation to occur there must be, "not only good, but warm, genuinely friendly, and . . . intimate relations" (1952: 206). Similarly, Pier Cesare Bori indicates that communication among members of diverse cultures requires creating a "common emotional *fabric*" (1994: 22).

Trust, as the Haudenosaunee show so well, is a key element in such communication among diverse peoples. It is through trust, built up through actual experience of shared practical action that the predictability of Transcommunal relationships, and therefore, their relative reliability, are formed. For example, S. D. Boon and J. G. Holms remind us that

> The prospective nature of trust implicates the importance of subjective forecasts of what the future holds. Patterns of responsiveness and validation that have characterized the relationship in the past lay the foundation for these forecasts. When a partner has proven over the course of time to be consistently responsive . . . a sense of security or confidence in the partner is likely to develop. (1991: 198)

Although most academic leftists and progressives generally pay little heed to the significance of friendship and trust as key elements in activism and coalition building, these and other interpersonal aspects are absolutely crucial to Trans-communality.

The Propulsion of Vision

Simultaneous with its down-to-earth practicality, Transcommunal action is propelled by a *visionary scope*. Transcommunalists aim at nothing less than social justice, equality, and peace. The Haudenosaunee classically engage in constant practical interpersonal action that is aimed at creating the "Great Peace" among all peoples. From the household to the nations, the Great Peace is a propelling motivation that is reinforced by and reinforces the practical everyday actions of interacting communities. Transcommunally, more immediate goals are oriented toward these principles. Consequently, mundane matters such as the organizing of an event, a meeting, a demonstration, or an educational class for a community that can be achieved in the near future with a great deal of certainty are fueled by a visionary future. Other objectives may be more intermediate, less predictable, but still conceivable within a near term. Still other objectives are essentially basic visionary principles, such as the making of egalitarian peaceful society. The vision of egalitarian nonviolent life is what pulls the Transcommunal activists toward the future while sustaining them with a profound sense of both responsibility and possibility. In its merger of immediate, near-term, and distant objectives and principles the Transcommunal association avoids a sterile overemphasis on utopian dreams that have no connection with the real world. It also escapes from the entrapment of a compulsively utilitarian outlook so rooted in the status quo that it goes nowhere and changes nothing. As John Dewey notes in *The Public and Its Problems*, "liberty and equality isolated from communal life are hopeless abstractions. Their separate assertion leads to mushy sentimentalism or else to extravagant and fanatical violence" (149).

The pragmatic doability of Transcommunal group action links the immediately possible to the more general goals and principles and so grounds the actions of Transcommunalists. They know that at least some small initial victories not only are possible but probable, while the more long-range objectives are not lost sight of, so giving a profound future-oriented spirit to the daily struggle.

The Engaged/Disengaged Flexibility of Transcommunality

A key feature of Transcommunal organization and action is its on again–off again structural potentiality. The Transcommunal multichapter organization does not require that all its units be "on-line," in direct contact at all times. Rather each chapter, facing its own particular local circumstances develops its own particular way of being. But the local chapter can also call on other individual chapters or the entire organization for assistance, advice, and support when necessary.

At the moment of such a call, the dormant but intact relationships are energized and the larger organization becomes visible. This on-off pattern is of great value because it allows each chapter to be directly responsive to its particular environment while also ensuring that no one chapter is isolated and overcome by its local conditions. It is this articulation/disarticulation that serves the Haudenosaunee well in maintaining multiple layers of local and national identities while also providing an overarching framework of the larger organization of the League "Longhouse" itself.[7]

The Widening Coordination of Locally Rooted Groups

The elements of autonomy and engagement/disengagement are in turn related to the way in which a Transcommunal organization allows local groups to operate quite independently, while also enhancing their coordination. Consisting of autonomous groups, which nonetheless maintain contact through interpersonal ties and shared practical action, Transcommunality draws on the strengths of grassroots activists who know their own particular situations, while also gaining strength from a coordination that enhances their individual positions. Without this coordination, Transcommunality would fracture into completely separate parts and could not possibly grow beyond them. It is precisely this coordinated aspect that allows the Haudenosaunee to simultaneously be rooted in the decision making of women and men in households and local kin groups, while operating as the league fashion over great distances. In contrast to the slogan "think globally, act locally," Transcommunal activists can think and act globally, regionally, and locally.

The Uses of Ambiguity against the Monotone of Elite Domination

Precisely because it is practical in its approach, Transcommunality recognizes the fluid complexity of life and is alert to ambiguity and contradiction. The Transcommunal view of the world recognizes the ravages of power, while also being cognizant that even the powerful cannot control every factor of life the way they want, no matter what resources they have at their disposal. The complexities of any social moment are such that fissures emerge and changes erupt that even the weak can use to challenge domination. The civil rights movement in the U.S. South, the Peoples' Power movement in the Philippines, the Zapatista and Mayan indigenous movements in Chiapas, Mexico, are all examples of this complexity that undermines the solid facade of authoritarian power by producing unexpected but tangible challenges to it. As Simone de Beauvoir suggests, an ambiguity-focused approach recognizes that "separate existences" can forge their own "true laws" in ways that totally counteract the dominant structures of elite power (1947: 25). Not surprisingly, those who benefit from tightly designed doctrines of elite domination, says Beauvoir, always attempt to "suppress ambiguity."

Consequently, transcommonalists embrace ambiguity unlike those philoso-phers, who John Dewey says avoid it. Dewey writes:

> strangely enough philosophers who call themselves realists, have constantly held that the traits which are characteristic of thinking, namely, uncertainty, ambiguity, alternatives, inquiring, search, selection, experimental reshaping of external condi-tions do not possess the same existential character as do objects of valid knowledge. (1958: 69)

The problem with an unambiguous world is its emphasis on clear-cut, nearly mechanical structures and processes that are generally devoid of human influ-ence. It was this mechanization of Marxist thought that Lenin and Gramsci ar-gued against in their emphasis on the potential of organized human will to change the world.[8] It was Marx's famous antidogmatic dictum that "philosophy has only sought to understand the world, our task is to change it" that propelled their concerns. As David Hecht and Maliqalim Simone note, the strength of the dispossessed comes in part from their use of "the ambiguity of reference," which allows them to both adopt and resist European culture even as it is forced upon them. For Hecht and Simone many "Africans . . . use and diffuse external pow-ers, thus changing their meanings, often to their own advantage. So, what looks like simple domination can/might/may have a subversive transformative mean-ing—hence its ambiguity even in the face of power" (1994: 37).

Similarly, the Haudenosaune, with their supple engaged/disengaged form of organization, infuse their social life with a well-organized ambiguity that allows for concomitant coordination and overarching identity on one hand and highly independent heterogenous activity on the other hand. Transcommunality also recognizes the swirling fluidity of often clashing currents of existence. Sometimes these may flow against what is being attempted. But always there is the possibility of openings, and changes, many of them unanticipated. All the more reason then to be well-organized across group lines, to have coordinated action based on in-terpersonal trust that can respond to and take advantage of shifting circumstances. Such ambiguity is vital to Transcommunality's ability to withstand shocks from outside. The flexibility of the Haudenosaunee, although sorely tested, over the past five hundred years contributes to their continued vitality and growth today.

TRANSCOMMUNAL COORDINATION: BEYOND UNITY

We have seen, on the preceding pages, the ways in which such coordination has been, is being, and can be developed. The question is one of how to make use of historic/contemporary models, along with the analytical understanding of Transcommunality, to enhance expanded positive interaction among this multi-tude of highly diverse, sometimes fundamentally divergent, organizations.

Transcommunally, such cooperation must not threaten their distinctive particular circumstances, objectives, and identities.

The courageous Mozambican revolutionary Samora Machel advised his comrades that "Solidarity is not an act of charity, but mutual aid between forces fighting for the same objectives" (Jordan, 1971: 119). But a unity built on the expectation that people must have the same objectives in order to cooperate is riddled with corrosive problems that can undermine the very interaction itself. There is a wide range of distinct, sometimes colliding, objectives among those who fight under the general principle of social justice. *We know that such variation is in fact essential and unavoidable if a truly comprehensive range of communities, organizations, and outlooks are to be really embraced.* Homogenizing unity, no matter how progressive its purpose, breaks that embrace. For example, for many indigenous activists "social justice" often entails spiritually infused community/cultural self-determination. Concomitantly, "social justice" can mean building strong unions for leftist and labor organizers. Accordingly, any alliances among such distinct vantage points must accept heterogeneity rather than homogenization. At best, such varied objectives have little connection with each other. At worst, they can be in conflict. For example, even a strongly progressive union might find itself fighting for the jobs of oilfield workers drilling on land considered sacred to a community of indigenous peoples.[9] It is these gaps between different social justice zones that must be grappled with directly.

The call for "unity," while positive in its intent, often requires a melting-pot homogenization that obliterates rather than resolves such problems in order to create the longed-for single whole, or "block." Unreflectively employed, the term *unity* emphasizes a massively consolidated "one-ness" of those inside the block and the subduing of their heterogeneity. For example, the heroic and thoughtful Gramsci, for all his important sensitivity to distinctions between rural and urban regions, "peasants" and "workers," nonetheless envisions the need for a solidified dominant party, led by the highly organized workers that will "stimulate the formation of *homogenous* [emphasis mine], compact, social blocks" (1971: 204–9). Following the spirit of Gramsci's vanguard model, it is such a "revolutionary social block" that Manning Marable calls for in his analysis of the need to unite "divergent class and racial groups" (1983: 258).[10]

But given the reality of highly varied community-rooted organizations struggling within a wide range of exploitative contexts, avoidance of reductionist calls for a "unity" that obliterates diverse organizational agendas is essential. As Mikhail Bakhtin, in *Toward a Philosophy of the* Act, notes within a very different context, but with the same angle of appreciation, "the very word unity should be discarded" (39). The abstract or theoretical principle of "unity" is far-removed from, and often hostile to, complex competing heterogeneity of the everyday lives of millions of peoples in different zones, communities, and affiliations. Consequently, Bakhtin notes the tactical dilemma that the "closer one moves to theoretical unity . . . the ultimate unity proves to be an empty . . . concept" (39). By contrast, as real dialogue, based on direct mutually transformative interaction, occurs among diverse participants, then, "the more concrete [unity] becomes."

As Bakhtin suggests, the participants in such practical dialogue constantly orient and reorient themselves in relation to each other, so creating a shared sense of commonality through action or "performance of an act." There are many different but interacting perspectives or "horizons," in dialogue says Bakhtin: "The speaker seeks to orient his discourse, and even the horizon that has determined his discourse, in relation to the horizon of the other" (cited in Tzvetan Todorov, *Mikhail Bakhtin: The Dialogical Principle*, 74–5).

In such mutual respect for, and recognition of, different "horizons" or points of origin of interacting speakers, there is, adds Bakhtin a, "reinforcement by fusion without [homogenizing] identification" (75). This "fusion" without homogenization can be put Transcommunally. In our terms here, such fusion involves simultaneous coordinated communication and interpersonal interaction, with maintenance of autonomy, and group identity, similar to the Haudenosaunee "Longhouse" federation infused with its distinctly autonomous, yet cooperative, multiple groups. It is this Transcommunal capacity to conceptualize and actualize fusion without homogenizing reduction that allows for a single structure that is actually many structures and many structures that are actually a single structure at different moments, under different circumstances.

Just as this Transcommunality differs methodologically from top-down homogenized approaches, so also is it fundamentally opposite to a free-floating cultural relativism marked by absence of common norms and beliefs. Transcommunal outlooks/methods emphasize shared beliefs in the importance of autonomy, decentralization, coordination, and mutual respect for difference that facilitate simultaneous fluidity and commonality. It is precisely these fluid, flexible, interactive elements that mark Transcommunal coordinated action as constructively different both from reductionist vanguardist approaches, such as Gramsci's "homogenous" social bloc, and from the chaotic relativism over which many of multiculturalism's advocates stumble.

To successfully resist the power of centralizing economic political giants in the twenty-first century will require a Transcommunal methodology that replaces increasingly outdated nineteenth-twentieth-century Leftist ideas of homogenized "unity," while also discarding the recent postmodern confusion that emphasizes diversity without practical methods for positive interaction among varied peoples. Methodologically, Transcommunality draws out the positive elements of both structured organization and heterogeneity while, at its best, avoiding both deadening uniformity *and* aimless celebration of diversity without ethical content. It is the ambiguity of Transcommunality's capacity for fusion that is also fission, for coordination that is also heterogeneity, for autonomy of multiple voices that are also in mutual dialogue, that we so desperately need to avoid the nightmare of a corporate world order dependent on our fragmentation and lack of interaction.

So our transformation of Machel's call for solidarity looks like this: Transcommunality is not an act of charity but of mutual coordination, sometimes activated, other times inactive, among distinct autonomous organizations and communities, many with very different objectives, but each fighting for social justice. So, through equitable coordination of diverse independent organizations, rooted in distinct circumstances, Transcommunality offers a constructive mode of thought and action.

There are encouraging examples of Transcommunalistic efforts that cross social diverse justice zones of diverse peoples, each with its own particular fundamental problems and solutions. They are Transcommunal in tendency because of their emphasis on community autonomy, decentralized forms of organization, respect for different objectives, or at least the willingness to wrestle with the reality of such difference, and in their emphasis on interpersonal linkages through shared practical action.

Jorge Castañeda notes that "The Confederation of Widows of Guatemala [or Conavigua] reflects the characteristics of repression in Guatemala extending to the indigenous peoples in the highlands, labor leaders, and peasant activists as well as middle-class intellectuals" (1994: 227–8). In Brazil, he observes that the Workers Party (PT) achieved some election victories in part through its significant linkage to poor and rural communities. "For the first time a significant sector of the poorest, most excluded part of Brazilian life voted with the most organized sectors. They cast their votes for the PT and emphasized the unsuspected strength of the Workers' Party in the rural areas" (227–8). This strength was directly connected, Castañeda points out to the long-term role of the grassroots progressive Catholic movement the ecclesiastical base communities—the communidades eclesias de base or CEBs.

Jeremy Brecher and Tim Costello point to examples of such "community-labor" interaction in the United States: "Often inter-movement cooperation has grown out of common or at least overlapping interests. . . . Employees, churches, government officials, and even merchants have often supported efforts by groups like the Naugatuck Valley Project and the Steel Valley Authority to save local plants via worker or community buyouts" (1990: 334).

In Quebec, and the states of Vermont and New York, coordinated actions of indigenous, environmentalist, and labor organizations were successful in blocking a major hydroelectric project of Hydro Quebec that, as Brian Toker says, would have caused devastation affecting "thousands of native Cree and Inuit people living in the Great Whale watershed." The interrelationships established by the antihydroelectric activists were "more diverse, colorful and decentralized than anything the region has seen for some time." Toker continues:

> Activists petitioned state officials and regulatory agencies. There were demonstrations in the streets of state capitals, at utility offices and at utility commission hearings and press conferences. Students at major universities initiated divestment cam-

paigns. Cree speakers appeared regularly throughout the region, and Cree and Inuit canoeists traveled up the St. Lawrence River, down Lake Champlain and the Hudson River to New York City, holding public receptions along the way. . . . Activists in Vermont and New York State forged alliances with labor around the issue of job losses from such large exports of public funds. . . . One town in Vermont established an ongoing student exchange program with a school in the Cree and Inuit town of Great Whale. (1995: 47–8)

Similarly, the "Peoples Plan for the Twenty First Century" (PP21), organized in Japan in August 1989, in conjunction with the Asia-Pacific Resource Center, brings together a vast array of grassroots organizations throughout South Asia and the Pacific. In Transcommunal fashion the networks of PP21 cross a variety of social justice zones as well as ethnic/racial/national ones. The PP21 1992 meeting in Thailand brought together a range of grassroots groups working on issues such as indigenous peoples, violence against women, peasant organizing, urban workers, and fisher-people.

Importantly, this meeting did not simply use Thailand as a setting for discussion of "broad issues" elsewhere. Rather, concerns of relevance to Thailand were made central to the conference. The conference made a clear effort to be organized "on the basis of the Thai reality and Thai peoples' movements." Thailand was, "not just venue but also the focus of the program" (Asia-Pacific Resource Center, 2). Consequently the conference was both wide-ranging and rooted in the immediate tangible situations of the Thai hosts while also bringing activists, in a diverse set of social justice zones, together to discuss their own particular grassroots situations. There was a high degree of diversity, autonomy, and coordination of the different grassroots organizations. In France, Catherine Withol de Wenden points out, as "working-class mobilisation had lost some of its potency, the religious dimension has abruptly appeared." Workers of North African descent, says de Wenden, have made the "struggles in the car industry" part of the "emergence of Islam at the work place; a kind of 'social syncretism' distinguished by the appearance of a joint religious and trade union leadership." This linkage of labor and religious activism was a direct outcome of creating space for cultural-religious diversity in the factories:

Prayer rooms were created inside factories, along with ones established in urban suburbs in the 1970's; the first factory mosque was opened at Renault-Billancourt in October 1976. It began to acquire visibility and legitimacy. . . . The main union, the CGT, decided to 'go along with' Muslim Renault workers, devising a unifying strategy in the name of culture and dignity. (1994: 103)

In Chiapas, the Mayan indigenous rights movement is directly confronting the issue of maintaining indigenous objectives while working with others for whom the goals are quite different. The mix of "peasant" or Campesinista and indigenous dimensions in this movement is a significant development. As Araceli Burgete says,

"the Campesina and Zapatista tradition has until now subjugated Indianist efforts."
He notes that there are "several important differences between the programs of the
Campesinista and Indianist organizations. Peasant demands focus on land distribution, agrarian reform, infrastructure improvement (roads, health care, etc.), and
guarantees of individual human rights." By contrast the Indigenous program set out
by the Independent Indian Peoples Front (FIPI) focus on changing the "relations
between the State and the Indigenous peoples which implies constitutional recognition of their right to self determination." FIPI also calls for:

> recognition of territorial rights of the Indigenous people of the country and of Chia-
> pas and establishment of pluri-ethnic Indigenous regions where the different Indige-
> nous identities and mestizos would live under equal conditions [and] modification
> of national laws to guarantee the participation of Indigenous representation in the
> legislative, executive and judicial branches of government at the federal and state lev-
> els. (1993, 11)

Similarly, Antonio Hernandez Cruz, *Maya Tololabal* and secretary general of
the State Indigenous and Campesino Council of Chiapas, emphasizes the fundamental issue of difference between Zapatista and indigenous collectivist concerns, when he says that the original Zapatista calls for individualized land reform
that would parcel out land to the peasants were "completely negative." Such demands, he points out, "will destroy our people; because it is a way of diving us into
pieces . . . because the land will be privatized" (14). Simultaneously, Hernandez
emphasizes the importance of "mutual respect" between indigenous and
campesino communities and organizations. He notes that now, "we are organizing at the level of both campesino and indigenous under the principle of mutual
respect. The intellectuals, the students, the allies, are all surprised that we are
more than they imagined" (14). It is a clear indication of Transcommunal efforts
when groups having different, even potentially opposed, objectives can create a
single organization and attempt to develop a mutual respect between diverse outlooks. Hernandez Cruz's emphasis on "mutual respect" between indigenous and
campesino outlooks is an important indication of an emphasis on autonomy and
coordination of these communities that seeks to establish some kind of mutually
cooperative balance between them rather than trying to reduce one to the other.
At the time of this writing there are strong indications that the Zapatistas have, in
true Transcommunal fashion, begun to refashion portions of their agenda in response to indigenous emphases of collective self-determination (personal communication, from Gaspar Rodriguez of the South/Meso American Indian Rights
Center, 1995).

So, an important issue of the struggle in Chiapas is the development of mutual
recognition and cooperation among these two outlooks (campesino and indigenous), each opposed to the status quo, but each having a distinct conceptualization of the land itself, and each in potential conflict with the other. In such set-

tings the actualization of Transcommunal autonomy oriented mutual respect for divergent objectives is truly being tested.

Meanwhile, in the battered labor movement in the United States, innovative efforts to bridge the gap between grassroots community groups and unions are being attempted. Steve Early and Larry Cohn point to the nationwide Jobs with Justice (JWJ) network that brings together "labor and community activists engaged in coordinated campaigns for worker's rights."

They continue:

> JWJ has developed a grassroots orientation and direct-action approach very different from that of so many "letterhead" organizations sponsored by unions in the past. The JWJ model of decentralized, bottom-up organizing represents an exciting alternative to traditional forms of cross-union activity. (1994: 8)

Similarly, the Southwest Network for Environmental and Economic Justice, and the Southeast Regional Economic Justice Network link a broad range of labor groups and communities around issues that span diverse settings from the workplace to the environment. Often these two networks find themselves the only means of labor organizing in Southeast and Southwestern localities in which unions no longer exist and strong pressures against labor dominate.

In some key instances, groups with particular agendas have overlapping secondary relations with other groups in other zones. For example, Nane Alejandrez, executive director of the Santa Cruz, California, Barrios Unidos chapter, focuses on community revitalization and the end of youth violence, while maintaining numerous overlapping ties with other organizations. He is a member of the Native American Treaty Rights Council, has worked closely in support of Indigenous land rights, has ties with the United Farm Workers, works closely with the African American community in the Los Angeles area and with the African American and white American church leaders, such the Rev. Mac Charles Jones and the Rev. Sam Mann in Kansas City, along with Jim Wallis of the ghetto-based, progressive Evangelical Christian group Sojourners. All these overlaps involve interpersonal ties built up through shared practical action, in which a variety of individuals with organizational roots in different communities develop direct links with each other. In typical Transcommunal organizational style, these links are activated at certain moments and may be inactive at others. The primary objectives of the various interacting groups remain central to them. But simultaneously they work cooperatively with other groups having different objectives. The autonomy of each group is maintained, but they are able to work cooperatively *as needed at the necessary moments.* A mere "organizational catalog" listing of Barrios Unidos, the United Farm Workers, the L.A. "Gang Truce" movement, Native American Treaty Rights, St. Stephen's Baptist Church, the Evangelical Lutheran Church, and the Sojourners organization would not by itself express these interpersonal and organizational relationships that link key people in these different settings. In fact, such a catalog would probably classify these groups under quite separate categories such as "religious," "indigenous," "inner city," and so forth, so missing the fluid Transcommunal linkages among them. What looks like "single issue" focus, such as ending gang violence, in reality is multidimensional with an array of complex cooperative ties to groups with a wide range of central social justice objectives.

Precisely because such Transcommunality is fundamentally action rather than theory, it cannot be architecturally laid out with an advance blueprint. Rather, it can only be enacted if it is to be understood in full. We can benefit from an illumination of the key elements in Transcommunality, such as has been developed on these pages. But such illumination only highlights the imperative of action from which those elements are drawn. I can only provide the "illumination" and analysis of Transcommunality because it is real and active. As the Native American Leni Lenape people say, "talk won't grow corn." In this vein we can profit from Bakhtin's advice that we avoid a "fatal theoreticism" that assumes the ability to abstract a formal ethics and set of directions in advance of action. Transcommunality is an approach like that described by Bakhtin, which "can orient itself only with respect to [the] actually performed act" (1993: 20). Words, as the Haudenosaunee Mother of Nations advised, only have meaning when they take form in the world. The task is to act Transcommunally, and so assist in the expanding cooperation of diverse communities, rooted in a multitude of settings, if we are to effectively fight for comprehensive social justice that can resist power-hungry globalized economic elites and their political guardians.

My friend, Guillermo Delgado pointed out to me that the indigenous Aymara people of the Andes employ a concept that in both its complexity and vision is cousin to Transcommunality.[11] The word *Aruskipaxidcajananakasakipunirakispawa* entails the multiple, yet linked requirements "that we communicate with each other/face to face/our feet rooted in the earth/with which we also must communicate/if we are to live." These requirements are in the essence of Transcommunality.

If there is hope against the ravages of gigantic centralizing militarized quick-profit power, it lies in all forms of action akin to *Aruskipaxidcajanakasakipunirakispawa*.

NOTES

*I owe a special thanks to Native American colleagues, Gerald Alfred (Mohawk Nation, Kahnawake, and Concordia University, Quebec), Lynne Williamson (Institute for Community Studies, Hartford), and Peter Jemison, manager of the Seneca Ganondagan Community Center, New York State, for their thoughtful commentary. Guillermo Delgado has provided invaluable dialogue. I also want to thank Jeremy Brecher and Martin Bresnick for their helpful comments. This chapter was aided by stimulating discussion at the 1995 symposium, "Asia-Pacific Identities: Culture and Identity in the Age of Global Capital," organized through the Duke University Department of History and the Asian/Pacific

Studies Institute, under the leadership of Arif Dirlik. This chapter is part of my general project on modes of Transcommunal cooperation and alliance building.

1. Simone Weil is an important thinker on the issue of diversity and cooperation whose work should be reinvigorated by new discussion.

2. The dates of the formation of the Haudenosaunee are of some debate. For various views on this issue, see for example, Matthew Denis, *Cultivating a Landscape of Peace*; Francis Jennings, *The Ambiguous Iroquois Empire*, and Paul A. Wallace (To-Ri-Wa-Wa-Kon), *The White Roots of Peace*. It is clear that by the time the Dutch, French, and English were pursuing their competitive conquest of North America, the well-established Haudenosuanee Confederacy was already a major force with which they had to contend and negotiate. The Haudenosaunee continue today to be a vital living reality.

3. The Haudenosaunee dwellings were longhouses occupied by several families in different compartments. Every two compartments shared a common cooking fire. In this way the interior of the longhouse allowed for each family to have its own space and to cooperate with their immediate neighbors. Overall the overlapping linkage of the different compartments tied everyone together inside the longhouse. The "Iroquois Confederacy," stretching from present day Buffalo to Albany, New York, and consisting sequentially from West to East of the Seneca, Cayuga, Onondaga, Oneida, and Mohawk, was politically/symbolically considered by them to be a "longhouse" with each nation occupying a "compartment," while being linked to its neighbors. The Tuscarora nation later joined the Longhouse to become the sixth compartment.

4. Lewis Henry Morgan's work, *The League of the Ho-di-no-sau-nee, or Iroquois* (1851) was used by Friedrich Engels, who, while seeing the significance of this society, mistakenly viewed them as examples of simple organization. Engels missed the supple complexity of Haudenosaunee organization.

5. Longfellow took the name "Hiawatha" from its Haudenosaunee setting and transferred it to the Cree people in his famous poem.

6. These Massachusetts Algonquins along with other New England Native Americans were part of a refugee group that became known as the "Brotherton Indians" in Brotherton, New York, on land provided by the Oneida nation.

7. As Arif Dirlik emphasizes such a focus and reliance on localism is a vital element in the development of progressive organizing. See for example Dirlik's "Post Socialism/Flexible Production: Marxism in Contemporary Radicalism," in *Polygraph*.

8. For an informative early example of Gramsci's critique of "mechanical Marxism" and its emphasis on automatic processes, see his article on the Bolshevik revolution entitled, "The Revolution against Capital," reprinted in, Pedro Cavalcanti and Paul Piccone, *History, Philosophy and Culture in the Young Gramsci*.

9. For some important discussion of such gaps see Ward Churchill's "Marxist Theory of Culture: a Cross Cultural Critique." Also useful is Maivan Clech Lam's "A Resistance Role for Marxism in the Belly of the Beast."

10. For an earlier discussion of mine on vanguardist perspectives, see my book, *Leadership, Conflict, and Cooperation in Afro-American Social Thought*.

11. Indigenous outlooks on inclusionary kinship, in which many individuals can be considered as "cousins," "sisters," and "brothers," can usefully be employed for mutual acceptance of different philosophical and ideological systems. To say that one ideology is "cousin" or "akin" to another allows for affinity without assumptions of sameness. Although the "kinship of ideologies" may strike some ears as strange, its effectiveness at creating wide-

ranging networks of mutual support when used in extended family structures is suggestive of its political potentiality.

REFERENCES

Asia-Pacific Resource Center. *Join the PP21 Thailand, Making the People Visible/More Power to the People, People's Plan for the 21st Century*. Bangkok, Thailand: National Organizing Committee, 1992.

Bakhtin, Mikhail B. *Toward a Philosophy of the Act*, Translated by V. Liapunov. Austin: University of Texas Press, 1993.

Beauvoir, Simone de. *Pour une morale de l'ambiguite*. Paris: Gallimard, 1947.

Boon, S. D., and J. G. Holms. "The Dynamics of Interpersonal Trust Resolving Uncertainty in the face of Risk." In *Cooperation and Prosocial Behavior*, edited by R. A. Hinde and J. Groebel. Cambridge: Cambridge University Press, 1991.

Bori, Cesare Pier. *From Hermeneutics to Ethical Consensus among Cultures*, translated by P. Leech, C. Hindley, D. Ward. Atlanta, Ga.: Scholars Press, 1994.

Brecher, J., and T. Costello, eds. *Building Bridges*. New York: Monthly Review Press, 1990.

Burgete, Araceli. "Chiapas: Maya Identity and the Zapatista Uprising." *Aby Yala News* 7(3/4) 1993: 9–12.

Castaneda, Jorge G. *Utopia Unarmed: The Latin American Left after the Cold War*. New York: Vintage, 1994.

Childs, John Brown. *Leadership, Conflict, and Cooperation in Afro-American Social Thought*. Philadelphia: Temple University Press, 1989.

Churchill, Ward. "Marxist Theory of Culture: A Cross Cultural Critique." In *Culture versus Economism: Essays on Marxism in the Multicultural Arena*, edited by Glenn Morris, Elisabeth Lloyd and Ward Churchill. Bouldrer, Colo.: Indigena Press, 1984, 27–40.

Cruz, Antonio Hernandez. "Interview from Chiapas." *Aby Yala News* 7 (3, 4) (1993): 12–14.

Delgado, Guillermo. Personal communication, 1995.

Denis, Matthew. *Cultivating a Landscape of Peace: Iroquois-European Encounters in Seventeenth Century America*. Ithaca, N.Y.: Cornell University Press, 1993.

Dewey, John. The Public and Its Problems. Denver: Allan Swallow, 1927.

———. *Individualism Old and New*. New York: Minton Balch, 1930.

———. *Experience and Nature*. New York: Dover Publications, 1958.

———. *The Quest for Certainty: A Study of the Relation of Knowledge and Action*. New York: Capricorn, 1960.

Dirlik, Arif. "Post Socialism/Flexible Production: Marxism in Contemporary Radicalism." *Polygraph* 6/7 (1993): 133–69.

Early, Steve, and Larry Cohn. "Jobs with Justice: Building a Broad-Based Movement for Worker's Rights." *Social Policy* (Winter 1994): 7–18.

Gramsci, Antonio. *Selections from the Prison Notebooks of Antonio Gramsci*, edited and translated by Q. Hoare and G. N. Smith. New York: International Publishers, 1971.

———. "The Revolution against *Capital*." In *History, Philosophy, and Culture in the Young Gramsci*, edited by P. Cavalvanti and P. Piccone, translated by P. Molajoni, M. A. Aiello-Peabody, P. Piccone, and J. Thiem. New York: Telos Press, 1975: 123–5.

Hecht, David, and Maliqalim Simone. *Invisible Governance: The Art of African Micropolitics*. Brooklyn, N.Y.: Automedia, 1994.

Holub, Robert. *Crossing Borders: Reception Theory, Poststructuralism, Deconstruction*. Madison: University of Wisconsin Press, 1992.

Illich, Ivan. *Tools for Conviviality*. New York: Harper and Row, 1973.

Jennings, Francis. *Cultivating a Landscape of Peace: Iroquois-European Encounters in Seventeenth Century America*. Ithaca, N.Y.: Cornell University Press, 1993.

———. *The Ambiguous Iroquois Empire*. New York: W.W. Norton, 1996.

Jeyifo, Biodun. "Introduction." In *Art, Dialogue, and Outrage: Essays on Literature and Culture*, edited by Wole Soyinka. New York: Pantheon, 1988, ix-xxix.

Jordan, Joseph. *Solidarity as an Organizing Principle*. New York: Broadside, 1971.

Kastoryano, Riva. "Mobilisations des migrants en Europe." In *Cartes d'identite: Comment dit-on "nous" en politique*, edited by Denis-Constant Martin. Paris: Presses de la Fondation Nationale des Sciences Politiques, 1994, 229–39.

King, Martin Luther Jr. *Where Do We Go from Here: Chaos or Community?* New York: Harper and Row, 1967.

Lam, Maivan Clech. "A Resistance Role for Marxism in the Belly of the Beast." In *Marxism beyond Marxism*, edited by S. Makdisi, C. Casarino, and R. E. Karl. New York: Routledge, 1996, 255–64.

Lyons, Oren. "The American Indian in the Past." In *Exiled in the Land of the Free: Democracy, Indian Nations, and the U.S. Constitution*, edited by O. Lyons. Santa Fe, N.M.: Clear Light, 13–42.

Marable, Manning. *How Capitalism Underdeveloped Black America*. Boston: South End Press, 1983.

Morgan, Lewis Henry. *The League of the Ho-di-no-sau-nee, or Iroquois*. Rochester, N.Y.: Sage, 1851.

Mowhawk Nation/Akwasasne. *The Great Law of Peace and the Constitution of the United States*. Akwasasne, N.Y.: Tree of Peace Society, no date given.

Patocka, Jan. *Philosophy and Selected Writings*, translated and edited by E. Kohak. Chicago: University of Chicago Press, 1989.

Pritchard, Evan T. *The Way of the Wabanaki: The Poetics of the Sacred in Northeast Native American Life*. Beacon, N.Y.: Resonance Communications, 1993.

Rodriguez, Gaspar. South/Meso American Indian Rights Center. Personal communication, 1996.

Sioui, Georges E. *For an Amerindian Autohistory*, translated by S. Fischman. Montreal: McGill-Queen's University Press, 1992.

Soloman, Maynard. *Marxism and Art*. Detroit, Mich.: Wayne State University Press, 1979.

Soyinka, Wole. *Art, Dialogue, and Outrage: Essays on Literature and Culture*. New York: Pantheon, 1988.

Tehanetorens. *Tales of the Iroquois*. Mohawk Nation, Rooseveltown, N.Y.: Akwasasnee Notes, 1976.

Todorov, Tzvetan. *Mikhail Bakhtin: The Dialogic Principle*. Minneapolis: University of Minnesota Press, 1984.

———. *On Human Diversity: Nationalism, Racism, and Exoticism in French Thought*, translated by C. Porter. Cambridge, Mass.: Harvard University Press, 1993.

Toker, Brian. "Grassroots Victories, Lobbyist Gridlock." *Z Magazine* (February 1995): 47–8.

Trask, Haunani-Kay. *Notes from a Native Daughter: Colonialism and Sovereignty in Hawaii*. Monroe, Maine: Common Courage Press, 1993.

Wallace, Paul A. *The White Roots of Peace*. Philadelphia: University of Pennsylvania Press, 1946.

Weil, Simone. *The Need for Roots*, translated by A. Wills. New York: Putnam, 1952.

Williams, Roberts. "Linking Arms Together: Multicultural Constitutionalism, a North American Indigenous Vision of Law and Peace." *California Law Review* (July 1994): 1–195.

Williamson, Lynne. "The Great Tree of Peace." In *Global Visions: Beyond the New World Order*, edited by J. Brecher, J. B. Childs, and J. Cutler. Boston: South End Press, 1993, 283–7.

———. Personal communication, 1995.

Withol de Wendent, Catherine. "Immigrants as Political Actors in France." In *Politics of Immigration in Western Europe*, edited by M. Baldwin-Edwards and M. A. Shain, Portland, Ore.: Finka Cass, 1994, 98–115.

Part IV

Concluding Essay

13

Rethinking Difference and Equality: Women and the Politics of Place

Wendy Harcourt

INTRODUCTION

The theory of the politics of place undergirding this book has a strong resonance with my own experience of women's attempts to reconfigure the power struggles of today's global network society. In reading in particular the opening theoretical chapters, I have been compelled to revisit my own work on gender and development and to explore how the politics of place offers a framework for understanding the set of resistances generated by the international women's movement in popular struggles for women's autonomy, rights, and livelihoods. Place-based consciousness offers an interesting way to rethink the type of politics and the production of knowledge that women NGOs and others involved in the women's movement are creating. As a way of complementing the issues raised by Arif Dirlik and Roxann Prazniak I will map out how the politics of place could be used to reconceive and reconstruct the world based on the visions and experiences of women around the world.

My argument is that there is a politics of place being advanced by women aided in particular by the new information technologies in the domains of violence against women, health, and environment. This place-based politics is very important for rethinking and advancing issues of difference and equality not only from a gender perspective but in general. Women's place-based politics is changing and redefining political experience in visible ways, effecting social change particularly through networking and providing new spaces for the transformation and construction of identity and rights.

WOMEN AND THE POLITICS OF PLACE

Taking up the premise of this book, the networking, building of solidarity, advocacy, lobbying, and envisioning radiating out from women's daily needs—their autonomy and rights of self, the home, the community—can be usefully labeled the politics of place.

I would suggest that in elaborating the concept as set out by Arif Dirlik in chapter 2 to take in the complexity of gender, the concept of place is played out on three levels in women's lives and struggles.

Women's bodies are the first level of place. It is the female body that defines women as the other, as the reproductive being, the mother, as the sexually desired. It is the body through which women mediate all gendered interactions, including those from which they defend and evolve their identity.

A second level is the domestic place of the home that for many women still defines their primary social and cultural identity and lived domain. The home and immediate community are usually the safe places for women to express themselves. It is here that women foster their own sense of power and knowledge and sustain their own and their family's livelihoods as they balance their productive and their reproductive work space. The "usually" is an important proviso given that gender inequalities also lead to very unsafe home environments with domestic violence and oppression of women. Even if it is through resistance to these factors, women act and live largely in the home, and so it is from this place that women find their strength.

The third place is that outside the home—the political and social public place—the male-dominated domain to which many women still have no access, and where most women find themselves silenced and few women rule. The women's movement for many years now has been creating diverse avenues for entry into that place, even if they too are often marginal to the pulse of political power. They need to help to redesign institutions where their voices are heard in ways that can mediate and radically change the public political domain.

The politics of place is advanced in local struggles that are then connected up through networks, weaving together different groups in ways that cannot be easily placed into "national," "regional," or "international" political categories. Nonetheless they expand the struggle to levels beyond the local. The politics of place deliberately challenges the sense of polarity between local and global—as if the local is here and the global far away. Instead it positions the global as very closely mapped onto the local. People live with the global in their own lives and indeed shape the global at the local level.

A place-based strategy for change in gendered difference toward greater equity is being mapped out by many women, both as individuals and groups, based on their everyday life realities, their resistance to hierarchies and gender bias, and their own activities. The current shift in historic private and public divides, the new technologies, the ambivalence around the role of the state, the possibilities for linkages across geopolitical borders—have created possibilities for women to negotiate new social and cultural positions.

At the basis of this movement are the community women's groups, networking within their community and among other women. Their activities defy definitions of women as simply the exploited victims of modernity. Instead they are creating and living the global in the local. Through organizing in NGOs or community voluntary organizations they are resisting the worst forms of global capital in the work, domestic, and marketplace and are taking advantage of some of the opportunities of the new information technologies and access to different lifestyles, ideas, and cultures. Through networking—making connections among different places—women are linking their place-based defense of communities in ways that are challenging and changing public institutional spaces. They are altering the boundaries between private and public in the three levels of place. For example, violence against women's bodies, either in the street or through sex, work, or in conflict situations, is now openly discussed. Women working in the home are linking with others for support in terms of managing children and other domestic pressures. Women in high tech factories in Asia are organizing across North-South lines with the international support of NGOs on health work conditions, including women's special needs, for example, on night shift. And using the UN process, women have brought local concerns to the forefront of the international agenda, analyzing women's needs in each region and connecting to political leaders willing to support a women's agenda internationally, at times in defiance of fundamentalist and antiwomen positions at home.

This politics of place is an important space both for understanding the predicaments of difference and equality and for transforming entrenched structures. In rethinking difference and equality we can explore these new forms of political activities. We can examine how women's engagement with local and global issues in conflictual situations at the three levels of body, home, and public spaces are often woven together in both daily and political practice, challenging and reconstituting gender relations. Modern forms of global capitalism are reconstituting the lived experiences of women at all three levels, and that is why women's bodies, the home, community, and environment are sites of contest and reappropriation by women from their different perspectives and understanding.

The following discussion presents the gender dimension of difference and equality from the perspective of the triple but interrelated politics of place through a series of examples from women's resistance and reappropriation of the conflicts they face in their lives.

WOMEN'S PLACE-BASED STRATEGIES IN RELATION TO VIOLENCE

One of the deepest and most difficult areas of conflict among the genders historically has been violence against women (VAW)—domestic violence, sexual harassment, civilian rape, and rape as an instrument of war. In the past decades it is in campaigns around VAW where women have fought many of the battles for their self-determination. Through these multifarious resistances, largely by women's groups in civil society, new political spaces have opened up that have forged legal, social, and cultural change. These changes though must be constantly defended as today's globalization processes bring about violence in women's lives in many new ways in all three levels of the body, home, and community and public space. In the last decades there has been a notable increase in domestic violence, rape, and drug and alcohol abuse, all of which have a detrimental effect on the well-being, health, and self-determination of women on the receiving end of such aggression.

In the escalating violent conflicts in the postcolonial era it is civilians—women and children—who are increasingly experiencing violence during war, and with it the systematic rape of women. Fast growing urban environments with slums and shantytowns, combined with the breakdown of family and community, expose women to violence and danger. An example of this is the recent rape crisis in Indonesia following the country's economic upheaval that led to the unavailability of the most basic commodities, food riots, and subsequently, the rape of the Chinese ethnic women whose families owned most of the businesses and shops (Women in Action, 1998: 61–3). In the free trade zones and multinational export-oriented industries, increasing numbers of young women are working night shifts. They are exposed not only to exploitative conditions but also to harassment and possibilities of attacks at night. The increasing economic poverty owing to retrenchments and shifts in productive patterns holds a double load for women with the increase of domestic violence. Growing economic liberalization has not only meant rising economic inequalities but also the displacement of a growing number of people from their homes. Women constitute a disproportionate number of such economic refugees. The sex industry has profited from increasing numbers of vulnerable and poor migrant women forced into sex work. Trafficking in women has increased in countries where the pressures of poverty and loss of livelihood drive women to the sex trade and risk of death because of the high incidence of HIV-AIDS and the spread of infectious disease (Subramaniam, 1999).

In contesting the growing violence that has come with modernity and in reappropriating their bodies, safe spaces in the home and community, women have brought the issue of violence to the public space. Through the networking and linking of issues women have ensured that rape, domestic violence, and harassment are no longer silenced or seen as isolated occurrences. Rape as a weapon in war is now acknowledged in the mainstream press and by the public and, as in the case of the former republics of Yugoslavia conflict, swiftly punished. Women's centers to help victims of rape in war have been set up across ethnic divides. They also deal with the internalized violence of women, which can be expressed in child abuse or neglect, elder abuse, self-mutilation, and in extreme cases, murder/suicide. Similarly crisis centers for women enduring domestic violence have been set up in many places learning and adopting from other country examples.

NGOs across the world support migrant women to make other choices than sex work or to help extricate them from difficult situations.

In the following I cameo a few of the many examples of women working in communities in NGOs, service centers, and other institutions striving to assist women exposed to VAW in areas of violent conflict, be it in war, in the street, or in their home.

FIJI WOMEN'S RIGHTS MOVEMENT

The Fiji Women's Rights Movement (FWRM) gives a definitive example of how the three environments of women are closely interlinked in the politics of place. The FWRM emerged from twin needs—to protect women from domestic violence and to protect them from being discriminated against as women workers in the tax-free zones (Women in Action, 1997: 58–60). FWRM includes in its lobbying platform constitutional reform and women's inequality in the workplace and home, including unpaid rural labor and domestic and community violence. Working with multiracial cross-section groups, FWRM has strongly lobbied for a minimum wage for garment industry women and has spearheaded inquiries into conditions for women working in tax-free zones as well as lobbying to obtain legal recognition for women's unpaid labor in the home, in subsistence farming and agriculture. They have run a public media campaign on rape entitled "Forceline" (a local term implying that rape is an acceptable cultural practice), reaching out to schools, medical personnel, police officers, and judicial personnel as well as rural women's groups. Drawing on international support the group has become the voice of Fijian women in the national media and political arena. Particularly around the problems of breaking the cultural acceptance of wife beating and rape, FWRM has opened up the spaces where women's three environments are politicized through the resistance to oppression.

WOMEN IN WAR AND VIOLENT CONFLICT

Women's experiences of violence in war and guerrilla conflict have become the subject of considerable concern given the escalation of conflicts in the postcolonial period and the far greater involvement of civilians, women, and children in war. In addition to suffering general violations (forced evictions, torture, loss of livelihoods, and loss of freedom of expression) women have also suffered gender-specific violations, including rape as a weapon of war, sexual slavery, and forced sterilization. Women's responses to war, however, have not always been as victims. There are many examples of how women have managed communities without their men, have reacted against the violence and rape. For example, in Sudan, which has experienced the longest civil war in Africa (started in 1955), women have evolved their own way of solving conflicts, especially at the household and community levels (Impact, 1999). They have provided income and basic necessities, running "women's courts" that run parallel to male-dominated official courts and deal with gender conflicts (fining men for wrongdoing, and solving cases of domestic violence, circumcision, unwanted pregnancy, and so on). Women have also organized themselves into solidarity groups that provide support for each other, deal with acts of violation against women, act as channels of communication for rebels, function as peace brokers, and provide livelihoods for the community as well as help in educating the children. These community courts and groups are recognized locally by the mayors and sultans and nationally have joined together as a force in trying to sustain peace and local trade. These Sudanese women illustrate how at the grassroots level women are changing traditional customs together in order to survive the oppression of long-term poverty and violence in their lives through place-based politics around gender relations in conflict.

Throughout Africa women have come together specifically around gender violence using the support of international organizations as well as local groups. ISIS-WICCE, an action, research, and information NGO based in Uganda, has been part of an African-wide response by women's groups to support women in resisting sexual violence in war as well as helping women in postconflict situations to continue to challenge oppressive gender relations. An example of their work is their intervention in the Luwero district, where their findings pointed to the need to raise awareness of reproductive health and psychosocial problems of women as major problems that are failing to be addressed. Working with women's networking groups as well as medical experts and psychologists, service facilities and support groups are being set up for the women, including sharing their experiences with other women from conflict situations in the ISIS-WICCE Exchange Programme.[1] In these exchange programs women from different conflict situations come together to share their experiences, discuss ways to overcome ongoing problems, and support each other in postconflict situations.

Moving to the civil war of the former republics of Yugoslavia, ongoing since 1992, as in African conflicts and wars, women have been raped and abused as a tactic of war. Women experienced the destruction of their families, livestock, and community as well as physical and psychological abuse. One example of women's response is in Zenica, a town in central Bosnia. Three multiethnic crisis centers were set up by an Italian woman with German funding and led by a team of seventy women doctors and therapists in order to help the survivors of rape and the trauma of war. The ethos of the center is not only to tackle the healing of the women, in terms of their physical and psychological needs, which were horrific enough to deal with. It also works toward empowering the women in the other environments—the home, the community, and the public space. It is, therefore, envisaged as more than a health center that aims to build up women's self-identity and integrity after tremendous loss, torture, and rape in order to build an autonomy that enables women to cope with the inevitable changes to family and community life in the wake of the war. This means working with the women in highly participatory ways to challenge and change the traditional family system of "zadruga" (a highly patriarchal family system) where women lack equality in order to renegotiate gender relations. Through different interactions among the different ethnic groups in the center, the women discuss their strategies on how, in the postconflict situation, to manage men who have been involved in such a gender-violent war and who come home feeling lost and perhaps threatened by the changes. In fact the increase of prostitution and domestic violence has become an issue in the center as the men return and as foreign men are based in Zenica. As a result, the center has gone beyond simply assisting or servicing the women to being highly politicized and vocal in all three environments of women's place-based politics: campaigning against violence in the home, working toward understanding between the different ethnic communities, and building new gender relations.

Through the work of the center, women have found not only care and help for their battered bodies but also support for changing gender relations in the home and communities. They join politically with other women's groups, such as those running the SOS hotlines being set up around the former republics of Yugoslavia, in the highly successful campaigns to have rape recognized and punished as a war crime (Cockburn, 1998: 175–210). This is an example of how the politics of place is interlacing different levels of women's lives, based on the immediate need to cope with the trauma of rape in war and moving on to challenge gender difference across the ethnic divides on which the war was being fought.

Women in Black (a heterogeneous group of women of ages ranging from 18 to 75), operating in Belgrade, is another example of how women in the former republics of Yugoslavia break ethnic barriers to serve as message carriers about equality and difference beyond the gender-specific torture of women. Their nonviolent protest was at first against their sons being involved in war, but from 1992 when the scale of rape as part of the "ethnic cleansing" became known, they linked their protest to VAW, focusing on rape as a weapon of war and also on domestic violence. Through the support of Women in Black, women who had been raped could speak out to the media. The coverage and consequent trials of the soldiers involved put VAW on the public agenda. The connection between military and domestic violence is an important link to other women's groups worldwide as Women in Black groups and strategies spread to other areas of violent conflicts. They maintain public consciousness of the barbarity of gender-specific torture and in doing so have become skilled negotiators in bringing women's place-based politics to the public agenda. As they said in a conversation with Cynthia Cockburn, "What we wanted to do was to work on building civil society and becoming a kind of messenger to the authorities point out the needs of the whole community . . . leaving out politics with a big P" (1998: 172–3).

An important feature of their success was not only the skillful use of the mass media but also the use of the new information technologies to make their work known and supported by contacts made on the Internet.

VAW AND THE INTERNET

The Internet has been an important political space for women's groups to bring VAW from the private space of the home and community to the public space of the media and political and legal institutions. Campaigns on the plight of women raped in the riots of Indonesia and in conflict areas of Afghanistan and Bosnia have involved thousands of women who responded to e-mail pleas for support. Individual women's detention, rape, or abuse by authorities is swiftly reported, and responses pour in. For example, in June 1999, Shirkat Gah, a women's NGO based in Islamabad, Pakistan, and a member of Women Living under Muslim Law as well as a partner of the Society for International Development, maintained an intense campaign around the murder of Samia Imran. A Pakistani woman, she was murdered by her family in her lawyer's office when she went there to ask for a divorce. As in most of these campaigns the women's group could swiftly send details of the case to the people in their network asking for letters of support to be faxed to the relevant authorities. Whereas before this request for support would have been confined to the domestic space, reaching local or national media at most — if the women had sympathetic media contacts — it can now be placed on the international agenda, with local women's groups using international agreements and international civil society support to pressure for domestic change and justice (Personal e-mail correspondence with Khawar Mumtaz).

Another creative use of the Internet to cross traditional geopolitical and cultural boundaries through politics of place strategies is the use of on-line conferences using chat rooms (Personal e-mail correspondence with Wanda Nowicka). Mira-Med, a Russian-based NGO, used the chat room format to open up a discussion on women and human rights organizations from the Former Soviet Union and Mongolia. The chat room session exposed the extent of the international trafficking of CIS women and children for purposes of forced prostitution in forty-three countries. The purpose of the Internet discussion was to create a combined strategy of collaboration between international organizations and local CIS organizations. The Internet allowed these groups to meet in cyberspace, using the free facilities of the University Internet Centers in fifty-five regions of the CIS.

The General Assembly Binding Women for Reforms, Integrity, Equality, and Leadership and Action (GABRIELA), based in the Philippines is fighting the more insidious use of the Internet in trafficking mail order brides on the information superhighway. GABRIELA has fought for the protection of women being "peddled" as part of the tourist industry under the Marcos regime, exploiting women wishing to escape poverty. The Internet is proving to be a more difficult space to protect women, because the legal ban on mail order brides in 1990 prevents residents of the Philippines from accessing the web sites that advertise the women. However GABRIELA counters this through its own international networking, asking women's groups outside the country to campaign against the mail order bride agencies (Langit, 1998, 6–7).

UNIFEM VAW CAMPAIGN

UNIFEM has brought many VAW experiences together in its recent campaign of ending violence against women, where they have addressed violence in the family, violence in war, economic discrimination, and political persecution and discrimination. Through regional campaigns and using the new international technologies—including an interagency global video conference—UNIFEM has made visible the work of many thousands of women against violence in their lives through training, education, advocacy, direct service provision, documentation, and initiatives to change social and cultural norms. Global organizing has crystallized around the annual 16 Days Campaign from November 25 through December 10, which has linked local, regional, and international groups around the 16 Days of Activism against Gender Violence. Set up by the Women's Global Leadership Institute in 1991, this multiple-level network, radiating from women's local concerns, is a telling example of how the politics of place operates to bring VAW into the public arena, changing cultural, legal, and social norms.

The range of women's groups that are involved in the campaign can be clearly seen in UNIFEM's Internet listserv working group, where more than 100 women and men working on VAW report how their links to the international level supported their local work on various fronts. The listserv discusses the different strategies used in an effort to support and strengthen local campaigns. For example, B.a.B.e., a strategic lobbying group in Croatia, used the 16 Days Campaign to hold media campaigns to raise awareness of women's experience of violence during the war and to force a new family law to incorporate restraining orders against men in domestic rape cases (UNIFEM, 1999: 25). In Lome WILDAF's West Africa Coordinator reported that the 16 Days Campaign enabled abused women to break the silence and talk about the violence in order to stop it, and the campaign has been a guide to all women in their struggle to be respected (UNIFEM, 1999: 26–7). In Italy, TV, radio, and newspapers are used to "send out the message to women that there is an alternative to a life of violence," looking in particular at the lives of young Albanian and Russian women forced into prostitution in Italy (UNIFEM, 1999: 53). In Lebanon, the Lebanese Council to Resist Violence against Women used international human rights law to protect a woman, who was abducted, raped, and thereby forced into marriage. The council through public pressure was able to have the marriage annulled by authorities (UNIFEM, 1999: 27). These are just some of the many VAW strategies that show women's initiative to help break silences and politicize the issue by working with teachers, health providers, police, judges, and religious leaders (UNIFEM, 1999: 36–8).

These examples show how women are responding to conflict at the level of the body, the community, and in the public arena by resisting VAW, reconfiguring their identity, and as a consequence changing gender relations. The three levels of women's environment are intermixed in the campaigns to reclaim women's bodily integrity, to support women's right to work and live safely in the home, and to create a public discussion around violence that breaks the shame and silence, as well as to create legal changes. The use of networking across countries and cultural experiences as well as the opportunities offered by UN agencies, such as UNIFEM, and the two decades of World Conferences on Women have come some way toward creating political spaces that challenge and change inequitable gender relations as well as traditional notions of private and public politics. They have also created opportunities for women to change their status and position in a positive way, as they confront the multiple-level impact violence has had on their lives. And ultimately they have shifted inequitable gender relations.

WOMEN'S PLACE-BASED STRATEGIES AROUND HEALTH AND ENVIRONMENT

Another traditional area of contest for women's autonomy and one where gender relations are clearly determined, is that of health—both reproductive and general. Healthy outcomes are linked closely in the process of economic change; changes in the environment and the resulting shifts in peoples' well-being have significant implications for women.

Women are mobilizing at the grassroots level in both the North and the South over the right to reproductive and sexual health as well as the right to live and work in a healthy environment. These collective actions of resistance and cooperation are reshaping gender relations as women develop strategic ways to meet their gendered concerns and needs. Through their local organizations, which are linked to a growing network of supporting institutions, women are beginning to find voice in the public arena, to shift the boundaries between public and private, and to raise as vital concerns the link between economic globalization, health, and environmental degradation.

The negative impact of economic globalization can be seen in the growing evidence of environmental hazards on health and well-being. Women's groups have tackled this both from an environmental and from a health perspective. The gendered effects of environmental damage as well as the deepening poverty and ill health resulting from misplaced public sector reforms have eroded universal access to quality health care and comprehensive reproductive health services.

The environmental changes resulting from development have exacerbated traditional problems related to poverty: lack of access to safe water, poor sanitation, pollution (such as pesticide contamination, lead poisoning, hazardous waste), and occupational hazards in agriculture and cottage industries. As caretakers and mothers, women have been at the frontline in protecting the environment for their and their families' survival and health. Pregnant women and nursing mothers are particularly vulnerable to environmentally caused illness. Studies have found in the highly polluted CIS countries that pregnant women suffer from infections more than the general population in addition to pregnancy complications and birth defects (WEDO, 1999: 15). Ecological disaster areas in the upper Silesian Industrial Zone in Poland, for example, are characterized by high cancer rates and lowered birthrates. Reproductive disorders are experienced as a result of chemical exposures and other occupational hazards (WEDO, 1999: 16). The use of pesticides has increased worldwide because of growing demands of globalization and export-oriented technologies. Long-term exposure to pesticides and fertilizer pollutants directly affects the health and fertility of women in the Third World who produce half the world's food. In the industrialized world, breast and other cancers are linked to environmental problems. And across the world accumulation of toxins has raised concerns about the safety of breast milk.

In response to the impact of development, economic globalization, and environmental change on themselves, their families, and localities, women have set in motion powerful and effective strategies, opening up an inclusive politics of place that closely links body, community, and wider public institutions. As in VAW there are many thousands of examples on which one can draw, particularly resulting from the impetus of the UN conferences held since UNCED, Rio 1992. I will touch on just a few as illustrations of women's place-bound politics.

ENVIRONMENTAL GROUPS

One of the most important women's groups operating in this area is Women's Environment and Development Organization (WEDO). With a network of more than 140 partners in as many countries, they have monitored women's active engagement in environment, health, and development issues since 1992. Their regular reports and caucuses at the international level build on women's NGOs' reports of activities that measure national gender equity, women's health issues, and environmental change. These reports are used as lobbying tools internationally but also nationally, supporting local women's needs and acting as a solid resource for policymakers open to addressing women's issues. WEDO is one of the clearest examples of women's place-based politics that respects cultural differences and viewpoints of the women's groups and has helped to bring about major changes in policy approaches to environment, health, and gender (WEDO, March and November 1998).

From the many WEDO partners, Mama-86, a Ukrainian women and environment NGO that was formed in response to the Chernobyl disaster can serve as an example of what members of WEDO achieve. Mama-86 works to put pressure on government to improve environmental conditions that are impacting women's health. Radiation and air and water pollution are chronic in the Ukraine. Mama-86 estimates that only one-quarter of the country's territory is safe for human health. The level of chronic pathology in the country that results from industrially produced ecological change can be measured by: the increase in number of spontaneous abortions, abnormal deliveries, maternal and infant illness, the doubling in recent years of reproductive system cancers and breast cancer, the lowering of the age of menopause, and a reduction in fertility (WEDO, 1999: 172, and Women's Global Network for Reproductive Rights (WGNRR, 1999: 10–12). As well as monitoring the health and well-being of women, Mama-86 runs education campaigns across sectors on approaches to social and economic sustainable development that would support local women's bottom-up initiatives on health and environment.

URBAN ACTIVISM

With the continuing restructuring of the state, economic globalization, and increasing environmental degradation, the local urban community has become a site for increased political action by women. In cities of the industrialized world and global south women are increasingly engaged in the politics of place through community-based protests and initiatives to increase women's equity and participation in urban decision making. The city has become a site of complex political struggles. Women's mobilization around provision of basic services, food, clean water, shelter, health care, and waste recycling has opened up a new political space for women in cities based on collective community and domestic responsibilities as well as the need for income generation (Horelli, 1998: 25–35). The critical element of this politics of place has been empowerment, but unlike with other social movements, there is also the political recognition of the public face of reproduction. Sites of resistance have formed around access to food, shelter, and the right to employment. This politics of place links economic growth, environmental health, and social equity. Women's groups, particularly in Northern Europe, have undertaken projects based on a political approach that integrate dwelling, care, and work in space and time, which are radically changing city planning. These groups have focused on gender planning, housing, and mobility issues in their efforts to create a more women-friendly city. Campaigning around the infrastructure of women's productive and reproductive daily life, projects in Italy, Germany, Austria, Finland, the UK, and Sweden have fought for different opening hours for schools, shops, and government offices, rescheduling of public transport, handling of waste, and more gender-aware housing and park facilities, being conscious also of the needs to protect working women's rights to family-friendly employment opportunities (Euro Fem, 1998: 44). These acts of resistance challenge the forces of globalization and economic restructuring that have increased homelessness, poverty, hunger, and environmental damage. The politics of place directed at ensuring food, shelter, health, and safety is part of an ethics of care that extends from the family to the immediate community to the environment.

One example from the Euro Fem network is the Women's Health Design Service, based in Camden, a suburb of London, England. The service has been working with women in ethnic minorities in order to improve their built environment. The group works with the migrant women's groups in order to identify what changes are needed in their local environment (better lighting, parks, transport, health centers, public shelters, and other facilities that are receptive to different ethnic needs) and then helps them negotiate with the authorities to bring about change. The women audit the local environment, looking at what is positive or negative about the neighborhood from their perspective. The results have been the provision of better community services and a healthier environment as well as the politicization of women from diverse cultural communities who are aware of their rights and are willing to engage in government and planning at the local level. The results of their project over the years have been linked through the Euro Fem network to other women's groups who are working in cities on environmental and habitat issues in the European community. The work of Euro Fem illustrates how women interlink body, housing, community, and public space in their place-based strategies for change.

ABORTION AND REPRODUCTIVE RIGHTS

Once taboo subjects such as abortion are now part of women's health agendas worldwide. Women's groups now link the politics of the body to the human rights agenda, to issues of citizenship, and to public political campaigns. For example, Grupo de Información en Reproducción Elegida (GIRE), working in Mexico City through media, seminars, and talks, has maintained intense discussion involving politicians and religious and cultural leaders, using the national elections to push the issue of abortion (Personal correspondence with Sharon Bissell). GIRE links safe legal abortion to women's self-determination and rights but also to equity, health care, social security issues, and civil society rights. GIRE campaigns have brought abortion rights into the public arena. Their strategy is to use the backing of international agreements to open up the local and national spaces for discussion while responding to economically poor women's needs for safe, sanctioned abortion, instead of unsafe, clandestine abortion.

WEDO has also broken silences and taboos around the links between breast cancer and environmental degradation, particularly in the industrial North (particularly Canada, the United States, and the UK). The Global Action Plan for the Eradication of Breast Cancer aims to identify and reduce incidences of exposure to potential causes of breast cancer alongside the search for better treatments and cures. Working with international NGOs, such as Greenpeace and the World Wild Life Fund, the campaign brings the concerns of local women's groups at the site of environmental degradation to the global level through media and advocacy work. The strategy is to graphically introduce the issue of private bodily concerns of women and reproductive illness into the public arena in order to pressure policy makers to ban carcinogens and long-lived toxic chemicals in industries. The campaign has forced women's specific concerns into the international environmental agenda, shifting the politics around toxic pollution to take up the usually hidden politics of the body (WEDO, 1999).

Based in Santiago, Chile, but reaching out to the entire region of Latin America and the Caribbean, the Women's Health Network takes up the whole spectrum of health concerns from a rights perspective that challenges the globalization of specific cultural images of women's identity, sexuality, and lifestyle. Their networking promotes an exchange of information and experiences of women's health, rights, and citizenship. They closely link women's bodily rights to their public rights as citizens, seeing women's health and reproductive choice as a tool for women's empowerment that will open up spaces for women's greater participation in public policy and decision making. Their focus is on support for local needs to reach out to national, regional, and international campaigns.

An example from their network is Red de Mujeres de Villas y Barrios (Network of Women from Neighborhoods and Towns) in Cordoba, Argentina, where community and women's organizations resisted a provincial law on reproductive and sexual health. The women successfully over turned a law that prevented the provision of family planning services in public hospitals. They fought under the banner of the right to build citizenship, the right to choose, as well as the right to have access to resources that guarantee true choice. The focus of the Red de Mujeres is on the needs of economically poor women living in generation-deep poverty, whose basic needs are unmet and who work in the informal sector with little access to health and family planning services. At the core of their demands is the concern that "despite the fact that these issues deal directly with our lives and bodies . . . we had to justify our right as citizens to decide on and control our own bodies . . . we had to put our bodies, brains and hearts everywhere" (Domínguez, Soldevila, and Acevedo, 1997: 65).

The women from the working-class neighborhoods and towns were the protagonists for the campaign locally and nationally. They worked in alliance with health workers and NGOs, such as Servicio a la Acción Popular (SAP, People's Action Service), unions, and the national women's movement networks: Red Nacional por la Salud de la Mujer and Red Nacional de Confluencia.

Because they work strategically on the local, national, and international levels, this campaign's success is an example of women's place-based politics around body, community, and the public arena. The linking of the gendered body to citizenship rights is an example of the political shift around notions of private and public. Working from grassroots women's needs, encouraging women's leadership in the campaign, and using national networks and international agreements is an example of a multifaceted strategy of place-based politics that does manage to change local realities. The local group's actions help shape global resistance and reappropriation of women's bodies as their success is taken up in other localities and discussed through network publications, workshops, and conferences at the national and international levels.

Another illustration of a women's network on health and reproductive rights that was built on local level campaigns around issues of abortion and damage to health because of shifts in the environment, is the Women's Global Network for Reproductive Rights (WGNRR). By weaving together local concerns with actions around the world, the WGNRR aims to fight the global trends of the withdrawal of state funding for health services, which has drastically reduced poor women's access to quality health care. Working with local women's groups to map out what services are needed, the network puts pressure on governments to prevent the rising cost of medical care, out-patient fees, and privatization of hospital facilities. A strong campaign has been around antifertility vaccines, linking members from Kenya, Brazil, the United States, Australia, India, and Europe. The network gathers information at the local level and takes it to the international arena, where the WGNRR is lobbying in particular the World Health Organization to review antifertility vaccines in relation to quality of care of reproductive services (WGNRR, 1999: 3).

BREAST MILK CAMPAIGNS

Resistance to the impact of the global market on breast milk has been one of the most successful civil society–led campaigns around women's health and rights in response to globalization. The International Baby Food Action Network (IBFAN) and the World Alliance on Breastfeeding Action (WABA) have responded to the opening up of new markets for breast milk substitutes with their dire implications for children and poor households. These networks have capitalized on the new information technologies to build vast networks that link local breast-feeding groups to international organizations such as UNICEF and WHO as well as campaigns that organized the famous boycott of Nestlé (the Infant Formula Action Coalition INFACT). Working together these civil society networks have pushed for and won the establishment of the International Code on the Marketing of Breastmilk Substitutes (1981) and the Innocenti Declaration of 1990 and Plan of Action at the World Food Summit of Rome to support, protect and promote breast-feeding. The network continues using these international agreements to encourage breast-feeding and to monitor companies, in particular Nestlé, who are fighting back strongly in Sweden, for example. Local groups respond and work with actors at the international level to help change infant feeding practices and to provide the necessary support for mothers to establish breast-feeding through mother-to-mother support groups (Chapman, 1999).

Breast-feeding campaigns are an interesting example of how the politics of place is replacing "top-down" instructions to women. There is growing awareness of the need not to admonish women to do "what is best" but to change behavior in a participatory and empowering way. For working mothers, breast-feeding can be a drain and difficult to establish, putting demands on physical health and time that they may not have. With the pressure of advertising and modernity, the bottle can seem a modern and effective advance for such women personally. There is need for support and time for women to choose breast-feeding for themselves if there is to be the necessary sustained cultural change and support for breast-feeding. There is now awareness that though international accords are needed, more important for a profound change, is that women have support for themselves at the community level—families, schools, pharmacists, and health workers. Conditions to choose have to be embedded in the wider political context. The constraints women face because of poverty, hazardous environment, nutrition, and ignorance about their rights have to be understood along with the provision of support and services for breast-feeding. Bringing breast-feeding into the public political domain, one of the first international political successes for civil society, is now happening at the grassroots level, linking the three environments of women's politics of place.

These movements are crossing borders and boundaries. Increasingly the boundaries of North and South have become blurred as women connect with and learn from one another and begin to create transnational frameworks and practices that challenge restructuring and economic globalization.

WOMEN CREATING NEW SPACES THROUGH COMMUNICATION AND INFORMATION TECHNOLOGIES

As many of the previous examples show, networking through the new information technologies has been a vital tool for linking the different sites of place-based politics. By connecting to other individual women and women's groups engaged in similar issues, sharing information and strategies in real time, women have been strengthened and empowered. The Internet has allowed women's groups to create channels for self-expression, communication, and political action as an integral part of the new global network society. These interconnections across geopolitical divides and across traditional boundaries of time and distance have fostered new identities, new knowledges, and stronger ways to confront and adapt globalization. Women as networkers and netweavers have become an important part of a cultural politics of cyberspace. The flows of communication in cyberspace seem to have suited and helped mold women's politics. Particularly in the last five years there has been an interesting interaction between cyberpolitics and place-based politics where the women work and live. At the 1995 Beijing Fourth World Conference on Women there was a spectacular use of cyberspace to defend place-based politics, with thousands, if not millions, of women's groups being linked in the process around the event.

> The Internet was being hyped and women's organizations were well prepared for action . . . electronic communication allowed women to bypass mainstream media and

still reach thousands . . . women who met on-line found an immediate network in Beijing. . . . One hundred thousand visits were made to the APC Website on the Conference. . . . When the International Women's Health Tribune Global FaxNet was posted on the Web, over 80,000 hits were recorded in the week before the Beijing Meetings. (Alice Gittler in Harcourt, 1999: 94–5)

The use of the Internet raises some interesting questions about how women can work in their own homes and communities and yet be linked to wider arenas. Are women, as they participate in cyberspace, changing local and global cultures that challenge the male bias of the global technocapitalism that is behind the Internet? How does women's work on the Internet create new types of political activity that are redefining the possibilities for women's politics of place? How do we connect women with few resources and access to the Internet so that it becomes an empowerment tool for both them and professional women already linked?

An experimental cybergroup "Women on the Net"[2] has brought together women and men who are self-consciously using the Internet to promote their place-based concerns around the body, environment, and public political agendas. It could appear to be a paradox to link place with cyberspace but the group's work illustrates how the Internet is a tool for strengthening place-based politics.

Laura Agustin (originally from Argentina) works with migrant women sex workers, primarily based in Spain and Mexico, to promote their rights and to let them tell their side of the story. Traveling from country to country she links different women migrants in a cyberspace group called Connexion for Migrants. In English and Spanish, these women, normally marginal in traditional political debates, discuss their concerns. As Agustin points out in her writing, these women are speaking; they are not silent. The question is, Who is listening? (Agustin in Harcourt, 1999: 149–55). Through her connections in cyberspace she sees herself (with other allies) opening up a space for migrants and sex workers to discuss their issues and make other groups listen without being biased by outsiders who assume certain things to be wrong or right. With NGOs and women's networks that she met through cyberspace, Agustin has been promoting the ILO recognition of the rights for sex workers to organize and be recognized as workers who should be able to work without stigma, fear of being arrested, or fear of being abused by traffickers. Her goal is to raise money to provide sex workers with mobile vans that could provide them with access to high-tech communication facilities that could help sex workers speak out, organize, and participate in actions that affect them.

Agustin's work with Connexions for Migrants is a fascinating example of how place-based politics in a globalized world implies a different sense of what is place. For these migrant women and also for Agustin in her work, place is constantly moving localities that are being linked and made real politically through the Internet. These women, isolated from their original birthplaces, are forging new places of work and survival based on the services they can offer with their bodies. In the globalized sex market they are linked through traffickers and crime. But in the space Agustin and others envisage and hope to offer, using the political mileage provided by the ILO publication "The Sex Sector" (Personal e-mail correspondence from Laura Agustin), they are reappropriating space for themselves as politicized actors. They are creating a community that argues for support for the choices they make (preferring flexible sex work that is freely chosen rather than ill-paid exploitative and dangerous work in factories and free trade zones). Through the Internet they have found a place for discussion, advocacy, and change that can give them a voice that offers an alternative and, Agustin argues, a more truthful version than the stories of unrelenting victimization and exploitation written on their behalf.

In Zanzibar, Tanzania, cyberspace is also offering another form for self-expression that strengthens and extends place-based traditional communication. The *kanga* is a traditional cloth worn by women in a country where women are not able to express their sentiments vocally, in a culture of silence. Every kanga has a philosophical saying drawn from Swahili culture. The sayings on the cloth are suggestive or reflective, depending on the mood of the woman wearing the kanga, and give clear messages to the men and women around them. The Internet is used to exchange new sayings, maintaining the flow of information about the latest kanga patterns, both in Zanzibar and among the Zanzibari community globally. Far from detracting from or destroying traditional cultural expressions, cyberspace provides the opportunity for a vibrant cultural community to build its creative wealth of sayings and debates in Kiswahili. Here the Internet is reinforcing women's expression of self and desire, molding together high-tech with traditional modes of communication, changing in the process the sense of a Zanzibarian community. The cyberspace expression of the kanga discussion is not a question of exploitation from the outside but of how our global network society is stretching the sense of cultural identity along communication nodes that have a politically place-based connection to the concrete locality (Fatma Alloo in Harcourt, 1999: 156–61).

This stretching of what is body, identity, and community can be seen in other Internet-connected communities. In outback Australia women in isolated rural homestead stations have been linked through an Internet feminist action research project to urban-based women. Three on-line discussion groups provide the means for women living thousands of kilometers apart to connect to discuss concerns about their daily lives—ranging from breast-feeding, menopause, and children's illnesses, to agricultural concerns and political issues around aboriginal land rights. Rural women used to living in complete isolation find themselves in daily conversation with other women about the most intimate areas of their lives—in conversations that would never happen face-to-face. Urban women linked into the discussions suddenly find themselves taking part in rural women's lives and concerns. These women have crossed boundaries of place, race, and culture, creating a sense of care and concern for women. "*We-link* is providing a significant means of giving voice to rural women; it gives much needed social support, helps to break down differences and stereotypes and to broaden perspectives" (June Lennie, et al., in Harcourt, 1999: 195).

The use of the Internet to build women's care for each other, support for personal issues, and networking beyond their localities is evident for many women—even when access to computer facilities is difficult. Internet service centers provide African women's groups with information about what is happening internationally. The information is downloaded and distributed to local groups so that instead of, for example, newspapers taking months to arrive, the women are immediately connected (Alice Gittler in Harcourt, 1999: 91–101). Women trained in international technology provide resources in training local NGOs to use Internet facilities. For example, Synergy Gender and Development, Environment and Development in the Third World (SYNEV ENDA), based in Senegal, focuses on environment and development issues that have to do with economic autonomy for women and women's health. It links up thirty organizations in West Africa and thirty-five links with women's groups in the rest of Africa, regularly sending out information downloaded from the web on reproductive rights issues and providing technical training for twenty-five women's groups (Nidhi Tandon in Harcourt, 1999: 140).

In the Arab world, the Internet provides an important space that gives women access to the public political arena from their private space in countries that restrict women's physical movement. The Internet can provide ways to get around fundamentalist concerns with Western cultural influences and provide a place for Arab women to speak to other women living in Muslim societies, strengthening their local struggle for women's autonomy and rights. "Potentially women can use the Internet to express themselves and their views on gender, political and economic equity which would be impossible—even dangerous—in the pubic sphere" (Lamis Alshejni in Harcourt, 1999: 218).

In Hawaii, Kekula Bray-Crawford has provided links to indigenous women's groups around the Pacific or "The Liquid Continent." The lobbying of her Internet network, the Netwarriors, an e-mail-based group that supports indigenous people's rights, activated when UN working groups on indigenous people require the immediate support of NGOs and others around the world, has proven remarkably successful (Harcourt, 1998: 11).

The group's conversations can be read as an experiment in women using technology as a cultural practice to empower women's place-based activities. Pi Villanueva, in a cyberspace conversation with Bray-Crawford (published in the ISIS journal *Women in Action*), says that technology is empowering women and:

> Allow[s] us to meet some of the challenges we are faced with "from the inside out" with common tools. Level the playing field . . . including technologies in our agendas is imperative in order to stand face to face, shoulder to shoulder, back to back with our sisters . . . to know (technology) is to understand our potential at this time . . . we are at the doormat for a number of situations and realities . . . from the homefront all the way to the global country/state/politic/religion/family of women. (Villanueva, 1998: 24–9)

In this conversation the new communication technologies symbolically and in reality represent the place-based position for women working in their own localities to reach out to the global community and, in using the technology, their voices transfer globalism itself.

These examples from women using the Internet are not intended, however, as a wholehearted celebration of the new technology. The difficulties of using the new information technologies are recognized—the huge inequities in terms of access to the resources needed, the control of these resources by global capitalism, technical and language barriers, the military use of the web, pornography, and the uncertainty of the service provision. In their conversations, published in the book *Women@internet: Creating New Cultures in Cyberspace* (Harcourt 1999), it is evident that the Internet is transforming these women's experience of the global from their own place as women working from their home, their office, their cybercafé, or their conference site. It is linking up these localities, allowing space for women to discuss different knowledges, cultural differences, and common goals for women in terms of their bodies, communities, and the public arena. It is very graphically breaking down the barriers between the private and the public in women's lives, along with the distances between North and South and the differences among age and ethnic groups.

SOME IMPLICATIONS OF WOMEN'S PLACE-BASED STRATEGIES

What does this skim through a fraction of some of the place-based strategies of women's groups in terms of violence against women, health and environment, and communications and networking suggest for revisioning difference in equality?

First these place-based political practices have effects of equality that are not impeded and do not deny difference. In many cases women act as "carriers" of equality across class, race, and ethnic divides. The Zenica shelters are an example of how women worked across ethnic divisions, over which the war was being fought, to provide support for women's psychological and social healing and ultimately the restructuring of their society. The violence against women along ethnic lines (in civil wars and also in economic and social distress, such as the rapes of Chinese ethnic women in Indonesia) is transfigured by women's response to rape as a weapon of war that commits a deeper violation of women's body and identity. In this discourse, groups such as Women in Black cross ethnic and public political divides to support all women as a strong political gesture. At the same time when discussing women's autonomy and rights in international spaces such as the big UN meetings from 1992 where women have been very vocal and effective largely because of their networking, difference among cultures has been strongly respected in negotiations for an agreed women's agenda. Women's spaces, such as the women's tents in the Rio de Janeiro conference (UN Conference on Environment and Development) in 1992, and all the NGO meetings since, have created, alongside traditional UN structures, alternative ways to bring in different community women's needs, breaking down as much as possible the dominance of Euro-American ways of working and issues and tackling the regionally diverse gendered aspects of the impact of transnational capital. Marginalized groups, particularly indigenous women's groups, have been invited to take up and use these spaces for their own political concerns. The paradoxes of women immersed in identity politics at the local level using UN events where vital livelihood-determining differences in the dominant debates are regularly dismissed in "North-South" tussles, are acknowledged by women entering into the discussion, and the contradictions become woven into the linking of different localities.

There is also an active dialogue around women's use of the politics of rights, framed most distinctly in the question, Who has the right to have rights? And which rights? Cultural rights can work pointedly against women's rights to reproductive and sexual health. The complex debate around female genital mutilation (FGM) is an example of how place-based politics by women has cut across traditional development policy "respecting" cultural difference at the expense of women's health and autonomy. The supralocal response of community women working with external support groups has brought the issue of sexuality and health of women into the public arena. FGM has been placed on the international agenda in support of women who have to challenge cultural traditions in those countries that continue the practice. Similarly, gendered conflicts around land rights have been politicized by women's movements supporting local women's demands for land rights in direct challenge to male-dominated state support for cultural practices that deny women's ownership of land.

The emergent identities from such processes cannot be adequately described by conventional models of political activity. There is a crossing of boundaries in time and space that has created a women's politics that is grounded in place and yet built into political negotiations that move at far more abstract levels. Again as the tremendous outreach and information sharing and ultimately political use of the UN conferences for women's local rights show, women are navigating and shaping this process as they go through a complex set of linkages in the thousands of networks being built up around reproductive rights, healthy environments, and violence against women. The identity of the women comes from their sense of self as women, formed by their own culture and environment but also from their linking to the wider women's movement. Their place-based political identity reconfirms their body, community, and citizenship needs in ways that are shaped by glocal negotiations.

Women's politics of place is creating and enabling reconstructions of place, identity, and public space that respect differences and are reshaping gendered relations. Place-based activities are stretching the boundaries of the body, identity, and public spaces. The body does not end in the skin, place does not end in the community, environment does not end in nature, and all of these are reconfigured in more gender equal ways. The crossing of geopolitical, social, and cultural borders and boundaries, in women's glocal responses to conflict, violence, and economic globalization, are producing new spaces where bodies and places are being metaphorically stretched to help resolve the very real problems of women's bodily integrity, livelihoods, and social existence posed by economic, social, and cultural manifestations of global capital.

CONCLUSION: POLITICS OF PLACE AS A CHALLENGE TO DEVELOPMENTALISM

These women's activities reflect the profound shifts in gender relations and new forms of cultural expressions that are emerging in response to economic global-ization. Women working from the grass roots in different economic, social, and cultural positions are creating a new form of politics that is changing women's sense of self and their place in the community and opening up new public places for negotiation for gender economic and social justice. Despite the backdrop of increasing economic poverty, exploitation and state restructuring, women are re-sisting strongly the negative impact of economic globalization in their lives through a place-based politics around the body, community, and the public arena. In engaging in a politics of place, women are redefining political action to take into account their gender concerns based on their own needs and responses to globalism as it is experienced at the level of their daily lives. At the same time this placed-based politics links localities into a glocal network society, redefining possibilities for women's sense of self, position in the community, and access to the public arena and decision-making venues.

Place-based politics is opening up possibilities for women's groups to make meaningful change at the local level in terms of VAW, reproductive health, and local habitat. Networking that is radiating out from place is enabling women to work in support and solidarity, across cultural differences and geographic dis-tances to make vocal the once unpoliticized issues around the body, reproductive health, and women's work in the home and in the community. In doing so women and other networks are creating a network of social spaces, parallel glocalities that are forming alternatives to the dominant globalizing network society.

In rethinking political responses to modernity and global capitalism it is im-portant to build on the knowledge and experience of women's groups engaged in place-based politics. The conflicts that women are experiencing at the different levels usher in new forms of cultural and political relations. Women as actors in their own lives are leading activities around the politics of the body, the home, the community, and local government. They are working together toward greater eq-uity, respecting and working with their cultural and other differences. Strategies for greater equity that respect cultural difference can be crafted from these supralocal connections.

Such strategies could well repudiate dominant development in the name of the autonomy of place, projecting place into spaces that are currently the domains of capital and modernity, in order to create new structures of power and perhaps even as a result, imagine an outside to global capitalism. As these cases demonstrate, the politics of place is a very practical politics, responding to conflicts and working with alliances and networks that form around those conflicts. The resulting reconfigurations have been both a response but also part of the vision that women have begun to project based on concepts such as the caring economy, cultural diversity, a sharing of reproductive and productive roles, a celebration of women's bodies and creative abilities. The idea of place conceived as a project is an essential step to critique developmentalism and to imagine alternatives to it. I hope this chapter has suggested ways in which women are beginning to envisage global lives in local spaces in ways that do not imprison but forge new gendered identities and new cultures.

I would like to illustrate this briefly, as any good feminist should, from my own personal experience, as a mother of two very young daughters, an Australian researcher and editor living in Italy, working in an international organization and deeply engaged in networking and learning through international information and communication technologies with women of all ages around the world. I am engaged in the politics of place in my negotiations on all levels—experiencing the changes of the body through pregnancy and motherhood, through friendships that are formed in cyberspace with men and women, sharing the joys and difficulties of birth, sleepless nights, and breast-feeding. I try to link that bodily experience to local community struggles for better health services and information in Rome, where caesarean sections make up a full third of births, and where breast-feeding is still not totally accepted. I take part in European networks alliance-building with southern women's groups on reproductive rights and environment as well as at the broader international level, contributing to campaigns on reproductive rights, health, and equity issues with research institutes and UN agencies. My work, I now see, is one of the many links in the new networks that are building the politics of place, mixing personal with public lives, supporting each other across distances, probing and challenging our glocalities.

NOTES

1. See the entries by Butega, Brunet, and Dundu in the publication of ISIS-WICCE, "Impact," 1999, 10–16.

2. This group was set up by UNESCO and the Society for International Development in 1997 to explore the cultural spaces women are shaping in cyberspace and the ways women are transforming the technical tool of the Internet into a political tool for advocacy for women in different regions.

REFERENCES

Chapman, Jennifer. "Civil Society Response to the Marketing of Breast Milk Substitutes in Ghana." Paper given at the SID-WHO-RF Roundtable "Responses to Globalization: Rethinking equity and health," Geneva, 1999.

Cockburn, Cynthia. *The Space between Us: Negotiating Gender and National Identities in Conflict.* London: Zed, 1998.

Domínguez, A., A. Soldevila, and P. Acevedo. "Building Citizenship: The Right to Choose." *Women's Health Journal* 97 (4), Latin American and Caribbean Women's Health Network, (1997): 62–8.

Escobar, A., guest editor. "Globalism and the Politics of Place." *Development: Journal of SID* 41(2). London: Sage, 1998.

Harcourt W., ed. *Women in the Digital Age.* Rome: Society for International Development, 1998.

———. *Women@Internet. Creating New Cultures in Cyber Space.* London: Zed, 1999.

Horelli, Lisa, ed. "Euro Fem Gender and Human Settlements Proceedings of the Euro Fem International Conference on Local and Regional Sustainable Human Development from a Gender Perspective." Helsinki: June 10–12, 1998.

IBFAN. *Africa News.* September/October 1997. (Entries detail activities of the IBFAN activities in Africa.)

ISIS-WICCE. *Impact* 1 (1) (1998).

Langit, R. "Filipinas on Sale on the Net." *Women in Action* 2 (1998) 6–7.

Subramaniam, Vanitha. "The Impact of Globalization on Women's Reproductive Rights and Health: A Regional Perspective." Paper given at the SID-WHO-RF Roundtable, "Responses to Globalization: Rethinking Equity and Health." Geneva, 1999.

UNIFEM. *Women@Work. Against Violence: Voices in Cyberspace.* New York: UNIFEM, 1999.

Villaneueva, P. "E-mails on the Edge." *Women in Action* 2 (1988): 24–9.

WEDO. *Risks, Rights and Reforms. A 50-country survey assessing government action.* New York: WEDO 1999.

WEDO. *New and Views* 12(3) (November 1998).

Women's Global Network for Reproductive Rights, Newsletter 65(1) (1999).

Women's Health Journal, Latin American and Caribbean Women's Health Network 4 (1997): 62-8.

Index

About the Contributors

John Brown Childs is professor of sociology at the University of California, Santa Cruz. He is the author of *Leadership, Conflict, and Cooperation in Afro-American Social Thought* (1989). His new book, *Transcommunality: From the Politics of Conversion to the Ethics of Respect* is fortchoming from Temple University Press. Childs works with interethnic organizations, including the National Coalition of Barrios Unidos, Escuela Esperanza in Watsonville, California, and the Advocacy Institute in Washington, D.C. He was awarded the Fulbright "Thomas Jefferson Chair of Distinguished Teaching" at the University of Utrecht in the Netherlands in 1997.

Arif Dirlik is professor of history at Duke University. He is the author of numerous works, including *Anarchism in the Chinese Revolution* (1991), *After the Revolution: Waking to Global Capitalism* (1994), and *The Postcolonial Aura: Third World Criticism in the Age of Global Capitalism* (1997). He was also editor of and contributor to *What Is in a Rim? Critical Perspectives on the Pacific Region Idea* (1998).

Arturo Escobar is professor of anthropology at the University of North Carolina, Chapel Hill. Among his publications are *Cultures of Politics/Politics of Cultures: Re-visioning Latin American Social Movements* (1998), *Encountering Development: The Making and Unmaking of the Third World* (1995), and *Power and Visibility: The Invention and Management of Development in the Third World* (1987).

Jonathan Friedman is directeur d'études at the Ecole des hautes en sciences sociales, Paris, and professor of social anthropology at the University of Lund, Sweden. He has done research and written on Southeast Asia, Oceania, and Europe and has written on more general issues concerning structuralist and Marxist theory, models of social and cultural transformation, and, for the past twenty years, on the anthropology of global process, cultural formations, and the practices of identity. He has contributed to international journals and books on issues ranging from globalization to ethnicity to the nature of political correctness. His books include *Cultural Identity and Global Process* (1994), *Consumption and Identity* (editor, 1994), *System, Structure and Contradiction in the Evolution of "Asiatic" Social formations* (1998), and, together with R. Denemark, B. Gills, and G. Modelski, *World System History: The Science of Long-Term Change* (2000).

Wendy Harcourt received her Ph.D. from the Australian National University in 1987. She joined the Society for International Development, based in Rome, as associate editor of *Development* and director of programs. Since becoming editor of *Development* in 1995 she has steadily steered the journal toward a more critical line on development, particularly examining the impact of globalization on the developing world. In addition to her work for the journal on globalization, her current research focus is on women and cyberculture; gender, health, and globalization; and adolescence and reproductive rights, and in all three areas she is leading a dynamic international group of women and men on some cutting-edge analysis and the setting of new political agendas. She is the editor of three books: *Feminist Perspectives on Sustainable Development* (1993), *Power, Reproduction and Gender* (1997), and *Women@Internet: Creating New Cultures in Cyberspace* (1999). All of her writings are self-consciously identified as part of the collective international exploration of alternatives to mainstream thinking on gender, economics, sustainable development, and population.

Peter Kwong is director of Asian American studies and professor of urban affairs and planning at Hunter College, City University of New York.

Russell C. Leong edits the *Amerasia Journal* at UCLA's Asian American Studies Center. His most recent book of fiction, *Phoenix Eyes and Other Stories* (2000), is on migration, sexuality, and samsara. Leong is an adjunct professor of English at UCLA and teaches classes in fiction, film, and poetry.

James H. Mittelman is professor of international relations at the School of International Service, American University. Among other works, he has published *The Globalization Syndrome: Transformation and Resistance* (2000), *Globalization, Peace and Conflict* (1997), and *Out from Underdevelopment Revisited: Changing Global Structures and the Remaking of the Third World* (1997).

Roxann Prazniak is Elliott Professor of history at Hampden-Sydney College. She is the author of *Dialogues across Civilizations: Sketches in World History from the Chinese and European Experiences* (1996) and *Of Camel Kings and Other Things: Rural Rebels against Modernity in Late Imperial China* (1999).

Elizabeth Rata teaches at the Auckland College of Education and is the author of *A Political Economy of Neotribal Capitalism* (2000).

Geoffrey M. White is professor of anthropology at the University of Hawaii and senior fellow at the East-West Center. He also serves as editor of *The Contemporary Pacific*. His publications include *Perilous Memories: The Asia-Pacific War* (edited with Takashi Fujitani and Lisa Yoneyama, 2000), *Chiefs Today: Traditional Chiefs in the Postcolonial Pacific* (edited with Lamont Lindstrom, 1997), and *Identity through History: Living Stories in a Solomon Islands Society* (1991).

Margaret M. Zamudio is assistant professor in the Department of Sociology at the University of Colorado, Boulder, where she teaches courses in race and ethnic relations, Latina/os in the United States, and classical and contemporary sociological theory. She is the author of *Organizing the New Otani Hotel in Los Angeles: The Role of Ethnicity, Race, and Citizenship in Class Formation* (1996).